Memory and Myth

Memory and Myth

The Civil War in Fiction and Film from *Uncle Tom's Cabin* to *Cold Mountain*

Edited by
David B. Sachsman
S. Kittrell Rushing
Roy Morris Jr.

Purdue University Press / West Lafayette, Indiana

Printed in the United States of America.

Clothbound ISBN 978-1-55753-439-2
Paperback ISBN 978-1-55753-440-8

Library of Congress Cataloging-in-Publication Data

Memory and myth : the Civil War in fiction and film from Uncle Tom's cabin to Cold mountain / edited by David B. Sachsman, S. Kittrell Rushing, and Roy Morris Jr.

p. cm.

Includes bibliographical references and index.

ISBN 978-1-55753-439-2 (casebound : alk. paper) -- ISBN 978-1-55753-440-8 (pbk. : alk. paper) 1. United States--History--Civil War, 1861-1865--Literature and the war. 2. American fiction--History and criticism. 3. Historical fiction, American--History and criticism. 4. United States--History--Civil War, 1861-1865--Motion pictures and the war. 5. War films--United States--History and criticism. 6. Historical films--United States--History and criticism. 7. United States--History--Civil War, 1861-1865--Influence. 8. War and literature--United States--History. 9. War in literature. I. Sachsman, David B. II. Rushing, S. Kittrell. III. Morris, Roy.

PS374.C53M46 2007
813'.08109--dc22

2006100291

Contents

Preface

David Sachsman

The Civil War is a central focus of American history and American historical scholarship, and yet our image of the time is of Scarlett O'Hara as much as it is of Abraham Lincoln, and the pictures in our head of Abraham Lincoln come from movies more than history books. Even our concepts of slavery come from fiction rather than history—just as they did in the 1850s in the North, where the dominant image of slavery was provided by *Uncle Tom's Cabin*.

The essence of great fiction may be its essential truth. Our best pictures of England in the nineteenth century are provided by Charles Dickens, just as our understanding of nineteenth century whaling is based on *Moby Dick*. We believe almost everything we read in *War and Peace*, especially its images of the essential feeling of war. Likewise *The Red Badge of Courage* is a meaningful, truthful picture of the Civil War. But are we equally well served by best-selling fictions . . . from *Gone With the Wind* to *Cold Mountain*? And can we put any trust at all in the stories and pictures of the Civil War provided by movies and television?

Our culture as a people—our national culture—is based on our collective memory. Should we be disturbed that our memory often is based on our stories rather than our history, or should we, like Robert Penn Warren, focus our interest on "the distinction between the historical importance and what might be called the appeal to the national imagination"?[1]

The annual Symposium on the 19th Century Press, the Civil War, and Free Expression in Chattanooga, Tennessee focuses on both our history and our fiction, our memory and the formation of our culture.[2] Most of its participants explore the history of the mass media, which themselves are creators and repositories of our memory and culture. Others are scholars who study the interplay of fiction and history. In 1998, for example, the symposium featured a panel of invited presentations on "Fiction and History: Does *Cold Mountain* Accurately Reflect Life During the Civil War?" and in 2000, it offered a panel on "Novels of Ideology—The Fiction of Slavery." The 2001 symposium included papers on *The Red Badge of Courage*, Upton Sinclair's Civil War fiction, the Reconstruction novel, and *Glory!* If we wish, we can call all these papers "cultural history," confusing matters still more. After all, our mass media and our fiction are at the heart of our popular culture and our collective memory.

Memory and Myth: The Civil War in Fiction and Film from Uncle Tom's Cabin to Cold Mountain consists of twenty-five chapters drawn from papers originally presented at the annual Symposium on the 19th Century Press the Civil War, and Free Expression in the past twelve years. They discuss the effects of fiction on the course of history, the creation of myths, the images of history in fiction, and the popular images created by motion pictures and television. It is said that when we watch a historical movie made in the 1950s, we learn more about the 1950s than we do about the era depicted. If this is so, then these chapters reflect the cultural history of America from the Civil War to today—telling us as much about the times in which these novels and films were created as they do about the Civil War, itself.

NOTES

1. Robert Penn Warren, *The Legacy of the Civil War*, a book that got its start as an essay for *Life* magazine on the occasion of the Civil War Centennial. James H. Justus, Introduction to *Wilderness: A Tale of the Civil War* by Robert Penn Warren (Knoxville: University of Tennessee Press, 1961, 2001).
2. Parts of this discussion were first presented at the Symposium on the 19th Century Press, the Civil War, and Free Expression, in Chattanooga Tennessee, November 8, 2001, and were published as part of a book review of Robert Penn Warren's *Wilderness: A Tale of the Civil War* in *The West Tennessee Historical Society Papers* 55 (December 2001): 131–132.

Acknowledgments

A work of the magnitude and complexity of *Memory and Myth* requires the talents, the dedication, and the hard work of a large number of people. *Memory and Myth* reflects the hopes and dreams of the scholars whose names appear as authors as well as those of research assistants, copy editors, secretaries, and families.

Memory and Myth is the culmination of more than a decade of scholarship beginning with a conversation between David Sachsman and me, that, over more than a decade, became more than wishful musing. We acknowledge here those who shared in the project for which the goal was to make concrete and lasting years of work—to make real those musings of years ago. We here acknowledge those without whom this book and what it represents would not exist.

In November 1993, a small group of journalism historians were invited to meet in Chattanooga, Tennessee, to organize what evolved into an annual meeting that has continued for more than a decade. Those who joined David and me in 1993 included David Mindich, then of New York University; Dwight Teeter, at the time the Dean of the College of Communication at the University of Tennessee at Knoxville; Ed Caudill, also of the University of Tennessee at Knoxville; Lloyd Chiasson, Nichols State University; Don Reynolds, East Texas State University; Edd Applegate, Middle Tennessee State University; Gene Wiggins, University of Southern Mississippi; Bob Dardenne, University of South Florida; Jim Ogden, United States Park Service; Joe Trahan, UT Chattanooga; Barbara Straus Reed, Rutgers University; and Leonard Ray Teel, Georgia State University.

The 1993 group issued a call for papers for a planned 1994 meeting. The hope was that the response would be sufficient to justify another meeting during which the group could share once again ongoing research into the roles played by nineteenth century media in the development of what became twentieth- and twenty-first-century attitudes, values, and realities. The response to that initial call justified a meeting, and each year thereafter interest and participation have more than met the initial expectations of the small group that met in 1993 to share and to critique the work of one another.

Through the years the membership of the symposium steering committee has grown from the original founders to a much larger number, all of whom have presented papers in Chattanooga. Those who have consistently worked to add to our understanding of the place and impact of nineteenth-century mass communication in our culture include Hazel Dicken-Garcia of the University of Minnesota; William Huntzicker, now at St. Cloud State University in Minnesota; Nancy Dupont, now at the University of Mississippi; Douglas W. Cupples, University of Memphis; Debra Reddin van Tuyll, Augusta State University; Phebe Davidson, University of South Carolina-Aiken; Bernell E. Tripp, University of Florida; Paul Ashdown, University of Tennessee at Knoxville; Holly Hodges, formerly the archivist of the University of Tennessee at Chattanooga Lupton Library; Stephen Cox, University of Tennessee-Chattanooga Lupton Library; Crompton Burton, Marietta College in Ohio; Menahem Blondheim, The Hebrew University of Jerusalem; and, of course, our friend and colleague Roy Morris Jr. of Chattanooga.

We should mention especially here two honor student workers who performed a great deal of the work in preparing the project. Meredith Jagger devoted months to collecting, organizing, and listing conference papers from 1993 through 2005. Autumn Dolan read each of the dozens and dozens of papers and reorganized the materials into logical divisions and categories. Without the work of Jagger and Dolan, the project might very well have remained only stacks of papers, computer disks and programs stored in file cabinets and cardboard boxes.

Administrative assistant Kelly Griffin continues to provide backbone support and managerial skills to the project. She has been supportive, dependable and knowledgeable about the business side of managing the conference on which this book is based.

Acknowledgment must also be made of the University of Tennessee at Chattanooga administrators who shared our dream and offered and continue to provide material and logistical support as well as encouragement. Fred Obear, Richard Brown, John Friedl, Herb Burhenn, Roger Brown, and the late Grayson Walker all contributed and supported the work that led to this publication.

We are appreciative, too, for a UTC Faculty Research Committee Grant supported by the University of Chattanooga Foundation. The grant made possible concentrated editing and supplemental research without which the project would not have advanced. We also appreciate and acknowledge the support and the presence of Peter Pringle, the Luther Massingill Professor of Communication (now emeritus) and the rest of the faculty of the UTC Department of Communication, and the support of Jerald Dauer, the former Provident Chair of Excellence in Applied Mathematics.

Of course, a list of acknowledgments can never be complete, and the danger always looms that significant contributors will be overlooked. Every member of the symposium steering committee deserves individual mention, as do many others, including Fran Bender and Judy Sachsman, who attended every conference.

Whatever the value of this project, these named and the many unnamed should receive credit. Whatever the failings of the effort, the responsibility must rest solely on the shoulders of the editors.

Kittrell Rushing

Introduction

— Roy Morris Jr. —

America was a myth long before she was a country, and she remains something of a myth today. Reality always intrudes, but the shining image of America as a land of freedom, wealth, and opportunity still survives in the hearts and minds of millions of people throughout the world. From the French Revolution onward, America has served as both example and inspiration to those seeking a greater say in their own lives and the lives of their countries.

All myths need a credible creation story to sustain them. America has had two: the founding of the republic in 1776 and the much-darker "rebirth of freedom" during the cataclysmic Civil War, nine decades after the Declaration of Independence. Increasingly, the Civil War has supplanted the Revolution as the preeminent event in American history, largely because—as the Founding Fathers worried at the time—the republic they had created was inherently flawed. That flaw, the "fire bell in the night," as Thomas Jefferson predicted, was slavery. There were other factors, of course, both economic and cultural, that divided the northern and southern sections of the country, but the constitutionally protected institution of slavery was the most fundamental. Abraham Lincoln succinctly formulated the American dilemma on the eve of the Civil War. "No nation," he said, "can exist half-slave and half-free." The subsequent war that his election as president made inevitable was a heartbreaking resolution of that essential dilemma.

From the time of her founding, America has challenged artists to confront both the reality and the myth of their native country. The chapters included in this book are all concerned, to one degree or another, with creative responses to the Civil War. Part 1, "So This Is the Little Lady Who Made This Big War," details the responses of writers in the years leading up to the Civil War, particularly their responses to slavery. Part 2, "Civil War Witnesses: Between Fiction and Fact," examines the works of writers during or immediately after the war, including some, like Ambrose Bierce and Albion Tourgée, who actually fought in the war. Part 3, "Let the Story Tellers Invent It All," concerns the struggles of modern writers to make moral and artistic sense of the national calamity. Part 4, "History with Lightning," looks at the wildly disparate ways the war has been rendered and remembered by succeeding generations of American filmmakers, including those working in the then comparatively new medium of television.

"So This Is the Little Lady Who Made This Big War"

How Americans responded to slavery was influenced to a great degree by a single novel, Harriet Beecher Stowe's 1852 best-seller, *Uncle Tom's Cabin*. That novel, which outsold every other book in the nineteenth century with the exception of the Bible, set the template by which millions of Americans thought—pro or con—about the institution of slavery. Indeed, its impact was so far-reaching that it was scarcely an exaggeration when Abraham Lincoln greeted the novel's author at a White House gathering at the height of the Civil War by saying: "So this is the little lady who made this big war."[1]

William E. Huntzicker's "'This Inherited Misfortune': Gender, Race, and Slavery in *Uncle Tom's Cabin* and *Gone with the Wind*" undertakes to examine how Stowe's revolutionary act of myth-making ultimately was superseded by southern-born author Margaret Mitchell's counter-myth of racial harmony, which Mitchell hoped would help "refute the impression of the South which people abroad gained from Mrs. Stowe's book." Both books reflect, perhaps unwittingly, the prevailing zeitgeist of their times, as well as the overarching shadow that chattel slavery has cast over the American experience.

Even a work as groundbreaking as *Uncle Tom's Cabin* had its roots in both historical fact and imagined "reality." As Lloyd Chiasson, Jr. reminds us in "Beyond *Uncle Tom's Cabin*," there was a long series of literary disputes over slavery, stretching back to the very end of the seventeenth century. "During the years before the Civil War," Chiasson writes, "the debate was constant and unflinching in virulence, propelled by a litany of events that began well before the Revolutionary War." Northern abolitionists, fueled by moral and religious opposition to slavery, were challenged by an array of pro-slavery publications, which sought to "prove" the superiority of the South's "peculiar institution" on economic and scientific levels.

That fear was reflected, Eve Dunbar recounts in "The Terror of Poe: Slavery, the Southern Gentleman, and the Status Quo," in the works of native southerner Edgar Allan Poe, a writer not normally associated with real-life issues. As Dunbar makes clear, the sense of dread that lay over the South, although based in fact, far exceeded the limits of rational thought. One might say that the fear of slave revolt and slave revenge had reached mythic levels in the decades before the Civil War.

One real-life person who became entirely consumed with this myth, and in so doing became mythic himself, was the northern abolitionist-turned-terrorist John Brown. Bernell E. Tripp, in "John Brown: The Many Faces of a Nineteenth-Century Martyr," considers the different ways in which the real John Brown was transformed into an avenging angel and religious warrior by the news media of his own time, and how that image has largely carried over in modern movies.

Robert Penn Warren struggled mightily with the largely favorable image of John Brown in his own 1929 biography, *John Brown: The Making of a Martyr.* Warren's struggles, occasioned in large part by his immersion in the Fugitive movement of the 1920s and 1930s, are documented in two chapters, Robert Blakeslee Gilpin's "The Fugitive Imagination: Robert Penn Warren's *John Brown*," and "The Search for Community and Justice: Robert Penn Warren, Race Relations, and the Civil War," by Edward J. Blum and Sarah Hardin Blum.

Civil War Witnesses: Between Fiction and Fact

Once the war had begun, reality superseded myth. New York newspaper editor Benjamin Wood attempted the difficult task of writing a novel that would contain both real and mythic elements. That novel, *Fort Lafayette*, was a notable if noble failure, its conventionally melodramatic plot undermining its scenes of literary realism. As Menahem Blondheim observes in "Between Fiction and Fact: Ben Wood, *Fort Lafayette*, and Civil War America," "The fictional plot could not possibly deliver the reader far enough from reality into a self-contained and seamless web of fiction. *Fort Lafayette*'s readers are constantly drawn back from the realm of imagination into the here and now."

The ongoing war, in a sense, was too real—or certainly too present—for creative artists to deal with successfully at the time. As Phebe Davidson and Debra Reddin van Tuyll note in "William Gilmore Simms: A Literary Casualty of the Civil War," Simms's failure was foreshadowed by the failure of his earlier novel, *Woodcraft, or Hawks about the Dovecote*, an inadequate fictional response to Harriet Beecher Stowe's *Uncle Tom's Cabin*. Simms's novel, the authors note, was an "idealized fantasy about the nature of the relationship between slave and master." As such, it reflected how far Simms and his native region had diverged from the American literary mainstream, as expressed by the northern-based publishing houses, reducing Simms from the front ranks to the dustbin of modern American literature.

As literary critic Daniel Aaron has noted in *The Unwritten War: American Writers and the Civil War*, the most talented American writers at the time of the war were either too old or too timid to take part in the war. (Who knows how many potentially great writers were killed in the war before having had the chance to develop their talents?) One of these "malingerers" was Henry Adams, who spent the Civil War years serving as his diplomat father's private secretary in London. In "Henry Adams's Civil War: Despair and *Democracy*," W. Scott Poole considers Adams's fictional response to the greatest crisis in American history. Adams's 1879 novel, *Democracy: An American Novel*, concerns itself with the dispiriting aftermath of the Civil War, which Adams sees as merely "one more moment in the degeneration of the American experiment." Adams's novel "reflects a growing sense . . . among many late-nineteenth-century writers and thinkers, that the Union victory had lengthened the shadows over the republic, not dispelled them." As such, it was a "novel of despair written on the verge of a new century he [Adams] would despise."

Adams's sense of disenchantment and disappointment was echoed by Civil War veterans such as Ambrose Bierce and Albion Tourgée, whose post-war fiction reflected a growing sense of the futility of the war and its terrible sacrifices to pave the way for a better country. For the darkly humorous Bierce, the war was an absurd, surreal experience whose horrors could best be suggested by stories in which the traditional protagonists suffered equally absurd fates. As Roy Morris Jr. points out in "'So Many, Many Needless Dead': The Civil War Witness of Ambrose Bierce," Bierce bolstered his absurdist fables with realistic details he had gained on the battlefield.

Tourgée, who like Bierce had fought in the Union Army in the western theater of the war, carried with him a similar disillusionment, one he extended to his experiences in the immediate post-war era. The principal target of Tourgée's anger, as expressed in his novels *A Fool's Errand* and *Bricks without Straw*, were the unreconstructed Southerners who refused to accept the war's verdict. Edward J. Blum's "Of Saints and Sinners: Religion and the Civil War and Reconstruction Novel" considers Tourgée's work in opposition to that of southern novelist Thomas Dixon, who served as an apologist for southern resistance to change.

The vastly more talented writer Stephen Crane used the experiences of others to write his own Civil War novel, *The Red Badge of Courage*. Crane biographer Roy Morris Jr. refutes the author's claims to have written his novel "on my own authority" by demonstrating how carefully Crane researched the war, basing his book on a wide variety of sources both oral and written, including the accounts of Civil War veterans in his hometown of Port Jervis, New York.

"On Whose Responsibility? The Historical and Literary Underpinnings of *The Red Badge of Courage*" concludes that Crane's critical and popular success was based in no small part on the works of Union veterans such as Bierce and John W. De Forest, who, like his fictional hero Henry Fleming, "had been to touch the great death."

"Let the Story Tellers Invent It All"

The continuing lure of the Civil War as a mythic subject can be seen in the works of such disparate modern writers as Upton Sinclair and F. Scott Fitzgerald. Sinclair, best known as a muckraking journalist, characteristically saw the war and its memory as a way in which modern Americans could "be redeemed from the sordidness and shame of the present." In "A Muckraker at Manassas: Upton Sinclair's Civil War Fiction," Jessica A. Dorman considers Sinclair's novels *Manassas* and *The Metropolis*, in which he examined the war's effect on a young Union soldier and the son of a Confederate soldier killed at Spotsylvania.

Fitzgerald, in his comparatively minor Civil War-related fiction, took from the war a renewed "sense of romantic possibility and a keen awareness of its elusiveness," scholars Marcia Noe and Fendall Fulton note in "Narrative Art and Modernist Sensibility in the Civil War Fiction of F. Scott Fitzgerald." For Noe and Fulton, Fitzgerald's towering achievement, *The Great Gatsby*, with its mythopoeic approach to American history and personal self-creation, owes much to his lifelong study of the Civil War. "For Fitzgerald," they write, "as Faulkner's Gavin Stevens notes, 'The past is never dead. It's not even past'; he viewed himself, his life, his family, his friends, and, above all, his subject matter, through the lens of American history."

The mythologizing impulse is seen in the various ways in which real historical figures such as John Singleton Mosby and Nathan Bedford Forrest have been transformed into barely recognizable stereotypes through the transforming constraints of popular art. Paul Ashdown and Edward Caudill examine the Mosby myth in "'Let the Story Tellers Invent It All': Col. John S. Mosby in Popular Literature." They find that Mosby, a successful but comparatively minor Confederate cavalry raider during the Civil War, became his own "chief mythmaker" following the war, outliving all other major Confederate military figures—including those who might have contradicted his heroic version of himself. At the same time, Mosby was a "remarkably protean figure" who could be "plotted as a cowboy hero, a spy, a villain, a metaphor, or a cat. He can be invoked on the boulevards of Paris or the mountains of Mexico. He can be an arsonist, a train robber, a kidnapper, a bomber, a torturer—even a rat killer. " This ability to change images insured that Mosby's story would remain fresh in the public mind.

Another Confederate cavalryman, Tennessee general Nathan Bedford Forrest, is the subject of Ashdown and Caudill's "Hydra or Heracles?: Mythologizing Nathan Bedford Forrest in Civil War Fiction." The authors argue that Forrest, while undeniably successful as a Civil War leader of mounted troops, "is as much literary myth as military hero . . . his complex reputation has been shaped largely by fiction writers from Joel Chandler Harris to Elmore Leonard." The Forrest that emerges in fiction, they note, "is both monster and hero, sinner and saint, devil and redeemer, depending on where one stands in relation to historical events."[2]

A legend of a different sort is seen in Mississippi novelist James Street's 1942 novel, *Tap Roots*. As Nancy Dupont demonstrates in "*Tap Roots* and the Free State of Jones," Street traded on an already existing legend, that of the supposed secession of Jones County, Mississippi, from the Confederacy during the Civil War, to chronicle the effects of the war on a single southern family. Whether or not the residents of Jones County actually seceded in an organized way, or merely hid out in the local swamps for the duration of the war, the myth has proved exceptionally long-lived, and twenty-first-century travel brochures still chronicle the "Free State of Jones." The fact that Street's novel was later made into a movie of the same name provides yet another layer to the myth.

This mythogizing of the Civil War has continued in the modern novel and movie, *Cold Mountain*, which is the subject a study by Paul Ashdown that consider how novelist Charles Frazier overlaid the actual Civil War with another layer of Homeric myth, and how he made use of his own relative's real Civil War experiences to create a best-selling novel. In "Savage Satori: Fact and Fiction in Charles Frazier's *Cold Mountain*," Ashdown suggests that "Frazier's real quest in *Cold Mountain* is the recovery of language and lost tradition . . . a tradition Frazier sees vanishing, if not already gone, but still worth remembering." Inevitably, Ashdown says, this raises questions about the historical accuracy of the events Frazier recounts.

"History with Lightning"

Myth-making of another sort can be seen in D.W. Griffith's 1915 movie, *The Birth of a Nation*, which was based in large part on Thomas Dixon's reconstruction-based novels, *The Clansman* and *The Leopard's Spots*. Phebe Davidson's study of Griffith's movie and its widely discredited sources, "'History with Lightning': The Legacy of D.W. Griffith's *The Birth of a Nation*," argues that while the movie "still retains great power due to its technical proficiency and innovations," it is "at best the 'record of a cultural illusion' and not, despite its claims, of history itself." It is, in other words, a myth, however modern it is in its chosen artistic medium of film.

Another Civil War myth was created by Atlanta author Margaret Mitchell, whose famous 1936 novel, *Gone with the Wind*, led to an even more famous movie version three years later. In "Hollywood Themes and Southern Myths: An Analysis of *Gone with the Wind*," William E. Huntzicker takes a look at Mitchell's mythologizing of the Old South, and how the movie was influenced in part by *The Birth of a Nation*. Like the earlier film, says Huntzicker, *Gone with the Wind* romanticizes a South that never was, imbuing it with a pervasive sense of nostalgia for a place and a way of life that never really existed in the first place.

Paul Ashdown further examines the way in which Mosby has been remembered in the more recent medium of television in "Knights in Blue and Butternut: Television's Civil War." Ashdown finds that the 1957–58 series about Mosby's exploits, *The Gray Ghost,* was the only TV series of its time to focus on the war itself. A plethora of other shows, from *The Rifleman* to *Yancy Derringer,* treated the Civil War as a past event in its heroes' lives. This was due partly, Ashdown says, to the fact that "stories placed during the Civil War required battle scenes and had to confront messy ideological issues. Stories set after the war emphasized reconciliation and renewal."

In "History Thrice Removed: Joshua Chamberlain and *Gettysburg*," Crompton Burton traces the ways in which an actual historical event, in this case Chamberlain's leadership of the 20th Maine Infantry during the second day of the Battle of Gettysburg, has been inevitably transformed as the story of the event has threaded its way from official reports through various memoirs, historical accounts, novels, and a movie screenplay. The process, says Burton, results in "history thrice removed . . . not a portrait of what happened but a story of what happened."

The book comes full circle with looks at the movie *Glory*, about the sacrificial service of black soldiers during the war, and the celebrated miniseries *Roots*, which created its own myth about the black experience of slavery and emancipation. As W. Scott Poole notes in "'Ain't Nobody Clean': *Glory!* and the Politics of Black Agency," such mythmaking "allows humans both freedom and absolution from the sins of history."

The particular historical sin of slavery—bad enough on its own—impelled Tennessee author Alex Haley to mythologize his own family's personal experience of slavery as a way of finding a moral meaning to the overwhelming experience of the Civil War itself. In so doing, William Huntzicker suggests in "Alex Haley's *Roots*: The Fiction of Fact," Haley simultaneously made a fiction of fact and a fact of fiction. Or, to put it another way, he used memory to create myth, which is something writers have been doing in one form or another since Homer sent Odysseus on his long way home from Troy.

Another southern novelist, Mississippi-born Shelby Foote, reluctantly found himself an overnight celebrity following the wildly successful 1990 television broadcast of filmmaker Ken Burns's multi-part documentary, *The Civil War*. As David W. Bulla points out in "A Voice of the South: The Transformation of Shelby Foote," Foote was just one of many expert commentators featured in the series, but his courtly demeanor and drawling southern accent made him seem almost a contemporary of such Confederate warriors as Robert E. Lee and Stonewall Jackson. It was a fame that Foote had neither expected nor sought, but the success of the television series illustrated yet again the unshakable hold the Civil War still has on the American psyche, nearly a century and a half after its conclusion.

The various artists featured in *Memory and Myth: The Civil War in Fiction and Film from* Uncle Tom's Cabin *to* Cold Mountain, working in their chosen media, have continued to examine that hold. Whether in fiction, non-fiction, television or film, artists are still attempting to make sense of the war, and to convey their findings to their readers and watchers—both in America and throughout the world.

Notes

1. This well-known quote has become part of the accepted lore surrounding Harriet Beecher Stowe and Abraham Lincoln, but no one can seem to agree on the exact wording—or even if Lincoln actually said it at all. There was, in fact, a meeting of the two in 1862 at the White House, where Stowe was introduced to the president by Massachusetts senator and family friend Henry Wilson, but no one bothered to take notes at the time. Stowe herself reported to her sister only that "It was a very droll time we had at the White House I assure you. I will tell you all about it when I get home." How the president's direct reference to *Uncle Tom's Cabin* entered the history books remains unclear, and the quote may indeed be apocryphal. Various versions have Lincoln saying either "So this is the little lady who made this big war"; "So this is the little woman who started this big war"; "So this is the little woman who wrote the book that started this great war"; "So you're the little woman who wrote the book that started this great war"; and "So you're the little woman who wrote the book that made this great war." David Herbert Donald, the dean of Lincoln biographers, renders it "So this is the little lady who made this big war" in his 1995 biography, and he should perhaps be given the final word. Tellingly, perhaps, Stowe's most recent biographer, Joan D. Hedrick, omits the quote altogether in her 1994 biography, although she cites Stowe's follow-up letter to her sister. Whatever the case—and no one will ever be able to say definitively—it certainly sounds like the sort of gracious and witty remark that Lincoln might have made, had it occurred to him at the time, and the sentiment was widespread on both sides of the Mason-Dixon line.
2. Paul Ashdown and Edward Caudill, "Hydra or Hercules? Mythologizing Nathan Bedford Forrest in Civil War Fiction," paper read at 9th annual Symposium on the 19th Century Press, the Civil War, and Free Expression, 31 October–2 November 2002, University of Tennessee, Chattanooga, Tennessee.

PART I

"So This Is the Little Lady Who Made This Big War"

"This Inherited Misfortune"

Gender, Race, and Slavery in *Uncle Tom's Cabin* and *Gone with the Wind*

— William E. Huntzicker —

Like the Old West, the Old South has often been a favorite fictional setting for novelists depicting the nation's tumultuous history. A New England abolitionist, Harriet Beecher Stowe, provided the first and arguably the biggest blockbuster story about the Old South. Her 1852 novel, *Uncle Tom's Cabin*, became the narrative against which future stories were measured, particularly in the antebellum era. The South's most successful response came long after the Civil War and Reconstruction, when Atlanta journalist Margaret Mitchell published *Gone with the Wind* in 1936. Each novel, in its own way, created vivid images of gender, race, and slavery in the Old South that still endure.

Few popular literary works have ever had such a powerful political impact or left such an enduring legacy as *Uncle Tom's Cabin*. Eric J. Sundquist has succinctly summarized the novel's immediate success:

> When it appeared in book form in 1852, 50,000 copies were sold within eight weeks, 300,000 within a year, and 1 million in America and England combined by early 1853. It added an entirely new dimension to a campaign that had often bogged down in internecine quarrels and useless theorizing. By giving flesh-and-blood reality to the inhuman system for which the Fugitive Slave Law now required the North, as well as the South, to be

> responsible, it became a touchstone for antislavery sentiment. Stowe was hardly the first to call attention to slavery's destruction of both black and white families, but her novel perfectly combined the tradition of the sentimental novel and the rhetoric of antislavery polemic. In scene after scene, the fragmentation of black households and the corrosive moral effect on white conscience is her focal point.[1]

Upon meeting Harriet Beecher Stowe, President Abraham Lincoln reportedly underscored the book's influence in polarizing the nation by commenting, "So this is the little woman who started this big war."[2]

Although very much a product of its time, *Uncle Tom's Cabin* painted powerful scenes and characters that both contemporary critics and future generations would find impossible to erase from public memory. Stowe told a sweeping and involving story into which she wove a strong political argument with religious overtones. People who have not read the book still recognize the main characters' names and associate them with certain personal characteristics and crucial scenes: Uncle Tom, the steadfastly loyal Christian and martyr; Eliza, the loving mother who flees across an icy river, risking her own and her baby's lives to avoid sale and separation; Little Eva, the saintly child whose death converts both her father and a heathen slave girl; Topsy, Eva's opposite, a trickster with little self-esteem who finds redemption in the end; and Simon Legree, the plantation overseer who has become the archetypal slave driver and tyrant in American fiction.

Religion not only puts the story on a moral plane, but also ties it to the mainstream of American history. Both religious leaders and historians in the nineteenth century saw their lives as being directed by the unseen hand of Providence,[3] and the wedding of theology and politics was part of Puritan theology from the very beginning of the republic. Jane Tompkins points out that *Uncle Tom's Cabin* fits into the "jeremiad" theme of American history, defined as "a mode of public exhortation" that joined "social criticism to spiritual renewal, public to private identity, the shifting 'signs of the times' to certain traditional metaphors, themes and symbols." The jeremiad theme, says Tompkins, explains why the novel was so phenomenally successful, using characters, settings, situations, symbols, and doctrines that fit within the religious values while attempting to move the nation in a particular political direction.[4]

Stowe came from a family of ministers, and the jeremiad was a prominent part of Puritan theocracy. "Its fusion of theology and politics is not only doctrinal—in that it ties the salvation of the individual to the community's historical enterprise—it is practical as well, for it reflects the interests of Puritan ministers in their bid to retain spiritual and secular authority," says Tomkins. "The sentimental novel, too, is an act of persuasion aimed at defining social reality; the difference is that the jeremiad represents the interests of Puritan ministers, while the sentimental novel represents the interests of middle-class women." Rhetoric defines reality and makes history by convincing people of its description of the world. "The sentimental novelists make their bid for power by positing the kingdom of heaven on earth as a world over which women exercise ultimate control."[5] Tompkins characterizes the novel as revolutionary in its call for a restructuring of society from a feminine (if not necessarily feminist) perspective.

Even considered within the context of her time, however, Stowe was not a radical feminist. Instead, she was the ultimate promoter of family values. A "radical conservatism" uniting the sacred and the secular, Eric Sundquist writes, lay behind the novel's "elevation of domestic Christian virtues associated with women over the failed political secular virtues associated with a patriarchal society." The "knotted complexity" of the relationships among women, blacks and the Christian tradition reveals "how inadequately *Uncle Tom's Cabin* has been understood and how central it is, as a literary and political document, to the American experience."[6]

Stowe's conservatism becomes clear when contrasted with the experiences of the sisters Sarah and Angelina Grimké, who also appealed to the national conscience and exhorted women to work against slavery. Unlike Stowe, they urged women to become involved in politics outside the home. Sarah Grimké, who grew up on a Charleston plantation, had abhorred slavery since her childhood, when she was given a slave to be her servant. Young Sarah, who had a passion for learning, treated the girl as a playmate and taught her to read in deliberate defiance of her parents' rules and South Carolina law. Sarah's sister, Angelina, born thirteen years later, developed the same revulsion toward slavery.

Sarah and Angelina eventually moved to Philadelphia, where they became outspoken abolitionists. At first the Grimkés were limited to speaking in private parlors. As their audiences grew, however, they moved their speeches into churches and other public auditoriums—a scandalous activity for proper young women of the time. Denied admission into the American Anti-Slavery Society, the sisters joined the Philadelphia Female Anti-Slavery Society. In 1836 they moved to New York to become the first full-time female abolition agents.[7]

Angelina Grimké insisted that women were not helpless even without the vote, and she appealed to southern women to exert their influence on slavery by reading on the subject, praying both publicly and privately, speaking out against it, and taking action. "It is through the tongue, the pen, and the press, that truth is principally propagated," she wrote. Angelina urged Southern women to speak to friends, relatives, and acquaintances calmly and forcefully about the sin of slavery. "Some of you *own* slaves yourselves," she said. "If you believe slavery is *sinful*, set them at liberty, 'undo the heavy burdens and let the oppressed go free.'" If the freed slaves wished to remain on the plantation, then their former owners should pay wages and educate them. Everyone had a duty to improve his own and others' mental faculties, Angelina argued, "and we commit a great sin, if we *forbid or prevent* that cultivation of the mind in others, which would enable them to perform this duty." Recognizing that freeing slaves and teaching them to read would violate some state laws, she added, "such wicked laws *ought to be no barrier* in the way of your duty, and I appeal to the Bible to prove this position."[8]

The Grimkés acted in accordance with their faith, a Quaker sect that encouraged women to become leaders and to speak out on public issues. The sisters presented their message in religious terms, but Massachusetts church leaders issued a pastoral letter deploring "the intimate acquaintance and promiscuous conversation of females" in assuming "the place and tone of a man as a social reformer." Such women threatened the social order by leaving the private sphere. Sarah Grimké shot back a long retort, citing scriptural incidents in which women bore God's tidings, and accused the ministers of creating scriptural differences between the genders where none existed. Furthermore, she wrote, interpretation of the scriptures would surely change as more women learned Greek and Hebrew to provide their own translations of the text.[9]

Literary critic Jean Fagan Yellin has highlighted the contrast between Stowe and the Grimké sisters by looking at the approach to social activism recommended in *Uncle Tom's Cabin*. Through the character of Ophelia and others, Stowe demonstrated that a person could make a difference by acting solely within the women's sphere. Forced to face her own prejudice by her brother, the benevolent slave owner Augustine St. Clare, Ophelia agrees to try to educate the rough black girl Topsy. Yellin notes that important scenes take place in kitchens, making the kitchen the center of the women's sphere, if not the universe. Non-whites, like women in Stowe's book, possess special attributes. Her hero triumphs in heaven after being persecuted on earth.[10] Elizabeth Ammons takes the feminine argument a step further, seeing Uncle Tom as a maternal savior in a world led by women in the home—a sacred place to Stowe. By contrast, Legree's greatest sin, Ammons argues, is to violate the sanctity of the home by bringing the marketplace into it with slaves as mistresses.[11]

Although Stowe presented her message in religious terms, she advocated working within the system. She did not advocate breaking laws or stepping out of the women's sphere, except to help slaves escape and to preserve their families. In this sense, Stowe was clearly not revolutionary in the political sphere, despite the strongest possible condemnation of slavery through both her narrative and sermonizing. "There are those living who know the mothers whom this accursed traffic has driven to the murder of their children and themselves, seeking in death a shelter from woes more dreaded than death," Stowe wrote. "Nothing of tragedy can be written, can be spoken, can be conceived, that equals the frightful reality of scenes daily and hourly acting on our shores, beneath the shadow of American law, and the shadow of the cross of Christ."[12]

Besides promoting religion, *Uncle Tom's Cabin* is astutely political. Despite her critics' allegations, Stowe carefully separated her attacks on slavery from her views of the South, and each of her characters represented archetypes in the slavery debates. Marie St. Clare, the whining household mistress, fits the mold of the Southern aristocrat spoiled by slavery. Similarly, Ophelia St. Clare represents a New England aristocratic abolitionist who has not yet confronted her own racism. Her brother, the good-hearted plantation owner, points out her hypocrisies while acknowledging weaknesses in the system of slavery. Augustine St. Clare also serves as a warning that one must not hesitate to do the right thing or it may be too late; he dies before he frees Uncle Tom as promised. The Shelbys, who appear at the beginning of the novel, also seem to be good people tricked into selling Uncle Tom out of economic necessity. The novel has many good people caught in a bad system, as well as bad people who exploit and perpetuate that system.[13]

The most important character in *Uncle Tom's Cabin*, of course, is Uncle Tom. Stowe herself, as well as subsequent literary critics, seemed to underestimate the power of the character she created, partly because they failed to understand the power of non-violence. Uncle Tom was no Uncle Tom, in the way that modern cultural memory has come to know him. Not even Stowe seemed to understand the source of his power. A year after her novel appeared, she published *A Key to Uncle Tom's Cabin; Presenting the Original Facts and Documents upon Which the Story Is Founded* to defend her characterization of slavery. In discussing the character of Uncle Tom, she defined the enduring Uncle Tom label. She cited a number of parallels to Uncle Tom, most notably the published memoirs of Josiah Henson, a Maryland native then living in Canada.

Henson's story began in slavery, when as a young boy he witnessed his father beaten by an overseer for protecting his mother from an attack by a white man. Raised a heathen, Henson converted to Christianity and became an overseer loyal to his master and to God. When his owner needed to move some slaves to Kentucky, Henson was placed in charge. "On the way thither they passed through a portion of Ohio," Stowe wrote, "and there Henson was informed that he could now secure his own freedom and that of all his fellows, and he was strongly urged to do it. He was exceedingly tempted and tried, but his Christian principle was invulnerable." As a result, he kept control over of the slaves because he had given his word to his master. This provided Stowe with another opportunity for a sermon: "Those casuists among us who lately seem to think and teach that it is right for us to violate the plain commands of God whenever some great national good can be secured by it, would do well to contemplate the inflexible principle of the poor slave, who, without being able to read a letter of the Bible, was yet enabled to perform the most sublime act of self-renunciation in obedience to its commands."[14]

If Uncle Tom had behaved as Josiah Henson did, he may have been long lost to oblivion. He did not. Uncle Tom is not a classic Christian martyr beaten to death for refusing to renounce his Christian faith, but one who gives his life to protect the hiding place of two slaves working to obtain their freedom and to protect the virtue of a young girl from the evil Simon Legree. Thus, he dies for God, country, friends, and principles—not to protect the rights of a master over his victims, as suggested in the Henson anecdote. Eventually, Henson earned his own freedom, but at the expense of keeping his fellow slaves in bondage. One cannot imagine Uncle Tom behaving in such a fashion. In any case, Uncle Tom's martyrdom was certainly no cowardly act.

Stowe's representation of African Americans stirred strong reaction among her contemporaries and for generations to come. As soon as it appeared, *Uncle Tom's Cabin* created a veritable industry of Southern responses. Between 1852 and 1861, at least twenty-seven novels by southerners worked to foster the image of a more pleasant plantation system in popular culture. In reviewing them, Thomas F. Gossett found that roughly half of the authors said their works were a direct response to *Uncle Tom's Cabin,* and another one-fourth attacked the novel directly. Gossett found that the Anti-Tom works created kinder, gentler plantations with fewer whippings, more thoughtful mistresses, and more pious, passive, and loyal slaves. Many of the slaves in these works declare their need for slavery, if not satisfaction and happiness with it.[15] The legacy of Uncle Tom as someone who sells out to the establishment may have come more from the characterizations of Uncle Tom in the Anti-Tom literature than from the original.

Whatever the case, the stereotype of the happy slave was safely ensconced in American popular culture by 1936 when the blockbuster novel *Gone with the Wind* was published. The author, Atlanta journalist Margaret Mitchell, had grown up listening to stories of the Confederacy and the Lost Cause. Eighty-five years after Stowe's novel appeared in serialized form, the South's most popular response appeared, but Mitchell clearly had not intended to write a cultural counterpoint to *Uncle Tom's Cabin.* She claimed that *Uncle Tom's Cabin* was irrelevant to her writing of *Gone with the Wind,* but she linked the two books together in a letter written two years after her novel was published. "It makes me very happy to know that 'Gone With the Wind' is helping refute the impression of the South which people abroad gained from Mrs. Stowe's book," she told a Berlin correspondent. "Here in America 'Uncle Tom's Cabin' has been long forgotten and there are very few people today who have read it. They only know it as the name of a book which had a good deal to do with the bitterness of the Abolition movement."[16]

Mitchell considered her book apolitical and appeared baffled that some African Americans did not like it. She again referred to *Uncle Tom's Cabin* in a 1939 letter to fellow Georgia journalist Susan Myrick, who was in Los Angeles to advise Hollywood on how to depict Mitchell's southerners on the big screen. "The Radical press tried to use 'Gone With the Wind' as a whip to drive the Southern Negroes into the Communist Party somewhat in the same manner that 'Uncle Tom's Cabin' was used to recruit Abolitionists," she complained. "Of course you know how happy it made me to have Radical publications dislike 'Gone with the Wind.'"[17] Those who criticized the novel were taking politics too seriously, she wrote.

Surprised by the reaction to her book by some African Americans, Mitchell concluded that some in the black press disliked the book because some characters used the pejorative terms "nigger" and "darky." "Regardless of the fact that they call each other 'Nigger' today and regardless of the fact that nice people in ante bellum days called them 'darkies,' these papers are in a fine frenzy," Mitchell observed, suggesting that those who objected to her book were trying to keep old conflicts alive. "But I do not intend to let any number of trouble-making Professional Negroes change my feelings toward the race with whom my relations have always been those of affection and mutual respect. There are Professional Negroes just as there are Professional Southerners and, from what I can learn from Negroes I have talked to, they are no more loved by their race than Professional Southerners are by us."[18]

This passage illustrates how Mitchell was both trapped by and sought to escape from Southern stereotypes. Ironically, in *Gone with the Wind*, the novel *Uncle Tom's Cabin* causes problems for Scarlett O'Hara when she encounters Northern women holding stereotypes created by the earlier book: "Accepting *Uncle Tom's Cabin* as revelation second only to the Bible, the Yankee women all wanted to know about the bloodhounds which every Southerner kept to track down runaway slaves. And they never believed her when she told them she had only seen one bloodhound in all her life and it was a small mild dog and not a huge ferocious mastiff." She resents their interest in branding irons and slave concubinage. "Especially did she resent this in view of the enormous increase in mulatto babies in Atlanta since the Yankee soldiers had settled in the town."[19]

In one conversation, three Northern women discuss the difficulty of finding a servant. "'That shouldn't be difficult,' said Scarlett and laughed. 'If you can find a darky just in from the country who hasn't been spoiled by the Freedmen's Bureau, you'll have the best kind of servant possible.'" The women become indignant, saying they would not trust blacks to handle their babies. "Scarlett thought of the kind, gnarled hands of Mammy worn rough in Ellen's service and hers and Wade's. What did these strangers know of black hands, how dear and comforting they could be, how unerringly they knew how to sooth, to pat, to fondle? She laughed shortly. 'It's strange you should feel that way when it was you all who freed them.'"[20]

The women quickly disavow any association with abolition. "I never saw a nigger till I came South last month," one of them says, "and I don't care if I never see another. They give me the creeps." Standing nearby, Uncle Peter hears the conversation, and one of the women then refers to him. "He had never had the term 'nigger' applied to him by a white person in all his life. By other negroes, yes, but never by a white person. And to be called untrustworthy and an 'old pet,' he, Peter, who had been the dignified mainstay of the Hamilton family for years!" The Maine woman says she would prefer "a good Irish girl," to which Scarlett replies that she had never seen a white servant and would not want one. "I assure you that darkies aren't cannibals and are quite trustworthy."[21]

Scarlett's thoughts turn angry and patronizing: "What damnably queer people Yankees are! Those women seemed to think that because Uncle Peter was black, he had no ears to hear with and no feelings, as tender as their own, to be hurt. They did not know that negroes had to be handled gently, as though they were children, directed, praised, petted, scolded. They didn't understand negroes or the relations between the negroes and their former masters. Yet they had fought a war to free them. And having freed them, they didn't want to have anything to do with them, except to use them to terrorize Southerners."

This terror is made implicit at the climax of the novel, when Scarlett is attacked by two men, one black and one white, while riding through the freedmen's Shantytown. Taking such a route, as Scarlett does to and from work, could be dangerous, and she runs the risk of getting raped—the word is not used—and thus invoking the wrath of the Ku Klux Klan in retaliation, which in turn would bring Union soldiers back down on Atlanta. This chain reaction begins with the attempted assault on Scarlett. She is rescued by Big Sam, who used to be a Tara field hand. Big Sam and the would-be rapist present a sharp contrast seen throughout the novel. The Civil War failed to end the distinction between field hands and house slaves, who remained loyal after emancipation. As a field hand, Big Sam breaks yet another barrier, becoming a loyal house slave by rescuing Scarlett—in effect, joining the family. Mammy, of course, was already part of the family, more of a parent than Scarlett's real parents. Another former slave, Peter, expresses a similar need to belong: "'No, Ma'm! Dey din' sot me free. Ah wouldn' let no sech trash sot me free,' said Peter indignantly. 'Ah still b'longs ter Miss Pitty an' w'en Ah dies she gwine lay me in de Hamilton buhyin' groun' whar Ah b'longs.'"[22]

Both Stowe and Mitchell remove the African Americans in their stories slightly from the mainstream racist images so popular in their times. Stowe's plantation slaves have different personalities and even some cultural nuances that were missed in contemporary works. Certainly, they were a useful antidote to the "coon songs," Stephen Foster melodies, and minstrel shows popular at the time. Mitchell's blacks lack the evil-incarnate character of those in D.W. Griffith's overtly racist movie *The Birth of a Nation*, but Mitchell still describes them as being one generation removed from the jungle and gives some of them animal characteristics. The loyal servants, on the other hand, are seen as benevolently childlike. Both books gave African Americans ample reason to be concerned about the appropriation of their images, but both also moved the culture forward, if ever so slowly.

Like most popular fiction, the novels provided scenes populated with good people—if not heroes—and hissable villains who profit from the loss of life or the breakup of families. They present people readers can care about, even if they don't necessarily identify with them. The books share some other characteristics. Contrary to what the critics said, *Uncle Tom's Cabin* does not depict most plantations as evil places, but it does present the *system* of slavery as evil. By contrast, *Gone with the Wind* does not present the unambivalent longing for the Old South that viewers of the more romanticized movie may expect from it.

Although each story challenges the stereotypes created by previous views of slavery and the Old South, they share some common traits and illustrate what Timothy B. Powell has characterized as the tension between "multiculturalism" and "monoculturalism." During the antebellum era, Powell contends, westward expansion brought new cultural groups and territories into the new nation, and the growing industrial revolution required cheap labor imported from abroad. Both trends created cultural diversity at the same time as "equally powerful forces of monoculturalism . . . sought to counter the increasing cultural diversity of the nation." The resultant conflicting interests of inclusion and exclusion can be seen in contemporary politics and culture.[23]

Gone with the Wind and *Uncle Tom's Cabin*, for all their differences in tone, outlook, and artistic merit, share similar assumptions about cultural superiority. And each shares, as well, the attitude of an unidentified journalist who as early as 1819 characterized slavery as "this inherited misfortune," a system of social and economic tyranny which already had outlived its usefulness.[24]

Notes

1. Eric J. Sundquist, ed., *New Essays on* Uncle Tom's Cabin: *The American Novel* (New York: Cambridge University Press, 1986), p. 18.
2. This quotation has been reported with minor variations over the years, referring to woman or lady, big war or great war, and with and without a reference to the book. Thus, it has often been reported as "So this is the little woman who made this big

war," as it is in Glenna Matthews, *The Rise of Public Woman: Woman's Power and Woman's Place in the United States 1630–1970* (New York: Oxford University Press, 1992), p. 88.

3. See the analysis in David W. Noble, *Historians Against History* (Minneapolis: University of Minnesota Press, 1965).
4. Jane Tompkins, *Sensational Designs: The Cultural Work of American Fiction 1790–1860* (New York: Oxford University Press, 1985), pp. 140–141; Sacvan Bercovitch, *The American Jeremiad* (Madison: University of Wisconsin Press, 1978), pp. xi, xiv, 9.
5. Tompkins, pp. 140–42.
6. Sundquist, pp. 6–7.
7. Miriam Gurko, *The Ladies of Seneca Falls: The Birth of the Woman's Rights Movement* (New York: Schocken Books, 1974), pp. 30–46. For similar connections between feminism and the civil rights movement of the 1960s and 1970s, see Sara Evans, *Personal Politics: The Roots of Women's Liberation in the Civil Rights Movement and the New Left* (New York: Alfred A. Knopf, 1979).
8. Angelina Grimké, Appeal to the Christian Women of the South, *The Anti-Slavery Examiner* 1:2 (September 1836): 16–26; *The Feminist Papers*, ed. Alice S. Rossi (New York: Bantam Books, 1974), pp. 296–304.
9. Sara M. Evans, *Born for Liberty: A History of Women in America* (New York: The Free Press, 1989), pp. 78–81; Rossi, pp. 305–318.
10. Jean Fagan Yellin, "Doing It Herself: Uncle Tom's Cabin and Woman's Role in the Slavery Crisis, in Eric J. Sundquist, ed., *New Essays on* Uncle Tom's Cabin: *The American Novel* (New York: Cambridge University Press, 1986), pp. 85–105.
11. Elizabeth Ammons, "Stowe's Dream of the Mother-Savior: *Uncle Tom's Cabin* and American Women Writers before the 1920s," in Sundquist, pp. 155–195.
12. Stowe, *Uncle Tom's Cabin*, "Chapter XLV: Concluding Remarks."
13. Stowe's views cited here are taken from *A Key to* Uncle Tom's Cabin: *Presenting the Original Facts and Documents upon Which the Story Is Founded* (Bedford, Mass.: Applewood Books, reprint of Boston: John P. Jewett & Co., 1853).
14. Stowe, *A Key to Uncle Tom's Cabin*, p. 26.
15. Thomas F. Gossett, *"Anti-Uncle Tom Literature,"* Chapter 12 of *Uncle Tom's Cabin and American Culture* (Dallas, Texas: Southern Methodist University Press, 1985), pp. 212–239. The books are listed on pages 429–431.
16. Richard Harwell, ed., *Margaret Mitchell's Gone with the Wind Letters 1936–1949* (New York: Collier Books, 1976), p. 217.
17. Harwell, pp. 273–274.
18. Harwell, pp. 273–274.
19. Margaret Mitchell, *Gone with the Wind* (New York: Warner Books, 1964 [1936]), Chapter XXXVIII, p. 662. Citations are from this inexpensive, paperback edition.
20. Mitchell, Chapter XXXVIII, p. 665.
21. Mitchell, Chapter XXXVIII, pp. 665–66.

22. Mitchell, Chapter XXXVIII, pp. 666–67.
23. Timothy B. Powell, *Ruthless Democracy: A Multicultural Interpretation of the American Renaissance* (Princeton, N.J.: Princeton University Press, 2000). Quotes from page 11.
24. From a 23-page review of the second annual report of the American Colonization Society, signed "T," probably Horace Holley, in *The Western Review and Miscellaneous Magazine* 1(3) (October 1819).

BEYOND *UNCLE TOM'S CABIN*

— LLOYD CHIASSON, JR. —

Perhaps no fictional characters in American literature have ever generated more emotion or controversy than those in Harriet Beecher Stowe's 1852 novel, *Uncle Tom's Cabin.* For many who opposed slavery, Stowe's creations—Tom, Legree, Eliza, and Little Eva—embodied real life, and the abuses they suffered represented an accurate portrayal of plantation life and were therefore more fact than fiction. Viewed from this perspective, *Uncle Tom's Cabin* was a form of nineteenth-century New Journalism; it was non-fiction fiction that was generally applauded in the North as revealed truth and reviled in the South as emotionalistic propaganda.

No matter how much *Uncle Tom's Cabin* may have galvanized public opinion in both regions, however, it would be a mistake to believe that any single work of literature had a lasting effect on the institution of slavery. This is not to say that authors in the North and South did not write extensively about the subject, or that the cumulative effect of their works was not profound in the course of events. During the years before the Civil War, the debate was constant and unflinching in virulence, propelled by a litany of events that began well before the Revolutionary War. Regional antagonism festered and moved inexorably toward conflict, growing stronger and harsher with a series of geographical compromises, the fear of slave insurrections, and a growing sense of righteous indignation and inevitability on both sides.

The election of a Republican in the 1860 presidential race was the culmination of events that began in 1820 with a legislative balancing act called the Missouri Compromise. To appease both regions by maintaining a balance between slave and free states, Congress allowed Missouri to enter the union as a slave state, while Maine came in as a free state. For the next forty years the slavery debate simmered and occasionally boiled. The Nat Turner slave uprising in 1831 aroused long-held southern fears of domestic violence. The Kansas-Nebraska Bill in 1854 called upon settlers to resolve the slavery question politically in their territories, and resulted in violence between pro- and anti-slavery forces in Kansas. In 1857, the anti-slavery factions railed against the Dred Scott decision, in which the Supreme Court ruled the Missouri Compromise unconstitutional and declared blacks non-citizens. Two years later, John Brown's failed slave insurrection at Harpers Ferry, Virginia, exacerbated old fears, inflamed rhetoric, and steeled both regions for a foreboding future.

Unrelenting propaganda during this period magnified each event and enlarged the debate. Most notable were the abolitionist journals that flourished in the northern states after 1830. Discussion about slavery was not confined to abolitionist newspapers and magazines, however. In various works of fiction and nonfiction, the slavery issue was articulated. Novels, monographs, children's books, and pamphlets reached an influential, educated audience. At the same time, tracts, almanacs, sermons, hymns and non-religious songs brought the pro- and anti-slavery messages to the common man. During the antebellum period, each of these became a meaningful lever of propaganda.

The literary dispute over slavery had a long history. Beginning in the colonial period, religion framed the debate, first in the pulpit, and then in literature. Samuel Sewell's *The Selling of Joseph, A Memorial*, a widely distributed anti-slavery pamphlet published in 1700, is an early example.[1] One year later, John Saffin wrote what was probably the first published defense of slavery in America, *A Brief and Candid Answer*.[2] *Answer* attempted to undermine the biblical arguments put forth in *Joseph*. More important, *The Selling of Joseph* and *A Brief and Candid Answer* set forth in clear terms the core issue, sustained for the next century and a half: God's will regarding man, master and slave.[3] Both Sewell and Saffin expressed simple, straightforward ideas. Sewell wrote about the equality of man in God's eyes, Saffin wrote of God's creation of different degrees of men.

It is no surprise that a religious group began the anti-slavery movement in this country.[4] The Quakers cited religious and moral reasons for the abolition of slavery in several pamphlets in the eighteenth century: *The American Defense of the Christian Golden Rule* by John Hepburn (1713);[5] *A Brief Examination of the Practice of the Times* by Ralph Sandiford (1729);[6] *Testimony against Making Slaves of Men* by Elihu Coleman (1733);[7] and *All Slave-keepers that Keep the Innocent in*

Bondage, Apostates by Benjamin Lay (1738).[8] Not only was the message spread throughout Quaker congregations in the colonies,[9] but Quaker and evangelical churches were influential in sustaining the movement into the nineteenth century, as exemplified in 1810 by Elias Hicks's influential pamphlet, *Observations on the Slavery of the Africans and Their Descendants*.[10]

Prior to 1820, opposition to slavery existed in every state and was based primarily upon the principles of individual liberty and human rights, although factors like the economic viability of slavery were questioned.[11] Primarily because of the influence of the evangelical churches,[12] abolitionist societies were numerous in the South until about 1830.[13] In fact, 106 of 130 abolitionist societies were located in Virginia, Tennessee, Kentucky, and the southern section of the Old Northwest,[14] although their actual influence was small and their approach conciliatory.[15] By the early 1830s, however, the abolitionist movement quickly lost force in the South. Southern abolitionists receded from the debate because of conflicts within the churches over the slavery issue, the extreme positions taken by northern abolitionists such as Benjamin Lundy and William Lloyd Garrison,[16] and the belief many southerners held that northern abolitionists were behind the Denmark Vesey slave insurrection in 1822 and the Nat Turner uprising nine years later.[17]

No event did more to quicken the end of the abolitionist movement in the South than the publication in 1829 of *Walker's Appeal*, David Walker's stirring message to the "Colored Citizens of the World."[18] Probably the first published criticism of slavery by a black man,[19] *Appeal* was a passionate denunciation of the racism Walker viewed as inherent in the institution. Walker immediately became a prominent figure in the early abolitionist movement, although even Lundy and Garrison considered *Appeal* too inflammatory when it first appeared.[20]

Appeal elicited the strongest response in the South, where copies were distributed among slaves and free blacks.[21] What may have attracted the most southern attention, however, was that a free black man was openly advocating an armed insurrection by the slaves.[22] Secret sessions of the state legislatures in North Carolina and Georgia were quickly convened to discuss ways to diffuse any threats the pamphlet might create in those states.[23] Since publication figures on *Walker's Appeal* vary, it is impossible to say how large a distribution the pamphlet had, but several thousand probably reached slaves and free blacks, the primary audience for whom Walker wrote.[24]

The appearance of *Walker's Appeal* coincides with the emergence of a national abolitionist movement, which replaced the loosely knit state organizations common to the first quarter of the nineteenth century.[25] By the early 1830s, the movement had two centers. In New England, Garrison's fire and brimstone rhetoric held sway,[26] while in what was known as the Old Northwest Territory,

Joshua Giddings and Salmon Chase of Ohio proved the abolition issue was a vehicle to elected office. By 1840 the Liberty Party became a national force when James Birney was named that party's presidential candidate.[27]

In the United States, a wave of abolitionist propaganda gained strength. Abolitionist societies became active in arranging public speakers, initiating petitions,[28] distributing tracts and publishing anti-slavery periodicals.[29] The American Anti-Slavery Society in 1837–1838 published 7,877 bound volumes, 47,256 tracts and pamphlets, 4,100 circulars, and 10, 490 prints. *The Anti-Slavery Magazine*, a quarterly publication by the society, had a circulation of 9,000. *Slave Friend*,[30] a children's publication, had a circulation of 131,050; the monthly *Human Rights* had a circulation of 189,400, and the weekly *Emancipator* had a circulation of 217,000. From 1854–58, the society spent more than $3,000, a considerable sum at that time, on a series of anti-slavery tracts.[31]

The anti-slavery crusade targeted everyone, including children. Stories aimed at teaching moral lessons to the young were common, as was with case with the following selected verses of the ABC's:

A is an Abolitionist
A man who wants to free
The wretched slave, and give to all
An equal liberty.

B is a Brother with a skin
of somewhat darker hue
but in our Heavenly Father's sight,
He is as dear as you.

C is the Cotton field,
to which this injured brother's driven,
When, as the white man's slave, he toils
From early morn till even

D is the driver, cold and stern,
Who follows, whip in hand,
To punish those who dare to rest, or disobey command.

I is the Infant, from the arms
of its fond mother torn,
And at a public auction sold
With horses, cows, and corn.

W is the whipping post,
To which the slave is bound,
While on his naked back, the lash
Makes many a bleeding wound.

Z is a Zealous man, sincere,
Faithful, and just, and true;
An earnest pleader for the slave—
Will you not be so too?[32]

Juvenile stories often mirrored or surpassed the graphic detail and emotionalism of *Uncle Tom's Cabin*. Tales, often accompanied with illustrations, depicted slave children who were horribly tortured and killed.[33] For example, *A Picture of Slavery for Youth* by Jonathan Walker painted a vivid portrait of the cruelties of slave life on slave children.[34]

Poetry also became a vehicle for propaganda. Such notables as Edmund Quincy, Ralph Waldo Emerson, John Greenleaf Whittier, Henry Wadsworth Longfellow, Charles Sumner, William Ellery Channing, and Theodore Parker published work supportive of the abolitionist movement.[35] Whittier's poem "The Branded Hand" told the story of John Walker, the "slave stealer" from Pensacola, Florida, who engineered an unsuccessful attempt to pirate seven slaves to freedom in 1844. Printed along with a picture of Walker's hand with the SS (slave stealer) brand, the poem appeared in newspapers across the country, and verses such as the following were recited by children for many years afterward.[36]

Why, that brand is highest honor!—than its traces never yet
Upon old armorial hatchments was a prouder blazon set;
And they unborn generations, as they tread our rocky stand,
Shall tell with pride the story of their father's BRANDED HAND![37]

An inexpensive form of propaganda used by both sides was the pamphlet. Some widely circulated pro-slavery pamphlets, many of which were compiled and published in book form, include *Review of the Debate in the Virginia Legislature of 1831 and 1832* by Thomas R. Dew (1832);[38] *Slavery, Justified, by a Southerner* by George Fitzhugh (1850);[39] *Scriptural and Statistical Views in Favor of Slavery* by Thornton Stringfellow (1856);[40] and *The Interest in Slavery of the Southern Non-Slave holder. The Right of Peaceful Secession. Slavery in the Bible* by J. D. B. DeBow (1860), the editor of *Debow's Review*.[41]

Less conventional means of spreading the anti-slavery message were also employed. Propaganda appeared in many almanacs, one of which graphically described a slave owner who hacked a slave to pieces after having hung him on a meat hook.[42] Far less descriptive but successful in reaching a mass audience was abolitionist music,[43] principally hymns set to traditional church music, praising God and freedom while lamenting sin and slavery. Books like George Clark's *The Liberty Minstrel* (1844)[44] and William Wells Brown's *The Anti-Slavery Harp* (1848)[45] concentrated on anti-slavery song and verse.

It was in the more traditional forms of literature, however, that the most far-reaching and pervasive pro- and anti-slavery propaganda could be found. Without question, one work stands out in this regard: *Uncle Tom's Cabin.*[46] Harriet Beecher Stowe's account of horrific slave life quickly became the best-selling novel of the century,[47] and undoubtedly the most controversial. Novels about the harsh existence of the slaves were nothing new, but not until Stowe's novel was published did a flood of emotional, propagandistic fiction pour out of the North.[48] It would be misleading to suggest that Stowe's novel, published in 1852, was the first of its kind. Besides *The Selling of Joseph*, notable works include *Northwood; or, Life North and South* by Sara Joespha Buell (1827).[49] Nine years later Richard Hildreth's *The Slave; or, Memoirs of Archy Moore*[50] was published. Probably the first notable anti-slavery novel, *Memoirs* was the moving story of a mulatto slave cruelly treated and sexually abused. Hildreth was more idealistic than realistic in his story-telling, a style common to *Uncle Tom's Cabin,* as well as most of the anti-slavery novels to which Stowe's famous novel gave birth.

Less emotional was *Swallow Barn, or a Sojourn in the Old Dominion* by John Pendleton Kennedy.[51] First published in 1832, this book met with increased success on its second publishing in 1856, and has since been much acclaimed. Kennedy described the book as a collection of travels, a diary, a collection of letters and a history, one that some literary critics believe was "the literary origin of the plantation model."[52] The book resists categorization in that it both criticizes and venerates life in the South.[53] Subsequent novels of note include *A Yankee Among the Nullifiers* by Asa Greene (1833);[54] *Ida May* by Mary Hayden Pike (1854);[55] *English Serfdom and American Slavery* by Lucien Bonaporte (1854);[56] *Caste* by Mary Hayden Pike (1856);[57] *Neighbor Jackwood* by John Townsend Trowbridge (1857);[58] and *Our Nig; or, Sketches from the Life of a Free Black, In A Two-Story White House, North. Showing that Slavery's shadows Fall Even There* by Harriet E. Wilson (1859).[59] Although *Our Nig* sold less than 100 copies,[60] it qualifies as one of the most interesting books of the period for several reasons. It was the first fiction published by an African-American in the United States; it received almost no attention,[61] probably because it criticized racism in both the North and the South and compared abolitionists to kidnappers "who didn't [*sic*] want slaves at the South, nor niggers in their own house, North."[62]

Not surprisingly, *Uncle Tom's Cabin* created a considerable stir in the South[63] and generated a not-so-romantic literary criticism of Stowe's portrayal of plantation life. It was condemned for being cheap, propagandist melodrama overflowing with lies.[64] George Frederick Hommes's review of *Uncle's Tom's Cabin* in the *Southern Literary Messenger* provides a gauge of the magnitude of emotion generated by Stowe's novel:

> It is a fiction throughout; a fiction in form; a fiction in its facts; a fiction in its representations and coloring; a fiction in its statements; a fiction in its sentiments; a fiction in its morals; a fiction in its religion; a fiction in its inference; a fiction equally with regard to the subjects it is designed to expound, and with respect to the manner of their exposition. It is a fiction, not for the sake of more effectual communicating truth; but for the purpose of more effectually disseminating a slander.[65]

Southern writers had been producing pro-slavery literature nearly two decades before Stowe's best-seller, however. In 1836 Nathaniel Beverley Tucker wrote *George Balcombe*[66] and *The Partisan Leader.*[67] *Letters of Curtius* by William John Grayson was published in 1851,[68] and a year later Mary Eastman's *Aunt Phillis's Cabin, or Southern Life as It Is* was printed as an answer to Stowe's *Uncle Tom's Cabin.*[69] What it lacked in narrative style, it compensated for in directness. For example, the final lines of the book read: "Let the people of the North take care of its own poor. Let the people of the South take care of theirs."[70] Occasionally authors wrote anonymously, as was the case with *The Yankee Slave-dealer; or An Abolitionist Down South, A Tale For The Times.* The author was simply identified as "A Texan."[71]

Far less overt but nonetheless effective propaganda were romantic novels set in the South. Works like *Alone* by Mary Virginia Terhune (1854)[72] exalted southern traditions and values while reaching a large audience. However, perhaps the most interesting novel published during the period was *Wild Southern Scenes* by John Beauchamp.[73] This fictionalized account of a civil war caused by regional controversy over slavery was published just one year before secessionists fired upon Fort Sumter.

Supplementing the emotionalism of anti-slavery fiction was an array of religious, economic, and scientific nonfiction literature. In fact, pro-slavery nonfiction was more common, probably because the debate was less abstract than in fiction. As slavery came under criticism in Europe and Latin American, as well in the South, proponents found themselves constantly defending southern values and traditions. From the 1830s to the Civil War, however, their writing turned more militant.[74] By 1835 it was clear that slavery and the South's sectional interests were one and the same. To many, criticism of slavery was criticism of the South. No longer were there concessions that slavery was evil; it was, instead, an institution with social, economic and religious merit.[75]

When the abolitionists argued that slavery was an outdated feudal system, proponents of slavery countered with "King Cotton," a theory that embraced the importance of slavery to world cotton trade. Prominent nonfiction by slavery proponents included *Slavery in the United States* by James K. Paulding (1836). What is most interesting about this book is that an earlier edition, *Let-*

ters from the South [1817], opposed slavery.[76] Other works included *Negro-mania Being an Examination of the Falsely Assumed Equality of the Various Races of Men* by John Campbell (1851);[77] *The Pro-Slavery Argument as Maintained by . . . Chancellor Harper, Governor Hammond, Sr. Simms, and Professor Dew* (1852);[78] *The Political Economy of Slavery; or, The Institution Considered in Regard to its Influence on Public Wealth and the General Welfare* by Edmund Ruffin (1853);[79] *Bible Defence of Slavery* by Josiah Priest,[80] *A South-side view of Slavery* by Nehemiah Adams (1854);[81] *A Treatise on Sociology, Theoretical and Practical* by Henry Hughes (1854);[82] *Types of Mankind* by Josiah Nott;[83] *Sociology for the South* by George Fitzhugh (1854);[84] *The Bible Argument: or, Slavery in the Light of Divine Revelation* by Thornton Stringfellow (1856);[85] *Cannibals All! or Slaves Without Masters* by Fitzhugh (1857);[86] *Black Diamonds Gathered in the Darkey Homes of the South* by Edward Pollard (1859);[87] *Liberty and Slavery or, Slavery in the Light or Moral and Political Philosophy* by Albert Taylor Bledsoe;[88] and *Cotton is King* by David Christy(1860).[89]

Reasons put forth in support of slavery were creative, insightful and varied. In *The Political Economy of Slavery*, Ruffin, a noted fire-eater, argued that slavery was superior to the capitalistic system in the North, since that system was based upon greed. *A South-side View of Slavery* by Nehemiah Adams gained favorable attention in the South primarily because Adams was not from that region but a New England minister who opposed slavery. Rather than a sociological or scientific treatise, this book presented the South as a region that was misunderstood and more harmonious than the North. A nearly flawless labor system in the South, one he didn't refer to as slavery but as "warranteeism,"[90] was the theme of Henry Hughes's *A Treatise on Sociology, Theoretical and Practical* (1854). *Types of Mankind* by Josiah Nott was a "scientific" treatise that attempted to explain why the black race was inferior to the white race. In *Sociology for the South*, George Fitzhugh argued that the values of a feudal system were superior to those of capitalism,[91] and in the more widely read *Cannibals All!* he attempted a more rigorous analysis of capitalism and asserted that laissez-faire would create a level of competition that would turn workers into "moral cannibals."[92]

Noteworthy for its religious analysis was Josiah Priest's *Bible Defence of Slavery*, a fifteen-point explanation of God's plan for slavery that included an outline by the Rev. W. S. Brown for the colonization and removal of the free blacks in the United States. Perhaps the most significant pro-slavery theology was Thornton Stringfellow's *Scriptural and Statistical Views in Favor of Slavery*. Easily the most popular book in support of the southern position was David Christy's *Cotton Is King*. It has been termed "the most brilliantly 'realistic' of all the arguments in support of slavery"[93] because of the far-reaching economic underpinnings Christy attributed to slavery. Christy argued that cotton was important far beyond the United States and that British prosperity depended on cotton textile manufacturing. The author reasoned that since Great Britain was inexorably tied to the South because of economics, it was in the best interests of the United States to support slavery.

Opponents to slavery were no less active in publishing nonfiction supportive of their beliefs. Significant publications include *Letters on Slavery* by John Rankin (1826),[94] and *Thoughts on African Colonization* by William Lloyd Garrison (1832), a treatise which denounced the concept of recolonization of slaves in Africa following their emancipation in the United States.[95] *Appeal in Favor of the Class of Americans Called Africans* by Lydia Maria Child (1833) used economic and anthropological arguments in opposition to slavery.[96] *The War in Texas* by Benjamin Lundy (1836) contended that slave holders planned that war,[97] while Lydia Maria Child advocated the gradual freedom of the slaves after an apprenticeship period in *Anti-Slavery Catechism* (1836).[98]

The Bible Against Slavery (1837)[99] and *American Slavery As It Is* by Theodore Dwight Weld (1839)[100] are significant since they may have served as the inspiration for *Uncle Tom's Cabin.* Two biographies which were widely read and which had an impact on the growing abolitionist movement were *Trial and Imprisonment of Jonathan Walker* by Jonathan Walker (1845)[101] and *Narrative of the Life of Frederick Douglass, An American Slave* by Frederick Douglass (1845), later revised and republished in 1855 as *My Bondage and My Freedom.*[102]

In *The Impending Crisis of the South*, Hinton R. Helper wrote in 1857 how slavery adversely affected poor southern farmers and landless whites.[103] The same year *Letters from the Slave States* by James Stirling[104] was published. This was a compilation of letters by Stirling, an Englishman who traveled across the United States but wrote most of his letters from the South. *The Southern Platform: or, Manual of Southern Sentiment on the Subject of Slavery* by Daniel Goodloes was an attempt to awaken in southern minds what the author considered "those noble and generous sentiments of freedom which animated their ancestors."[105] Finally, *Plea for Captain John Brown* by Henry David Thoreau was one of several publications that portrayed the leader of the Harpers Ferry raid as a martyr.[106]

An important category of anti-slavery nonfiction was slave stories written by slaves. These were the slave narratives, the best-known of which was *My Bondage and My Freedom* by Douglass. The growth of the slave narrative genre was tied closely with the desire of anti-slavery societies to generate autobiographies that described the "hard facts" of slavery, although at times the authors were extensively edited by white publishers who felt the white reading public wanted facts rather than blacks' perceptions of slavery and society.[107] In fact, the quality as well as the veracity of many slave narratives were compromised because they were ghost-written by white writers. Blacks who persisted in keeping their original works untainted often found it difficult to be published without agreeing to extensive rewriting. To avoid such heavy-handed treatment, authors such as Harriet E. Nelson, who wrote *Our Nig*, sometimes published at their own expense.[108]

Some black narratives met with great success, however, and in the late 1840s autobiographies by Frederick Douglass, William Wells Brown and James W. C. Penningston outsold Thoreau, Melville and Hawthorne during the same period.[109] This was not the case for most. Except for use as propaganda, slave narratives, as well as any other genre produced by slaves and free blacks, had little chance of being published.[110] This did little to deter African-Americans who continued, with varying degrees of success, to publish slave narratives.[111] Some of the more prominent include *Narrative of William W. Brown, A Fugitive Slave, Written by Himself*;[112] *Incidents in the Life of a Slave Girl, Written by Herself* by Harriet Jacobs;[113] *Narrative of the Life of Frederick Douglass, An American Slave, Written by Himself (1845)*;[114] *Narrative of the Life and Adventures of Henry Bibb* (1850);[115] *Twelve Years a Slave* by Solomon Northup (1853);[116] *My Bondage and My Freedom* (1855);[117] *Sketches of Slave Life* by Peter Randolph (1855);[118] *The Refugee: or the Narratives of Fugitives Slaves in Canada Related by Themselves*, by Benjamin Drew (1856);[119] *Fifty Years in Chains: or, The Life of an American Slave* by Charles Ball;[120] *Autobiography of a Female Slave* by Mattie Griffiths (1857);[121] and *A Narrative of the Life of Rev. Noah Davis, A Colored Man, Written by Himself, At the Age of 54* (1859).[122]

Clearly, the dominant theme in antebellum American culture, as well as in American literature, was slavery. The institution created religious discord, fostered discussion about the origin of man, and led to economic debate over the value of capitalism as compared to a socialistic feudal system. Anti-slavery sentiment in the North gave birth to a wave of propaganda, and the literature was, at its core, critical of the southern way of life. At the same time, pro-slavery sentiment in the South became more militant. Its literature was apologetic for neither southern values nor southern traditions. In pamphlet and novel, song and poem, tract and almanac, the message from both sides was clear: our way of life is best. Given the strength of feelings in both regions, and the vast amount of propaganda unleashed in sustaining those emotions, it was probably inevitable that the war of words would end in a war of guns.

Notes

This essay was originally published as a chapter in *Three Centuries of American Media* (Englewood, CO: Morton Publishing, 1999).

1. Samuel Sewell, *The Selling of Joseph, A Memorial* (Boston, 1700). Reprinted from an original in George H. Moore's *Notes on the History of Slavery in Massachusetts* (New York, 1866), pp. 83–87.

2. John Saffin, *A Brief and Candid Answer to a late/ Printed Sheet, entitled/The Selling of Joseph/whereunto is annexed, /a True and Particular Narrative by Way of Vindication of the /Authors Dealing with and Prosecution of his negro Man Servant/for his vile and exorbitant Behavior towards his Master and his/Tenant, Thomas Shepard; which hath been wrongfully represented/to their Prejudice and Defamation* (Boston, 1701).
3. William Sumner Jenkins, *Pro-Slavery Thought in the Old South* (Chapel Hill: University of North Carolina Press, 1935), pp. 4–5.
4. Ibid., p. 7.
5. John Hepburn, *The Christian Golden Rule* (London, 1713). As cited in Jenkins's *Pro-Slavery Thought in the Old South*, p. 7.
6. *The Works of Benjamin Franklin* (Sparks, ed.) (1844), vol. 10, p. 403.
7. Jenkins, *Pro-Slavery Thought in the Old South*, p. 9.
8. Ibid.
9. Ibid., p. 11.
10. Elias Hicks, *Observations on the Slavery of the Africans and Their Descendants* (New York, 1810). See also Louis Filler's *The Crusade Against Slavery, 1830–1860* (New York: Harper & Brothers, 1960), p. 112.
11. Avery Craven, *The Coming of the Civil War* (Chicago: The University of Chicago Press, 1942), p. 118.
12. Merton L. Dillon, *Slavery Attacked: Southern Slaves and Their Allies, 1619–1865* (Baton Rouge: Louisiana State University Press), p. 117. See also Craven's *The Coming of the Civil War*, p. 119.
13. Herbert Aptheker, *One Continual Cry* (New York: Humanities Press, 1965), p. 30. See also Alice D. Adams's *The Neglected Period of Anti-Slavery in America* (Gloucester: Peter Smith, 1964).
14. Craven, *The Coming of the Civil War*, p. 119. See also Filler's *The Crusade Against Slavery*, pp. 18–19.
15. Filler, *The Crusade Against Slavery*, pp. 18–19.
16. Craven, *The Coming of the Civil War*, p. 120.
17. Ibid.
18. David Walker, *Walker's Appeal in Four Articles; Together with a Preamble to the Coloured Citizens of the World, but in particular, and very expressly, to Those of the United State of America, Written in Boston, State of Massachusetts, September 28, 1829* (Boston: David Walker, 1830), title page. See also Herbert Aptheker's *One Continual Cry, David Walker's Appeal to the Colored Citizens of the World, 1829–1830* (New York: Humanities Press, 1965), pp. 45–53.
19. Aptheker, *One Continual Cry*, p. 54.
20. Ibid., p. 2.
21. Ibid., p. 45.
22. Ibid., pp. 45–53.
23. Ibid., p. 49.
24. Ibid., p. 45.
25. Craven, *The Coming of the Civil War*, pp. 120–134.

26. Ibid., p. 135.
27. Ibid., p. 141.
28. Filler, *The Crusade Against Slavery*, 97. See also Craven's *The Coming of the Civil War*, p. 145.
29. Craven, *The Coming of the Civil War*, p. 145.
30. Filler, *The Crusade Against Slavery*, p. 97. See also Craven's *The Coming of the Civil War*, p. 145.
31. Craven, *The Coming of the Civil War*, p. 145.
32. *The Anti-Slavery Alphabet* (Philadelphia, 1847).
33. Booklet of Anti-Slavery Children's Poems in Huntington Library, as cited in Craven's *The Coming of the Civil War*, p. 452
34. Jonathan Walker, *A Picture of Slavery For Youth*. Reprinted in *Negro Protest Pamphlets* (New York: Arno Press and the New York Times, 1969).
35. Robert Spiller, Willard Thorpe, Thomas Johnson, Henry Seidel Canby, Richard Ludwig, eds., *Literary History of the United States*, 3rd ed., revised (New York: Macmillan, 1963), p. 564.
36. Joe Richardson, *Trial and Imprisonment of Jonathan Walker at Pensacola, Florida for Aiding Slave to Escape from Bondage* (Gainesville: University of Florida Press, 1974), pp. viii–xi. (A facsimile reproduction of the 1845 edition.)
37. Whittier, "The Branded Hand," *The Early Poems of John Greenleaf Whittier Comprising Mogg Megoe, The Bridal of Pennacook, Legendary Poems, Voices of Freedom, Miscellaneous Poems, and Songs of Labor* (Boston: Houghton, Mifflin and Company, 1891), p. 194.
38. Thomas R. Dew, *Review of the Debate in the Virginia Legislature of 1831 and 1832* (Richmond, VA: T.W. White, 1832).
39. George Fitzhugh, *Slavery, Justified, by a Southerner* (Fredericksburg: Recorder Printing Office, 1850).
40. Thornton Stringfellow, *Scriptural and Statistical Views in Favor of Slavery* (Richmond, VA: J.W. Randolph, 1856).
41. J. D. B. DeBow, *The Interest in Slavery of the Southern Non-Slave Holder: The Right of Peaceful Secession. Slavery in the Bible* (Charleston, SC: Evans & Cogswell, 1860).
42. *Abolitionist's Library*, no. 1, January 1834. See also Craven's *The Coming of the Civil War*, p. 452.
43. Filler, *The Crusade Against Slavery*, 184–185. See also Craven's *The Coming of the Civil War*, pp. 144–145.
44. George Clark, *The Liberty Minstrel* (New York: Leavitt & Alden, 1844).
45. William Wells Brown, *The Anti-Slavery Harp* (Boston: B. Marsh, 1848). For additional information concerning songs by slaves and free blacks, see Vernon Loggins' *The Negro Author: His Development in America to 1900* (Port Washington, NY: Kennikat Press, Inc., 1964).
46. Harriet Beecher Stowe, *Uncle Tom's Cabin; or Life among the Lowly* (New York: Dodd, Meade & Company, 1952).

47. In the first year of publication, *Uncle Tom's Cabin* sold more than 300,000 copies in the United States and one million in England. See Josephine Donovan's *Uncle Tom's Cabin: Evil, Affliction, and Redemptive Love* (Boston: Twayne Publishers, 1991), p. 11.
48. Robert Spiller et al., *Literary History of the United States,* p. 567.
49. Sara Joespha Buell, *Northwood; or, Life North and South* (Freeport, NY: Books for Libraries Press, 1972). See also Lucien Bonaparte Chase, *English Serfdom and American Slavery* (New York: H. Long & Brother, 1958).
50. Richard Hildreth, *The Slave; or, Memoirs of Archy Moore* (New York: Negro Universities Press, 1969).
51. John Pendleton Kennedy, *Swallow Barn, or a Sojourn in the Old Dominion* (Baton Rouge: Louisiana State University Press, 1986).
52. Kennedy, *Swallow Barn,* introduction by Lucinda MacKethan, p. xviii.
53. Ibid., p. xi.
54. Asa Greene, *A Yankee Among the Nullifiers* (New York: W. Stodart, 1855).
55. Mary Hayden Pike, *Ida May* (Boston: Phillips, Sampson, 1854).
56. Lucien Bonaparte, *English Serfdom and American Slavery* (New York: H. Long, 1854).
57. Mary Hayden Pike, *Caste* (Boston: Phillips, Sampson, 1856).
58. John Townsend Trowbridge, *Neighbor Jackson* (Boston: Phillips, Sampson, 1857).
59. Harriet E. Wilson, *Our Nig, or, Sketches from the Life of a Free Black: in a Two-Story White house, North, Showing That Slavery's Shadows Fall Even There* (Boston: G.C. Rand & Avery, 1859).
60. Kari Winter, *Subjects of Slavery, Agents of Change* (Athens: University of Georgia Press, 1992), p. 34.
61. Ibid.
62. Wilson, *Our Nig,* p. 129.
63. J. C. Furnas, *Goodbye to Uncle Tom* (New York: William Sloane Associates, 1956), p. 7.
64. Stowe, *Uncle Tom's Cabin,* introduction by Langston Hughes, p. 1.
65. "Uncle Tom's Cabin," *Southern Literary Messenger* 18 (December 1852), p. 721.
66. Nathaniel Beverley Tucker, *George Balcombe* (New York: Harper, 1836).
67. Nathaniel Beverley Tucker, *The Partisan Leader* (Chapel Hill: University of North Carolina Press, 1971).
68. William John Grayson, *Letters of Curtius* (Charleston, SC: A. E. Miller, 1851). Originally published in the Charleston *Courier.*
69. Mary Henderson Eastman, *Aunt Phillis's Cabin, or Southern Life as It Is* (Philadelphia: Lippincott, Grambo & Co., 1852).
70. Ibid., p. 280.
71. *The Yankee Slave-dealer; or, an Abolitionist down South, A Tale for the Times* by A Texan (Nashville, TN: Published for the Author, 1860).
72. Mary Virginia Terhune, *Alone* (Richmond, VA: A. Morris, 1854).

73. John Beauchamp, *Wild Southern Scenes* (Philadelphia: T.B. Peterson & Brothers, 1859).

74. Albert Fried, *John Brown's Journey: Notes and Reflections on His America and Mine* (Garden City, NY: Anchor Press, 1978), p. 228.

75. Ibid.

76. James K. Paulding, *Slavery in the United States* (New York: Harper & Brothers, 1836).

77. John Campbell, *Negro-Mania Being an Examination of the Falsely Assumed Equality of the Various Races of Men* (Philadelphia: Campbell and Power, 1851).

78. *The Pro-Slavery Argument as Maintained by . . . Chancellor Harper, Governor Hammond, Sr. Simms, and Professor Dew* (Charleston, SC: Walker, Richards & Co., 1852). This compilation, the most noteworthy of which was Dew's "Review of the Debate In the Virginia Legislature," is a strong defense of southern institutions.

79. Edmund Ruffin, *The Political Economy of Slavery; or, The Institution Considered in Regard to Its Influence on Public Wealth and the General Welfare* (Washington, DC: Lemuel Towers, 1853).

80. Josiah Priest, *Bible Defence of Slavery* (Glasgow: Rev. W.S. Brown, 1853).

81. Nehemiah Adams, *A South-side view of Slavery* (Boston: T.R. Marvin & B.B. Mussey, 1854).

82. Henry Hughes, *A Treatise on Sociology, Theoretical and Practical* (Philadelphia: Lippincott, Grambo & Co., 1854).

83. Josiah Nott, *Types of Mankind* (Philadelphia: J.B. Lippincott, Grambo & Co., 1854).

84. George Fitzhugh, *Sociology for the South* (New York: Burt Franklin, 1854).

85. Thornton Stringfellow, *The Bible Argument: or, Slavery in the Light of Divine Revelation. Included in Compilation for Cotton is King and Pro-Slavery Arguments,* Ed. E. N. Elliott (Augusta, GA: Pritchard, Abbott & Loomis, 1860). Reprinted by The Basic Afro-American Reprint Library.

86. George Fitzhugh, *Cannibals All! or Slaves without Masters* (Richmond: A. Morris, Publisher, 1857).

87. Edward Pollard, *Black Diamonds Gathered in the Darkey Homes of the South* (New York: Pudney & Russell, 1859).

88. Albert Taylor Bledsoe, *Liberty and Slavery: or, Slavery in the Light or Moral and Political Philosophy* (Augusta, GA: Pritchard, Abbott & Loomis, 1860).

89. David Christy, *Cotton Is King: Or the Culture of Cotton, and Its Relation to Agriculture, Manufactures and Commerce of the Free Colored People: and to Those Who Hold That Slavery Is in Itself Sinful* (Cincinnati, OH: Moore, Wilstach, Keys & Co.).

90. Hughes, *A Treatise on Sociology, Theoretical and Practical*, pp. 207–289.

91. Fitzhugh, *Sociology for the South*, pp. 7–79.

92. Fitzhugh, *Cannibals All!* pp. 7–20.

93. Eric L. McKitrick, ed., *Slavery Defended, The Views of the Old South* (Englewood Cliffs, NJ: Prentice-Hall, 1963), p. 111.

94. John Rankin, *Letters on Slavery* (Newburyport, MA: Charles Whipple, 1837).

95. William Lloyd Garrison, *Thoughts on African Colonization* (Boston: Garrison and Knapp, 1832).
96. Lydia Maria Child, *Appeal in Favor of the Class of Americans Called Africans* (Boston: Allen and Ticknor, 1833).
97. Benjamin Lundy, *The War in Texas* (Upper Saddle River, NJ: Literature House, 1970).
98. Lydia Maria Child, *Anti-Slavery Catechism* (Newburyport, MA: Whipple, 1836).
99. Theodore Dwight Weld, *The Bible Against Slavery* (New York: R.G. Williams for the American Anti-Slavery Society, 1837).
100. Theodore Dwight Weld, *American Slavery As It Is* (New York: American Anti-Slavery Society, 1839).
101. Jonathan Walker, *Trial and Imprisonment of Jonathan Walker* (Boston: Dow & Jackson's Power Press, 1845).
102. Frederick Douglass, *Narrative of the Life of Frederick Douglass, An American Slave* (Boston: Anti-Slavery Office, 1845). Later revised and published in 1855 as *My Bondage and My Freedom.*
103. Hinton R. Helper, *The Impending Crisis of the South* (New York: Burdick Brothers, 1857).
104. James Stirling, *Letters from the Slave States* (London: John Parker and Son, 1857).
105. Daniel Goodloes, *The Southern Platform: or, Manual of Southern Sentiment on the Subject of Slavery* (Boston: John P. Jewett co., 1858), preface.
106. Henry David Thoreau, *Plea for Captain John Brown* (Boston: D.R. Godine, 1969). Lecture read to the citizens of Concord, Massachusetts, on October 30, 1859; also the fifth lecture of the Fraternity Course in Boston, November, 1859.
107. Winter, *Subjects of Slavery, Agents of Change*, p. 36.
108. Harriet E. Nelson, *Our Nig.*
109. John Sekora and Darwin Turner, eds., *The Art of Slave Narrative: Original Essays in Criticism and Theory,* Essays in Literature Series (Macomb: Western Illinois University, 1982). From an essay by Lucinda H. MacKethan, "Metaphors of Mastery in the Slavery Narratives," 55. See also Winter, *Subjects of Slavery,* pp. 35–38.
110. Winter, *Subjects of Slavery,* p. 34.
111. Ibid.
112. William W. Brown, *Narrative of William W. Brown, A Fugitive Slave, Written by Himself* (Boston: Anti-Slavery Office, 1847).
113. Harriet Jacobs, *Incidents in the Life of a Slave Girl, Written by Herself,* ed. L. Maria Child (Boston: Published for the Author, 1861).
114. Douglass, *Narrative of the Life of Frederick Douglass.*
115. Henry Bibb, *Narrative of the Life and Adventures of Henry Bibb* (New York: The Author, 1849).
116. Soloman Northup, *Twelve Years a Slave* (Auburn: Derby and Miller, 1853).
117. Frederick Douglass, *My Bondage and My Freedom* (New York: Miller, Orton & Mulligan, 1855).

118. Peter Randolph, *Sketches of Slave Life* (Boston: Published for the Author, 1855).
119. Benjamin Drew, *A North-side View of Slavery. The Refugee: or the Narratives of Fugitive Slaves in Canada Related by Themselves* (Boston: John Jewett and Co., 1856).
120. Charles Ball, *Fifty Years in Chains; or, The Life of an American Slave* (Indianapolis, IN: Dayton & Asher, 1859).
121. Mattie Griffiths, *Autobiography of a Female Slave* (New York: J.S. Redfield, 1857).
122. Noah Davis, *A Narrative of the Life of Rev. Noah Davis, A Colored Man, Written by Himself, At the Age of 54* (Baltimore, MD: J. F. Weishmapel, Jr., 1859).

The Terror of Poe

Slavery, the Southern Gentleman, and the Status Quo

— Eve Dunbar —

In the introduction to their essay "Beyond 'The Problem of Poe,'" Shawn Rosenheim and Stephen Rachman note that the "critical dismissal of [Edgar Allan] Poe has followed from Poe's own seeming disengagement with American Culture."[1] Although his supposed disengagement grants Poe a certain amount of chilling universality and timelessness, there is nevertheless a definite need to examine the ways in which Poe's involvement in his culture, the antebellum South, helped to shape some of his most disturbing work.

Poe is rarely taught as a southern writer, and readers are rarely asked to consider how his self-ascribed position as a southern gentleman may have shaped his writing. Ishmael Reed, himself a contemporary southern author, prompts his readers to examine Poe's implication in slavery. In his novel *Flight to Canada*, Reed questions how Poe could be overlooked as the chief biographer of the horrors of slavery. Reed asks:

> Why isn't Edgar Allan Poe recognized as the principal biographer of that strange war? Fiction, you say? Where does fact begin and fiction leave off? Why does the perfectly rational, in its own time, often sound like mumbo-jumbo? Where did it leave off for Poe, prophet of a civilization buried alive, where, according to witness, people were often whipped for no reason. No

> reason? Will we ever know, since there are so few traces left of the civilization the planters called "the fairest civilization the sun ever shown upon," and the slaves called "Satan's Kingdom." Poe got it all down. Poe says more in a few stories than all of the volumes by historians. Volumes about the war. The Civil War. The Spirit War.[2]

Reed sees in Poe's writings the terror and cruelty inherent in the institution of slavery, and questions whether Poe's gothic terror is really senseless or merely a product of his implicit association with slavery. Much like Rosenheim and Rachman, Reed is interested in restoring Poe to his culture by calling into question what some describe as the "reasonlessness" of violence in many of Poe's works. Although the excessive violence may seem unreasonable in many of Poe's tales, reason can be restored if one considers his stories in the light of the antebellum South. If these tales are read in the contexts of the time and place of the writer, the terror of Poe is ultimately the terror felt by white culture and coming to terms with the end of the institution of slavery.

Poe spent much of his life roaming in search of work between Richmond, Virginia, and the major cities of New England,[3] but he always considered himself to be a southerner, and is regarded as such by most critics. This self-proclaimed southerner status has many implications that must be considered if one is to examine Poe's literary involvement with his culture. Poe, who is described as having a "zeal for slavery,"[4] was self-consciously a southern gentleman. Joseph Osgoode, a writer intent on restoring the South to a respectable place in American history, describes Poe as a "true type of the Southern gentleman . . . in literature an exponent of the independent thought, free outlook, original conception, genial humor, unobtrusive yet commanding dignity, exquisite refinement, and sound and penetrating judgment characteristic of a true son of the South."[5] To be a "son of the South," a southern gentleman, one must "possess every quality which the Yankee lacked: honor and integrity, indifference to money and business, a decorous concern for amenities, and a high sense of civic and social responsibility."[6] In addition, history has made it clear that one of the most prominent characteristics of the southern gentleman was his pro-slavery stance. To be a true southerner one must stand for state sovereignty and, with it, the right to own slaves.

It is in Poe's review of J. K. Paulding's *Slavery in the United States* and *The South Vindicated* that one may examine how well the author fits into any discussion of southern gentry and slavery. In this review in the *Southern Literary Messenger,*[7] a literary journal based in Richmond, Poe is less intent on reviewing or recommending the works in question than he is on begging "leave to add on a few words of our own . . . because there is a view of the subject most deeply interesting to us."[8] In doing so, Poe offers a revealing commentary on the necessity of slavery and the inability of the outsider to understand the true bond created between slave and master. Citing the French Revolution, Poe's ultimate goal is to persuade his readers that the ownership of property brings true happiness to man; property and happiness become interchangeable. Poe claims that property is that thing at which "all men aim, and their eagerness seems always proportioned to the excitement, which . . . may for the time prevail. Under such excitement, the many who want, band themselves together against the few that possess; and the lawless appetite of the multitude for the property of others calls itself the spirit of liberty."[9] It is natural for man to gather possessions—ownership equals happiness—and those lacking property intended to deny happiness and liberty to all property owners.

Throughout his review, Poe pays little attention to the humanity of the slaves because he does not consider them anything other than property. Poe critiques those white men who argue that "they [the slaves] are, like ourselves, the sons of Adam, and must therefore, have like passions and wants and feelings and tempers in all respects." He continues, "This, we deny, and appeal to the knowledge of all who know."[10] Concerned with the essential differences between the white man and the black,[11] Poe is adamant in retaining those cultural constructions that require blacks to maintain the subservient status of property. He argues that the slave and his master create a bond that demonstrates a "degree of loyal devotion on the part of the slave to which the white man's heart is a stranger, and on the master's reciprocal feeling of parental attachment to his humble dependent."[12] The bond created by master and slave is dearer than those bonds between whites, he says, because the slave will always remain dependent—a belief widely held by many of the master class. [13]

Poe then explores the inability of the northerner to understand the deep devotional attachment between master and slave. In his southern gentlemanly way, Poe sarcastically thanks Mr. Paulding, a northern man, "for the faithful picture he had drawn of slavery as it appeared to him in his visit to the South."[14] Although Paulding's review was in favor of slavery and southern gentry, Poe does not embrace Paulding, whose work he finds inadequate in his rendering of southern slave-and-master relationships. However favorable Paulding's review of the South and slavery may be, Poe cannot laud Paulding's insight. Instead, Poe accuses Paulding and any other northerner who might decide to write a book concerning the southern plantation system of coming in "the names of our common Redeemer and common country—seeking our destruction under the mask of Christian Charity and Brotherly Love."[15] These northerners are not only inadequate learners of southern society, they are inherently out to destroy all that the South holds dear—chiefly, the institution of slavery.

Although Poe would like to believe that an affectionate bond exists between master and slave, he seems to realize that there is an uncontrollable darkness inherent in the relationship. Poe cites the "recent events in the West Indies, and the parallel movement here" as giving "an awful importance to these thoughts in our minds. They superinduce a something like despair of success in any attempt that may be made to resist the attack on all our rights, of which that on Domestic Slavery (the basis of all our institutions) is but the precursor."[16] The jovial relationship that Poe refers to in his review is undercut with despair and fear of the outside world's infringement on the southern status quo.

About a year before Poe published his review of Paulding in the *Southern Literary Messenger*, the British Parliament granted "qualified slave emancipation on August 1, 1834, and full freedom four years later"[17] to the historically rebellious slaves in the West Indies. This emancipation, prompted by continuous uprisings in the West Indies, especially the 1831–1832 Baptist War in Jamaica,[18] may be one of the "recent events in the West Indies" to which Poe refers. Emancipation in the West Indies would indeed be "awful" for any southern gentleman desirous of keeping his plantation running under the status quo and free of revolt.

The fear of rebellion, and ultimately emancipation, that Poe describes lay closer to home than many realized at the time. When Poe warns about the "parallel movements here," he is likely referring to the Nat Turner Rebellion of 1831, which took place in Southampton, Virginia, on August 21–22, seventy miles outside of Richmond, a rebellion well-known by many of his readers.[19] Many local newspapers covering the story describe the excitement and fear that must have been instilled in the hearts of every southern gentleman when Nat Turner's name was uttered. Almost all the papers carried some coverage of the insurrection. *The Petersburg Intelligencer* noted: "A great excitement has prevailed in this town for some days past, in consequence of the receipt of information on Monday night last, that an insurrection had broken out among the negroes in Southampton. The rumors have been so numerous and contradictory that we are unable to state to our readers, at present, the precise state of affairs in that county." *The Richmond Enquirer* added: "What strikes us as the most remarkable thing in this matter is the horrible ferocity of these monsters. They remind one of a parcel of blood-thirsty wolves rushing down from the Alps; or rather like a former incursion of the Indians upon the white settlements. Nothing is spared; neither age nor sex is respected—the helplessness of women and children pleads in vain for mercy. . . .The case of Nat Turner warns us."[20]

Although Turner was soon tried and put to death, the Richmond area was still alert and taking precautions when Poe decided to write his article for the *Southern Literary Messenger.* Ultimately, Poe's review in the *Southern Literary Messenger* establishes him as not merely a slavery advocate and idealizer, but also a writer with a deep understanding of the fear and loathing that claimed the hearts of many southern plantation owners when confronted with the twin specters of emancipation and rebellion. It is in "The System of Doctor Tarr and Professor Fether" that we realize Poe's justification for the institution of slavery, the bond between slave and master, the inability of visitors to grasp the inner workings of the institution, and the ultimate subduing of the institutionalized. What is impressive is the way in which Poe manages to comment on the fears of southern culture without ever mentioning slavery.

It can be argued that the mentally institutionalized and those institutionalized by slavery become confounded in the narrative of "The System of Doctor Tarr and Professor Fether." Critic Joan Dayan notes that "animality, after all, emerges for most nineteenth-century phrenologists, theologians, and anthropologist in those beings who are at once man and beast: lunatics, women, primates, black men, and children."[21] To confound the institutionalized, the insane, and blacks is not such a strange idea in light of southern culture. It does not seem unreasonable that Poe would, consciously or subconsciously, group the insane and slaves in a similar category. The setting of the narrative is important in linking it to southern slave culture. As the narrator states, he is "on tour through the extreme southern provinces of France."[22] It becomes suddenly apparent that the landscape and location of this narrative must have greater implications. In comparing the difference between northern France and southern France, *Life World Library: France* says that it is

> wise to begin by noting that the great dividing line is between the North and South, with the Loire River as a kind of Mason-Dixon Line. South of the Loire is the country of grapevines, orange trees and olive groves, and the mulberry trees that sustain the silkworms. . . . The French South, like the American South, has many modern areas and many centers of progress, but—again like the American South—it is for the most part poor economically and somehow out of the stream of things.[23]

Although this is a fairly essential description of the differences between the north and south of France, it sheds light on why southern France may have been chosen as the setting for Poe's narrative, and why the narrator must be coming from the metropolis of Paris. Southern France and the American South are both agricultural centers of their countries, and both are looked down upon by their northern counterparts.

Poe also links France to the South in his review in the *Southern Literary Messenger.*[24] There is a link between the south of France and the American South that allows the reader to explore "Doctor Tarr and Professor Fether" in the context of southern society, with all of its connotations. In fact, because the South desired to distinguish itself from the North, it used Europe as its mirror. Europe becomes, for Poe and his culture, "a mirror which threw back a distorted image of what was happening to the South, an image which threatened revolution, class warfare and the extinction of polite culture."[25] Not only is southern France of a similar agricultural and economic constitution as the American South, it is also experiencing similar civil traumas.

Poe's treatment of the narrator in "Doctor Tarr and Professor Fether" should be read in light of his well-established distrust and resentment of the visiting northerner in the South. The narrator of this story, much like Mr. Paulding in Poe's review, is visiting the southern "extremes" in order to experience the institution. Throughout the tale the narrator is shown to lack all understanding of the institution and its workings, and it is his lack of understanding that allows him to be duped by the institutionalized. All around him there are signs that would expose the truth to anyone with knowledge of how such an institution works. One example takes place when the narrator is at dinner with the people he assumes to be sane friends of the master of the asylum. The narrator notes that

> there was an air of oddity, in short, about the dress of the whole party, which, at first, caused me to recur to my original idea of the "soothing system", and to fancy that Monsieur Maillard had been willing to deceive me until after dinner . . . but I remembered having been informed, in Paris, that the southern provincialists were a peculiarly eccentric people, with a vast number of antiquated notions; and then upon conversing with several members of the company, my apprehensions were immediately and fully dispelled.[26]

The narrator notices the extravagance of dress, food, music, and character, but never concludes that there is something wrong with the situation. Even when the dinner party's attendants begin acting out their neuroses under the guise of imitating the truly insane, the narrator never allows himself to believe that these people and their actions are abnormal for the South. Some may argue that Poe is merely pointing out the problem with believing stereotypes, but he is also addressing Paulding and all the other northerners who visit the South to examine and change a system about which they have no knowledge. Poe would like his readers to believe that the fact that the institutionalized have the power to plan a rebellion, confine and punish the true masters on the institution, and remain in power for an extended amount of time is the true horror of his tale. The terror of uprising in the tale's institution is comparable to the terror he evokes in the *Southern Literary Messenger.* In both instances, Poe desires to make his reader fearful of what the world might become when it is out of the hands of the white, male patriarch.

In both fictional and factual rebellion, the reversing of power comes when those keepers begin to trust the institutionalized. The first mistake of the madhouse, Maison de Santé, was to practice the "soothing system." The system is one in which "all punishments were avoided—that even confinement was seldom resorted to—that patients, while secretly watched, were left much apparent liberty, and that most of them were permitted to roam about the house and grounds, in the ordinary apparel of persons in right mind."[27] In the same way that Nat Turner was permitted to preach around the Virginian countryside, the patients are allowed all the freedom of the sane in the hope they might recover. And just as it proved to create a rebellion in Southampton, the asylum is soon overthrown by the insane. It seems as if Poe is criticizing any method that allows institutionalized freedom and equality between the keeper and the kept.

Ironically, once the institutionalized gain control, they begin to resort to some of the same methods used by southern slave owners and traders—tarring and feathering was a common practice in the American South when runaway slaves were recaptured. It is after this practice that Maillard names his alternative method the Doctor Tarr and Professor Fether system. Maillard's method requires constant imprisonment of the insane because "a lunatic may be 'soothed,' as it is called, for a time, but in the end, he is very apt to become obstreperous. His cunning, too, is proverbial, and great . . . when a madman appears thoroughly sane, indeed it is high time to put him in a strait-jacket."[28] Even the institutionalized seem to comprehend the need for firm and constant punishment and imprisonment. Only a northerner would continue "soothing" the institutionalized.

Soon after Maillard exposes the truth behind the institution to the dense, and still clueless, narrator, the real asylum keepers break into the party. These men, who have been tarred and feathered, have managed to escape from their imprisonment and are able to reclaim their positions of power. As they break through the windows of the dinning room the narrator describes them as "Chimpanzees, Ourang-Outangs, or big black baboons of the Cape of Good Hope."[29] This is a problematic image, since such characteristics were often used to describe blacks during the nineteenth century. One explanation for this trope reversal may lie in Poe's fears of slave rebellion. The author seems to fear that if slaves were to revolt and gain control, the whites would be reduced to the status of slaves. The great horror of his tale is one of retribution by the institutionalized and an end to the status quo.

"The System of Doctor Tarr and Professor Fether" is a prime example of Poe's innate understanding of the southern plantation owner's fear of slave revolt and emancipation. It demonstrates Poe's own reservations about a system upon which he has vested his whole existence as a southern gentleman. He encourages his readers to consider the consequences of an institution's falling into the hands of the institutionalized. It is difficult to argue that Poe had no interest in the issue of slavery in light of his personal history, his article in the *Southern Literary Messenger,* and "The System of Doctor Tarr and Professor Fether." Dayan notes that "Poe must have frequently walked past the Richmond slave market, which was only two blocks from the offices of the *Southern Literary Messenger.* He doubtless witnessed the slave auctions, and experienced the terror of those led through the streets, chained in slave coffles, readied for their journey to the Deep South."[30] It is doubtful that these images failed to speak to him as he wrote his narratives. Poe was a man of his culture: a southern gentleman, a frequent reader of the news, an anti-abolitionist, and a professional writer. These factors combined to produce a work of fiction that is, as Ishmael Reed contends, more factual "than all of the volumes by historians."[31]

Notes

This essay was previously published as "Disciplining and Punishing in Edgar Allen Poe's 'The System of Dr. Tarr and Professor Fether': The Southern Origins and Implications of Poe," *The Southern Historian* 24(1) (Spring 2002): pp. 6–15.

1. Shawn Rosenheim and Stephen Rachman, eds., *The American Face of Edgar Allan Poe* (Baltimore: Johns Hopkins University Press, 1995), p. ix.
2. Ishmael Reed, *Flight to Canada* (New York: Random House, 1995), p. 10.
3. *The Heath Anthology of American Literature* does a good job of giving a brief, but concise, documentation of Poe's life and his various moves around the country.
4. W. J. Cash, *The Mind of the South* (New York: Vintage Books, 1941), p. 96.
5. Joseph Osgoode, *Tell It In Gath* (Sewanee, Tenn.: The University Press of Sewanee, Tennessee, 1918), p. 142.
6. William Taylor, *Cavalier and Yankee: The Old South and American National Character* (New York: Doubleday, 1963), p. 73.
7. There seems to be some debate over whether or not Poe is the actual author of the review on slavery in the *Southern Literary Messenger.* Dana Nelson (*The Word in Black and White: Reading "Race" in American Literature,* New York: Oxford University Press, 1992) exposes the controversy that surrounds Poe's review of Paulding in her essay "Ethnocentrism Decentered: Colonialist Motives in *The Narrative of Arthur Gordon Pym.*" The debate seems to stem from those critics who desire to disassociate Poe with Southern culture. Nelson concludes that authorship is of little matter because these same feelings on slavery can be seen in many of Poe's personal writings to friends and family. Thus, Nelson takes on the task of exploring Poe's use of color and race in *The Narrative of Arthur Gordon Pym.*
8. Edgar Allan Poe, "Slavery," *Southern Literary Messenger,* vol. 2 (Richmond: T.W. White Publishers, 1835–46), p. 338.
9. Poe, "Slavery," p. 337.
10. Poe, "Slavery," p. 338.
11. Although I do understand that the term "Negro" is out of date, I use the term at this point in my paper because it seems more fitting to the time period of which I am writing and it keeps with Poe's own voice.
12. Poe, "Slavery," p. 338.
13. Joan Dayan deals explicitly in "Amorous Bondage: Poe, Ladies, and Slave" *The*

American Face of Edgar Allan Poe (Baltimore: The Johns Hopkins University Press, 1995). Her essay has been helpful in my understanding of Poe's culture and his relation to slavery and slaves.

14. Poe, "Slavery," p. 337.
15. Poe, "Slavery," p. 338.
16. Poe, "Slavery," p. 337.
17. Michael Craton, *Testing the Chains: Resistance to Slavery in the British West Indies* (Ithaca, NY: Cornell University Press, 1982), p. 291.
18. The Baptist War involved 60,000 slaves in an area of 750 square miles, killing 540 slaves and 14 whites (291 Craton). This was just one of the many revolts that took place in the West Indies, but it is probably one of which Poe may have had some knowledge.
19. For more information on Nat Turner and his rebellion refer to *The Confessions of Nat Turner and Related Documents* ed. Kenneth Greenberg (New York: Bedford Book of St. Martin's Press, 1996).
20. Henry Tragle, *The Southampton Slave Revolt of 1831: A Compilation of Source Material* (Amherst: University of Massachusetts Press, 1971), pp. 43–44.
21. Dayan, "Amorous Bondage," pp. 183–84.
22. Edgar Allan Poe, "The System of Doctor Tarr and Professor Fether," in *The Complete Edgar Allan Poe Tales* (New York: Avenel Books, 1981), p. 527.
23. D.W. Brogan, *Life World Library: France* (New York: Times Incorporated, 1966), pp. 11–12.
24. His linking between the American South and France is based upon his citation of the French Revolution—property as happiness.
25. William Taylor, *Cavalier and Yankee: The Old South and American National Character* (New York: Doubleday and Company, 1963), p. 29.
26. Poe, "Dr. Tarr and Professor Fether," *The Complete Edgar Allan Poe Tales* (New York: Avenel Books, 1981), p. 530.
27. Poe, "Dr. Tarr and Professor Fether," p. 528.
28. Poe, "Dr. Tarr and Professor Fether," p. 536.
29. Poe, "Dr. Tarr and Professor Fether," p. 538.
30. Dayan, "Amorous Bondage," p. 204.
31. Reed, *Flight to Canada*, p. 10.

John Brown

The Many Faces of a Nineteenth-Century Martyr

— Bernell E. Tripp —

Combatants on both sides brandish rifles and pistols as the battle rages around the larger-than-life figure towering over the action from his position at the center of the scene. His stark white beard flutters in the breeze, while his eyes fixate on a point far into the horizon. Smoke from the battle swirls around him as the folds of the American flag billow to his right. With arms outstretched and a determined scowl upon his face, Captain John Brown grips a rifle in one hand and a Bible in the other. Several slaves huddle near his feet, like small children clutching at their father's pant legs for protection, as the Rebels try to pry them from their perch. It's all part of *The Tragic Prelude (John Brown),* a mural by John Steuart Curry housed, appropriately enough, in the state capitol in Topeka, Kansas.[1]

Years after Brown's prophetic raid at Harpers Ferry, Virginia, African-American orator and abolitionist Frederick Douglass noted during a speech on the site before the public and students of Storer College:

> If John Brown did not end the war that ended slavery, he did at least begin the war that ended slavery. . . . Until this blow was struck, the prospect for freedom was dim, shadowy and uncertain. The irrepressible conflict was one of words, votes and compromises.
>
> When John Brown stretched forth his arm the sky was cleared. The time

> for compromises was gone—the armed hosts of freedom stood face to face over the chasm of a broken Union—and the clash of arms was at hand.[2]

Such was one of the traditional depictions of Brown in both words and pictures. Black journalists and other supporters would later perpetuate similar images to their audiences, bestowing this idealistic honor upon "Old Osawatomie Brown" as they recounted tales of his antislavery activity and his improbable rise to martyrdom. By the time of his execution in December 1859, and continuing into the twenty-first century, several distinctive images of Brown would be manifested in the pages of newspapers and on canvases throughout the country, including avenging angel or savior; loyal patriot or founding father; and surrogate father or benevolent uncle.

Long before Brown's emergence as a radical and violent abolitionist, the country was already charged with controversy surrounding slavery. Newspapers, as well as citizens, were choosing sides as either pro-slavery advocates or abolitionists. The last thing slavery sympathizers needed was another martyr.[3] However, Brown, a man who had been raised to abhor slavery and discrimination in all forms, would become more than that to millions of people.

Brown was born May 9, 1800, in Torrington, Litchfield County, Connecticut, the second son of Owen and Ruth Mills Brown. His father, a tanner and shoemaker, had also been an abolitionist, a legacy that his son would pass on to his own children.[4] By 1856, Brown and his family had made names for themselves among blacks and whites in both the North and the South, not only for contributing items and support to several black and abolitionist newspapers,[5] but also for massacring five pro-slavery settlers near Osawatomie, Kansas. The following year, President James Buchanan labeled Brown an outlaw and offered a reward for his capture.[6] Remaining free in the North and in Canada until October 1859, Brown waited and planned for his next major revolutionary action—the taking of the arsenal at Harpers Ferry, Virginia. Only 12 of the 21 men with Brown survived, and Brown would lose two sons, Watson and Oliver, as casualties of the raid.[7]

Media coverage of Brown's daring attack at Harpers Ferry, followed by the loss of his sons and the shoddy treatment of the prisoners, contributed significantly to the development of Brown's multifaceted image. Brown's personal press conferences in his cell, stressing that he had committed no acts of violence except for those necessary to implement his plans, contributed to the blurring of the lines between savior and sadist.[8] Abolitionist Charles H. Langston, who was one of Brown's recruiters, declared that Brown's actions were derived not from a single source, but from three sources, only the third of which was abolition. He proclaimed that "[n]ow it is plain to be seen that Capt. Brown only carried out in his actions the principles emanating from these three sources, viz: First—The Bible. Second—The Revolutionary Fathers. Third—All good Abolitionists."[9]

Of Langston's first source, few people who knew Brown would disagree. Staunchly religious, Brown believed himself to be a tool wielded by the hand of God,[10] and as such, he was often compared to characters of Bible lore. In eulogizing Brown, the Reverend J. Sella Martin likened his death to the decision that led to Jesus' crucifixion, the question being whether the country "would give up the Barabas of Slavery, or the John Brown of Freedom?" The correspondent covering the speech continued with Martin's allusion:

> The speaker compared Brown with John the Baptist, claiming for the martyr of to-day an equal devotion to a great cause. John Brown had been beheaded; so was John of old. He had fallen a sacrifice to the great sin of the nation. His life was the failure which pertains to all great and devoted lives. History will place it in the same category with the life of Christ who died on the cross.[11]

This merging of religious service and fighting spirit coalesced into the reigning image of religious zealot so prevalent in the "John Brown" characters of Hollywood.[12] Among the multitude of portrayals, one of the most notable was Raymond Massey and his dramatization of Brown in two films—*Santa Fe Trail* (1940) and *Seven Angry Men* (1955).[13] Massey's personal brand of overacting—complete with scowling face, billowing white hair, and thundering voice—lent an air of fanaticism that rendered Brown's determination to end slavery entirely plausible to the other characters, as well as the viewing audience.

In the earlier film, West Point graduates James Ewell Brown "Jeb" Stuart (Errol Flynn) and George Armstrong Custer (Ronald Reagan), along with many others in the all-star cast, are asked to express their feelings toward slavery, which are noncommittal by comparison to former cadet Rader (Van Heflin), a radical abolitionist who secretly supports Brown's bloody campaign in Kansas. Reagan's Custer, displaying genuine sympathy for the old man, sheds light on Brown's contradictory personality by pointing out several times in the movie that there was a "purpose behind that madness." After Brown's execution, it is also Custer who corrects Stuart's boast that the old man's cause is "broken for good" by prophesying, "Nothing will ever break the force of John Brown . . . not even death."[14]

Massey's Brown took center stage again in *Seven Angry Men*, produced fifteen years after his appearance in *Santa Fe Trail*. Chronicling Brown's crusade for freedom, from his rampage through Kansas to his own personal Waterloo at Harpers Ferry, the movie invoked sympathy for Brown without ignoring his murderous fanaticism. Brown's relationships with his family (including performances by Jeffrey Hunter, Dennis Weaver, Larry Pennell, James Best, Guy Williams, and Tom Irish as his sons) and a romantic subplot between Owen Brown (Hunter) and his sweetheart Elizabeth (Debra Piaget) served to soften, and ultimately humanize, what had become the stereotypical representation of an old man driven mad by his intense devotion to stopping the evil force of slavery. As the story progressed, Brown grew more and more violent in the service of his cause, readily explained away by the Bible verses he espoused.[15]

Despite his violent nature, Brown was generally portrayed in reality and fiction as the benevolent protector and surrogate father to the slaves he sought to free. Noted as a conscientious benefactor of runaways and Canadian refugees, Brown provided both money and words of comfort to his charges, who readily equated many of his most brutal actions to those of a father willing to do anything necessary to protect the lives of his children. Consequently, black editors and community leaders fondly referred to him as "father" or "uncle," a highly valued member of the family.[16]

One ironic manifestation of this surrogate father image was created by Brown himself, through his guise of "Sambo," an old black man who sought to share the life lessons he had learned with his younger brethren. Brown biographers have attributed his empathy for blacks to the idea that he had divested himself of all "color prejudice" by the time he reached manhood.[17] Thus, feeling no discomfort at being in their presence, he often sought them out, including *Ram's Horn* editor Willis A. Hodges.[18] Through this relationship, Hodges convinced Brown to publish his famous essay, "Sambo's Mistakes," in *The Ram's Horn* early in 1848.[19] Biographer F. B. Sanborn concluded that this somewhat lengthy "unfinished pamphlet" was a major undertaking for Brown, who so disliked the act of writing that everything he penned was short—an important illustration of Brown's dedication to the antislavery cause.[20]

In "Sambo's Mistakes," Brown addressed northern blacks as peers, blatantly pointing out their weaknesses in dealing with whites, as well as certain character flaws that allowed them to buy "expensive gay clothing, nice canes, watches, safety-chains, finger-rings, breastpins, and many other things of a like nature" and rendered them unable to benefit their "suffering brethren" in the South. The essay was filled with common-sense advice and kindly sayings reminiscent of Benjamin Franklin's "Poor Richard." Offering his brethren the benefit of his experience, Sambo advised:

> Mess. Editors, Notwithstanding I may have committed a few mistakes in the course of a long life like others of my colored brethren yet you will perceive at a glance that I have always been remarkable for a seasonable discovery of my errors and quick perception of the true course. I propose to give you a few illustrations in this and the following chapters.[21]

Almost like a grandfather rebuking his younger progeny, Sambo admonished blacks for trivial shortcomings, as well as larger transgressions. In each example, Sambo confessed his own errors and assured the reader that he had learned his lessons. In this way, Sambo (or Brown) spoke not from an outsider's vantage point, but from the midst of argument, as guilty as any other who had committed the same acts. He continued:

> Another error of my riper years has been, that when any meeting of colored people has been called in order to consider any important matter of general interest, I have been so eager to display my spouting talents, and so tenacious of some trifling theory or other that I have adopted, that I have generally lost all sight of the business at hand, consumed the time disputing about things of no moment, and thereby defeated entirely many important measures calculated to promote the general welfare; but I am happy to say I can see in a minute where I missed it.[22]

Each of Sambo's "blunders" chastised blacks' inaction and encouraged them to consider bolder activities, philosophies shared by both Brown and Hodges. Brown often criticized blacks and other abolitionists for relying too much on rhetoric. He once compared his form of antislavery activity to "[gun]powder confined in rock." At a public debate on slavery in 1859, he interrupted the meeting with shouts of "Talk! talk! talk!—that will never set the slave free."[23] While seemingly frivolous at some points, Sambo revealed the true spirit of Brown and his revolutionary fervor through the vitriolic words of the final chapter. He concluded:

> Another trifling error of my life has been that I have always expected to secure the favour of the whites by tamely submitting to every species of indignity, contempt & wrong, instead of nobly resisting their brutal aggressions from principle & taking my place as a man & assuming the responsibilities of a man, a citizen, a husband, a father, a brother, a neighbour, a friend as God required of every one (if his neighbour will allow him to do it;) but I find that I get for all my submission about the same reward that the Southern Slaveocrats render to the Dough-faced Statesmen of the North for being bribed & browbeat, & fooled & cheated, as the Whigs & Democrats love to be, & think themselves highly honored if they may be allowed to lick up the spittle of a Southerner. I say I get the same reward. But I am uncomm[on] quick sighted I can see in a minute where I missed it.[24]

Sentiments of Brown's fatherly nature were also exemplified in both black and mainstream newspapers that included accounts of Brown's behavior toward a black mother and her child in the crowd as he left the jail on the day of his execution. The often-reprinted article described:

> His thoughts at that moment none can know except as his acts interpret them. He stopped for a moment in his course, stooped over, and with the

> tenderness of one whose love is as broad as the brotherhood of man, kissed the child affectionately. That mother will be proud of that mark of distinction for her offspring.[25]

The words were fitting for the man who earlier had refused to be accompanied by white clergy, "those whose robes are dyed in the guilt and sin of slavery." After demanding that the priests leave his cell, he supposedly uttered what nearby reporters labeled as among his last words. He implored, "I would prefer rather to be accompanied to the scaffold by a dozen little slave children and a good old slave mother, with their appeals to God for blessings on my soul, than all the eloquence of the whole clergy of the Commonwealth combined."[26]

Undoubtedly, these tales sparked numerous illustrations of Brown with the distraught mother and her child. In one painting, a stoic and determined Brown stands poised at the door of the jail, while a soldier in full dress regalia angrily beckons him forward. However, the abolitionist casts a fatherly glance upon the barefoot young mother in a flowing dress offering her naked, cherubic baby up to Brown.[27] A similar painting shows Brown flanked by heavily armed soldiers as he pauses on the steps to kiss one baby as the slave mother, wearing tattered rags, carries yet another child in a harness on her back.[28]

Brown's radical spirit had infected many abolitionists, particularly blacks, who responded to his insurgent words and those of other such revolutionaries as *Liberator* editor William Lloyd Garrison. These followers maintained little hope that moral suasion alone would convince slaveholders to part with millions of dollars in property and believed that intersectional violence was inevitable.[29] Brown's revolutionary attitude and his railings against societal, as well as legal, injustices offered hope for blacks who were fast becoming disillusioned with the white-dominated abolitionist movement. To these followers, he became their own George Washington, defending their rights to be free.

Many editors rationalized that Brown was simply continuing the fighting spirit that had been embodied by those who fought in the Revolutionary War. He was often compared to heroes from that war. At a Pittsburgh meeting to honor Brown, a "conferring committee on the part of the colored residents of Allegheny City" resolved "[t]hat we see in the Harper's Ferry affair what Daniel Webster saw when speaking of Crispus Attucks, the black Revolutionary martyr, who fell in Boston—viz.: the severance of two antagonistic principles. . . . That John Brown, in taking up arms to liberate the slaves, only acted upon the maxim that 'resistance to tyrants is obedience to God.'"[30]

Brown's old friend Frederick Douglass selected a different hero of the Revolutionary War. Sharing the speaker's platform at Storer College with the state attorney who had prosecuted Brown, Andrew Hunter, Douglass deemed

Brown's death as "a foregone conclusion" because of his dauntless spirit, and envisioned Brown as assuming a well-earned place in American history. Douglass observed:

> He [Brown] had practically illustrated a truth stranger than fiction,—a truth higher than Virginia had ever known,—a truth more noble and beautiful than Jefferson ever wrote. He had evinced a conception of the sacredness and value of liberty which transcended in sublimity that of her own Patrick Henry and made even his fire-flashing sentiment of 'Liberty or Death' seem dark and tame and selfish. Henry loved liberty for himself, but this man loved liberty for all men, and for those most despised and scorned, as well as for those most esteemed and honored. Just here was the true glory of John Brown's mission.[31]

Ironically, the earliest known portrait of Brown, a daguerreotype created in 1846 or 1847 by black abolitionist Augustus Washington at his studio in Hartford, reveals him in a standard patriotic pose. The portrait shows a grimly determined Brown, with his customary furrowed brow, penetrating eyes, and tightly drawn lips.[32] His right hand is raised as if uttering a pledge of allegiance, while his left hand grasps the pole of a banner or flag. This is the portrait most often used by historians to illustrate Brown's resolve to end slavery by any means necessary.[33]

By his very nature, Brown easily inspired blacks to rally in support of his efforts. To black Americans, the leader of the raid at Harpers Ferry was a symbol who conferred dignity and worth upon his followers. This devotion to Brown, with his condemnation of slavery as the sin of all sins, motivated many blacks to follow him without question.[34] Years later, when followers wanted to raise funds for a monument to honor Brown, black readers were assailed with the exchange between Frederick Douglass Jr. and *New York Age* editor T. Thomas Fortune over who had made the greater sacrifice to end slavery, John Brown or Nat Turner.[35] For many, the answer was an easy one. No other white man had given up his life and the lives of his sons to defeat a system that had no direct impact on their existence.

Thus, while Brown's raid on the federal arsenal at Harpers Ferry failed, it acted as a catalyst that forced the country to address the inevitable violent end to slavery. Andrew Hunter, appointed as special prosecutor by Virginia Governor John Letcher, later agreed that Brown and his raid was not "the insignificant thing which it appeared to be before the public, but that it really and truly was the incipient movement of the great conflict between North and South and that it evidently resulted in the war."[36]

For blacks, the role John Brown played in changing the course of their lives was threefold. When Brown raised his hand at Harpers Ferry, the time for compromise was gone, and slaves had a champion who was simultaneously a nurturer, revolutionary, and prophet. On the subsequent "Martyr Day," blacks met to "acknowledge the person of John Brown a hero, a patriot, and Christian—a hero because he is fearless to defend the poor; a patriot because he loves his countrymen, acknowledging the truth of the brotherhood of man; and a Christian because he loves his neighbor as himself, and remembered those in bonds as bound with them."[37]

Notes

1. "The Tragic Prelude (John Brown)," Mural by John Steuart Curry, in State Capital of Topeka, KS, ca. 1937–42. Reprinted from National Archives and Records, Washington, DC.
2. Frederick Douglass, "John Brown: An address by Frederick Douglass, at the fourteenth anniversary of Storer College, Harper's Ferry, West Virginia, May 30, 1881." Reprinted as part of the African-American Perspectives: Pamphlets from the Daniel A.P. Murray Collection, 1818–1907, Library of Congress. Douglass presented the manuscript of the speech to college officials to be sold, with the proceeds to be used to endow a John Brown Professorship.
3. The 1837 murder of editor Elijah P. Lovejoy had already provided the abolitionists with a martyr and concrete evidence of the brutality of those who promoted the continuance of slavery practices.
4. Oswald Garrison Villard, *John Brown, 1800–1859: A Biography Fifty Years After* (Boston: Houghton Mifflin Co., 1910), 478–479. Stephen B. Oates, *To Purge This Land with Blood: A Biography of John Brown* (New York: Harper & Row, 1970), p. 238. F. B. Sanborn, *The Life and Letters of John Brown, Liberator of Kansas, and Martyr of Virginia* (Boston: Roberts Brothers, 1891), p. 12.
5. Bernell Tripp, *Origins of the Black Press in New York, 1829–1849* (Northport, AL: Vision Press, 1992), pp. 52–53.
6. Lloyd Chiasson Jr. (ed.), *The Press in Times of Crisis* (Westport, CT: Greenwood Press, 1995), p. 69.
7. Truman Nelson, *The Old Man: John Brown at Harper's Ferry* (New York: Holt, Rinehart & Winston, 1973), 198. Baltimore *Patriot*, 17 October 1859; Baltimore *American*, 18 October 1859; Baltimore *Exchange*, 18 October, 19 October 1859.
8. Nelson, 198, 207. See also New York *Times*, October 21, 1859; New York *Herald*, October 20, 1859; Hartford *Evening Press*, October 20, 1859.
9. *Cleveland Plain Dealer*, 18 November 1859.
10. *North Star*, 15 December 1851.
11. *The Liberator* (Boston), 9 December 1859; *Weekly Anglo-African*, 17 December 1859; *Douglass' Monthly*, December 1859.
12. Several noted character actors played Brown in popular films, television series, and theater productions. John Anderson, best known for his recurring role as "Harry" on the *MacGyver* television series, and famed horror film and dramatic actor John Carradine produced two such memorable portrayals. See also Royal Dano, *The Skin*

Game (1971); John Cromwell, *Abe Lincoln in Illinois* (1940); Johnny Cash, *North and South* (television miniseries, 1985); Sterling Hayden, *The Blue and the Gray* (television miniseries, 1982).

13. Massey also portrayed Brown in the theatrical production of "John Brown's Body," along with Tyrone Powers.
14. *Santa Fe Trail*, Michael Curtiz (B&W, Warner Bros., U.S., 1940), starring Errol Flynn, Olivia de Havilland, Raymond Massey, Ronald Reagan, Alan Hale, and Van Heflin.
15. *Seven Angry Men*, Charles Marquis Warren (B&W, Allied Artists, U.S., 1955), starring Raymond Massey, Debra Piaget, Dennis Weaver, Jeffrey Hunter, Larry Pennell, James Best, and Guy Williams.
16. Martin Delany often used the term "Uncle" for Brown. Delany had met Brown when the old man had gone to Chatham, West Ontario, to recruit followers. Afterwards, Delany maintained contact with Brown and his lieutenant, John Henry Kagi. See, for example, letter from M. R. Delany to J. H. Kagi, Aug. 16, 1858, reprinted in Dorothy Sterling (ed.), *Speak Out in Thunder Tones: Letters and Other Writings by Black Northerners, 1787–1865* (Garden City, NY: Doubleday, 1973; repr., New York: Da Capo, 1998), pp. 276–277. See also, for example, Agnes Mary Grant to Wendell Phillips, in care of the Office of the Anglo African. From the Blagden Papers collection, Harvard College, reprinted in Irving H. Bartlett (ed.), *Wendell & Ann Phillips: The Community of Reform, 1840–1880* (New York: W.W. Norton & Company, 1979), pp. 75–76.
17. F. B. Sanborn, ed., *The Life and Letters of John Brown, Liberator of Kansas, and Martyr of Virginia* (Boston: Roberts Brothers, 1891), p. 128. John Brown Jr. later remarked that the first time he saw his father kneel in prayer was in about 1837 when Old Brown explained to his oldest children his goal to stage a war against slavery (ibid., 39); James Redpath, *The Public Life of Capt. John Brown, with an Auto-Biography of His Childhood and Youth* (Boston: Thayer and Eldridge, 1860), p. 59; Villard, *John Brown*, pp. 49–50; Robert Penn Warren, *John Brown: The Making of a Martyr* (New York: Payson and Clarke, 1929), pp. 18–20.
18. Willard B. Gatewood, Jr. (ed.), *Free Man of Color: The Autobiography of Willis Augustus Hodges* (Knoxville: University of Tennessee Press, 1982), p. xliii.
19. Alexander Moore, *Nelson-Hodges Papers, 1773–1936* (New York: Long Island Historical Society, n.d.), Addendum, I. Brown, who at the time maintained a wool business in Springfield, Massachusetts, was one of many businessmen associated with the abolitionist movement who received complimentary copies of *The Ram's Horn*. After receiving the complimentary copies, Brown sent a list of names and some money to the paper, along with the request that copies be mailed to people on the list for one year. According to Alexander Moore, Hodges's descendant, the two later met in the office of the *Ram's Horn* "as brothers, parted as friends; they related their past life, their futures were full of hope, their past histories had been different, their hopes were the same."
20. Sanborn also compared "Sambo's mistakes" to the advice and wisdom in "Poor Richard's Almanack." Sanborn, p. 131.

21. Reprinted in Sanborn, pp. 128–131.
22. Ibid.
23. Ibid., p. 131.
24. Sanborn, p. 129. This was Brown's only known journalistic endeavor. Not long after, Brown moved part of his family from Springfield, Massachusetts, to North Elba, New York, to settle among blacks on land granted to them by abolitionist and philanthropist Gerrit Smith. He eventually moved his family to the Adirondacks near the site where Hodges later settled. *The Ram's Horn*, 5 November 1847.
25. *Weekly Anglo-African*, 10 December 1859; *Harper's Weekly*, 14 December 1859; *Anglo-African Magazine*, December 1859; *Philadelphia Bulletin*, 3 December 1859. The scene has also been depicted many times in paintings and other artwork. Compare the painting of John Steuart Curry, circa 1859, to that of Louis L. Ransom, circa 1863.
26. *Weekly Anglo-African*, 17 December 1859.
27. *John Brown, The Martyr* (New York: Currier and Ives, 1870), Prints and Photographs Division, Library of Congress (127).
28. *John Brown on His Way to His Execution*. Oil painting by Thomas Hovenden, 1884. Historic Photo Collection, Harper's Ferry NHP.
29. See, for example, Samuel J. May, *Some Recollections of Our Anti-Slavery Conflict* (Boston: Fields and Osgood, 1869), p. 27.
30. *Weekly Anglo-African*, 17 December 1859. Editor Thomas Hamilton coordinated correspondents in providing coverage of the John Brown memorial services from various cities throughout the North, including Cleveland, Detroit, Pittsburgh, Philadelphia, Albany, New Haven, and Boston.
31. Douglass, "John Brown," Storer College.
32. *John Brown Portrait*, Augustus Washington. From a quarter-plate daguerreotype, circa 1846/47. National Portrait Gallery, Smithsonian Institution, Washington, DC.
33. Producers for the documentary *John Brown's Holy War* also used this portrait to illustrate the moment at the memorial for slain abolitionist editor Elijah Lovejoy when Brown pledged his life to ending slavery.
34. Benjamin Quarles (ed.), *Blacks on John Brown* (Urbana, IL: University of Illinois Press, 1972), p. xiii.
35. See *New York Age*, 12 January, 29 January 1889; Washington *National Leader*, 19 January 1889.
36. Quoted in Nelson, *The Old Man*, p. 200.
37. *Weekly Anglo-African*, 17 December 1859.

The Fugitive Imagination

Robert Penn Warren's *John Brown*

— Robert Blakeslee Gilpin —

Robert Penn Warren, the only writer to receive Pulitzer Prizes in both fiction and poetry, was personally and professionally preoccupied with the memory of the antebellum South throughout his life. While Warren is remembered primarily for his novel *All the King's Men,* the native Kentuckian spent much of his life wrestling with the South's legacy in nonfiction. His explorations found their most forceful expression in his early work, particularly his first book, the 1929 biography *John Brown: The Making of a Martyr.*

Warren's choices as a writer and historian are vitally important, especially in appreciating the evolving attitudes towards race, religion, and reform in the early-twentieth-century South. Warren confronts these issues both implicitly and explicitly in *John Brown*. His values and assumptions, particularly in his early work, were firmly rooted in his Fugitive experience, the collective project of southern writers Allen Tate, John Crowe Ransom, Donald Davidson, and Andrew Lytle at Vanderbilt University in Nashville, Tennessee. Louis Rubin, who has studied Ransom, Davidson, Tate, and Warren, argues that the only influence that the Fugitives had on Warren was stylistic; his deep friendships simply "taught him to be a literary craftsman."[1] To Rubin, Warren is the ultimate immaculate literary conception, springing full-born into genius, a portrait that conveniently disregards the problematic texts and influences of his early career.

The reality was much different. To fully grasp the meaning of Warren's early career, it is necessary to look at Nashville in the early twentieth century.

Warren wrote in 1963 that Nashville is "the city I know—or knew—best in the world, the city which more than any other, with all the thinning of old ties and the work of time, was still 'home.'"[2] Nashville in 1914 was a city that aspired to be more than it was. True, the self-proclaimed "Athens of the South" had constructed a replica of the Parthenon in the city's main public park (alongside the cabin that Jefferson Davis grew up in, transported from Kentucky and rebuilt). But aside from a collection of emerging universities, Nashville had little to distinguish itself from other southern cities. In the midst of significant changes, Vanderbilt University, under the progressive vision of Chancellor James Kirkland, soon emerged as a destination for southern intellectuals.

By the end of World War I, John Crowe Ransom and Donald Davidson, both native Tennesseans, were teaching at Vanderbilt and running biweekly literary sessions at Nashville clothier James Frank's house. In November 1921, at the urging of Davidson, the group invited a precocious Vanderbilt undergraduate named Allen Tate to join their discussions. By February 1922, Tate and his compatriots had written so much that Sidney Hirsch suggested they publish a magazine. In April of that same year, *The Fugitive*, a small blue booklet named after one of Hirsch's poems, was published. The publication of this first issue, however, was not the most significant development in the history of the Fugitives. It was their next recruit, a lanky, red-haired Kentuckian named Robert Penn Warren, who would secure them more than a footnote in southern literary history.

In the spring of 1923, Tate was typing a poem when a "physically uncoordinated and socially awkward" boy approached him from behind, asking quietly if he might like to trade poems.[3] A friendship was immediately struck and Warren, a sixteen-year-old from Guthrie, Kentucky, who called himself "Red," moved in with Tate and his roommate one week later. Tate nurtured Warren's writing and boosted the nervous freshman's confidence in his work. Tate soon told the Fugitives that the "boy is a wonder . . . and deserves election to the board."[5] Within the year, Warren had been made a full member of the Fugitives. Tate had a ready ally in Davidson, who was teaching Warren in his freshman English class. Davidson, who admitted to being a bit intimidated by Warren's precocious ambition, described him as "a freckled, angular, gawky boy, yet a prodigy whom at birth the Muse had apparently vested with complete literary equipment."[6] Davidson would further comment that Warren was "the brightest student they had ever seen around here."[7]

While Warren's poetry was still rough, the group took quickly to him. Tate made the case to Davidson that "Red is pretty close to being the greatest Fugitive poet."[6] But when Warren joined the Fugitives, he was very much in the process of developing and harnessing his gifts, and he eagerly absorbed the influences of his new peers. He spoke admiringly of Ransom's work and spurred Tate to write as much as possible. In addition to writing and editing, Warren also began to bring qualified undergraduates to meetings, including a classmate named Andrew Lytle, who would become a fast friend of Warren and Tate. Warren, just eighteen, spent his evenings with established poets and intellectuals, quickly becoming focused on a single career. As he described those early days, "Ransom was writing his best poems then, and Tate was just finding himself," and Warren soon decided that "this is what I'm going to do."[8]

In July 1925, Tennessee was thrust into national headlines. John Scopes, a Rhea County biology teacher, was charged with illegally explaining evolution in his high school science class. The trial became a national showcase for modern values, religion and the enduring sectionalism of American life. H. L. Mencken, a journalist for the *Baltimore Sun* and the country's best known columnist, aggressively chronicled what he saw as the perfect encapsulation of an American backwater: the South. Mencken's columns on the trial were filled with references to the "yokels," "primates," "morons," "half-wits," and "hillbillies" who populated America beneath the Mason-Dixon line.[9]

For southerners, the trial also became, in the words of Fred Hobson, "a prototypic event, the single event that more than any other of the 1920s brought to the surface all of the forces and tensions that had characterized the post-war South, the event that most forcefully dramatized the struggle between southern provincialism and the modern, secular world."[10] In the wake of the Scopes trial, an increasingly combative southern intellectual movement crystallized. Since the early Fugitive days, Ransom, Tate, and Davidson had all sought in various ways to plumb the lost honor of the Old South. This passion for the past found new purpose in the post-Scopes South. The Fugitives began to eagerly seek forums to contrast the halcyon antebellum years and the encroaching problems of the industrial North. Often rendered in the language of the Civil War itself, the Fugitives saw their intellectual, spiritual, and emotional legacy being hijacked by a marauding North. They argued with increasing anger that they must either take control of their past or suffer a second defeat.

A crucial meeting took place in 1926, when they started referring to themselves as the brethren.[11] After the Scopes debacle, Tate had written some of his compatriots to try to organize a "Southern Symposium" to confront some of the issues raised by the trial and the infuriating northern press treatment.[12] Andrew Lytle, by now a dedicated comrade, was promoting "the formation of a society, something like the *Action Française* group" with "a whole religious, philosophical, literary and social program."[13] Warren went him one better when he wrote to Tate. "The Nashville brothers," he wrote, "are on fire with crusading zeal and the determination to lynch carpet baggers."[14] Davidson, for his part, related his profound visit to a Confederate graveyard. Walking through the markers, he became convinced that the Old South would rise again, reading inscriptions of "bold, generous and free" soldiers, "firm in conviction of the right, ready at their country's call, [and] steadfast in their duty."[15] As Davidson proudly wrote to his fellow Fugitives, "the principles for which they fought can never die."[16]

There was nothing novel about the ideas the Fugitives started advocating in the 1920s. David Blight's deft analysis of Lost Cause beliefs highlights how similar ideas had facilitated the South's quick and effective organization after the war. As Blight writes, "a nostalgic Lost Cause reinvigorated white supremacy" with "arguments [that] reinforced Southern pride, nationalized the Lost Cause, and racialized Civil War memory for the postwar generations."[17] The most ingenious aspect of Lost Cause ideology was the siege mentality it encouraged, convincing southerners that they were constantly under attack from the North. The Fugitives took this concept and twisted the endpoint to produce an entirely different dynamic. Tate, Ransom, Davidson, Lytle, and Warren all saw themselves at the vanguard of something quite different—a progressive movement that was not mired in the past, but selectively drew from it. The Fugitives cast their efforts as part of a new age, something beyond the stigma and overt racism of previous Lost Cause organizations.

Serious developments were on the horizon. Not long after Tate graduated from Vanderbilt, he managed to secure a book contract for a biography of the Confederate war hero Stonewall Jackson. Even before Tate started writing, he had reached his conclusion, writing to Davidson that "we should now be a separate nation."[18] "I'm doing a stirring partisan account," he added, "the stars and bars forever!"[19] Tate's 1928 biography of Jackson held true to his claims. Tate's book made Unionists the true traitors, "northern rebels" who were "destroying the long standing balance between the states and the federal government" and trying to create a new Constitution.[20] Portraying Jackson's life as a story of the tragic decline of the South, Tate sought to revive the Old South, "if only through memory."[21] To pursue this agenda and in service of a larger southern myth, Tate explained that enslaving blacks was a "positive good" because "it had become a necessary element in a stable society."[22] For Tate, slavery was merely "benevolent protection: the elite man was in every sense responsible for the Black—the Black man, 'free,' would have been exploited."[23]

Tate's biography got mixed reviews, especially in the northern press, but the book sold extremely well. Earle Balch, Tate's publisher, soon convinced him to begin another biography. Tate decided to use his unused notes from *Stonewall Jackson* for a biography on Jefferson Davis. Louis Rubin argues that both of these biographies were only done in the spirit of "exercise[s], done to earn bread and to shock the Brahmins . . . game[s] played for the fun of it."[24] Unfortunately, dismissing the biographies as exercises or fun and games ignores the polemical nature of Tate's arguments and descriptions just as it trivializes their impact and influence. By making these books out to be incidental exercises, Rubin and others fail to grasp the very real propagandistic program that lay behind their writing. As Tate wrote in 1927, "interesting things are, I believe, at last stirring in the South, and in that part of the South which we cannot help taking about with us forever, wherever we may go."[25]

Tate convinced his publishers to give Andrew Lytle a contract to write the life of Nathan Bedford Forrest. He had not forgotten about Warren, and strongly pushed him in conversations with Mavis MacIntosh, a literary agent in New York. Soon, Warren had a contract with Payson and Clarke for a biography of the abolitionist John Brown, with an option for a book of poetry to follow.[26] From the very first, the Brown biography was conceived as a southern project. In place of such southern heroes as Stonewall Jackson, Jefferson Davis, and Nathan Bedford Forrest, Warren, ever the iconoclast, had chosen a northern abolitionist, but one whose life could be made to argue the same points. As Warren recalled, he felt specially drawn to Brown, who held a "sentimental appeal and [provided] an attempt to relive something—to recapture, to reassess."[27] Warren's biography was explicitly tied to the shared speculations and conversations of the Fugitives.[28] The long friendship of these writers was powerfully entwined with their collective journey to rescue the southern past.[29]

Tate and Lytle, on a 3,500-mile tour of Civil War battlefields, met up with Warren in late 1928, as he was soaking up Brown tales at Harpers Ferry, and the men discussed their common pursuit of southern history.[30] As Tate commented, "here we are all working on the same idea."[31] For Warren and the others, biography provided a real opportunity to showcase an accurate version of the war, a war northern historians had been manipulating for too long. Thus, Warren sought to dislodge abolitionist narratives that had corrupted historical visions of the war. Beyond his belief that Brown was nothing more than a common criminal, Warren professed to abhor people using the past to further their beliefs.[32] For Warren, Brown was a symbol of and representative for this abolitionist failing, men who were willing to follow their beliefs to extreme lengths, regardless of the effects. Warren was disgusted and fascinated to equal degrees by the beliefs and hubris of the northern martyr, just as he was deeply angered by the way Brown had helped begin the Civil War.

Lytle articulated this shared Fugitive sentiment in a letter to Tate, in which he decried the North's "short-sighted greed" in the "murder of the South."[33] Lytle expressed his horror that "we've had to submit to our enemies in the presentation of our case to the world."[34] But they would submit no longer. Finally, the southern case was being pursued with their biographies. While the battlefield rendezvous had brought a thematic and spiritual coherence to Warren's work, his encounter with Tate and Lytle did not help with the most serious task of the John Brown biography: the accumulation of factual information. But beyond his trip to Harpers Ferry and a single interview, Warren conducted most of his research in the best-known biographies of Brown.[35] As Warren noted in a September 1928 letter, "the material in the Yale library was not very helpful—business letters for the most part, which had, unhappily, no bearing on the sundry swindling operations of our hero."[36]

While Warren's published and private writings from this period obviously reveal the influence of the Fugitives, the strength of these associations is frequently downplayed.[37] Actually, Warren's Fugitive connections were being reinforced in the late 1920s. Tate spent "a good portion of his time" visiting with Warren and reading drafts of the Brown biography, giving Warren notes on improving various aspects of the book. [38] As Tate wrote to Lytle in May of 1929, "I am all applause. [*John Brown* is] a great piece of work—very deceptive at first glance . . . but very soon you are amazed at the subtlety of the presentation—at the way small facts connect with other small facts further on, and at the quiet, dawning case that is being built up against the pseudomartyr. It's going to be a great book."[39]

Warren began *John Brown: The Making of a Martyr* with an ironic device. He told the story of the execution, in 1511, of a man in Kent, England, named John Brown who held so tightly to his conception of God that he was put to death. In addition to establishing the aggressively ironic tone that characterizes the biography, Warren used this story as a narrative hook and a thematic trope. Pointing out that the John Brown of Harpers Ferry fame erroneously claimed to descend from a Mayflower passenger named Peter Brown, Warren suggested that it would be equally ridiculous, but perhaps more in keeping with the "higher law" proclamations of Brown, if he had claimed to descend from his executed Kent namesake.

Warren continued the story with a skeptical rendering of the Brown family's Revolutionary War involvement and Brown's birth in West Simsbury, Connecticut, a portrait based mainly on pointing out the incongruities between Harpers Ferry, Kansas, and the Revolutionary War. Warren showed particular delight in pointing out the absurdities of the Brown legend, and because Brown was a vigorous self-promoter, there are countless opportunities. Brown's hagiographic tales of his own life included an entry from his time in Ohio, when a runaway slave appeared at his family's door and young Brown took the man in, hiding him in the underbrush. Brown recalled later of "hearing his heart beating before I reached him."[40] In addition to parodying Brown's superhuman hearing, Warren was pleased to point out that this occasion allowed the abolitionist to seize "the opportunity to again swear eternal enmity against slavery."[41] Warren made it plain that he considered tales like these to be the inventions of a deluded and misguided zealot. However, Warren did not simply refute the story, because the facts did not exist to do so. Instead, he used language to great dramatic effect, successfully dressing these passages with enough sarcasm to render Brown's story ridiculous. His skills entreat his readers to agree.

Moving on to Ohio, where Brown lived in the 1830s, Warren described the restrictive laws passed because "free negroes were generally unpopular in Ohio."[42] Of course, Warren asserted, "black laws or no black laws, Ohio was a better home to them than the jungle."[43] Thus, not only are Warren's northerners hypocritical opponents of slavery passing racist laws, but blacks in *John Brown* are hardly human—unthinking, unwitting participants in a drama they cannot really understand. Warren's treatment of the blacks who joined Brown on the abortive Harpers Ferry raid provides an excellent example of the racial dynamics of *John Brown*. Describing the mixed feelings of the raiders, Warren argued that "the negroes, knowing nothing of Harper's Ferry, naturally held no opinions."[44]

What many have failed to notice in *John Brown* are Warren's sustained arguments that the Civil War was unnecessary, slavery was benign, and the marauding North ruined the show for everyone. By treating slavery exclusively as an economic and social system with no human side, Warren created an utterly ahistorical picture. While Warren's language argued for slavery to be considered "in the more human terms of its practical workings" and not in an abolitionist's conception of its "abstract morality," Warren blithely depicted the slave as a happy and contented creature "never bother[ing] his kinky head about the moral issue[s of slavery]."[45] For the slaves, being held in bondage was merely a matter "of convenience" and freedom would only bring "inconvenience."[46] Southern slavery, Warren claimed, had none of "the horrors of West Indian slavery" because "immediate contact existed between master and slave," encouraging "an exercise of obligation [that] reached downward as well as upward."[47]

While Warren was willing to admit that "the system was subject to grave abuse," he argued that "the negro's condition was tolerable enough."[48] In Warren's view, basic economics meant that there could not be serious mistreatment, "for the slave was valuable property and it was only natural that the master would take care to give his property such treatment as would not jeopardize its value."[49] Warren summed up the meaning of the Civil War for blacks in much the same way. "There was, by consequence," he wrote, "no great reservoir of hate and rancor which at the least opportunity would convert every slave into a soldier; when the war came the masters marched off, leaving their families and estates in the care of those same negroes for whose liberty, presumably, the North was fighting."[50]

Warren argued that in addition to Brown's actions contributing momentum towards war, it was the North's immediate mythologizing of Brown's life that was particularly inexcusable and contributed mightily to the beginning of the war. Describing his disdain for James Redpath's celebratory biography, Warren wrote that "the Civil War, which confounded so many problems and clarified so few, followed close on the heels of Redpath's book to supplement the confusion which [Brown] had already contributed."[51] Warren distinctly echoed Tate's efforts, arguing that the war itself was unjust and imposed upon the nation by a misguided North. But while Warren only occasionally drew on the typical southern apologist vision of the horror and injustice of Reconstruction, he did subscribe to the notion that in the aftermath of the war, blacks had been given too much freedom, unleashing concepts and opportunities they were unprepared to accept. For Warren, blacks had become totally "accustomed to explicit directions" under slavery.[52] Thus, in *John Brown*'s worst moments, Warren concluded that "the negroes, as the experience of emancipation was to show, could not work for themselves."[53]

Often, and to Warren's credit as a stylist, the invective was much more subtle. While the main agenda of the biography was chastising the North for the Civil War and excusing slavery, John Brown the scoundrel provided the means to those larger ends. Indeed, Brown's "dishonest" business practices were Warren's favorite trope in the biography. For Warren, Brown's financial affairs, in which he saw dishonesty and deception where others have seen mere incompetence, hold the key to Brown's entire life. After describing the bloody killings at Pottawatomie Creek, Warren described Brown stealing his victims' horses and trading them immediately into a criminal network. Warren's writing powerfully recalled his influences. "The terms of the transaction will never be known," Warren wrote, "the sons who survived John Brown even denied for years his presence on the Pottawatomie on the night of May 25. When the truth was out at last and the world had prepared a motive—a motive which would fit the martyr—there were confessions from the sons. The world had justified the murderer; the Browns knew that it was a little more difficult to justify a horse thief. When daylight came, the evidence was gone. For the stolen horses were well on their way north to be sold."[54]

With the North thus condemned, and the war thus decided, Warren went on to describe Brown in even starker terms:

> As the years passed, he had tried many ways to get to the head of the heap and had failed and failed again, but with each failure the desire had become more insatiable, more absolute. The desire was susceptible to meanness,

> to chicanery, to bitter, querulous intolerance, to dishonesty, to vindictive and ruthless brutality.[55]

This was the John Brown that Robert Penn Warren left to the ages.

With the publication of *John Brown* in November 1929, Warren moved to the forefront of Fugitive efforts. To his compatriots, Warren's biography was firmly rooted in their shared intellectual project. Dealing indirectly with the Civil War, the book was just the first of his many attempts to confront the enduring legacy of that enormously influential chapter in the nation's history. Unfortunately for Warren, confronting the myth was going to be harder than simply writing the Brown biography. His publisher, Payson and Clark, was bankrupted by the stock market crash.[56] Not surprisingly, Payson and Clark's fiduciary troubles had a debilitating effect on the prospects of *John Brown*. The company was in a state of serious disarray, and book distribution was plagued with difficulties. A letter to Warren from Donald Davidson underscored the problems with Payson and Clark. Davidson wrote of his trouble procuring a copy to review, even when he offered to pay for it, and summed up by saying they were simply "bad people to deal with."[57] But Davidson had bigger concerns than the availability of Warren's book. The book kicked Davidson's crusade into high gear. Labeling a negative review of *John Brown* in the *New York Times* "an abomination," Davidson offered to "waive my lack of qualification and proceed to the discussion myself . . . of [Warren's] very substantial, well-balanced, and intelligent biography." "I am full of admiration," Davidson added, "the book is a remarkable performance all the way through, and it means, among other things, that you are able to do practically anything you wish in a literary way."[58] Davidson added that this "sentiment only confirms a feeling that all of your old Fugitive comrades have had: the world is your apple, Red."[59]

Davidson's review soon made appearances in dozens of papers across Tennessee, rallying support for Warren's book under a pro-southern banner. For Davidson, Warren's book "emphasizes once more a profound difference in historical point of view between the North and South. This difference is not now of a sort that will lead, as it once did, to a tragic effusion of blood; but it is still much more than a cold academic matter. It relates to differences of temper, social tradition, economics, geography, and much more."[60] In Davidson's opinion, Warren's book was not overtly southern at all. Warren merely "does not feel obliged to find excuses for John Brown's villainies . . . it is not a wrathy, fire-eating book, but a cool, thoroughly documented study, covering every detail of Brown's career."[61] Finally, Davidson laid out his earnest hope, "that Mr. Warren's excellent book will disturb and dislocate the legend . . . if anything will lay John Brown's ghost, this book will."[62]

At the time of Warren's death in November of 1989, Mark Winchell, an English professor at Clemson, was writing a biography of Donald Davidson. When the author contacted Warren's daughter for an interview, he came face to face with the whitewashing of Warren's past. Rosanna Warren curtly told Winchell that "Donald Davidson was a racist whose name was never spoken in our house."[63] Such an approach to Warren's life, work and his ultimate legacy is devastating and unfortunate. Perhaps Warren's daughter never thumbed through her father's notebooks. If she had, she might have seen the one where he had jotted hundreds of pages of affectionate memories for an unfinished essay on Davidson, his old mentor at Vanderbilt.[64]

Concerned with how history would judge his early works, Warren refused to bring them back into print during his lifetime. But Warren himself believed passionately that the past held valuable answers and myths. His Fugitive imagination, nurtured in the intellectual flowering of the 1920s, shaped his belief that America's national myth would ultimately be found in the South. Warren finished *All the King's Men* with a meditation on history, writing that events move quickly "out of history into history and into the awful responsibility of Time."[65] When exploring Warren's varied career, readers must share in this web of responsibility, especially if they hope to understand the interrelated and problematic memories of slavery, abolition, and the Civil War that shaped Warren as the southerner he so proudly was.

Notes

1. Louis Rubin, *The Wary Fugitives: Four Poets and the South* (Baton Rouge: Louisiana State University Press, 1978), 336
2. Robert Penn Warren, "Episode at the Dime Store." unpublished essay, Robert Penn Warren Papers, Beinecke Library, Yale University, YCAL MSS 51, Box 232, Folder 4391.
3. Thomas Underwood, *Allen Tate: Orphan of the South* (Princeton: Princeton University Press, 2000), p. 73.
4. Underwood, p. 74.
5. Mark Winchell, *Where No Flag Flies: Donald Davidson and the Southern Resistance* (Columbia: University of Missouri Press, 2000), pp. 18–19.
6. Winchell, p. 19.
7. Ibid., p. 73.
8. Ibid., p. 43.
9. http://www.law.umkc.edu/faculty/projects/ftrials/scopes/scopes.htm.
10. Fred C. Hobson, *Serpent in Eden: H. L. Mencken and the South* (Baton Rouge: Louisiana State University Press, 1974), p. 148.
11. Louis Rubin, *The Wary Fugitives: Four Poets and the South* (Baton Rouge: Louisiana State University Press, 1978), p. 229.

12. Joseph Blotner, *Robert Penn Warren: A Biography* (New York: Random House, 1997), p. 98.
13. Ibid., p. 98.
14. Ibid., p. 98.
15. Winchell, p. 157.
16. Winchell, p. 157.
17. David W. Blight, *Race and Reunion: The Civil War in American Memory* (Cambridge, Mass.: Belknap Press of Harvard University Press, 2001), p. 273.
18. Tate quoted in ibid., p. 130.
19. Ibid., p. 131.
20. Winchell, p. 129.
21. Ibid., p. 129.
22. Allen Tate, *Stonewall Jackson: The Good Soldier* (New York: Minton, Balch, 1928), p. 39.
23. Tate, p. 39.
24. Rubin, p. 98.
25. Thomas Daniel Young and Elizabeth Sarcone, eds., *The Lytle-Tate Letters: The Correspondence of Andrew Lytle and Allen Tate* (Jackson: University of Mississippi Press, 1987), p. 5.
26. Joseph Cullick, *Making History: The Biographical Narratives of Robert Penn Warren* (Baton Rouge: Louisiana State University Press, 2000), p. 30.
27. Ibid., p. 20.
28. Ibid., p. 20.
29. L. Hugh Moore, Jr., *Robert Penn Warren and History: The Big Myth We Live* (Paris: Mouton, 1970), p. 12.
30. Ibid., p. 134.
31. *The Lytle-Tate Letters*, p. 26.
32. Moore, p. 133.
33. *The Lytle-Tate Letters*, p. 16.
34. Ibid., p. 16.
35. James Redpath, *Echoes of Harpers Ferry* (Boston: Thayer and Eldridge, 1860); Oswald Garrison Villard, *John Brown, 1800–1859: A Biography Fifty Years After* (New York: Knopf, 1910); Franklin Sanborn, *Life and Letters of John Brown: Liberator of Kansas, and Martyr of Virginia* (Boston: Roberts Brothers, 1891); Richard Hinton, *John Brown and His Men: With Some Account of the Roads They Traveled to Reach Harpers Ferry* (New York: Funk and Wagnalls, 1894); Hill Peebles Wilson, *John Brown, Soldier of Fortune: A Critique* (Lawrence, KS: H. P. Wilson, 1913).
36. Robert Penn Warren to W. F. Payson, Correspondence. Box 93.
37. Leonard Casper, *Robert Penn Warren: The Dark and Bloody Ground* (Seattle: University of Washington Press, 1960), p. 40.
38. Underwood, p. 140.
39. *The Lytle-Tate Letters*, p. 26.

40. Robert Penn Warren, *John Brown: The Making of a Martyr* (Nashville: J.S. Sanders, 1993), p. 21.
41. Ibid., p. 21.
42. Ibid., p. 38.
43. Ibid., p. 32.
44. Ibid., p. 339.
45. Ibid., pp. 331–32.
46. Ibid., p. 332.
47. Ibid., p. 332.
48. Ibid., p. 332.
49. Ibid., p. 332.
50. Ibid., p. 332.
51. Ibid., p. 441.
52. Ibid., p. 283.
53. Ibid., p. 283.
54. Ibid., p. 166.
55. Ibid., p. 350.
56. William Bedford Clark, *The American Vision of Robert Penn Warren* (Lexington: University Press of Kentucky, 1997), p. 43.
57. "Donald Davidson to Robert Penn Warren, January 20, 1930," Correspondence, Robert Penn Warren Papers, Beinecke Library, Yale University, YCAL MSS 51, Box 93, Folder 1745.
58. Ibid.
59. Ibid.
60. Donald Davidson, "John Brown's Ghost is Laid," *Commercial Appeal*, Memphis, Tenn., Feb. 9, 1930 (printed in several other Tennessee papers, *Knoxville Journal*, 2-9-30, *Nashville Tennesean*, 2-9-30 and others).
61. Ibid.
62. Ibid.
63. Winchell, p. 298.
64. "Donald Davidson—Untitled Essay," Robert Penn Warren Papers, Beinecke Library, Yale University, YCAL MSS 51, Box 232, Folder 4387.
65. Robert Penn Warren, *All the King's Men* (New York: Harcourt, Brace, 1946), p. 464.

The Search for Community and Justice

Robert Penn Warren, Race Relations, and the Civil War

— Edward J. Blum and Sarah Hardin Blum —

"The Civil War is urgently our war, and . . . reaches in a thousand ways into our blood stream and our personal present," wrote Robert Penn Warren, one of America's greatest men of letters and, alongside William Faulkner, perhaps the most respected literary voice of the American South in the twentieth century. Beginning with childhood stories told to him by his grandfather, the Kentucky-born Warren always loved history, especially the Civil War. To him, the war influenced every aspect of society, even when he began writing about it nearly one hundred years later. "[T]he effects of the war, for better and worse, permeate American life and culture," he noted. For Warren, the Civil War stood as the central aspect of American history, the fulcrum upon which the entire society hinged, and remembering it constituted the most critical aspect of national identity: "To experience this appeal, in fact, [is] the very ritual of being American."[1]

But though Warren cherished history, historians have not always cherished Warren. In fact, when he published his first historical study at the youthful age of twenty-four, leading historians blasted him. His biography of abolitionist-turned-martyr John Brown garnered the derision of several prominent scholars, including Avery Craven, Allan Nevins, Florence Finch Kelly, and Sterling A. Brown. Writing for the *New York Times Book Review*, Kelly labeled Warren a young scholar whose work was superficial. "And still they come," Kelly chided, "these young iconoclasts, aflame with crusading zeal and bent on telling the oldsters where they got off with their historical hero-worshiping."[2] Sterling Brown claimed that Warren's study was a "masterpiece of detraction" written from "an obvious" pro-southern bias. "The biography," he concluded, "leaves the ranks of important interpretations, and becomes more of a Southerner's confession of faith."[3] As Warren's career progressed, he continued to receive extensive criticism. Some reviewers denounced his 1961 fictional account of the Civil War, *Wilderness*, as "inexorably didactic."[4]

But such reviews fail to recognize Warren's brilliance as a historian. Indeed, he was a superb chronicler of the past. For over five decades during the middle of the twentieth century, Warren demonstrated all of the skills necessary to be considered a master scholar of the Civil War and nineteenth- and twentieth-century America. He tackled difficult historical questions and issues, including the justness of southern segregation, the origins of the civil rights movement, and the social and cultural meanings of the Civil War. He employed historical methodologies such as oral history well before they became historically fashionable. He looked beyond the rhetoric of sectional glorifiers and challenged their basic premises. In short, Warren asked good questions, forged powerful and creative tools, and sought underlying meanings.

Beyond these traits, however, Warren stood out as a marvelous scholar because he interpreted the characters and plots of American history and the Civil War in order to help build stronger and deeper communities within the United States. Indeed, creating a "usable past" was always part of Warren's agenda. An analysis of several of Warren's key historical works, in comparison with similar studies by preeminent American historians, shows Warren to be one of the nation's finest students of the past.

Throughout his career, Warren challenged what usually was seen as unchallengeable in the South: the system of Jim Crow segregation. Long before the Supreme Court ruled against segregation *de jure* in the epochal 1954 *Brown v. Board of Education of Topeka, Kansas* decision, Warren had questioned racial separation. In 1930 he contributed an essay to a collaborative indictment of industrialization, titled *I'll Take My Stand*, by his colleagues at Vanderbilt University. While other contributors longed to maintain the traditional southern way of life, Warren's article, "The Briar Patch," disputed the justness of southern race relations. Warren examined how segregation hurt the region's economy. He argued that Jim Crow left blacks unhappy and eager to move to cities, depriving their previous homeland of a willing and qualified work force. To avoid this exodus, Warren urged white farmers to find a place for African Americans. He suggested that unchecked industrialization would lead to tension and competition between poor white and black farmers. To him, only racial cooperation could thwart the ills of industrialism.

Warren's call for the inclusion of African Americans into southern society was quite radical at the time—in fact, it almost led to its exclusion from *I'll Take My Stand*.[5] Warren's analysis, however, was not entirely free from prejudice. He paternalistically maintained that blacks were better off as farmers and should remain in rural areas rather than live and work where they wished. In addition, Warren's arguments against segregation were not derived from a moral compulsion that Jim Crow hurt African Americans, but from the idea that segregation damaged the region's economy and white farmers. In short, he attacked Jim Crow because it damaged whites, not blacks.[6]

Warren's views changed, however, as he listened to African Americans discuss and attack segregation and racism. In fact, he actively sought out blacks to learn from their experiences. Just two years after *Brown*, Warren conducted a series of interviews of whites and blacks in Tennessee, Kentucky, Arkansas, Mississippi, and Louisiana, during which he probed the social and spiritual ramifications of Jim Crow. In the work that emerged from these interviews, *Segregation: The Inner Conflict in the South*, Warren decreed that Jim Crow was no longer just an economic problem; it was a moral dilemma. He posed insightful questions to a wide variety of people: ministers, college students, planters, workers, white organizers, and black leaders. These questions, critically important to understanding southern race relations, included: Why do whites want segregation? What do African Americans want? Is there any difference between the exclusion felt by African Americans and that felt by a white man?

Warren discovered a complex web of answers, ranging from God's sanctification of segregation to an insistence by African Americans for fair opportunities. In his final interview, Warren proposed these same questions to himself and flatly denounced segregation. Warren's answers demonstrated that his own racial views had changed substantially. Now, African Americans were not the problem—whites were. "I don't think the problem is to learn to live with the Negro," Warren concluded. "It is to learn to live with ourselves."[7]

Warren's "Briar Patch" essay and *Segregation* were not his final words on racial separation. He took up the issue again in *Who Speaks for the Negro?*, a study of the origins of the civil rights movement. To write it, Warren interviewed prominent African American leaders, such as Martin Luther King, Jr., Stokely Carmichael, Malcolm X, Roy Wilkins, and Robert Moses. He explained, "I have written this book because I wanted to find out something, first hand, about the people, some of them anyway, who are making the Negro Revolution what it is—one of the dramatic events of the American story."[8] Warren's questions were both broad and narrow, and he was especially curious about the divisions between organizations, members, goals, and achievements in the movement as a whole. Ultimately, Warren made important conclusions for 1965: "It is not true that the colored folks invariably just love the white folks. It is not true that just a few 'bad niggers' are making all the trouble."[9] What was true, he discovered, was that countless blacks from a variety of backgrounds were willing to agitate and sacrifice for civil rights.

Historians after Warren have asked similar questions and employed similar methodologies in order to understand southern race relations. In fact, although most scholars point to C. Vann Woodward's *The Strange Career of Jim Crow* (1955) as the seminal study of southern segregation, Warren scrutinized many of the same aspects of segregation that Woodward examined. He too investigated who initiated racial separation, and why they did it. Yet Warren's analysis of the cultural cores of Jim Crow probed deeper than Woodward's legalistic analysis. Jim Crow and civil rights stood at the spiritual core of the South, Warren suggested. While whites defended segregation as ordained in heaven, African Americans saw their freedom crusade as akin to the biblical exodus. Warren's oral histories revealed that more than politics was at stake in the maintenance of racial exclusion. Instead, he found a moral component in the rigid separation of the races.[10]

Warren's use of extensive interviews to study the civil rights movement preceded the path-breaking work of historian William Chafe, who used scores of oral histories to write his award-winning study of the civil rights crusade in Greensboro, North Carolina, *Civilities and Civil Rights*. Asking similar questions about the origins of the movement, Chafe, like Warren, went to the African American community to tell a story of the black freedom struggle. While Warren focused on the dominant figures of the movement and discovered that "there is, in one sense, no Negro leader . . . [for] there are, merely, a number of Negroes who happen to occupy positions of leadership," Chafe uncovered the rank and file of the civil rights struggle. His interviews revealed an active group of parents, school teachers, students, and church leaders working to break the barriers of Jim Crow. Through their use of oral histories, Warren and Chafe provided intricate portraits of different aspects of the struggle. Taken together, these works are a kaleidoscope of the civil rights movement, displaying multiple constellations of colors, organizers, leaders, and participants.[11]

Warren also showed brilliant methodological innovation in studying the Civil War, especially in his 1979 essay on Jefferson Davis and his 1929 biography of John Brown. In 1979, after the United States Congress officially restored Davis's citizenship, Warren wrote a lengthy article for the *New Yorker*, which was later published as a book. Warren titled the magazine piece "Jefferson Davis Gets His Citizenship Back," but it was much more than a tale of the president of the Confederate States of America. Warren's essay was actually a lengthy reflection upon history, southern honor, and the power of myths and symbols. In it, Warren mused about his boyhood trip to Fairview, Kentucky, to view a partially completed statue to Davis. Looking at the figure, Warren confronted a host of important historical and cultural concerns, including the meaning of the Civil War, the nature of sectional tensions, and the relationships between history and myth. Warren used the statue as a jumping off point to discuss these issues and others. "Who is this Jefferson Davis?" he asked. What does the statue mean? How do public commemorations and displays reveal historical and social meaning?

To answer these questions, Warren recounted both Davis's personal history and the public history of Davis in the minds of southerners. He contended that Davis differed from his counterpart Abraham Lincoln in that he did not hold a "pragmatic" view of the Civil War, in which any tactic was permissible, even total war and emancipation. Rather, Davis sought to uphold a "chivalric tradition" in which honor and fixed principles were more important than victory. Rather than accept a federal pardon and tacitly admit wrong, Davis asserted the rightness of his cause while imprisoned briefly after the war. Ultimately, to Warren, Davis's life and his statue drew Americans back to a time before big technology and big business, a time when honor mattered more than capital.[12]

In addition to using architecture as an entry into historical study, Warren also demonstrated methodological innovation in his often-derided 1929 biography, *John Brown: The Making of a Martyr.* In it, Warren assaulted the image of Brown as an abolitionist solely committed to the anti-slavery cause. Such a favorable, indeed almost sanctifying, depiction was merely the creation of Brown and several of his earliest biographers, including Oswald Garrison Villard, Warren concluded. To him, the fiery Brown was little more than a hypocritical Puritan more interested in financial gain and in feeding his own ego than in saving those in human bondage. Perhaps more important than Warren's de-mythologizing of Brown, however, was his analysis of the ways Brown formed his own public image. Warren examined the ways Brown constructed himself as a Moses-like and Christ-like figure. Brown's intense reading of history and the Bible, Warren asserted, led him to dramatize himself and his actions in his letters and during a widely publicized interview before his execution. Moreover, Warren pointed out how Brown hired a press agent to chronicle his activities. In short, Brown purposefully manufactured an image for posterity with his words and actions.[13]

Although contemporary scholars rarely acknowledge methodological debts to Warren, in the 1980s and 1990s several of them followed his analyses of sculptures and self-constructions. Both Gaines Foster and Kirk Savage, in *Ghosts of the Confederacy* and *Standing Soldiers, Kneeling Slaves,* respectively, used Civil War statues as starting points for the study of post-Civil War America. To Foster and Savage, northerners and southerners commemorated in stone the war and its warriors to make sense of how the war drastically affected society. Just as Warren mused over the symbolic meanings of the motionless Davis in Kentucky, Foster and Savage focused on what the monuments tell historians about postwar attitudes on southern identity and race relations.

Other scholars have probed how famous nineteenth-century abolitionists constructed similar images to Warren's Brown.[14] In *Sojourner Truth: A Life, A Symbol*, acclaimed historian Nell Irvin Painter explored the ways in which northerners before and after the Civil War fashioned a variety of images of abolitionist and women's rights activist Sojourner Truth to further their causes. Truth herself, Painter showed, perpetuated such myths through her autobiography and her self-portraits. For instance, although Truth often had reading glasses in photographs, she was illiterate. Indeed, as Painter suggested, Truth presented herself as a "respectable, middle-class matron" rather than a poor abolitionist. Like Warren's Brown, Painter's Truth specifically fashioned herself in ways to appeal to northern audiences.[15]

As Warren used creative methodologies to analyze the Civil War and some of its key figures, he also challenged the deepest myths, conceptions, and perceptions of both northern and southern society. Although usually viewed as a southern partisan, Warren sought to debunk sectional myths created by both the North and the South. In 1961, he fired his most powerful volleys at the regional myths of both sides in *The Legacy of the Civil War*. In it, he examined the formation and implications of the southern Lost Cause ideology, a belief that although the Confederacy was destined to lose the war, it nonetheless waged a noble and holy crusade. Warren pointed out how a unified, "solid South" arose only after Robert E. Lee had surrendered at Appomattox Courthouse in 1865. "[O]nce the War was over," Warren wrote, "the Confederacy became a City of the Soul, beyond the haggling of constitutional lawyers, the ambition of politicians, and the jealousy of localisms."[16] But the Lost Cause hindered the South more than it helped, Warren proclaimed, functioning as a psychological "Great Alibi" that permitted inhumane racial actions while silencing criticism. "[T]he most painful and costly consequences of the Great Alibi are found," he wrote, "in connection with race." Indeed, he lamented that the Lost Cause and the Great Alibi sanctified atrocity: "[A]ny common lyncher becomes a defender of the Southern tradition." The Great Alibi, Warren concluded, "trapped" the South "in history."[17]

Northern myths were equally devastating for the nation, Warren believed. While the South excused white-supremacist behavior in the name of southern tradition, the North advanced a civilization built upon avarice and de-humanization under the rubric of a false righteousness acquired in the Civil War. Northerners believed they had obtained what Warren called a "Treasury of Virtue" because of the abolitionist implications of their cause. Northerners "feel redeemed by history, automatically redeemed," Warren maintained, but they were not above reproach. Most northerners were not against slavery, Warren rightly pointed out, and Union soldiers exhibited as much racism as their southern counterparts.

Warren further examined the depths of northern white racism in his 1961 Civil War novel, *Wilderness.* The protagonist of *Wilderness*, Adam Rosenwieg, leaves Germany to join the Union Army because he believes that the mission of the Federal government was to emancipate the slaves. But Rosenwieg's high ideals of freedom and justice stand in stark contrast to the realities of racial hatred in the North. Soon after he arrives in America, Rosenwieg stumbles upon the remains of a lynching victim. It is a black man, the first he has ever seen. Rosenwieg immediately blames the Rebels for the racial violence, but soon discovers that a northern mob protesting conscription laws had committed the heinous crime. Indeed, they were responsible for the deaths of a host of blacks in the city.

Although Rosenwieg does not join the army because of a lame foot, he takes a job as a sutler, supplying goods to the soldiers. As he follows the army, Rosenwieg witnesses numerous other instances of white racism. In the camps, other whites scoff at Rosenwieg's proselytizing about freedom for African Americans. At one point in the novel, Rosenwieg looks on in horror as several high-ranking Union officers humiliate and abuse a group of African Americans, in a sick game of bobbing apples in which the white soldiers threaten to suffocate the blacks by holding their heads underwater. Throughout the novel, Rosenwieg struggles with the endemic racism he witnesses all around him.[18]

In many ways, Warren's suggestions regarding northern Negrophobia and social segregation squared with the findings of Leon Litwack's *North of Slavery: The Negro in the Free States, 1790–1860*, also published in 1961. Litwack detailed how racism and mistreatment of African Americans was a national problem, showing that segregation and racial exclusion existed in northern cities before the Civil War. Prior to the war, Litwack maintained, many northern whites believed that African Americans were naturally inferior to whites and needed whites to help keep them in their proper places. Therefore, whites initiated separate schools, churches, residential areas, and public transportation for African Americans. Employment restrictions also limited the jobs available to free blacks. Both Warren's novel and Litwack's study revealed a similar phenomenon: a violent white racism that ran rampant through the antebellum North as well as the South. For Warren, both regions were guilty of perpetuating destructive, self-exculpatory myths that needed to be debunked by historians and in novels such as his. [19]

Warren was a superb historian because he believed in the power and presence of the past. He lamented the fact that Americans had little interest in their history, charging that they "knew, by and large, as little about the history of their nation as about the difference between the doctrine of transubstantiation and that of consubstantiation."[20] To Warren, a properly informed understanding of the past was crucial to the creation of a moral modern society. Warren, however, did not hold a naïve notion that merely by studying the past one could have all of the answers to present crises. "History cannot give us a program for the future," he concluded, "but it can give us a fuller understanding of ourselves, and of our common humanity, so that we can better face the future."[21]

Warren encountered such an understanding in the characters and times of the Civil War, and he hoped that twentieth-century Americans could learn from what he called the nation's "Homeric period." The heroes and heroines of the fratricidal conflict, Warren maintained, had what Americans in the twentieth century desperately needed, a sense of kinship forged amid fire. As northern and southern soldiers marched off to war, they formed bonds of unity, expressed love for their regions, and honored duty and loyalty. And in the war, Americans rose to new levels of courage and bravery. They found "a strength," Warren wrote, "somehow earned out of inner turmoil."[22] Americans of the mid-nineteenth century felt a closeness lacking in the twentieth century. "In our world of restless mobility, where every Main Street looks like the one before and the throughway is always the same, of communication without communion, of the ad-man's nauseating surrogate for family sense and community in the word *togetherness*, we look back nostalgically on the romantic image of some right and natural relation of man to place and man to man, fulfilled in worth action."

Only through historical study and belief, Warren concluded, "can our hope that somehow in our modern world we may achieve our own new version . . . of identity and community." Yet Warren recognized that Civil War-era notions of community were too limited to serve the people of the twentieth century. Neither in the North nor the South did whites readily accept African Americans into their communities as equals. For this reason, Warren fused his desire for community with an intense longing for racial justice. As late as 1961, Warren regretted the fact that the United States had not fully learned the lessons of the Civil War. "We have not yet achieved justice," he maintained. "We have not yet created a union which is, in the deepest sense, a community. We have not yet resolved our deep dubieties or self-deceptions."[23] Only when all peoples of the nation were treated equally and fairly, Warren concluded, could true community be obtained.

In his myriad novels, essays, and works of nonfiction, Warren sought to locate that true community. It was a frustrating, often contradictory quest, but one that he worked toward consistently throughout his career. For that reason, if no others, Warren should be considered not merely one of America's greatest fiction writers, but also an insightful and trailblazing historian who asked brilliant questions, probed difficult issues, and used various types of innovative methodologies—all in the interest of community and justice.

Notes

1. Robert Penn Warren, *The Legacy of the Civil War: Meditations on the Centennial* (New York: Random House, 1961), pp. 101, 77, 78.
2. Florence Finch Kelly, "John Brown Sits for a Critical Portrait: Mr. Warren Explains Him in Terms of an 'Enormous Egotism,'" *New York Times Book Review,* 12 January 1930, p. 7.
3. Sterling A. Brown, "Unhistoric History," *Journal of Negro History* (Apr., 1930), pp. 152–154.
4. Robert Penn Warren, *Wilderness: A Tale of the Civil War* (Knoxville: The University of Tennessee Press, 2001), p. x. Not all historians have criticized Warren as harshly as these reviewers. Beginning in the 1950s, C. Vann Woodward showed an intense and favorable interest in Warren's studies of history. In fact, Woodward had such an appreciation for Warren that he dedicated a collection of his essays to Warren. See C. Vann Woodward, *The Burden of Southern History* (Baton Rouge: Louisiana State University Press, 1960); by the end of Warren's career, other historians had joined Woodward in praising Warren's historical prowess. Reviewing one work by Warren, Robert Durden wrote, "As always, Robert Penn Warren's thoughts about the nation's cruelest testing time are profound and enriching." Robert F. Durden, review of Robert Penn Warren, *Jefferson Davis Gets His Citizenship Back, The South Atlantic Quarterly,* Winter 1983, pp. 104–105.
5. See Daniel J. Singal, *The War Within: From Victorian to Modernist Thought in the South, 1919–1945* (Chapel Hill: University of North Carolina Press, 1982).
6. Robert Penn Warren, "The Briar Patch," in *I'll Take My Stand: The South and the Agrarian Tradition, By Twelve Southerners* (New York: Harper & Brothers, 1930).
7. Robert Penn Warren, *Segregation: The Inner Conflict in the South* (New York: Random House, 1956), p. 63.
8. Robert Penn Warren, *Who Speaks for the Negro?* (New York: Vintage Books, 1965).
9. Ibid., p. 423.
10. C. Vann Woodward, *The Strange Career of Jim Crow* (New York: Oxford University Press, 1955).
11. William H. Chafe, *Civilities and Civil Rights: Greensboro, North Carolina, and the Black Struggle for Equality* (New York: Oxford University Press, 1980).
12. Robert Penn Warren, *Jefferson Davis Gets His Citizenship Back* (Lexington: The University Press of Kentucky, 1980).
13. Robert Penn Warren, *John Brown: The Making of a Martyr* (Nashville: J. S. Sanders & Company, 1993).
14. Gaines M. Foster, *Ghosts of the Confederacy: Defeat, the Lost Cause, and the Emer-*

gence of the New South, 1865 to 1913 (New York: Oxford University Press, 1987); Kirk Savage, *Standing Soldiers, Kneeling Slaves: Race, War, and Monument in Nineteenth-Century America* (Princeton, N.J.: Princeton University Press, 1997).

15. Nell Irvin Painter, *Sojourner Truth: A Life, A Symbol* (New York: W.W. Norton, 1996), pp. 184–199.
16. Warren, *Legacy of the Civil War*, p. 14.
17. Warren, *Legacy of the Civil War*, pp. 55–57.
18. Warren, *Wilderness.*
19. Leon F. Litwack, *North of Slavery: The Negro in the Free States, 1790–1860* (Chicago: University of Chicago Press, 1961).
20. Warren, *Jefferson Davis Gets His Citizenship Back*, p. 111.
21. Warren, *Legacy of the Civil War*, p. 100.
22. Warren, *Legacy of the Civil War*, p. 84.
23. Warren, *Legacy of the Civil War*, p. 107.

PART II

Civil War Witnesses: Between Fiction and Fact

Between Fiction and Fact

Ben Wood, *Fort Lafayette,* and Civil War America

— Menahem Blondheim —

"American literature," mused Theodore Parker in 1846, "is found only in newspapers and speeches, perhaps in some novel, hot, passionate, but poor and extemporaneous."[1] New York *Daily News* editor Benjamin Wood's 1862 novel, *Fort Lafayette,* certainly fits Parker's characterization. Featuring love and lust, intrigue and violence, devotion and death, the novel is indeed "hot" and "passionate." *Fort Lafayette* is also decidedly extemporaneous, in both its setting and its shallowly disguised purpose, a story about the outbreak of the Civil War and the early stages of the fighting. The novel was composed shortly after those events took place, and was published in New York in January or February 1862.[2] But the novel not only reflected and addressed extemporaneous events, it also wanted to affect them. It was designed to persuade its readers of the moral wrong, folly, and dangers to republican government of war in general, and of a war between America's two sections in particular.

As Wood's career demonstrates, there were significant parallels between the three components of what, according to Parker, constituted American literature—newspaper, speech, and one kind of novel. An able practitioner of all three, Wood was fully aware of the inter-media affinities. In *Fort Lafayette*, he often points out the similarity between speeches and newspapers in their power to mobilize masses.[3] Moreover, in his single extended authorial intervention in the novel's flow of narrative and dialogue, Wood highlights the link between the speech, the newspaper, and the novel.

Wood acquired a controlling interest in the *Daily News* in 1860, as a generation of intersectional controversy was reaching an impasse. From the start, his editorial policy was sympathetic to southern discontents within the Union, stopping just short of supporting secession. On the eve of the fateful election of 1860, the *Daily News,* after a period of equivocation, decided to support Stephen A. Douglas, the northern candidate for the presidential nomination of the Democratic Party, over the candidate nominated by the southern wing of the party, John C. Breckinridge. The newspaper declared itself opposed to secession, even in the case of a Republican victory in the fall elections, yet it expressed no doubt that should Abraham Lincoln be elected, the entire South would secede and war would come.

When it came, the *Daily News* placed the responsibility squarely on the North. More specifically, Wood singled out the anti-slavery and abolitionist movements as the main culprits, and emphatically identified Lincoln and his "Black Republican" supporters with abolitionism. There were three prominent elements in the *Daily News*'s verbal campaign against the war in the spring and summer of 1861. One was a recurring argument that war was not merely unjust, but that fighting it was an evil exercise in futility. Enraging even northerners critical of the war, the *Daily News* reviewed, time and again, the balance of power between the sections, and found the South stronger. The newspaper even seemed to take a perverse pleasure in repeatedly predicting heavy northern casualties in combat and an inevitable southern victory.

The second dominant feature of the *Daily News*'s coverage of the war was its focus on the role of the executive branch and particularly on the chief executive, featuring vicious *ad hominem* attacks on Lincoln. At times it depicted the newly elected president as a bumbling, grossly incompetent, even pathetic statesman, at other times as a scheming, sly, and extremely effective knave. The newspaper's handling of Lincoln could well be considered seditious. Ominous statements such as "Mr. Lincoln . . . has committed high treason, and for similar conduct Charles I of England lost his head" were characteristic of the newspaper's repeated attacks on the beleaguered president.[4]

Finally, and most daringly, the *Daily News* called for action from its readers. To stop the slaughter and government's harassment of civilians—North and South—the newspaper preached resistance to government in its prosecution of the war. "He is no Democrat who will enter the army or volunteer to aid this diabolical policy of Civil War," announced the *Daily News* on April 15, 1861. By July 16 it was calling for something in the nature of a public uprising:

> It is time! Wait no longer! Democrats, arise in your might. Throw off your allegiance to the vampires of your party and declare yourselves free men! . . . Thus will you tame the hyenas of war and give strength to the advocates of peace. . . . Each man who assents in stopping this horrible, bloody, and damnable Civil War, will enroll his name by the side of those of his political fathers, as a savior of his country.

As political conflict gave way to fighting, the message of peace as sounded by Wood in the *Daily News* was transformed in the popular mind from a legitimate opposition platform to a posture of questionable loyalty. Those who sounded it as persistently and vehemently as Wood became suspected of disloyalty to their section. Scorn was not the only feedback anti-war activists received. Shortly after the outbreak of hostilities, angry street-mobs attacked the *Daily News* for its opposition to the war. More pensive individuals, equally outraged by Wood's positions, wrote letters to the State Department, then in charge of policing disloyal activities in the North, and urged it to arrest Wood and close the *Daily News*. Still others chose the path of legal action against the *Daily News* and its like. In August 1862, a New York grand jury issued a presentment against five local anti-war dailies. Lincoln's postmaster general took the presentment as authorization to suspend the privilege of mail delivery for the *Daily News* and four other anti-war newspapers. Unable to deliver its copies to readers outside New York City—at least one-third of them in southern states—the *Daily News* ceased publication on September 14, 1862.

Wood, deprived of his newspaper, could no longer appeal directly to like-minded Americans in an attempt to mobilize them to the anti-war cause. But as a duly elected congressman representing New York's Third District, he had another forum for his dissent. Wood's orations in Congress focused on three themes: the injustice of war, its inner contradictions, and its dire consequences.[5] Wood ably challenged the Republican position on slavery and states' rights, and rebuked its thesis that the Union was indivisible. In pushing his argument beyond this well-covered ground, Wood baldly argued that the administration's goals, however misguided, could not possibly be accomplished by war. With remarkable foresight for someone evaluating the probable course of the war soon after its outbreak, Wood predicted a protracted military struggle and deemed its outcome too close to call.

Whatever the outcome on the battlefield, Wood argued, the Union's cause was destined to failure. Should the South win the war, there would be no union.

If northern arms carried the day, the result would be subjugation of the South, not reunion. In support of his prediction, Wood presented a brilliant analysis of the balance of power between the two sections and the grand strategy it dictated to either side. Through this analysis, Wood accurately forecast the nature the war would take. Southern strategy, he suggested, would inevitably build on the section's homogeneity, solidarity, and desperation. It would offer unrelenting resistance to northern invasion by its entire population. The only strategy that would yield a northern victory in such circumstances, according to Wood, was the waging of total war. The North would have to forcefully recruit its superior resources in manpower, financial assets, industry, and infrastructures, and bring them to bear on the prosecution of the war. The Union could then transfer its superiority to the strategic level, enveloping the South and pushing full-force all along the line, until the entire region was conquered.

The costs of this strategy to northern society, in particular to the lower classes of the North, would be staggering, Wood warned. Besides impoverishing the North, fighting a total war to victory would necessarily involve the devastation of the South in the process of conquering it. Achieving victory in this way would result in a complete and enduring rupture between the two sections. Under the hard hand of protracted war, all bonds of solidarity and fraternity between the sections would be severed, and the links of cross-sectional friendship and kinship would be shattered forever. Reconstruction would bring the subjugation of an estranged, humiliated, and inevitably spiteful enemy, rather than the reunion of true brethren. The end result would be conquest and coercion rather than cooperation and fraternity. Under the circumstances, such a victory would paradoxically defy the very purpose for waging war.

In developing his thesis, which in effect called for letting the South go in peace, Wood's fundamental focus was on American unity, not southern separateness. He highlighted the revolutionary heritage common to both sections and their shared political philosophy, and resorted to the future-oriented vision of manifest destiny. His main premise in arguing for peace was the organic nature of American society. "For after all, they are our brothers," he exclaimed, calling on his colleagues to "rekindle the old brotherly flame." War was an aberration, considering the deep bonds between individuals on either side of the sectional line: "Every drop of blood that is shed in this struggle will weaken the keystone of the fabric for whose sake the blood is pretended to be shed."

Fort Lafayette represented a renewal of Wood's direct appeal to a public audience, similar to his role as newspaper editor. Nevertheless, the novel's themes amplify Wood's reasoned anti-war oratory in Congress, rather than his belligerent appeals to the people in the pages of the *Daily News*. In the novel, Wood supplements the three main arguments against the war as developed in his congressional orations—the injustice of war, the inner contradiction in its goals, and its threat to republicanism—with an intriguing fourth argument. This added theme, a moral and ideological rejection of war and violence, is sounded in *Fort Lafayette* by the novel's tragic martyr and fictional exponent of Wood's own voice, Arthur Wayne. Wayne, the conscientious anti-war northern hero, crystallizes a complex and composite moral opposition to war in a single phrase. Peace, he claims, would "best obey the teachings of Christianity, the laws of humanity, and the mighty voice that is speaking from the soul of enlightenment, pointing out the errors of the past, and disclosing the secret of human happiness for the future." Toward the end of the novel, Wayne manages to convince his pro-war northern opponent and friend, Harold Hare, that Peace, with a capital P, was "sacred."[6]

Just as ably, the novel's characters lucidly walk readers through Wood's usual arguments against the war. Wood had consistently argued that the northern cause was unjust and illegitimate. In the novel, the main characters as well as lesser ones provide an elaborate and comprehensive canvass of the conflicting political arguments prominent in either section. Indeed, the exposition of the conflicting political positions in *Fort Lafayette* is, if anything, even more sophisticated, comprehensive, and ingenious than in Wood's congressional orations. Remarkably, it is also more fairly and evenhandedly presented. It has no resemblance at all to the fiery, one-sided coverage of the intersectional debate in the pages of the *Daily News* or to Wood's editorials about the war after the *Daily News* resumed publication in May 1863.

Nevertheless, with all the prominence of political discourse in the novel, its real focus lies elsewhere. To go along with the virtually pacifist position Wood developed, *Fort Lafayette* posits two central arguments that Wood had developed in his political orations: the inevitable failure of the North's cause and the disastrous consequences of war to civil liberties. In fact, the plot of *Fort Lafayette* is a powerful dramatization of Wood's thesis on intersectional fraternity and the danger of estrangement that war posed to it, as well as the danger to civil liberties. In their fictional adventures, the novel's protagonists demonstrate how deep-seated but fragile the personal ties across sectional boundaries could be. And in its tragic unfolding, the story highlights the calamitous implications of the demise of the rule of law and the rise of arbitrary executive and military power in war-torn America.

At the core of *Fort Lafayette*'s plot stands the fate of intersectional ties of kinship, friendship, and love, as challenged by political adversity and war. The novel tells the story of four friends: Beverly Weems and his sister Oriana, proud slave-holding Virginians, and Beverly's northern college friends, Arthur Wayne and Harold Hare. Hare, a Rhode Islander, and Oriana are engaged to be married.

The story begins with the reunion of the four friends in the Weemses' Riverside manor overlooking the James River, at the height of the Fort Sumter crisis. The political situation generates vigorous arguments among the four, each holding a different position: Harold and Oriana are extremists; although engaged, each espouses the uncompromising stands of his/her native section. Beverly is a moderate opposed to secession; Arthur, a native of New Hampshire, is opposed to war altogether. The heated political situation prompts neighboring Virginians to attack the guests from the North. Led by Seth Rawborn, Oriana's rejected suitor, jealousy and political enmity culminate in a violent ambush on Oriana, her fiancé, and their friend. Arthur, the anti-war northerner who was thought by Oriana to be a coward because of his objection to war, saves the company from Rawborn's vicious attack in a daring act of physical courage, suffering severe injuries in the attack, and remains in Virginia while Harold returns north to go to war. Oriana and her convalescing savior become emotionally involved.

Recovered sufficiently to return to the North, Arthur is contacted in New York by Beverly, who asks him to perform a delicate personal mission: to dissuade his orphaned cousin Miranda Aylaff from developing a relationship with Philip Searle. Searle, a veteran knave and forger, covets Miranda's inherited wealth, and begins courting her even though he is already married. Wayne fails his mission and through Searle's machinations is suspected of treason and thrown into the fort, still not yet fully recovered from the injuries he suffered in Virginia. With Beverly in the Confederate Army and Wayne effectively taken care of, Searle snares Miranda. With the help of Oriana and Beverly, Harold manages to escape Confederate captivity, and in an effort to save Arthur he attempts to cross the lines back to the North. Pursued by his old Virginia enemy Rawborn, Harold manages to reach Arthur. But the latter's arbitrary arrest and incarceration in the Federal fort dooms him. On his deathbed, Arthur assures Harold of Oriana's ultimate loyalty to him. He also succeeds in convincing Harold of the futility and evil of war generally and of the Civil War in particular.

The first of Wood's two main programmatic themes in *Fort Lafayette* was the depth of connections between northerners and southerners, and the danger of their severance by war. And indeed, *Fort Lafayette*'s entire cast of main characters—angelic heroes as well as satanic villains—consists of sectional boundary-spanners. All have some of their closest personal contacts across the sectional line. The two southern heroes of the novel—Oriana and Beverly Weems—return to their home state from extended sojourns in institutions of higher learning in the Northeast shortly before the Sumter crisis. Beverly became acquainted in college with Arthur and Harold, and they became his best friends. After college Harold, the northerner, found employment in the South, doing survey work in western Virginia. The depth of cross-sectional ties is most effectively represented in the novel by the engagement of Harold and Oriana. This emblem of intersectional fraternity is buttressed by the emotional involvement that develops between Oriana and Arthur.

The novel's villains are also attached to both sections, but their cross-sectional ties are of a very different nature. While the heroes are all loyal to their respective native sections, notwithstanding their deep intersectional connections, the villains are disloyal. The novel's two main scoundrels abandon their respective native states and cast their lot with the opposite section. Seth Rawborn, the violent and ruthless Virginian, comes to Dixie from the North in pursuit of profits from the slave trade and other shady commercial schemes. This fanatic convert to the southern cause is portrayed by Wood as a scheming scavenger, applying sharp Yankee commercial acumen to live off a naive, pre-modern agricultural sanctuary. Philip Searle, the northern scoundrel, is a native of Virginia who has gone north in pursuit of white slavery, abandoning his sick mother to the throes of deadly illness in their Manassas home. In the course of the war Searle changes sides yet again, deserting a commission in the Union Army (which he had attained through blackmail) and crossing over to Confederate General P. G. T. Beauregard's army. Searle not only deserts his adopted section's army, but betrays it by bringing along to the Rebel camp the most sensitive intelligence of Brig. Gen. Irvin McDowell's secret military preparations.

Fort Lafayette's portrayal of the prevalence and depth of intersectional ties serves to highlight how anomalous a war between the sections really was. Over the backdrop of intersectional fraternity, the war emerges as a preposterous exercise in unnecessary fratricide. Wood has no hesitation in bringing this point home to readers in the most melodramatic fashion when Harold Hare and a comrade, a young Union lieutenant of southern descent, take part in the First Battle of Bull Run. As Harold and the lieutenant charge the Confederate positions, their unit is challenged by a young southern officer and his force, occupying the high ground. The Union forces under Harold advance, and their charge on the line commanded by the Confederate officer yields a fierce, deadly clash, as well as a dramatic encounter:

> The mutual fire was delivered almost at the rifles' muzzles, and the long sword-bayonets clashed together. Without yielding ground, for a few terrible seconds they thrust and parried with the clanging steel, while on either side the dead were stiffening beneath their feet, and the wounded, with shrieks of agony, were clutching at their limbs. Harold and the young Southron [officer] met; their swords clashed together once in the smoke and dust, and but once, when each drew back and lowered his weapon, while all around were striking. Then, amid that terrible discord, their left hands were pressed together for an instant, and a low "God bless you!"

> came from the lips of both. "To the right, Beverly, keep you to the right!" said Harold, and he himself, straight through the hostile ranks, sprang in an opposite direction.[7]

But Wood does not settle for a near-deadly encounter between two friends and future brothers-in-law to illustrate the anomaly of war. His narrative goes on to play out the whole ancient pageant as it echoes the stories of Abel and Cain, Cain and Lemech, Absalom and David. At Harold's side, his friend the young Union lieutenant is also charging the hill at the head of his platoon. Reaching the Confederate line, the lieutenant fires, practically point-blank, into the face of the Confederate soldier facing him:

> So close were they, that the victim of that shot, struck in the center of the forehead, tottered forward and fell into his arms. There was a cry of horror that pierced even above the shrieks of the wounded and the yells of the fierce combatants. One glance at that fair, youthful face sufficed—it was his brother—dead in his arms, dead by a brother's hand. . . . "Charley! Oh God! Charley! Charley!" was all that came from his white lips, and he sat there like stone, with the corpse in his arms, still murmuring "Charley!" unconscious that blades were flashing and bullets whistling around him. . . . He only bent a little lower and his voice was fainter; but still he murmured "Charley! Oh God! Charley!" and never unfolded his arms from its embrace. And there, when the battle was over, the Southernors found him, dead—with his dead brother in his arms.[8]

Fort Lafayette's melodramatics have an underlying political message. By establishing the pattern of brotherhood between the sections, war brought about by politics emerges as a crime. In contrast, the moral virtue imperative for sustaining intersectional bonds inevitably becomes politically incorrect and represents a crime against government. Expressions of love and care between individuals separated by a political border and a military frontier thus become the focus of conflict between good and evil, morality and politics. Crossing the lines emerges as a central theme in the novel, signifying the point of conflict between the humane and moral imperative on the one hand and the combination of political and military power and criminal malevolence on the other. The novel's heroes trespass across sectional lines for noble causes. *Fort Lafayette* begins with northerners reuniting with their southern friends, only to be sent back north by local villains stirred by political demagoguery and a sectional call to arms. Towards the end of the novel, Beverly Weems and Arthur Wayne communicate across the lines in an effort to deliver Miranda from Searle's clutches; Hare helps Miranda cross the lines to reunite with her Virginia kin on her death bed; Beverly and Oriana help Hare flee to the North to try and save Wayne's life.

In contrast, the villains, like their respective governments, try to prevent the crossing of the lines. Rawborn, whose first encounter with the northern heroes is an effort to make them leave their friends and return north, finds his death in an attempt to prevent Hare from escaping military prison and crossing over to the North to rescue Wayne. Similarly, Searle tries to prevent Miranda's return to the South. A victim of his assault and battery, the dying Miranda is escorted to Virginia by Searle's bordello manager and lawful wife, Moll. Searle discovers Moll en route to Virginia and has her killed, although Miranda manages to cross the lines and die there, united with Beverly and Oriana, her closest kin. The contrast between humanity and political villainy is highlighted by Searle's own crossing of the lines. He has done so not in the cause of exalted humane service, but in an act of political and military treachery.

Arthur Wayne's delivery to the fort through Searle's machinations dooms him. While real enough to spell a death verdict to Wayne, the fort is not specifically identified in the text of the novel. Rather, it represents a vague, sinister pall over wartime life in the North, a shady danger lurking in the background. In Wood's congressional orations, too, the fort is seen as manifest evidence of despotism and is endowed with political and historical symbolism by being referred to as the "American Bastille," invoking French absolutism. Only in the novel's title does the fort emerge from its shadowy symbolism as Fort Lafayette. As the title of the novel, the real presence of the fort serves as an emblem of the ultimate consequence of war.

As the foregoing demonstrates, there was a clear and tight fit between the themes and morals of Wood's exercise in fiction, his political oratory, and his editorial writing. All three responded to contemporaneous events, most notably to sectional strife, secession, and war. In all three genres, Wood tried to make sense of tangled events—real or imagined—to find a coherent theme and relate their meaning to broader ideological and political precepts. Primarily, he ventured to use his media as a mobilizing force that could affect the course of history. But overall, Wood's efforts to mobilize Americans to the anti-war cause proved a failure. As we know by hindsight, the Copperhead war-resisting movement failed to carry the day, remaining a small minority in the wartime Union.

The reader of *Fort Lafayette*, 145 years after its composition, may well be struck by the dissonance between its hard-nosed realism and the fantastic hyperbole of its melodramatic plot. The novel's setting could have been extracted from any daily newspaper of the times. The political and moral dilemmas debated in its pages were central issues on the public agenda, discussed in the press, in the halls of Congress, and in the public sphere. The fictional plot could not possibly deliver the reader far enough from reality into a self-contained and seamless web of fiction. *Fort Lafayette*'s readers are constantly drawn back from the realm of imagination into the here and now. This dissonance is exacerbated by the minimal masking of the novel's political purpose as a work of propaganda, intended to convert readers and mobilize them to the cause of peace. Consequently, the novel's author cannot be considered a coherent teller of tales. His twin identities as a journalist and political activist are too inextricably meshed.

From Edgar Allan Poe, through Mark Twain and Stephen Crane, to Jack London and Ernest Hemingway, a remarkable number of American writers grew into practicing novelists from newspaper reporters, giving their literary texts the unmistakable taste of realism in the process. These journalists-turned-authors, Shelly Fisher Fishkin has suggested, had become frustrated with the restrictions that journalism placed on their literary creativity.[9] They responded by abandoning journalism, even if journalism and its realism never fully abandoned them. The case of Benjamin Wood as an author of fiction is different. He turned to fiction not out of a rejection of journalism but out of frustration at not being able to continue his chosen profession due to political restrictions and censorship. He went through the motions of *belles lettres*, but he remained a newspaper editor even as he was writing fiction.

The powerful links between *Fort Lafayette* and the stirring events of the day cannot be easily severed in readers' imaginations. The author's primary identity as a newspaperman makes for a blurring of boundaries between journalism and literature, between fact and fiction. Consequently, the plot of the novel, in its relation to ongoing events, could be, and apparently was, read as a mere reporting of contemporary events and their editorial interpretation. It was simple to relate Wood's fiction to the real world and see aspects of its intricate plot as elements of reality. That in turn weakened the impact of Wood's admittedly "hot, passionate, but poor and extemporaneous" Civil War novel for readers of his own time, even as it gives it a certain cross-genre relevance today. *Fort Lafayette*, like Wood's pleas for peace, was a quixotic failure.

Notes

This essay forms part of the introduction to *Copperhead Gore: Benjamin Wood's Fort Lafayette and Civil War America*, edited with an introduction by Menahem Blondheim (Bloomington & Indianapolis: Indiana University Press, 2006).

1. Theodore Parker, "A Speech on the 'Mercantile Classes'," in Henry Steele Commager, ed., *Theodore Parker: An Anthology* (Boston: Beacon Press, 1960), p. 149.
2. This dating reflects the fact that reviews of the book, copyrighted in 1862, appeared as early as 8 February 1862.
3. E.g.: "You will see it in every column of your daily prints, you will hear your statesmen urging it in your legislative halls and your cabinet ministers making it their theme"; *FL*, p. 262. Cf. *FL*, pp. 29–30, 238, 292.

4. *New York Daily News*, 15 April 1861.
5. Wood's two prominent Congressional orations are reproduced and annotated in Menahem Blondheim, *Copperhead Gore: Benjamin Wood's Fort Lafayette and Civil War America* (Bloomington & Indianapolis: Indiana University Press, 2006), pp. 255–83.
6. *FL*, pp. 66, 295.
7. *FL*, pp. 228–29.
8. *FL*, pp. 229–30.
9. Shelley Fisher Fishkin, *From Fact to Fiction: Journalism & Imaginative Writing in America* (Baltimore, MD: Johns Hopkins University Press, pp. 3–10.

William Gilmore Simms

A Literary Casualty of the Civil War

— Phebe Davidson and Debra Reddin van Tuyll —

Like many other southern writers in the first half of the nineteenth century, William Gilmore Simms was a casualty of the Civil War. In his day, Simms had been considered easily in the same class as James Fenimore Cooper, Edgar Allan Poe, and Nathaniel Hawthorne. His early fiction exemplifying American national values set against the backdrop of the South was eagerly sought by readers in other sections of the country who wanted an authentic picture of the region. As the sectional conflicts of the first half of the nineteenth century became more pronounced, Simms was drawn unavoidably into them. A South Carolinian by birth and, as Maurice Cullen put it, "by profession,"[1] Simms created a body of work intended to espouse the values and ideologies of his own region, particularly his home state. As a result, Simms's fiction, which promulgated ideas that ultimately were rejected by American society, now falls outside the canon of standard American literary works.

One of his later novels, *Woodcraft, or Hawks about the Dovecote,* is a good example of how far out of step Simms became with mainstream thought. In *Woodcraft,* Simms's answer to *Uncle Tom's Cabin,* the author attempts to hold up slavery as a benign institution, ordained by God as the best state for both the slave and his master. These were the arguments southerners commonly made to defend slavery.[2] Louisa McCord, one of the South's premier intellectual writers of the antebellum period, marshaled the same arguments as Simms in her spirited refutation of *Uncle Tom's Cabin*, published in the January 1853 edition of the *Southern Quarterly Review*. McCord likewise argued that slavery was a holy institution designed as a means of caring for the weak. McCord put into straightforward prose what Simms couched in fiction: "The negro, left to himself, does not dream of liberty. . . . In his natural condition, he is, by turns, tyrant and slave."[3]

Subsequently, the Civil War exacerbated these sectional conflicts, putting southern writers in an awkward position with regard to the national literary scene. With *Woodcraft*, Simms weighed in on the many sectional and political debates that preceded the Civil War. Given the political nature of so much of his work, to assess Simms's position one must consider not only the man and his work, but also the political culture within which he operated. His 1854 novel, *Woodcraft, or Hawks about the Dovecote,* originally published in 1852 as *The Sword and the Distaff, or Fair Fat and Forty*, is a good place to start.

A few personal details may offer insight into Simms's writings. He was born in 1806, the second and only surviving son of William Gilmore Simms, Sr., and Harriet Ann Singleton Simms. His mother died in 1808, when Simms was two. His bereaved father, a small mercantile dealer, left Charleston to live on the southwestern frontier, placing his son in the care of his maternal grandmother, Mrs. Jacob Gates. Simms was educated in Charleston public and private schools, and later read law. Although he visited his father a couple of times during his late adolescence and early manhood, observing his father's frontier life in Mississippi, Louisiana, Alabama, and Georgia, there was never any question that Simms's home and destiny were in Charleston. His grandmother, whose family had been active in the Revolutionary War and who once had rowed American spies out of Charleston harbor during the British occupation, instilled in Simms the patriotic zeal of his forebears.[4]

In 1826, Simms married Anna Malcolm Giles, who bore him three children before dying in 1832 of tuberculosis, leaving behind one surviving daughter. In 1836, Simms married Chevillette Eliza Roach, the daughter of a wealthy planter. She would bear him fourteen children, five of whom lived.[5] Chevillette died unexpectedly of appendicitis in 1863. His marriage to Chevillette Roach marked a substantial rise in social position for Simms. He and his wife took up residence at Woodlands, one of the Roach family plantations. Woodlands was to be Simms's residence for the remainder of his adult life, and his move to Woodlands marked the beginning of his role as a proponent of the planter's point of view rather than the city dweller's.[6]

Throughout his adult life, Simms remained involved in civic affairs and public life. His writing career began in 1825 with the publication of his first book,

Monody, on the Death of General Charles Cotesworth Pinckney.[7] His journalistic career was launched in late 1829 when he bought into the Charleston *City Gazette*, one of the city's older daily newspapers.[8] It was in the pages of the *City Gazette* that Simms supported the Union in the Nullification Crisis, a stand that caused him to be threatened by mob violence.[9] From then until virtually the end of his life, Simms wrote and published prodigiously, supplying his readers with more than eighty separate books, including eighteen volumes of poetry, three dramas, thirty-five novels and novelettes, ten histories and biographies, and at least eleven miscellaneous pieces, all of which marked for him "a renowned placed in nineteenth century American literature."[10]

Politically, Simms was at first a Jacksonian Democrat. With the passage of time, his political positions shifted in accord with what he thought were the South's best interests. In the 1840s, he was active in state politics, serving as an adviser to South Carolina governor James Henry Hammond. He served a term in the state legislature from 1844 to 1846, and in the latter year he was narrowly defeated for the post of lieutenant governor. In 1848, Simms supported Whig presidential candidate Zachary Taylor. Although Simms had hoped for a diplomatic appointment from Taylor, one was not forthcoming. Simms's political star may have fizzled at least in part because of his close association with Hammond, whose own career was brought to an abrupt halt by the revelation that he had dallied with four of his nieces, all daughters of the prominent South Carolina politician Wade Hampton. Additionally, Simms stood in opposition to South Carolina political icon John C. Calhoun, without whose imprimatur few political stars rose or fell in the Palmetto State. In the first secession crisis of the 1850s, Simms was a cooperationist, opposing secession and favoring the Union.

Throughout the ongoing sectional debates, Simms remained a strong supporter of slavery. As the sectional conflicts became shriller, so too did Simms's literary output, culminating in 1854 with his idealized fantasy about the nature of the relationship between slave and master, *Woodcraft.* This novel depicts a relationship that most southerners knew in their hearts was little more than fiction. *Woodcraft* offered a strong defense of slavery, portraying loyal bondsmen who were content in their enslavement. The benign picture Simms painted of slavery contrasted drastically with the reality of the South's "peculiar institution" and the acrimonious debates it engendered. The bitter conflict over the annexation of Texas and the expansion of slavery into the territories were fueled by white fear. Slaves were a resource that renewed itself. If slavery was bottled up in the existing slave states, whites feared that they would soon be outnumbered—as they were already in Simms's home state. In 1860, South Carolina's population included twice as many blacks as it did whites. In some of the Low Country parishes, slaves accounted for as much as 80 to 90 percent of the population. These facts, perhaps more than any other, were responsible for the rise of radicalism among southerners, particularly in South Carolina.[11] Southerners were not so much afraid of abolitionist tampering with cherished familial relationships, despite their public protestations, as they were of slave insurrections that might occur should their bondsmen be let loose upon society.

The size of South Carolina's black population was, in large measure, responsible for the unusual amount of homogeneity in thought among the state's white citizens, who lived with constant reminders that they existed "in an enemy camp."[12] Arson linked to disaffected slaves was common. Overseers, and sometimes masters, were murderously attacked by allegedly docile and happy slaves. As historian Stephen Channing has observed, "The mere physical presence of these familiar, and yet strangely frightening people was itself a source of anxiety." John Brown's 1859 raid on Harpers Ferry transformed this anxiety into widespread panic, as Channing further observed: "John Brown had plunged a knife deep into the psyche of Southern whites, and life would never be quite the same again."[13]

The planter elite were not the only ones who panicked after Brown's raid. All whites viewed slavery with a fearful eye, even those who owned no slaves. Further, even those lower-class whites who owned no slaves had a vested interest in the perpetuation of slavery: it was the institution upon which they staked their claims to equality with their betters, an equality that was the basis of the South's alternative version of American republicanism. Like their northern brethren, southerners believed that all men were created equal—so long, of course, as the men were white, propertied, and male. While there was an economic aspect to white equality in the antebellum South—certainly a yeoman farmer had far less political power than his slave-owning planter neighbor—it was not acknowledged as such.

Equality was signified by masterhood. If one was white, male, and propertied, one was a master, if only over one's wife and children, and thus shared certain political and cultural values with other white men, regardless of their economic situations. In reality, this equality did not extend beyond the front gate of one's homestead, but that was sufficient to maintain the illusion. This atmosphere, coupled with his rise to the planter elite through his marriage to Chevillette, would have been an important contributor to Simms's conversion from a Unionist in his youth to a fire-eating secessionist in his later years. As news of Brown's raid spread, so did rumors and whisperings of "unsound" strangers in the vicinity, and emissaries of Brown's army sneaking around to do "the devil's work." Southerners scrutinized every crisis for evidence of work by Brown's imagined army. Public sentiment coalesced around the perceived threats from outsiders.[14]

Ultimately, Simms was to be disappointed in both his political and his literary ambitions. During the 1840s, he had been closely associated with the rise of a national literature, one that arose from American rather than European soil, from the experiences, emotions, and beliefs of the American populace rather than those of England. The latter half of the nineteenth century produced a number of titles that have endured as major texts in American literature, among them Nathaniel Hawthorne's *The Scarlet Letter*, Herman Melville's *Moby Dick*, and Mark Twain's *The Adventures of Huckleberry Finn*. Other titles have fared less well in canonical status, including Harriet Beecher Stowe's *Uncle Tom's Cabin* and Simms's fictional retort, *Woodcraft, or Hawks about the Dovecote.* Simms's book was initially published in 1852 as *The Sword and the Distaff or Fair, Fat and Forty: A Tale of the South at the Close of the Revolution*, and was reissued as *Woodcraft, or Hawks about the Dovecote* in response to the publication of Stowe's book, and upon the advice of Hammond, who suggested to Simms that his first title was vulgar.

In addition to the political and social issues suggested by slavery as a literary topic, there were the practical logistics of publishing and distribution to be considered. Like many of his fellow writers, Simms faced financial hardship after the panic of 1837 and the serious depression that ensued.[15] During the 1840s, however, Simms was able to travel to northern publishing centers to secure advantageous book contracts, and was published by such notable houses as Harper and Brothers and Wiley and Putnam. On these visits, he met and befriended fellow authors, among them William Cullen Bryant and Edgar Allen Poe, along with Washington Irving, Fitz-Greene Halleck, and James Fenimore Cooper.[16] In terms of literary culture, Simms's star was dimmed by the political leanings of the heavily industrialized North, and once the Civil War was underway, he was no longer able to travel to secure the contracts that were crucial to literary success and continued income.

Further, Simms's literary aspirations were hampered by his political and social views, which were never very far from the surface of his fiction, but which were very much out of step with northern sentiments. Nowhere is this more obvious than in *Woodcraft.* The book offers readers a historical romance that includes an analysis of southern plantation life in the South Carolina Low Country as a microcosm of both the nation in general and the South in particular. The novel was the product of a sectional conflict of the first order, one that nearly resulted in the South's secession. The battles between abolitionists and pro-slavery forces were heating up, and more and more southern literary and journalistic output was designed to defend the region's "peculiar institution." *Woodcraft* was Simms's contribution to the debate—in his own words, "probably as good an answer to Mrs. Stowe as has been published."[17]

To be sure, Simms and Stowe weighed in on opposite sides of the slavery dispute. Stowe's 1852 novel, which secured for her great international recognition, was published with the express goal of alerting the general populace to what she perceived as the intolerable moral evil of slavery. Stowe carefully undermines the idealized representation of the plantation as a locus of happily managed human relations between master and slave that is typical of plantation fiction. Simms, by contrast, portrays slavery as beneficial to slaves as well as to their owners, a position he underscores by creating black characters who are incapable of managing for themselves as free men, or if they do possess the requisite degree of intelligence and self-direction, view freedom as a burden they would rather not assume. In Stowe's novel, even the best of slave owners cannot guarantee the safety of their property. In Simms's book, even when they could easily have abandoned their owner, Captain Porgy's slaves choose to remain with him. As in most plantation fiction, the southern plantation in *Woodcraft* is viewed as an Edenic site in which whites care for their dependent blacks as for children, while the blacks prosper under their rule.

Simms is often credited with being the first southern writer to include fully developed black characters in his fiction, but he was also a writer who presented them in a fashion calculated to advance the pro-slavery argument. Thus, Pompey, the remarkably gifted fiddler among the slaves of the Glen-Eberley plantation, is absolutely devoid of any sort of self-discipline, incapable of seeing a task to completion or of supplying his own material needs. By contrast, Tom, who is Porgy's chief favorite among the slaves, is a natural leader. He ensures the welfare of his fellow slaves and is clearly a more able manager than some of his poor-white social betters. During the Revolution, he serves in the field with Porgy under Francis Marion, distinguishing himself as a cool, reliable hand under fire and the best cook in the army. Yet when the question of his own liberty arises, Tom declares that he could not stand to be his own master. He also insists, when Porgy seeks to protect him from seizure by selling him to a neighboring widow, that he would rather be dead than be ruled by a woman. The black women in the novel do not come off any better. When Sophy, Porgy's old wet nurse, returns to the plantation from the swamp, she mistakes a stranger for Porgy, insisting that he is "her own chile" despite his denials, and when Porgy identifies himself, repeats the melodramatic welcome all over again. While her emotional investment in her master is perhaps touching, it also carries an implication that she doesn't really know one white man from another.

Other secondary characters of interest are the poor whites. Milhouse, a one-armed veteran returning from service under Marion with Porgy, sees himself as Porgy's future overseer, someone who can look out for Porgy's practical interests better than Porgy himself. The problem with Milhouse, however, is that he has no appreciation of the intellectual and ethical standards of the planter class; he is a good man, but only in his place. One of the novel's villains is the squatter Bostwick, who works in collusion with the Scotsman McKewn. Both are, in some way, pretenders. McKewn's goal is to achieve planter status in his own right, something he seeks to do by stealing slaves and selling them to the British for transportation to the West Indies. Bostwick, his henchman, occupies a plantation neighboring Porgy's, where he abandons his wife and daughters, visiting them only when some need sends him home. As an individual he is petulant, greedy, and irresponsible in the extreme. His wife and daughters survive only through the kindness of their neighbors, the Widow Everleigh and Captain Porgy. The implication is that Bostwick is in his unenviable position in society because he deserves to be. The fact that he loves one of his daughters, Dory, with a tremendous and sentimental love, does not redeem Bostwick. Dory, who is the counterpart of Beth in *Little Women* and Eva in *Uncle Tom's Cabin*, a girl child who is almost too good for this earth, must be severed from her father forever if the moral scheme of the novel is to be upheld. This is accomplished with Bostwick's death by smallpox, a contagion the other characters miraculously escape.

Of the two plantation owners limned in *Woodcraft*, the Widow Everleigh is the more practical and the more provident. The widow of a distinguished British officer, she is able to maintain a delicate stance that honors her husband's memory and at the same time allows her to be a dedicated American patriot. When her slaves are stolen and sold for transportation to the West Indies as the British evacuate Charleston, she has both the wit and the force of character to recover them, along with some slaves belonging to her neighbor, Porgy. Her plantation is well-stocked and well-managed. She is both courteous and courageous, and as her plantation adjoins that of the bachelor Porgy, there is speculation among the lower orders of Porgy's followers that the two should marry.

In contrast to the widow, Porgy is a corpulent old soldier of exceedingly prodigal habits. Raised to a life of indolence, he was never taught how to work and has never chosen to learn. His plantation is encumbered with debt to an extent that makes its foreclosure all but inevitable. Returning to his desolate home after the campaign with Marion, he is dependent on the Widow Everleigh for provisions. To his credit, he is a clear-seer and a hero of sorts. Thus, when the estimable widow is kidnapped by Bostwick and his cronies, who would re-steal her slaves, it is Porgy who rescues her. For all his faults, the two most notable being gambling and a fondness for drink, Porgy is a gentleman. He gives to the wife and children of Bostwick guineas he can ill afford. Like his underlings, he considers marriage to the widow, but she turns him down. When he seeks to console himself with another, less socially elevated widow, he finds her already spoken for.

Between them, Widow Everleigh and Captain Porgy present a clear analogy for the state of the American nation. In Widow Everleigh, we perceive the dependent who is now free of old encumbrances. Her lack of a husband nicely parallels America's rejection of British sovereignty. Her provident management of the land coincides with the agrarian view of America, a view of particular strength in the American South. In Porgy we observe the philosophical understanding, the kindness, and the ethical strength required if the new nation is to survive and prosper. In Porgy, also, we see the military strength and the soldierly tactics that will bring the nation, and his own Low Country home, safely into the garden of peace.

Still, while the novel, which is loosely classified as a "historical romance," is set in the immediate post-Revolutionary period, it was written and published on the eve of the Civil War, so that the Revolution also comes to represent the South's war for independence from northern domination. Porgy, then, becomes an idealized patriarchal figure of the old South, just as the Widow Everleigh becomes an idealized matriarch who will take good care of all the South's sons (even Porgy) as the new struggle draws near. The sticky matter in this analogy is that the South's impending war for its own liberty is based on the institution that denies liberty to virtually the entire class of African Americans. That Simms was unable to see this, despite his southern rearing and his own ascension to the planter class, is difficult to understand. Perhaps he saw the oppressive side of southern liberty, but saw no reasonable alternative to it. Whatever the case, his literary output is overtly political in its racial and social positions.

The fratricidal carnage of the Civil War produced many casualties, not all of whom were soldiers. A way of life, a variant of American political philosophy, and a regional literary tradition that had been on equal footing with that of New England also died in the war over conflicting views of what America meant. At one moment in history, Simms stood shoulder-to-shoulder with the likes of Poe, Melville, Hawthorne, and Cooper. After the defeat of southern slave ideology and the region's variant view of republicanism, Simms's work, for the most part, was relegated to the B-list of American fiction. Racism was a fact of life in nineteenth-century America, and hints of it can be seen in the literature of both sections. However, bondage based on racism was not an American value and had been controversial since the first steps toward nationhood were taken with the writing of the Declaration of Independence in 1776. That the South's literary tradition so clearly embraced slavery as a positive good that was essential to the well-being of a particular race is evidence that the political culture of the region was deeply embedded in its elite literary and intellectual circles. As an important member of that circle, Simms suffered much the same fate personally as the South did politically. Neither recovered entirely from the Civil War.

Notes

1. Maurice Cullen, "William Gilmore Simms: Journalist," *Journalism Quarterly* 64 (Summer 1961), p. 298.
2. Stephen Channing, *Crisis of Fear: Secession in South Carolina* (New York: W.W. Norton & Co., 1974), p. 66.
3. Richard C. Lounsbury, ed., *Louisa S. McCord: Selected Writings* (Charlottesville: University Press of Virginia, 1997), p. 118.
4. Charles S. Watson, "Introduction: *Woodcraft*" (Albany, NY: New College and University Press, 1983), pp. 9–10.
5. Mary Ann Wimsatt, "Introduction: *Tales of the South*" (Columbia, SC: University of South Carolina Press, 1996), p. 14.
6. Watson, p. 11.
7. Wimsatt, p. ix.
8. Cullen, p. 299.
9. Watson, p. 10, Cullen, p. xx.
10. Cullen, p. 198.
11. Channing, pp. 22, 213, 263; Stephanie McCurry, *Masters of Small Worlds: Yeoman Households, Gender Relations, and the Political Culture of the Antebellum South Carolina Low Country* (New York: Oxford University Press, 1995), p. 5.
12. Lacy K. Ford, Jr., *Origins of Southern Radicalism* (New York: Oxford University Press, 1988), p. 123.
13. Channing, pp. 22–23.
14. Channing, p. 24.
15. Johanna Nicol Shields, "Tales of the South," *Southern Cultures* 4 (Spring 1998), p. 129.
16. Watson, p. 13.
17. Mary C. Simms Oliphant, Alfred Taylor Odell and T.C. Duncan Eaves, eds., *The Letters of William Gilmore Simms* (Columbia: University of South Carolina Press, 1952–1982), vol. 5, p. 286.

Henry Adams's Civil War

Despair and *Democracy*

— W. Scott Poole —

Henry Adams has been called, by one of his admirers no less, "the most irritating person in American letters." It should be added that the same critic went on to refer to Adams's oeuvre as "the zenith of American civilization."[1] This fourth-generation member of one of America's great political dynasties very likely was a little of both.

The irritation that critics have felt for Adams comes, in part, from his often enigmatic nature and vocation—or vocations (he seemed to have several). Adams was one of the finest historians this country has ever produced; his *History of the United States during the Jefferson and Madison Administrations* is unmatched in its interpretive sophistication and narrative power. In his most famous work, *The Education of Henry Adams*, Adams perfected the postmodern memoir before there was even such a thing as the postmodern memoir. Briefly an academic, Adams came close to spending his days in Cambridge, Massachusetts, filling a prestigious Harvard professorship. But he dropped it all to become a sort of puritan bohemian, writing art and literary criticism. His writing on Chartres and Mont St. Michel not only represents architectural and cultural history of a very high order; it also manages to bridge art history and cultural criticism, very similar to Charles Ruskin's *Stones of Venice*. And Adams's famous dichotomy, "the Virgin and the Dynamo," still shapes much of our understanding of change in Western civilization.[2]

If Adams was not, perhaps, "the zenith of American civilization," he can still be positioned at the apex of the American intellectual tradition. Why, then, did Adams not write a clear interpretation of the most cataclysmic event of his generation, the American Civil War? In his histories, Adams seems to live more in the early Federal period or in the Europe of the thirteenth century than in his own time. Even in *The Education of Henry Adams,* the war seems a kind of bit player, a background to the unfolding tale of Adams's growing quarrel with the world. Not only his talents, but also his position in life would seem to have given him an important vantage point on the conflict. He was the son of Charles Francis Adams, who held perhaps the most important diplomatic post of the war and, one could argue, one of the more important diplomatic posts in American history—minister to the Court of St. James during the Civil War. The elder Adams's mission was to ensure that Great Britain not take the fatal step of recognizing the Confederacy. Henry and brothers Brooks and C. F. Adams, Jr., joined their father in England for that endeavor.[3]

Given his central vantage point, the question remains: Why did Adams not give us something more on the ultimate crisis of the American Union? He does, in fact, include some tantalizing chapters in his *Education*, and there are a couple of articles related to the diplomatic history of the war. But readers could be excused for wanting more from Adams, since he was, after all, a philosopher of history as much as a historian. He certainly suggests that the conflict had a profound meaning for American life when he writes that, upon his return from England in 1867, he discovered that America had given itself to "the great mechanical energies" and ignored "agriculture, handwork and learning." Adams describes his own self-consciousness at the time as being "no worse off than the Indian or the Buffalo who had been ejected from their heritage by his own people."[4]

This sense of disjuncture between the old republic and the new realities of post-bellum America undergirded Adams's novel, *Democracy: An American Novel.* This work belongs to an entire genre of Gilded Age literature that is accurately, if rather clunkily, described as "northern Lost Cause literature." At times it seemed that northern artists and intellectuals were not terrifically excited about the Union victory in the war and were willing to romanticize the southern struggle to further their own aesthetic and ideological ends. Intellectuals were not the only group willing to give the South a break. Indeed, the late-nineteenth-century northern public had become quite sentimental about the South that they had recently expended so much blood and treasure to vanquish.[5]

Such misplaced romanticism about the South is perhaps best explained by the North's growing disgust with the Gilded Age. This resulted in a number of works in which northern authors engaged in what already had become a favorite southern hobby—using representatives of the South, sometimes even of the Confederate Army, as spokesmen from whom to criticize the corruption and the materialism of late-nineteenth-century America. C. Vann Woodward's essay "A Southern Critique for the Gilded Age" notes that while it was not strange for the South to maintain its sense of identity by a "running critique of Yankee morals," it was rather peculiar that northerners should join in. Woodward, in fact, calls particular attention to Adams and sees in his use of the southern tradition an effort to recover an antique America.[6]

Adams conjures an even darker vision in *Democracy*, an ironic vision, as Woodward asserts, but one in which the very heart of the American experiment is imagined as unutterably corrupt. This would become the primary contention of a number of American writers who seemed to join the South in asserting the decline of the American republic, its rapid degeneration under pressure from a piratical economic system, a corrupted political system and a new citizenry who lacked the republican virtues of an older America. Written only three years after the end of Reconstruction, *Democracy* concerns itself with three characters, each of whom embodies a different aspect of Henry Adams's America. Adams, strangely, deals little with the war itself or its underlying issues and causes. Significantly, most of the novel's discussion of the war focuses on corruption in northern politics, a corruption that Adams sees working at the very heart of democracy itself.[7]

The central figure, as in many of Adams's works of fiction, is a female character in search of meaning, ultimate metaphysical meaning. Madeline Lee is the widow of a Confederate veteran, a Virginian whose blueblood family is a branch on the same tree as Rebel warlord Robert E. Lee. Madeline herself is a northerner by birth, an interesting reversal with regard to much of the popular fiction that played on northern and southern imagery. In most of these works, as historian Nina Silber has noted, the "romance of reunion" involves a northern male marrying a southern belle, often metaphorically subduing her rebellious tendencies. In Adams's telling, Madeline Lee's southern lover is dead, and is only a brooding presence in the novel. Combined with the recent loss of her only child, this tragedy has brought Lee to the edge of despair, a sense of ennui that leads her to the study of German philosophy, the works of Herbert Spencer, philanthropy, and even the ultimate disgrace—flirting with stockbrokers. Having tried all these avenues, she confesses feeling only continued despair.[8]

Lee's search for meaning takes her to Washington, D.C., of all places. This is the part of Adams's novel with which many modern readers have enormous difficulty. How could anyone possibly believe that existential angst could be healed by politics? Adams wanted to believe just that. His post-puritan notion of keeping the covenant he inherited from his illustrious ancestry forced him to believe in political salvation. His deep disillusionments, and the harsh cynicism burning like acid on every page of the novel, grew in part from the degradation of politics in the late nineteenth century. Adams, being an Adams, had little difficulty believing that politics should provide the individual with cosmic meaning. Thus, Lee's search turns to questions about politics: What is the meaning of America, and, in particular, what is the meaning of American democracy?[9]

Seeking to answer these questions, Lee seeks out Senator Ratcliffe, better known as the "Prairie Giant of Peonia, [Illinois]." The persona Adams creates is a fairly thin disguise for James G. Blaine, a man who would be the Republican Party's presidential candidate in 1884, and someone Adams believed represented the most corrupt face of the Grand Old Party. The character Ratcliffe is the very personification of corrupt Gilded Age politics, wielding his considerable power for the benefit of corporate interests, while justifying his actions with a sort of Machiavellian pragmatism. Ratcliffe becomes Madeline's suitor and midwestern Svengali. At various salons and soirees, Madeline learns from the senator that the American government works by means of corruption. Ratcliffe shows her that politics, in Adams's recounting, is little more than "human nature in its naked deformity playing pranks with the interest of forty million people."[10]

Ratcliffe carefully hides from Madeline his own turpitude in a concerted effort to win her hand. It might be assumed that his attentions would have little effect, that the "Prairie Giant of Peonia" would cause only revulsion in Madeline Lee, child of the eastern aristocracy. On the contrary, she finds herself in sympathy with Ratcliffe, attracted by his influence and knowledge of the world. This is one of the more sophisticated conceits in the work. Adams could have created a kind of American Pamela in Madeline Lee, but instead he goes for a gritty realism. He asserts that she is interested in Ratcliffe because she believes that he represents what she is seeking, an understanding of "the tremendous forces of government, and the machinery of society, at work." Adams even simplifies his description of her ambition. "What she wanted," he writes "was power."[11]

John Carrington serves as Adams's foil to Ratcliffe and to the larger Washington scene. The young lawyer is a Virginian and a Confederate veteran who had "shouldered his musket in a campaign or two" and is a distant relation of Madeline's dead husband. Carrington is a sort of sad-eyed, depressive figure, a common quality that northern authors frequently attributed to Confederate veterans. Carrington's air of sadness is not so much cynicism as it is wisdom about the fleeting nature of things and the more unfortunate aspects of human nature. This introduces a notion that would become a common one in writing about the South—the idea that the South, because of a combination of defeat in war, racial guilt, and severe economic difficulty, had somehow acquired a hard-earned wisdom of experience not known to the rest of the country. It was the notion, again to quote C. Vann Woodward, of "the burden of southern history."[12]

Carrington represents not only the South for Adams; he also embodies the best of an older America. He is described as having a "formality" and a "stiffness" that leads Madeline to proclaim him as "George Washington at thirty." He attempts to answer Madeline's search for meaning in American politics by providing her with the speeches of the famous senators Daniel Webster and John C. Calhoun, monumental representatives of the old republic. Most interesting of all, Adams, the archetypal Yankee WASP, allows Carrington to describe northerners as those with "cold eyes . . . steel grey . . . diabolic in passion, but worst when a little suspicious; then they watch you as though you were a young rattlesnake, to be killed when convenient." Not only does he put this harsh indictment in the mouth of a sympathetic character, he also seems to use Ratcliffe's moral failings to prove his point.[13]

Significantly, *Democracy* creates another sympathetic male character in Baron Jacobi, an Eastern European who speaks for the conservative aristocracy of the Old World, even as Carrington speaks for the conservative aristocracy of the Old South. Jacobi delights in humiliating Ratcliffe with witty salon repartee and, toward the end of the novel, gives Ratcliffe a caning that causes the corrupt senator to flee shamelessly. Adams's readers would have immediately recalled the caning of Massachusetts senator Charles Sumner by South Carolina congressman Preston Brooks on the floor of the Capitol in 1856, an incident that horrified Adams at the time, but one that he saw in a different light in the post-bellum world of corrupt politics.[14]

Adams's willingness to make a grumpy Eastern European aristocrat a sympathetic, if not indeed heroic, figure is no surprise in hindsight. He would soon turn to thirteenth-century Europe as a paradigm preferable to the corrupt society in which he lived. However, the creation of an admirable Confederate veteran should surprise all those familiar with the larger body of Adams's work, or at least those primarily familiar with the *Education.* In a famous and often-quoted description of his Harvard classmate William Fitzhugh Lee, son of Robert E. Lee, Adams wrote that southerners are unable to analyze ideas, and "strictly speaking, the southerner had no mind, only a temperament." Somewhat less famously, but perhaps making the point even more pungently, Adams wrote of southern statesmen that "no one learned a useful lesson from the Confederate school except to keep away from it." He concluded of the southern cotton planter that one could learn nothing "but bad temper, bad manners, poker and treason" from such a person.[15]

Making use of a Confederate veteran to critique Gilded Age America reveals the depths of Adams's own despair with American politics and the national experiment itself. A number of writers turned to images of the Civil War seeking some new foundation for American nationhood, nationhood built on soldiers' bravery or on the willingness of the two regions to reconcile, shaking hands and embracing across the bloody chasm. Adams turned to the Civil War only to find a solitary, sad-eyed figure to mock the politics and culture of a corrupt nation. This theme is evident throughout Adams's later work. He tells us in the *Education*, for example, that by 1870 he had come to believe American democracy, perfectly embodied by Ulysses S. Grant, could best be described as "inarticulate, uncertain, distrustful of itself, still more distrustful of others and awed by money." Political Washington was no more than "work, whiskey and cards." He would even assault Darwinian evolution by wryly noting that "the progress of evolution from President Washington to President Grant, was alone evidence enough to upset Darwin."[16]

Clearly Adams had become convinced in his cynicism by 1879. It is a cynicism that runs far deeper than we would imagine politics could go, down into the core of personal meaning. When Madeline Lee discovers that Ratcliffe has taken a bribe in order to push through legislation for a corporate interest, she rages at him, at herself, and at all American institutions. She also rages at the universe itself in a moment of transcendent despair, a kind of despair with which Adams himself was quite familiar. "Oh what a vile thing life is," Madeline rages. "Oh how I wish I were dead! How I wish the universe were annihilated!" Adams gives his heroine a good dose of despair, an existential and spiritual despair that he describes in *Education* as being part of his own experience.[17]

Madeline realizes that she has implicated herself in the corruption of late-nineteenth-century politics. Adams scholar George Hochfield writes that Madeline's own ambition for power was of a different order that Ratcliffe's, that she saw in American democracy a means to attain power and use it for the good. Hochfield also notes that Adams uses Madeline's experience to suggest that this is impossible, that power is by its very nature a corrupting influence. No more radical critique of the American experiment could be imagined in the late nineteenth century, when the desire for economic, political and social power seemed to be running like mercury through the American bloodstream.[18]

William Dean Howells once said that what Americans desire in a novel is "a tragedy with a happy ending." Adams gives us the tragedy but refuses the happy ending. Readers of post-bellum fiction would have expected, with Ratcliffe unmasked, that Madeline would turn naturally to Carrington. Such is not the case. "I want to go to Egypt," Madeline tells her sister, "democracy has shaken my nerves to pieces. Oh, what rest it would be to live in the Great Pyramid and look out for ever at the polar star." Madeline leaves America, leaves her hopes for finding meaning in democracy or in love and perhaps leaves the search for meaning altogether. She goes on an extended tour of the Nile River valley and the ancient Near East, seeking out the pyramids and their timelessness—she is not looking for meaning, nobility or a cause, she is looking for rest.[19]

The concluding chapter of the novel is a letter from Madeline's sister to Carrington. She gives no hint that Madeline has discovered meaning in her flight from the West, only that she is well. The only hope for a romantic denouement is a single "P.S." in which she hints that Carrington may want to "try again," in the sense of pressing a suit with Madeline, after she returns from her travels. Madeline also includes a postscript to the letter, the final line of the novel, in which she says, speaking of her refusal to marry the powerful and corrupt Ratcliffe, "the bitterest part of all this horrid story is that nine out of ten of our countrymen would say I had made a mistake."[20]

The Civil War, in Adams's time, was becoming for both sides an exercise in nostalgia. The United States was moving into what would become the *Pax Americana* of the twentieth century. Leaders like William Randolph Hearst, Theodore Roosevelt, and Josiah Strong, though very different men in very different fields, all had visions of an American empire. The war played the role of regenerative conflict in this vision, the moment in which America proved its manhood and then reconciled its differences. Henry Adams said no. Post-bellum America reflected moral failings, he believed, that drove the best into a crisis of meaning and elevated the worst to positions of power and influence. Henry Adams's Civil War was simply one more moment in the degeneration of the American experiment, producing political scandal and frustrated reformers. *Democracy* reflects a growing sense in Adams's own mind, and among many late-nineteenth-century writers and thinkers, that the Union victory had lengthened the shadows over the republic, not dispelled them. Nowhere does Adams's alienation show more clearly than in *Democracy*, his novel of despair written on the verge of a new century he would despise.[21]

Notes

1. Walter Susman, *Culture as History: The Transformation of American Society in the Twentieth Century* (New York: Pantheon, 1984), p. 5.
2. A good review of Adams's work and its importance can be found in George Hochfield, *Henry Adams: An Introduction and Interpretation* (New York: Barnes and Noble Inc., 1962); the contemporary biography that best explores his most creative period is Edward Chalfant, *Better in Darkness: A Biography of Henry Adams, His Second Life, 1862–1891* (Hamden, CT: Archon Books, 1994).
3. Adams's discussion of this episode appears in *The Education of Henry Adams,* in *Henry Adams* (New York: The Library of America, 1983), pp. 809–51.
4. Adams, *Education*, pp. 939–40.
5. "Reunionist culture" and the cynicism of writers such as Adams, Crane, Bierce, and

Twain should not be confused. Both genres did, however, share the tendency to either excuse the south for its failings or to suggest a moral equivalence between north and south (Nina Silber, *Romance of Reunion: Northerners and the South, 1865–1900* [Chapel Hill: University of North Carolina Press, 1993], pp. 66–92, second quote on 92); David Blight describes American culture in the 1880s and 1890s as "awash in sentimental reconciliationists' literature." He notes that, as part of this process, "southern writers and themes became the darlings of American fiction as never before." See Blight, *Race and Reunion: The Civil War in American Memory* (Cambridge, MA: Harvard University Press, 2001), pp. 238–9.

6. C. Vann Woodward, "A Southern Critique for the Gilded Age," *The Burden of Southern History*, 3rd ed. (Baton Rouge: Louisiana State University Press, 1993), pp. 109–140.
7. Adams's changing ideas about the American experiment, and the thinkers who influenced him, receive a clear explication in Stow Persons, *The Decline of American Gentility* (New York: Columbia University Press, 1973); see especially pp. 204–217. The southern "Lost Cause" movement focused on the defeat of the Confederacy the defeat of virtue. See Charles Reagan Wilson, *Baptized in Blood: The Religion of the Lost Cause, 1865–1920* (Athens, GA: University of Georgia Press, 1980) and my *Never Surrender: Confederate Memory and Conservatism in the South Carolina Upcountry* (Athens, GA: University of Georgia Press, 2004).
8. Henry Adams, *Democracy: An American Novel*, in *Henry Adams* (New York: Library of America, 1983), pp. 3, 8. The suicide of Adams's wife certainly influenced his choice of characters and their struggles with meaning. See also his novel *Esther* (New York: Library of America, 1983), pp. 185–336, in which the central character is another woman in search of meaning.
9. This interpretation of Adams's famous disillusionment draws heavily from George Hochfield's excellent study, *Henry Adams: An Introduction and Interpretation*, pp. 87–99.
10. Adams, *Democracy*, p. 8.
11. Ibid.
12. Adams, *Democracy*, pp. 12, 13; C. Vann Woodward, "The Search for Southern Identity," *The Burden of Southern History*, pp. 3–25.
13. Ibid., p. 15.
14. Sumner, a former friend and political ally with whom Adams had had a falling out, figures in other ways in the novel, including some of the more scandalous aspects of his failed marriage to former Adams neighbor Alice Mason; see Chalfant, *Better in Darkness*, pp. 128–29.
15. Adams, *Education*, pp. 772, 811.
16. Adams, *Education*, pp. 991–92; Adams had an extreme distaste for Grant and the scandals of his administration. See Hochfield, *Henry Adams*, pp. 125–29.
17. Adams, *Democracy*, p. 166.
18. Hochfield, *Henry Adams*, pp. 29, 32–33; Adams seems to have had complex views on this point, and his politics sometimes took him close to the notions of "Ameri-

can Empire" held by his brother Brooks. John Carlos Rowe notes the links between Adams and important political figures in the crucial 1898–1905 years of growing American imperialism. See John Carlos Rowe, "Henry Adams's *Education* in the Age of Imperialism," in *New Essays on the Education of Henry Adams*, ed. John Carlos Rowe (Cambridge, UK: Cambridge University Press, 1996), pp. 87–114.

19. Adams, *Democracy*, p. 182; Woodward's discussion of the novel includes the odd assertion that Lee "fled to Europe" at the end of the affair and suggests that it ends with the "romantic hint" that Carrington and Lee will eventually be together. In truth, it ends with no denouement for Carrington and Lee other than separation by time and space and an outright assertion of American venality. See Woodward, "A Southern Critique," 109–140.
20. Ibid., pp. 183–84.
21. Hochfield, *Henry Adams*, pp. 126, 127.

"So Many, Many Needless Dead"

The Civil War Witness of Ambrose Bierce

— Roy Morris Jr. —

Of the more than three million soldiers, Union and Confederate, who served in the Civil War, only one—Indiana native Ambrose Bierce—made anything approaching great art from the defining national tragedy. A few others—Connecticut novelist John DeForest, Georgia poet Sidney Lanier, Supreme Court Justice Oliver Wendell Holmes—also fought in the war and later wrote, sometimes memorably, about their experiences in it. But only Bierce brought the war home, in all its hideous details, to the genteel readers of the Gilded Age. In an era dominated by female readers accustomed to "the drama of a broken teacup [and] the tragedy of a walk down the block," Bierce's graphic accounts of wounds and death were nothing short of revolutionary. Like the family dog who carries a dead rabbit into the parlor and drops it unceremoniously in its mistress's lap, Bierce took great pains—and no doubt great pleasure—in shocking the more squeamish and refined sensibilities of the age. But his reputation for premeditated offensiveness notwithstanding, he had more in mind than mere offense. Only by showing war's effects, "the sickening 'spat' of lead against flesh," could Bierce give his writings "the air of reality" that Henry James considered "the supreme virtue" of all good fiction. And only by showing what the war had done to him and his fellow soldiers could he ultimately keep faith with "those many, many needless dead" who, unlike him, had not survived the Civil War.[1]

As modern critic Daniel Aaron has pointed out, Bierce was an unlikely candidate to become the foremost chronicler of the Civil War. The four dominant literary figures of the postwar era—three of whom Bierce actively despised, the fourth he probably never heard of—were Mark Twain, Henry James, William Dean Howells, and Henry Adams. They were, in Aaron's view, "the men probably best endowed, if not the most temperamentally suited, to record the war in history or fiction." The only problem was that they "never got close enough to the fighting to write about it." Howells and Adams sat out the war in European drawing rooms, James nursed his "obscure hurt" in the peaceful environs of Harvard Yard, and Twain "lighted out for the Territories" with his equally unmilitant brother Orion. With the problematical exception of Twain's highly—and perhaps wholly—fictionalized account of his brief fling with pro-Confederate rangers in his hometown of Hannibal, Missouri, "A Short History of a Campaign That Failed," none of the four "malingerers," as Aaron styles them, ever wrote a word about the most dramatic event of their lifetime. "The Civil War," notes Bernard DeVoto, "did not greatly disquiet most of our authors."[2]

It did disquiet Ambrose Bierce, who certainly got close enough to the fighting to write about it with the hard-earned authority of the veteran. In a military career that lasted almost as long as the war itself, from April 1861 to January 1865, Bierce saw action on such terrible fields as Shiloh, Stones River, Chickamauga, Missionary Ridge, Resaca, Pickett's Mill, Franklin, and Nashville. He narrowly escaped death from a Confederate minié bullet at Kennesaw Mountain, where his head was "broken like a walnut," and in short order he went from a callow Indiana farm boy to the ranks of "hardened and impenitent man-killers, to whom death in its awfulest forms is a fact familiar to their every-day observation; who sleep on hills trembling with the thunder of great guns, dine in the midst of streaming missiles, and play cards among the dead faces of their dearest friends." Gloomy and saturnine to begin with, he discovered in the war a bitter confirmation of his darkest assumptions about man and his nature. It did not necessarily make him a pacifist—he cared too little about himself and others to place much value on human life—but it did prepare him to write about the war with a bluntness and honesty hitherto unheard of in American literature.[3]

No one, perhaps not even Bierce himself, expected him to make much of a mark in the war. The youngest child of fanatically religious parents, he left home at the age of fifteen to work as an apprentice on the local abolitionist newspaper, the *Northern Indianan*. Following a dispute with the paper's publisher (legend has it that Bierce was wrongly accused of theft and resigned in a huff after being cleared of the charges), he left his hometown of Warsaw, Indiana (near South Bend) and went to live with his uncle, Lucius Verus Bierce, the mayor of Akron, Ohio, and a personal friend of the infamous John Brown. After completing a one-year stint at the Kentucky Military Institute, he returned to Indiana with no particular prospects and was working as a waiter at an ice cream parlor in Elkhart, thirty miles from Warsaw, when the Civil War erupted in the spring of 1861. The second man in his county to enlist in the Union Army after Abraham Lincoln's call to arms, Bierce advanced rapidly through the ranks of the Ninth Indiana Infantry, serving successively as a private, sergeant, sergeant major, second lieutenant, first lieutenant, and topographical engineer. He eventually joined the staff of Brigadier General William Hazen, a tough, no-nonsense fighter who considered Bierce "a brave and gallant fellow" and became his "master in the art of war." Justifying his commander's approving view, Bierce was decorated repeatedly for courage on the battlefield, twice rescuing wounded comrades under fire, and he might have made the army his lifelong career had it not been for a misunderstanding about his postwar rank. Offered a second lieutenant's commission in the regular army, Bierce "respectfully decline[d] the appointment" because it was not for a captaincy, as he had been led to expect.[4]

By that time, late 1866, a Hazen-led scouting survey of western forts had brought Bierce to San Francisco, where, except for brief intervals, he was to make his home for the next three decades. Largely self-educated—the only good thing he could say about his father was that the elder Bierce had maintained a surprisingly good library for a pious rustic—Bierce took a job as a night watchman at the U.S. Mint and began contributing to such local publications as the *Golden Era*, the *Californian*, and the Bret Harte-edited *Overland Monthly*. In December 1868 he became editor of the *San Francisco News Letter and Commercial Advertiser*, known familiarly as the *News Letter*. Founded in 1856 by English journalist Frederick Marriott, the weekly publication was modeled after Marriott's earlier London ventures, the *Illustrated News* and the *Morning Chronicle*. Within a decade it had grown from a hand-folded, one-page sheet of advertisements into a sixteen-page mixture of literary criticism, theatrical reviews, broadbrush satire, and local news, which it duly reported under the catch-all heading, "The Cradle, the Altar, and the Tomb." Bierce, who from childhood had exhibited an obsessive and rather creepy interest in the macabre, quickly put his own distinctive stamp on the *News Letter*, transforming his regular new column, the "Town Crier," into a gleefully mordant "Criminal Market Review" of robberies, burglaries, arsons, suicides, and murders. Coupled with his regular bludgeoning of elected officials, corrupt policemen, too-ardent clergymen, and rival journalists, the "Town Crier" became an immediate sensation, and Bierce gloried in his newfound fame as "the Laughing Devil," the "Diabolical Bierce," and "the Wickedest Man in San Francisco."[5]

Except for a three-year sojourn in London in the early 1870s, Bierce spent the next thirty years plying his trade as an unrepentant controversialist at a succession of Bay Area publications, including the *Argonaut*, the *Wasp*, and, from 1887 to 1905, William Randolph Hearst's San Francisco *Examiner.* His caustic and fearless wit was directed at anyone, great or small, who happened to attract his predatory gaze. Presidents, kings, and captains of industry competed daily with obscure poets, religious crusaders, liberated women—even dogs, for which humble creatures Bierce inexplicably developed a lifelong hatred. Not even the English language was safe from assault. One of his most popular ventures was *The Devil's Dictionary*, a collection of cynical redefinitions published serially in the *Wasp* and the *Examiner*, and later brought out in book form as *The Cynic's Word Book* (a less demonic title that Bierce loathed). A few examples may serve to give the flavor of the author's distinctive world view. He defined *love* as "a temporary insanity curable by marriage." *Marriage* itself was "a community consisting of a master, a mistress and two slaves, making in all, two." A *bride* was "a woman with a fine prospect of happiness behind her." Under *husband*, he advised, "see brute." A *year* was "a period of 365 disappointments," a *day* was "a period of 24 hours mostly misspent," a *saint* was "a dead sinner revised and edited," *once* was "enough," *twice* was "once too often," *peace* was "a period of cheating between two periods of fighting," and *president* was "the leading figure in a small group of men of whom—and of whom only—it is positively known that immense numbers of their countrymen did not want any of them for president." The *Senate* was "a body of elderly gentlemen charged with high duties and misdemeanors," a *lawyer* was "one skilled in circumvention of the law," *litigation* was "a machine which you go into as a pig and come out of as a sausage," and a *Christian* was "one who follows the teachings of Christ in so far as they are not inconsistent with a life of sin."[6]

But Bierce did more than write stinging newspaper columns and idiosyncratic dictionaries. Beginning in his mid-forties, he commenced work on a series of short stories, later collected and published in two volumes, *Tales of Soldiers and Civilians* and *Can Such Things Be?* Included in the works were seventeen stories set in the Civil War (two other war stories, the uncharacteristically humorous "Jupiter Doke, Brigadier-General" and "The Major's Tale," appeared in his *Collected Works* under the pointed rubric, "Negligible Tales"). As literature, the stories are of variable, if generally high, quality. At least two, "Chickamauga" and "An Occurrence at Owl Creek Bridge," will probably endure as lasting works of art—certainly, the latter is one of the most widely anthologized and best-known short stories in the English language. (No less a judge than Stephen Crane once gushed, "That story has everything. Nothing better exists.") Viewed as a whole, particularly within the context of the age in which they were written, the brutal, graphic, doom-laden stories are so different from the typical sunny domestic fare as to seem almost unprecedented. They function not as drawing room entertainments, but as messages smuggled from the front lines of hell, courageous and humane acts of witness by a writer not ordinarily noted for his humanity.[7]

Bierce first revisited the war in a non-fiction account, "What I Saw of Shiloh," published in the December 25, 1881, issue of the *Wasp*. A terse, vivid, sometimes stomach-turning account of his first major Civil War battle, at Shiloh, Tennessee, in April 1862, the story is definitely not the standard Victorian Christmas fare. Nor is it, as Bierce alleges at the beginning of the piece, "a simple story of a battle . . . told by a soldier who is no writer to a reader who is no soldier." In fact, the story and its effects are far from simple, and the person telling the story is indeed a writer, one working at very nearly the peak of his powers.[8]

Bierce begins his account, as Crane would begin *The Red Badge of Courage* a decade and a half later, with a Union army lolling peacefully around its morning campfires. "The men were idling about the embers of their bivouac fires," he writes; "some preparing breakfast, others looking carelessly to the condition of their arms and accoutrements . . . still others . . . chatting with indolent dogmatism on that never-failing theme, the end and object of the campaign." The calm is broken by "a dull, distant sound like the heavy breathing of some great animal below the horizon." The headquarters flag—another Crane-like touch—"lifted its head to listen," then "flapped excitedly, shaking out its blazonry of stars and stripes with a sort of fierce delight." Knots of concerned-looking officers dash to and fro, mounted messengers tear off in huge clouds of dust, and bugles begin blaring the call to arms.[9]

By the time Bierce's regiment, in Major General Don Carlos Buell's relief column, reaches the battlefield, it is dusk, and the new arrivals are ferried across the Tennessee River on two small steamboats, while enemy shells geyser the water around them. Along the riverbank a maddened crowd of refugees, shirkers, and walking wounded, "deaf to duty and dead to shame," attempts to fight its way onto the boats, meanwhile "express[ing] their unholy delight in the certainty of our destruction by the enemy." Bierce and his comrades struggle ashore and trudge into line on the Union left. As lightning flares the pitch-black sky, Bierce spies a collection of dimly lit tents, with stretchers of wounded men lying around them. "These tents were constantly receiving the wounded, yet were never full," he writes; "they were continually ejecting the dead, yet were never empty. It was as if the helpless had been carried in and murdered, that they might not hamper those whose business it was to fall tomorrow."[10]

Worse sights await the men at dawn. The battlefield is littered with the unmistakable evidence of a Union rout—abandoned equipment, broken-down wagons, slaughtered horses, and dead soldiers. While waiting to start the attack, Bierce comes across a mortally wounded sergeant, "a fine giant in his time," who is lying face-up on the ground. The man is dying slowly and terribly, "taking his breath in convulsive, rattling snorts, and blowing it out in sputters of froth which crawled creamily down his cheeks, piling itself alongside his neck and ears. A bullet had clipped a groove in his skull, above his temple; from this the brain protruded in bosses, dropping off in flakes and strings." Bierce marvels that anyone "could get on, even in this unsatisfactory fashion, with so little brain." One of his men offers to put the sergeant out of his misery, but Bierce refuses the request on the grounds that "it was unusual, and too many were looking."[11]

During a lull in the fighting, Bierce's regiment falls back to a hill overlooking a deep ravine. There, on the opening day of the battle, the 55th Illinois Regiment had been caught and butchered as it attempted to retreat. Confederate marksmen lining the ravine had shot the men like fish in a barrel as they attempted futilely to escape. Surveying the awful scene, Bierce stumbles upon a sight he would never forget: hundreds of dead and wounded soldiers burned to cinders by a quick-moving brushfire. Ankle-deep in their ashes, he surveys the charred remains of his fellow soldiers: "Their clothing was half burnt away—their hair and beard entirely; the rain had come too late to save their nails. Some were swollen to double girth; others shriveled to manikins . . . their faces . . . bloated and black or yellow and shrunken. The contraction of muscles which had given them claws for hands had cursed each countenance with a hideous grin. . . . I cannot catalogue the charms of these gallant gentlemen who had got what they enlisted for."[12]

Shiloh was a shocking, even unprecedented battle—more Americans died in the fighting there than had died in the American Revolution, the War of 1812, and the Mexican War combined—and it was a watershed event for Ambrose Bierce, making his earlier, almost picturesque service in West Virginia seem like a boyish idyll by comparison. Twenty years later, that sense of shock is still evident in his writing. "What I Saw of Shiloh," although not generally included in a short list of the author's best stories, remains an underrated masterpiece. The unmistakable work of a seasoned veteran, it represents the first time in American literature that anyone had written about warfare in such realistic detail. (One wonders what San Francisco readers, lingering over their Christmas breakfast, made of all the oozing brains and burning bodies.) Its influence may be seen most clearly in *The Red Badge of Courage*, which virtually duplicates Bierce's laconic beginning, the anthropomorphic animism of the headquarters flag and the "terrified" river, and the disorienting sense of having suddenly entered a battle over which the commanding generals have lost all control. Its effects may also be seen in the work of another Bierce disciple, Ernest Hemingway, whose celebrated novel *A Farewell to Arms* includes a surrealistic account of the Italian retreat at Caporetto that closely echoes, in its nighttime scenes along the riverbank, the chaotic arrival of Bierce's regiment at Shiloh and the total breakdown of military discipline.

In the decade to come, Bierce would return to the war again and again as he completed with remarkable rapidity the series of stories—not all of them set in the war—that comprised his first published collection, *Tales of Soldiers and Civilians*. Most of the stories appeared first in the San Francisco *Examiner*, whose Sunday supplement actively encouraged the outré and the shocking. Non-fiction accounts of lurid murders, premature burials, unexplained disappearances, and sensational executions competed for space with eerie short stories from Sir Arthur Conan Doyle, Guy de Maupassant, and other masters of the literary form. Ironically, given today's more sensitive editorial practices, the fact that the stories were published first in a newspaper rather than a book allowed their author greater artistic freedom, and Bierce took full advantage of the opportunity. Consider, for example, his famous story "Chickamauga," which appeared in the January 20, 1889, edition of the *Examiner*. Bierce, of course, had fought at Chickamauga, and he later wrote an effective non-fiction account of his role in the battle, "A Little of Chickamauga," for the January 24, 1898, issue of the newspaper. The short story, which concerns a lost little boy wandering about the battlefield, may be read on one level as that archetypal American coming-of-age story, the innocent youth confronting the violent frontier. That confrontation occurs unforgettably when the child, who is six, encounters a puzzling procession of strange men moving with painful slowness through the woods around his home. Unknown to the child, the men are wounded soldiers dragging themselves to the rear in search of a quiet place to lie down and die. To the child's uncomprehending eyes, the blood-streaked men resemble the clowns "he had seen last summer at the circus."[13]

Nothing else in Bierce's writings approaches the poignant simplicity of the hushed procession. As the boy watches, fascinated, the men "crept upon their hands and knees. They used their hands only, dragging their legs. They used their knees only, their hands hanging idly at their sides. They strove to rise to their feet, but fell prone in the attempt. They did nothing naturally and nothing alike, save only to advance foot by foot in the same direction. . . . Occasionally one who had paused did not again go on, but lay motionless. He was dead. Some, pausing, made strange gestures with their hands, erected their arms and lowered them again, clasped their heads; spread their palms upward, as men are sometimes seen to do in public prayer."[14]

Not knowing what he is witnessing, the child jumps atop one of the wounded men, hoping for a piggyback ride like those his father's slaves had often given him. The soldier collapses from the jolt, flings the boy aside, "then turned upon him a face that lacked a lower jaw—from the upper teeth to the throat was a great red gap fringed with hanging shreds of flesh and splinters of bone. . . . The man shook his fist at the child; the child, terrified at last, ran to a tree nearby, got upon the farther side of it and took a more serious view of the situation." The dying soldier shaking his fist is strikingly similar to the famous scene in *The Red Badge of Courage* when the protagonist, Henry Fleming, comes upon his mortally wounded friend Jim Conklin and shakes his own fist impotently at the sky, muttering the tersely eloquent word, "Hell!"[15]

The child, no longer innocent, returns home and finds his house on fire and his mother lying dead in the yard: "There, conspicuous in the light of the conflagration, lay the dead body of a woman—the white face turned upward, the hands thrown out and clutched full of grass, the clothing deranged, the long dark hair in tangles and full of clotted blood. The greater part of the forehead was torn away, and from the jagged hole the brain protruded, overflowing the temple, a frothy mass of gray, crowned with clusters of crimson bubbles—the working of a shell." The child, now revealed to be a deaf-mute, has come face to face with the terrible reality of war, not unlike Bierce and the other Boys of '61, who had rushed romantically off to the front, only to discover too late that there was little glory and no romance in it. Alone, orphaned, and terrified, the child utters "a series of inarticulate and indescribable cries—something between the chattering of an ape and the gobbling of a turkey—a startling, soulless, unholy sound, the language of a devil." Such language, Bierce implies, is all too appropriate to the battlefield.[16]

The various protagonists of Bierce's other Civil War stories are all older than the boy in "Chickamauga," but they too are trapped in an explicable nightmare world of sudden and often random destruction. The critic Ernest Hopkins has suggested that the stories be read as a sort of disguised novel in discrete chapters, a work which "would constitute the most enduring anti-war document in American literature." Bierce himself had little use for the novel form, defining it in *The Devil's Dictionary* as "a short story padded," but Hopkins is right in seeing in the stories a consistent—one might say a compulsive—theme. In one way or another, all concern men who are, like the doomed sniper in "One of the Missing," "caught like a rat in a trap." The trap may be literal, like the heavy wooden beams that pin the sniper beneath them, or it may be figurative, the product of misplaced patriotism ("A Horseman in the Sky"), curdled idealism ("An Affair of Outposts"), excessive pride ("Killed at Resaca," "A Son of the Gods"), a too-punctilious sense of duty ("The Affair at Coulter's Gulch," "One Kind of Officer"), or an overly developed imagination ("A Tough Tussle," "One Officer, One Man"). As Bierce scholar Cathy Davidson has maintained, the author "structures nearly all of his stories around breakdowns in perception . . . because those crises dramatize the limits of perception and reveal the fatuity of such language and most reason—the clichés of word and response." The failure of reason leads in turn to the failure of language, the result, says Davidson, of the mind's "incapacity to deal with the perceptual horrors it confronts." The lost generation of writers who served in World War I faced a similar dilemma—how to make sense (and literature) from what was essentially an insane situation, the mud and blood of no man's land. One need only read the too-pretty verses of Wilfred Owen, with their regular rhyme schemes and sonorous rhythms, to be struck by the severe disjunction between what Owen is describing and how he is describing it.[17]

It is just such a breakdown—or derangement—of perception that permeates Bierce's most celebrated story, "An Occurrence at Owl Creek Bridge." The plot of the story is deceptively simple: it opens with a pro-Confederate civilian named Peyton Farquhar about to be hanged from a northern Alabama railroad trestle for attempting to burn down the bridge the night before. Waiting wordlessly for the execution to take place, the condemned man feels his senses heighten preternaturally; the ticking of his pocket watch sounds like a blacksmith's thunderous anvil strokes. As the Union sergeant steps back from the plank on which Farquhar is standing, the story flashes back to the events leading up to Farquhar's fatal decision. The hanging proceeds as planned, but the rope breaks and Farquhar plunges to the bottom of Owl Creek, where he frees himself from his ropes and resurfaces with a shout. Desperately, he swims away as soldiers pepper the stream with rifle fire. Somehow, he makes good his improbable escape and eventually finds his way home. His wife is waiting for him on the steps of the veranda, and Farquhar steps forward to embrace her. Then, "he feels a stunning blow upon the back of his neck; a blinding white light blazes all about him with a sound like the shock of a cannon—then all is darkness and silence." The story concludes with one of the most famous sentences in American literature: "Peyton Farquhar was dead; his body, with a broken neck, swung gently from side to side beneath the timbers of the Owl Creek bridge." The escape had been an illusive dream.[18]

Careless readers have misinterpreted the story as being merely a bit of O. Henry-like legerdemain, a straightforward account of a botched hanging, followed by a trick ending. A closer reading of this most carefully written story reveals that the ending is no trick—except on the unfortunate and dull-witted Farquhar. Everywhere along the way Bierce prepares the reader for the story's only possible conclusion, an *occurrence*—a hanging—*at* Owl Creek Bridge. Moreover, in the frequently misread middle section of the story, Farquhar is revealed to be just the sort of self-deluding fool who would most likely imagine such a preposterous escape. The story, and Farquhar's self-created story-within-a-story, ends with a jolt, but not a surprise.

In fact, "An Occurrence at Owl Creek Bridge" ends twice, and both times identically. The third and final section of the story opens with a remarkably graphic and convincing account of Farquhar's actual death by hanging. "A sharp pressure upon his throat, followed by a sense of suffocation," is accompanied by "keen poignant agonies [that] seemed to shoot from his neck downward through every fibre of his body and limbs." These in turn are followed by "a feeling of fullness—of congestion" in his head, and a sense of swinging "through unthinkable arcs of oscillation, like a vast pendulum." Finally, he feels himself shoot upward with "a frightful roaring in his ears," until "all was cold and dark." At this point, Farquhar is dead and the real story is over, but it is Bierce's brilliant achievement to show how a dying man might, in the split second of life remaining to him, mistake the sensation of falling, being strangled, and being yanked upward again at the end of a rope for a saving plunge into deep water. No one knows if death by hanging really mimics death by drowning (probably it does not), but the similarity of the two is beside the point: it is Farquhar's dream we are experiencing, and since he is being hanged from a bridge over water, it is only natural that he would imagine himself falling into the water to escape, and that he would confuse the congestion of suffocation with that of drowning.[19]

The rest of the story occurs not in real time but in the instant that Farquhar is dropping through space to the literal end of his rope. Again, he experiences the sensation of hanging: "His neck ached horribly; his brain was on fire; his heart, which had been fluttering faintly, gave a great leap, trying to force itself out of his mouth. His whole body was racked and wrenched by insupportable anguish." Recent studies of near-death experiences have revealed a consistent pattern of similar sensations, of falling (or rising) through darkness toward a distant, all-encompassing light, which some have suggested are simply repressed memories of birth. And while Bierce could not have been exposed to such studies in his own lifetime, it is significant that a "blinding white light" does blaze around Farquhar at the exact moment that he hears "a sound like the shock of a cannon"—his neck breaking. Since Bierce never wrote about his own near-death experience at Kennesaw Mountain, it is impossible to say whether he was relying on personal knowledge in describing Farquhar's final moments, or was simply using the artist's creative prerogative. Certainly he used other personal experiences in writing the story: the real Owl Creek, which borders the battlefield at Shiloh; his regiment's railroad-guarding service in northern Alabama, which exactly corresponds to the time of the story; the various hangings he witnessed as a soldier in the army and as a reporter in San Francisco; even the miraculous "escape" from hanging that is the basic plot contrivance of the obscure eighteenth-century play *Ambrose Gwinett; or A Sea-Side Story*, from which he derived his name. The accretion of realistic details gives added weight to the unreal instant at the heart of the story. We believe it because, like Farquhar, we want to believe it.[20]

In a way, "An Occurrence at Owl Creek Bridge" has poorly served Bierce's academic standing by giving him an undeserved, if understandable, reputation for literary sleight of hand. This is unfortunate, since it obscures his true historical worth as the direct forerunner of the great American modernists. His realistic portrayal of war, his hard-earned cynicism, and his keen insight into the minds of soldiers facing the overwhelming existential crisis of the battlefield are now commonplace in literature. Prior to Bierce, they were not. He could write of the Civil War with such authenticity because he had been there, literally on the front lines, while others of his generation were carefully holding back. When the timeworn image of "Bitter Bierce, the devil's lexicographer," is stripped away, what finally remains is 1st Lt. Ambrose Bierce, Ninth Indiana Infantry, a young man who had seen war on a scale—both large and small—that no other American writer could even imagine in the half-century prior to World War I. His true significance as an artist, in contrast to his undeniable quotability as a drawing room curmudgeon and infernal wit, will forever rest on his pride of place as the first surviving witness to modern war, and the evil banality with which men die.

Notes

1. Frank Norris, "A Plea for Romantic Fiction," in *Anthology of American Literature*, vol. 2, George McMichael, ed. (New York: Macmillan, 1980), p. 874. "What I Saw of Shiloh," in *The Collected Works of Ambrose Bierce*, vol. 1 (New York: Neale Publishing Company, 1909–1912), p. 255. Hereafter cited as *Works*. Henry James, "The Art of Fiction," in McMichael, *Anthology of American Literature*, vol. 2, p. 719. "A Son of the Gods," in *The Collected Writings of Ambrose Bierce*, Clifton Fadiman, ed. (New York: Citadel Press, 1946), p. 29. Hereafter cited as *Writings*.
2. Daniel Aaron, *The Unwritten War: American Writers and the Civil War* (New York: Oxford University Press, 1973), p. 92. Bernard DeVoto, *Mark Twain's America* (New York: Harper and Brothers, 1933), p. 112.
3. "A Son of the Gods," *Writings*, p. 26.
4. Paul Fatout, *Ambrose Bierce: The Devil's Lexicographer* (Norman: University of Oklahoma Press, 1951), pp. 15, 33. William B. Hazen, *A Narrative of Military Service* (Boston: Ticknor & Company, 1885), pp. 264–265. "The Crime at Pickett's Mill," *Works*, 1: 284. M. E. Grenander, *Ambrose Bierce* (New York: Twayne Publishers, 1971), p. 29.
5. Franklin Walker, *San Francisco's Literary Frontier* (New York: Alfred A. Knopf, 1939), pp. 248–249. *News Letter*, February 13, 1869.
6. All definitions are taken from *The Devil's Dictionary*, in *Writings*, pp. 189–392.
7. John Berryman, *Stephen Crane* (New York: World Publishing Company, 1962), p. 170.
8. "What I Saw of Shiloh," *Works*, vol. 1, p. 234.
9. "What I Saw of Shiloh," pp. 234–236.
10. "What I Saw of Shiloh," pp. 245–247.
11. "What I Saw of Shiloh," pp. 254–255.

12. "What I Saw of Shiloh," pp. 261–262.
13. Richard Saunders, *Ambrose Bierce: The Making of a Misanthrope* (San Francisco: Chronicle Books, 1985), p. 50. "Chickamauga," *Writings*, pp. 20–21.
14. "Chickamauga," p. 20.
15. "Chickamauga," p. 21. Stephen Crane, *The Red Badge of Courage*, in McMichael, *Anthology of American Literature*, vol. 2, p. 820.
16. "Chickamauga," p. 23.
17. Ernest Jerome Hopkins, *The Complete Short Stories of Ambrose Bierce* (Lincoln: University of Nebraska Press, 1970), p. 261. *The Devil's Dictionary*, p. 313. "One of the Missing," *Writings*, p. 34. Cathy N. Davidson, *The Experimental Fictions of Ambrose Bierce* (Lincoln: University of Nebraska Press, 1984), pp. 2, 25.
18. "An Occurrence at Owl Creek Bridge," *Writings*, pp. 9–18.
19. "An Occurrence at Owl Creek Bridge," p. 13.
20. "An Occurrence at Owl Creek Bridge," pp. 14, 17–18.

Of Saints and Sinners

Religion and the Civil War and Reconstruction Novel

— Edward J. Blum —

When film director D. W. Griffith transformed Thomas Dixon's inflammatory Reconstruction novel *The Clansman* into the blockbuster 1915 motion picture *The Birth of a Nation*, he included most of Dixon's cast of villains. A coterie of poor southern white "scalawags," sexually charged African Americans, diabolical radical Republicans, and greedy northern "carpetbaggers" conspired together to demoralize the beaten South. Griffith, however, omitted one group that Dixon adamantly blamed for the evils of Reconstruction—northern Protestant ministers. In fact, Dixon—a minister himself—held these pastors and their Easter Sunday sermons after Abraham Lincoln's Good Friday assassination directly responsible for embittering northern sentiment against the South. As he described it, "Fifty thousand Christian ministers stunned and crazed by insane passion stood before the altars of God, [and] hurled into the broken hearts before them the wildest cries of vengeance—cries incoherent, chaotic, unreasoning, blind in their awful fury."[1]

In contrast to Dixon's appraisal, admitted carpetbagger and novelist Albion Tourgée offered a quite different interpretation of the Christian response to the war's end and Lincoln's assassination. "Perhaps there has been no grander thing in our history," he penned, than when "[t]he civilization of the North in the very hour of victory threw aside the cartridge-box, and appealed at once to the contribution-box to heal the ravages of war." Specifically, he praised northern Protestants for sending capital and missionaries to the South to help African-American freedmen. To Tourgée, "It was the noblest spectacle that Christian civilization has ever witnessed."[2]

While modern scholars would find little shocking about interpretive differences between Tourgée and Dixon, most would be surprised by the intensity with which these authors described religion and religious characters. An examination of the ways Tourgée and Dixon depicted religious ideologies, characters, and institutions suggests that faith affected regional relationships and conceptions more than current historical scholarship indicates.[3]

For the most part, post-1960 studies of Civil War and Reconstruction novels have focused on gender and racial issues. Whether analyzing the countless cross-sectional romantic relationships or the images of menacing African-American freedmen terrorizing white women, scholars have rightly pointed out how gender and racial ideologies deeply influenced northern and southern views of one another and regional reconciliation.[4] Indeed, both Tourgée and Dixon employed gender metaphors and racial imagery to narrate the story of Civil War and postbellum America. Their strong feelings about ministers and missionaries, however, indicate that along with race and gender, religion also played a pivotal role in regional conceptions, animosities, and resolutions.

An exploration of the most noteworthy novels of Tourgée, *A Fool's Errand*, and *Bricks without Straw*, and of Dixon, *The Leopard's Spots* and *The Clansman*, adds religious ideologies to the story of postwar America, and reveals the intersections of race, gender, and religion in the texts. While Dixon described northern faith as corrupt, Tourgée viewed southern Christianity as hypocritical. Although Dixon mocked Yankee missionaries to the South as idiotic blunderers, Tourgée praised them as angels sent from above. These differences, however, should not obfuscate the points the two writers shared. Both depicted the Ku Klux Klan as a quasi-religious organization; both acknowledged the crucial position of southern churches as locations of cultural hegemony; and, finally, both believed that religion and the Protestant God must play a role in regional reconciliation. In short, the novelists used religion as a way to articulate regional differences and regional reconciliation.

A brief look at Tourgée's and Dixon's personal histories makes their emphasis on religion less surprising. Born in the 1840s, Tourgée came from a long line of French Huguenots, and his parents inculcated him with Protestant values from his boyhood. In his semi-autobiographical *A Fool's Errand*, Tourgée referred to himself as "an active member of the church . . . and superintendent of its Sabbath school."[5] Like his carpetbagger counterpart, Dixon also came from a religious background; his father, Thomas Dixon, Sr., was a renowned Baptist minister, and young Dixon spent much of his childhood at church, Sunday school, and other religious functions. After graduating from Wake Forest and passing the bar exam with the intent of practicing law, Dixon decided instead to enter the ministry. During the 1880s, he was one of the Gilded Age's most promising young ministers, preaching to large congregations in Boston and New York. These religious backgrounds are clearly visible in their writings.[6]

In their Civil War and Reconstruction novels, Tourgée and Dixon often described the North and the South as regions whose conflicting religious ideologies kept them culturally separated. Tourgée portrayed southern religion as hypocritical and fraudulent. Marveling at and lamenting the way that southern white Christians despised and subjugated African Americans, he railed against their tacit acceptance of lynching. "He could not understand how men of the highest Christian character," Tourgée wrote of the carpetbagger protagonist in *A Fool's Errand*, "could be the perpetrators, encouragers, or excusers" of a lynching. "Yet the pulpit kept silent," he grieved.[7] Tourgée also bemoaned the southern belief in the divine nature of slavery. He wrote his most bitter invective against southern religion in *Bricks without Straw:* "Ah God! how sad that history should be compelled to make up so dark a record, abuse, contumely, violence! Christian tongues befouled with calumny! Christian lips blistered with falsehood! Christian hearts overflowing with hate!"[8]

Unlike Tourgée's stinging appraisal, Dixon believed that southern religion and racial segregation were sanctified and in step with biblical teachings. Portraying Abraham Lincoln as a southerner (something Dixon often enjoyed doing), he placed religious arguments for racial segregation in the president's mouth in his novel *The Clansman*.[9] After a radical Republican defended African-American equality by claiming that "God hath made of one blood all races," Lincoln promptly responded, "Yes—but finish the sentence—'and fixed the bounds of their habitation.' God never meant that the negro should leave his habitat or the white man invade his home."[10] To Dixon, racial segregation was not immoral; it was ordained in heaven. Moreover, he depicted the white South as a religious community and equated holiness with whiteness and manliness. Southerners, he contended, were "a sturdy, honest, covenant-keeping, God-fearing, fighting people."[11] Connecting religion, virtue, and manhood, Dixon maintained that southerners were God's chosen people.[12]

As they varied in their interpretations of southern religious ideology, Dixon and Tourgée also offered contradicting depictions of northern religious and missionary activities in the South. To Dixon, northern religion was pharisaical and only interested in punishing the South. In *The Clansman*, he used the radical Republican leader Thaddeus Stevens[13] as the epitome of corrupted Yankee religion. Stevens was more than a political leader to Dixon; he was an evil prophet.

On one occasion, Dixon had Stevens comment to his Republican colleagues: "I preach equality as a poet and seer who sees a vision beyond the rim of the horizon of to-day." Stevens continued, arguing that "[i]t is but the justice and wisdom of Heaven that the negro shall rule the land of his bondage."[14]

But to Dixon, Stevens was no angel of light. Rather, he was a tool of darkness, and Dixon pointed toward Stevens's infidelism by painting him as a friend of the evils of Roman Catholicism. "Among his many charities," Dixon wrote of Stevens, "he had always given liberally to an orphanage conducted by a Roman Catholic sisterhood." To many nineteenth- and early-twentieth-century evangelical Protestants, support for Catholicism was tantamount to blasphemy. Thus, rather than signifying piety, such contributions expose Stevens's villainy.[15] By the end of *The Clansman*, however, Stevens realized his mistaken war against the white South and sought to atone. He found a southern Presbyterian minister and begged for forgiveness. "I wish to confess to you," Stevens cried, "and set myself right before God." Not truly interested in black rights all along, Stevens admits his evil demagoguery: "Three forces moved me—party success, a vicious woman, and the quenchless desire for personal vengeance."[16] Only through religious confession, Dixon narrated, does Stevens both admit his wrong and reconcile himself with his southern brethren. For the remaining portion of the book, Stevens not only ceased his attacks against white southerners, but also came to embrace them.

Tourgée presented a much different appraisal of northern religion and religious figures. To him, northern Christians were genuinely interested in African-American rights and were not mere demagogues. "The North . . . was . . . honest in its conviction with regard to the wickedness of slavery," he wrote.[17] Furthermore, northern Christians carried the banner of African-American racial uplift into the South. Northern missionaries were, in Tourgée's opinion, the truest disciples of Jesus Christ. He describes one in *Bricks without Straw:* "The gentle child felt called of God to do missionary work for a weak and struggling people. She thought she felt the divine commandment which rested on the Nazarene."[18] After the war, Tourgée suggested that northerners who set out to alter the South were prompted by sincere faith. "The first step," he argued in *Bricks without Straw*, is the commitment to legal marriages for freed people. "It was prompted by the voice of conscience," he said, "long hushed and hidden in the master's breast. It was the protest of Christianity and morality against that which it had witnessed with complacency for many a generation. All at once it was perceived to be a great enormity that four millions of Christian people, in a Christian land, should dwell together without marriage rite or family tie."[19]

Northern allegiance to African Americans, however, did not stop at the marriage altar. Yankee Protestant missionaries also brought education, and Tourgée viewed these missionaries as "on a noble errand . . . doing God's work in teaching" the southern freed people. "As the North gave, willingly and freely, men and millions to save the nation from disruption," he penned, "so, when peace came, it gave other brave men and braver women, and other unstinted millions to strengthen the hands which generations of slavery had left feeble and inept." To Tourgée, these Yankee schoolmarms embodied virtuous religion: "Thousands of white-souled angels of peace, the tenderly reared and highly-cultured daughters of many a Northern home, came into the smitten land to do good to its poorest and weakest." And these missionaries left a lasting legacy. "Even to this day," Tourgée maintained, "two score of schools and colleges remain, the glorious mementoes of this enlightened bounty and Christian magnanimity."[20] Tourgée's appreciation for the Yankee schoolmarms squared with his intense belief in the importance of education for African Americans. As biographer Otto Olsen maintains, Tourgée considered education the key ingredient to African-American rights. The missionaries, then, stood as the radical vanguard for racial justice, carrying the awesome power of the cross and the spelling book into the South.[21]

Dixon held quite a different view of Yankee schoolmarms and their efforts. Though not as sinister as the radical Stevens, they nonetheless stood as misguided fools and were viewed as being somewhat less than female. To discredit such women, Dixon described their physical appearance as unattractive and unfeminine. Missionary "Susan Walker of Boston," he wrote, "fell just a little short of being handsome and [her] nose was responsible for the failure. It gave to her face when agitated, in spite of evident culture and refinement, the expression of a feminine bulldog."[22] Although Yankee schoolmarms may appear respectable, when agitated, their bodies exposed their lack of womanliness.

In addition to mocking the unattractiveness of the schoolmarms, Dixon also denounced their mission. To him, black education constituted one of the most repugnant aspects of radical Republicanism. He believed that schooling would ultimately destroy African Americans. "Education," he wrote, "increases the power of the human brain to think and the heart to suffer. Sooner or later these educated Negroes feel the clutch of the iron hand of the white man's unwritten laws on their throats. They have their choice between a suicide's grave or a prison cell. . . . The South is kinder to the Negro when he is kept in his place."[23] Educated African Americans, he argued, would have no other choice but to end their lives when they realized their political and social position as second-class citizens.

While Dixon and Tourgée disagreed on their interpretations of northern missionaries and regional ideologies, they did in fact make some parallel arguments. While preeminent historians of Reconstruction like Willie Lee Rose have suggested that Dixon's and Tourgée's novels had nothing in common, an analysis of the religious motifs and arguments they used to describe white terrorism, southern churches, and southern political culture actually reveals several similarities.[24] In fact, both writers described white terrorist organizations like the Ku Klux Klan as quasi-religious bodies that appealed to southern white Christians. After the death of a young white woman at the hands of an African-American man, Dixon wrote that "The trumpet of the God of our fathers call[ed] the sleeping manhood of the Anglo-Saxon race to life again."[25] The answer to God's call came clothed in the regalia of the Ku Klux Klan. Mixing religion and gender, as he had in his description of the southern community and the northern missionaries, Dixon depicted the Klan as battling "for their God, their native land, and the womanhood of the South!"[26]

On another occasion, he compared Klan members to "the Knights of the Middle Ages [who] rode on their Holy Crusades."[27] Linking masculinity and religious mission, Dixon viewed Klan members as Christian warriors. Furthermore, he often described local ministers sanctioning the Klan's white supremacist activities and Klan assemblies beginning with chaplain's prayers.[28] Likewise, Tourgée described the Klan as a religious body, albeit a heinous and vile expression of faith. In *A Fool's Errand*, he called them a "band of Christian Thugs."[29] He recognized that Christian men readily joined the Klan: "Grave statesmen, reverend divines, legislators, judges, lawyers . . . all who could muster a good horse, as it would seem, joined the [Klan]." In *Bricks without Straw*, he noted, "They are most of them church-members, and all of them respectable."[30]

In addition to agreeing that the Ku Klux Klan constituted a quasi-religious organization, both Tourgée and Dixon portrayed white churches as a powerful force in southern social life, one that offered southern whites a geography of resistance against northern intruders. For Tourgée, these churches functioned as the symbolic location of either social acceptance or social ostracism for northern immigrants. When southern whites sought to "expel" any invaders who desired to better African-American lives, the first step involved rejection from the church. In *A Fool's Errand*, southern whites initially show their disdain for the northern protagonist and his wife at church. "We do not often go to church now," the carpetbaggers lament, "there is constant coldness, which says, plainer than words can, that we are not wanted."[31]

Other northerners also complain about religious ostracism. One man comments that his name was immediately "dropped from the church-roll" after he had defended black manhood suffrage,[32] while others "were excluded from the Lord's Communion for establishing Sabbath schools for colored people."[33] Such isolation, Tourgée maintained, deeply affected northern whites in the South, as Yankee schoolmarms found ostracism heart-wrenching. Tourgée described one female missionary's response to separation: "Her heart was sick of the terrible isolation that her position forced upon her."[34]

Through a more positive portrayal, Dixon similarly described the southern church as a powerful institution. "In the village," he penned, "the church was the center of gravity of the life of the people.... [E]verybody who could... went to church."[35] Along with the church's preeminent role, Dixon considered the southern pastor a critical molder of public opinion: "As an organiser and leader of opinion he [The Preacher] was easily the most powerful man in the county, and one of the most powerful in the state."[36] In sum, Dixon and Tourgée positioned the southern church as the hegemonic arbiter of southern mores and practices.

Tourgée and Dixon also recognized an interconnection between faith and politics in both white and black southern culture. African-American society, Tourgée said, fused the secular and the sacred. Describing an African-American political rally, he contended that "the political and religious interests and emotions of this people are quite inseparable.... Their religion is tinged with political thought, and their political thought shaped by religious conviction." Due to this connection, Tourgée suggested that "in this respect the colored race in America are the true children of the Covenanters and the Puritans."[37] African-American freed people, he maintained, were the religious progeny of the colonial Puritans, who sought to create a religio-political "city on a hill." The influence of black preachers, moreover, "was very great" and had incredible power in shaping the African-American community.[38] Postwar African-American culture, Tourgée observed, intertwined religion and politics.

Dixon recognized a similar phenomenon in southern white society. In an exchange between two southern whites about religion and politics, one contends that the emergence of free African-American voters made politics a religious arena. "To me," he claimed, "politics is a religion.... I believe that the State is now the only organ through which the whole people can search for righteousness." In short, only through politics could southern whites save their beloved racial hierarchy and redeem the South. Freed blacks, thus, had sanctified white supremacist politics.[39]

Finally, both Tourgée and Dixon, with their radically different racial attitudes, looked to religion as a means of reuniting the North and the South. For Dixon, the Spanish-American War of 1898 stood as the culminating event of regional reconciliation because it was at heart a holy crusade of racial imperialism. "We believe that God has raised up our race," he noted, "as he ordained Israel of old, in this world-crisis to establish and maintain for weaker races, as a trust for civilization." Later, one of Dixon's pro-imperialist characters proclaims that "I believe in God's call to our race to do His work in history."[40] Although Tourgée wrote his Reconstruction novels well before the Spanish-American War, he also believed that religion would be necessary for regional reconciliation. Unlike Dixon, though, he saw faith as a critical component for future African-American equality and for the dismantling of white racism. Concluding *Bricks without Straw*, he looked forward to a time when religious virtues would triumph over prejudice: "The soil which slavery claimed, baptized with blood becomes the Promised Land of the freedman and poor white.... Ignorance marvels at the power of Knowledge. Love overleaps the barriers of prejudice, and Faith laughs at the impossible."[41] Paralleling the critical virtues articulated by St. Paul in I Corinthians of "faith, hope, and love," Tourgée invoked those of faith, knowledge, and love as the key ingredients to an egalitarian and reunited America.

Clearly, religious motifs, characters, institutions, and ideologies played an important role in how Tourgée and Dixon articulated racial, gender, and sectional issues after the war. Both men would have agreed with another postwar novelist, Paul Laurence Dunbar, when he concluded that "it was not flesh and blood, but soul and spirit that counted now."[42] Ultimately, such attention to "soul and spirit" can open new doors for interpretations of Civil War and Reconstruction novels and the damaged society they sought to reflect.

Notes

This essay was originally published in the *Journal of Religion & Society* 4 (2002), http://www.creighton.edu./JRS.

1. Thomas Dixon, *The Clansman: An Historical Romance of the Ku Klux Klan* (Garden City, N.Y.: The Country Life Press, 1905), p. 83; D. W. Griffith (producer and director), (1915), *The Birth of a Nation* [film], Los Angeles: Republic Pictures Home Video, [1991].
2. Albion Tourgée, *Bricks without Straw: A Novel* (Ridgewood, N.J.: The Gregg Press, 1967 [1880]), p. 133.
3. Some of Tourgée's contemporaries recognized the religious overtones in their works. *The Century*, for instance, considered *A Fool's Errand* "a vigorous burst of righteous wrath." See "The Native Element in American Fiction," *The Century: A Popular Quarterly*, July 1883, p. 367.
4. For the best analysis of gender and race in the Civil War and Reconstruction novels, see Nina Silber *The Romance of Reunion: Northerners and the South, 1865–1900* (Chapel Hill: University of North Carolina Press, 1993). In analyzing Dixon's work, Silber pays especial attention to issues of masculinity, pp. 185–187. For a similar interpretation of his novels, see Glenda Elizabeth Gilmore, *Gender and Jim Crow: Women and the Politics of White Supremacy in North Carolina* (Chapel Hill: University of North Carolina Press, 1996), pp. 66–70, 135–136; Maxwell Bloomfield, "Dixon's 'The Leopard's Spots': A Study in Popular Racism," *American Quarterly* (Autumn, 1964): 387–401.
5. Albion W. Tourgée, *A Fool's Errand: A Novel of the South* (introduction by George M. Fredrickson: New York: Harper Torchbooks, 1961 [1879]), p. 13; for more on Tourgée's religious upbringing, see Otto H. Olsen, *Carpetbagger's Crusade: The Life of Albion Winegar Tourgée* (Baltimore: The Johns Hopkins University Press, 1965), pp. 10–11, 290–291, 300–301.

6. For more on Dixon's religious background see Raymond A. Cook, *Thomas Dixon* (New York: Twayne Publishers, Inc., 1974), pp. 40–51; and Bloomfield, "Dixon's 'The Leopard's Spots,'" pp. 388–391.
7. Tourgée, *A Fool's Errand*, p. 316.
8. Tourgée, *Bricks without Straw*, 134; for a similar argument, see Tourgée, *A Fool's Errand*, p. 321.
9. Dixon actually wrote one entire novel arguing that Lincoln was a southerner. See Thomas Dixon, *The Southerner: A Romance of the Real Lincoln* (New York: D. Appleton and Company, 1913). For the southern trend to depict Lincoln as a southerner, see Michael Davis, *The Image of Lincoln in the South* (Knoxville: The University of Tennessee Press, 1971), p. 150.
10. Dixon, *The Clansman*, p. 47.
11. Dixon, *The Clansman*, p. 188.
12. For another discussion of how Dixon pits southern moral strength and Christianity versus the evils of northern capitalism and urbanization, see F. Garvin Davenport, Jr., "Thomas Dixon's Mythology of Southern History," *The Journal of Southern History* (Aug. 1970): 357–360.
13. In *The Clansman*, Dixon renames Thaddeus Stevens "Austin Stoneman," but the introduction makes it quite clear that Stoneman is Stevens. In reality, Stevens did not do or say most of the things that Dixon claims.
14. Dixon, *The Clansman*, pp. 182–183.
15. For two discussions of anti-Catholicism in nineteenth-century America, see Jenny Franchot, *Roads to Rome: The Antebellum Protestant Encounter with Catholicism* (Berkeley: University of California Press, 1994) and D. G. Paz, *The Priesthoods and Apostasies of Pierce Connelly: A Study of Victorian Conversion and Anticatholicism* (Lewiston, N.Y.: E. Mellen Press, 1986).
16. Dixon, *The Clansman*, p. 371.
17. Tourgée, *A Fool's Errand*, pp. 139–140.
18. Tourgée, *Bricks without Straw*, pp. 134–135.
19. Tourgée, *Bricks without Straw*, p. 35.
20. Tourgée, *Bricks without Straw*, pp. 132–133.
21. See Olsen, *A Carpetbaggers' Crusade*, pp. 242–251.
22. Dixon, *The Leopard's Spots*, p. 45; Dixon regularly used the nose as a distinctive feature which revealed the differences between "true" southern whites and northern carpetbaggers or southern scalawags. For another instance, see Thomas Dixon, *The Sins of the Father: A Romance of the South* (New York: Grosset & Dunlap, Publishers, 1912), p. 71.
23. Dixon, *The Leopard's Spots*, p. 265.
24. Willie Lee Nichols Rose, *Race and Region in American Historical Fiction: Four Episodes in Popular Culture* (New York: Oxford University Press, 1979).
25. Dixon, *The Leopard's Spots*, p. 128.
26. Dixon, *The Clansman*, p. 338.

27. Dixon, *The Clansman*, p. 316.
28. Dixon described the Klan as a group of Christian ministers in some of his other Reconstruction novels. See, for example, Dixon, *The Sins of the Father*, pp. 22–23. With the resurgence of the Ku Klux Klan in the 1920s, Dixon began differentiating the Klan of the 1860s with the latter one. In fact, he despised the twentieth-century Klan because it targeted groups other than African Americans. For a discussion of this point, see Bloomfield, "Dixon's 'Leopard's Spots'," p. 395.
29. Tourgée, *A Fool's Errand*, p. 247
30. Tourgée, *A Fool's Errand*, p. 304; Tourgée, *Bricks without Straw*, p. 252.
31. Tourgée, *A Fool's Errand*, p. 104.
32. Tourgée, *A Fool's Errand*, p. 107.
33. Tourgée, *A Fool's Errand*, p. 142.
34. Tourgée, *Bricks without Straw*, p. 218.
35. Dixon, *The Leopard's Spots*, p. 38.
36. Dixon, *The Leopard's Spots*, p. 37.
37. Tourgée, *Bricks without Straw*, p. 184.
38. Tourgée, *Bricks without Straw*, p. 68.
39. Dixon, *The Leopard's Spots*, p. 284.
40. Dixon, *The Leopard's Spots*, pp. 439–440.
41. Tourgée, *Bricks without Straw*, p. 521.
42. Paul Laurence Dunbar, *The Fanatics* (New York: Dodd, Mead & Co., 1901), p. 90.

On Whose Responsibility?

The Historical and Literary Underpinnings of *The Red Badge of Courage*

— Roy Morris Jr. —

Few American novels are as famous—or mysterious—as Stephen Crane's *The Red Badge of Courage*. From the day it was first published in October 1895, the novel has been justly praised for its vivid battle scenes, penetrating psychological insights, and sepia-tinged historical accuracy. So powerful are the novel's effects that one Civil War veteran, a Union colonel, claimed to have served with the author at the Battle of Antietam in 1862—nine years before Stephen Crane was born.[1]

How was it possible for a twenty-two-year-old New Jersey bohemian, who freely admitted that he had "never smelled even the powder from a sham battle," to have written about the Civil War with such seeming authority? The short answer is that Stephen Crane was a genius. The longer answer is that Crane, like all good historical novelists, did his homework. Far from "writing a story of the war on my own responsibility," as he told a friend, Crane based his novel on a variety of sources, both oral and written, including the accounts of Civil War veterans in his adopted hometown of Port Jervis, New York, and the firsthand experiences of his prep school history professor, a true veteran of the Battle of Antietam. In addition, Crane pored over volumes of *Battles and Leaders of the Civil War*, a collection of reminiscences by Union and Confederate veterans, as well as the fictional works of such former soldiers as John W. De Forest and Ambrose

Bierce. A closer look at Crane's sources makes it apparent that while he supplied the genius, many others supplied the "responsibility." This does not diminish in any way the author's astonishing literary achievement, but it does help to explain how Crane, in the words of Bierce, came to be "drenched with blood [although] he knows nothing of war." With apologies to William Randolph Hearst, Crane might almost have said, "You furnish the war, I'll furnish the pictures."[2]

The Red Badge of Courage made Stephen Crane famous, but he had already attained a certain notoriety within the closed world of the New York literary scene by virtue of his scandalous first novel, *Maggie: A Girl of the Streets.* In many ways, *Maggie* was even more remarkable than *The Red Badge of Courage*—Crane's self-appointed mentor, William Dean Howells, for one, always considered it a better novel. But *Maggie*, a scathing account of a young woman's descent into poverty, prostitution, and death, sold few copies, and its almost literally starving author was reduced to burning pages of the book in the fireplace of his Bowery apartment for warmth. Barely scraping by as a freelance journalist for various New York newspapers, Crane mordantly observed, "I'd sell my steps to the grave at ten cents per foot."[3]

In the winter of 1893, Crane dropped by the art studio of his friend Corwin Linson at the corner of Broadway and 30th Street. Linson supported himself by doing illustrations for magazines, and he avidly collected back issues of the leading journals of the day. ("Old magazines flew at me from bookstalls," he said in a phrase he might have borrowed from Stephen Crane.) On this March afternoon, the writer's attention was caught by a stack of *Century* magazines lying scattered on the floor. The magazine featured a popular, long-running series, *Battles and Leaders of the Civil War.* Crane had been entertaining thoughts of writing a war story of his own, "a potboiler, something that would take the boarding school element." He picked up an issue of the magazine—and the course of American literature changed. The more Crane read of the war, the more he became fascinated by the great event. "I got interested in the thing in spite of myself," he recalled, "and I had to do it my way." He began steeping himself in the legend and lore of the Civil War.[4]

It was an opportune time to begin such research. After nearly two decades of studiously avoiding the war—one modern historian has aptly termed the immediate postwar period "the Hibernation"—aging veterans had begun writing down their experiences for posterity. From the best-selling memoirs of Generals Ulysses S. Grant and William Tecumseh Sherman to the self-published reminiscences of the humblest private in the ranks, old soldiers were assiduously recording their memories. As Daniel Aaron has observed in his groundbreaking study of Civil War literature, *The Unwritten War:* "Anyone growing up in Crane's America could hardly have remained deaf to the echoes of that event. Memoirs, biographies, regimental histories, multivolumed chronicles, pamphlets, poems, diaries poured from the presses. The land swarmed with veterans more than ready to reminisce about the most exciting years of their lives."[5]

Crane, a congenital outsider with a great distrust of authority figures, naturally gravitated to the stories of the little men. One series of articles, in particular, caught his attention. It was the seven-part installment entitled "Recollections of a Private," by Warren Lee Goss of the 2nd Massachusetts Heavy Artillery. Goss had seen a good deal of action in the Civil War, and later had written a hair-raising account of his days as a prisoner at the infamous Confederate prison camp at Andersonville, Georgia. His series for *Century*, however, was more light-hearted, dealing mostly with his early days as a green recruit. Goss recounted the common experiences of incoming soldiers everywhere: the patriotic rush to the recruiting office, the tearful farewell to family and friends, the endless drilling and marching, the nervous waiting on the eve of battle. Modern critic Stanley Wertheim has pointed out that there was "a distinct literary convention for Civil War narratives" at the time; Wertheim said Crane might have used any number of different accounts as background for *The Red Badge of Courage*. However, the testimony of Linson—and of Crane himself, who personally thanked Mrs. Olive Brett Armstrong for loaning him her bound copies of *Battles and Leaders of the Civil War*—pinpoints Goss's work as an important primary source for the novel.[6]

A closer comparison of the two works strengthens that assumption. Readers of *The Red Badge of Courage* will remember the famous opening of the book, when the untried soldiers in the 304th New York Infantry of the Union Army of the Potomac, resting in their winter camp along the Rappahannock River in northern Virginia, are aroused by rumors of an impending battle: "The cold passed reluctantly from the earth, and the retiring fogs revealed an army stretched out on the hills, resting. As the landscape changed from brown to green, the army awakened, and began to tremble with eagerness at the noise of rumors." In the second installment of "Recollections of a Private," Goss remarks similarly that "in a camp of soldiers, rumor, with her thousand tongues, is always speaking. The rank and file and under-officers of the line are not taken into the confidence of their superiors. Hence the private soldier is usually in ignorance as to his destination. What he lacks in information is usually made up in surmise and conjecture; every hint is caught at and worked out in possible and impossible combinations. He plans and fights imaginary battles." This is precisely what the young protagonist in *The Red Badge of Courage*, Henry Fleming, finds himself doing in response to the rumors. Indeed, the central issue in the book involves the interior struggle that Henry fights with himself over the question of his moral and physical courage. In chapter 1 he is pictured lying on his bunk "in a little trance of astonishment. . . . He tried to mathematically prove to himself that he would not run from a battle. Previously he had never felt obliged to wrestle too seriously with this question. In his life he had taken certain things for granted, never challenging his belief in ultimate success, and bothering little about means and roads. But here he was confronted with a thing of moment. It had suddenly appeared to him that perhaps in a battle he might run. He was forced to admit that as far as war was concerned he knew nothing of himself." Goss admits to having similar doubts. "It is common to the most of humanity," he notes, "that, when confronted with actual danger, men have less fear than in its contemplation. . . . I have found danger always less terrible to face than on the night before the battle."[7]

There are other notable similarities between the two works. Both Goss and Crane describe the new recruits bidding farewell to their former schoolmates. In Goss's account, it is the students who are fatuous—"All our schoolmates and home acquaintances 'came slobbering around camp,' as one of the boys ungraciously expressed it. We bade adieu to our friends with heavy hearts." Crane, by contrast, stresses Henry's ridiculous self-inflation: "From his home he had gone to the seminary to bid adieu [note the identical phrasing in both accounts] to many schoolmates. They had thronged about him with wonder and admiration. He had felt the gulf now between them and had swelled with calm pride. He and some of his fellows who had donned blue were quite overwhelmed with privileges for all of one afternoon, and it had been a very delicious thing. They had strutted." Both accounts feature, as well, scenes where the soldiers' mothers send them off to war with a jar of preserves (Henry's mother packs him "a cup of blackberry jam" in his bundle). It can be argued that such gifts were commonplace in rural nineteenth-century America, but it is upon such small but authentic touches that the novelist builds a plausible narrative, and that is what Crane takes from Goss's "Recollections."[8]

Other similarities in the two accounts include descriptions of the long tedium of drill, the soldiers discarding their heavy backpacks during the march to the battlefield, and their first encounter with a dead man in the field. Again, the differences are as instructive as the similarities. In Goss's account: "We came upon one of our men who had evidently died from wounds. Near one of his hands was a Testament, and on his breast lay an ambrotype picture of a group of children and another of a young woman. We searched in vain for his name." In *The Red Badge of Courage*, Henry's regiment marches past a dead Confederate skirmisher: "He lay upon his back staring at the sky. He was dressed in an awkward suit of yellowish brown. The youth could see that the soles of his shoes had been worn to the thinness of writing paper, and from a great rent in one the dead foot projected piteously. . . . The ranks opened covertly to avoid the corpse.

The invulnerable dead man forced a way for himself. The youth looked keenly at the ashen face. . . . He vaguely desired to walk around and around the body and stare; the impulse of the living to try to read in dead eyes the answer to the Question." Goss's account is straightforward, matter-of-fact; one recalls Crane's complaint while reading *Century* magazine: "I wonder that some of these fellows don't tell how they *felt* in those scraps. They spout eternally of what they *did*, but they are emotionless as rocks."[9]

Crane's emphasis in his work is entirely upon how, and what, Henry is feeling at any particular time. This is particularly true in the most famous set-piece of the novel, when the youth comes upon a decaying body lying undisturbed in a cathedral-like clearing in the forest. It is, in a way, the heart of the novel, where Henry confronts his deepest fears, and Crane lavishes upon the scene all his remarkable descriptive powers:

> At length he reached a place where the high, arching boughs made a chapel. He softly pushed the green doors aside and entered. Pine needles were a gentle brown carpet. There was a religious half light. Near the threshold he stopped, horror-stricken at the sight of a thing. He was being looked at by a dead man who was seated with his back against a columnlike tree. The corpse was dressed in a uniform that once had been blue, but was now faded to a melancholy shade of green. The eyes, staring at the youth, had changed to the dull hue to be seen on the side of a dead fish. The mouth was open. Its red had changed to an appalling yellow. Over the gray skin of the face ran little ants. One was trundling some sort of bundle along the upper lip. The youth gave a shriek as he confronted the thing. . . . He remained staring into the liquid-looking eyes. The dead man and the living man exchanged a long look. Then the youth cautiously put one hand behind him and brought it against a tree. Leaning upon this he retreated, step by step, with his face still toward the thing. He feared that if he turned his back the body might spring up and stealthily pursue him. . . . He imagined some strange voice would come from the dead throat and squawk after him in horrible menaces.[10]

Like all great creative artists, Crane first gets the physical details right, then uses those details in the service of a larger emotional truth. He doesn't care so much what Henry sees as how it makes him feel and, through those feelings, act. Some critics have complained that *The Red Badge of Courage*, judged strictly as a Civil War novel, is deficient in its historical scope. The main incidents in the book, says Daniel Aaron, "might have occurred at Sevastopol or Sedan. . . . Negroes and Lincoln and hospitals and prisons are not to be found in Crane's theater; these and other matters were irrelevant to his main concern—the nature of war and what happens to people who engage in it. . . . The war served only as his setting for an antiwar tour de force in which deluded people misread the laws of the universe and were overwhelmed." Crane would have shrugged off the first part of Aaron's criticism, but one imagines he would have agreed completely with the last. As he said himself about his earlier novel, *Maggie: A Girl of the Streets*, his overriding intent was to demonstrate that "environment is a tremendous thing in the world and frequently shapes lives." Still, he devoted a great deal of care toward getting the physical details of that environment right, whether it was a Civil War battlefield or a New York slum.[11]

Goss was not the only old soldier whose wartime memories Crane mined for his book. As a boy living for a time in Port Jervis, New York, he had listened avidly to the stories told by veterans sitting around the Orange County courthouse. Most of these men, as historian Charles LaRocca observes, had served in the 124th New York Volunteers, nicknamed the "Orange Blossoms." The regiment's first battle, a literal baptism of fire, was at Chancellorsville, Virginia, in May 1863. There, much like Crane's 304th New York, the regiment had marched, countermarched, and fought a desperate rearguard action near the Plank Road on the battlefield following the rout of the all-German XI Corps by Lt. Gen. Stonewall Jackson's Confederates. (Significantly, Henry encounters a terror-stricken German babbling, "Where de plank road," during his own panicky peregrinations.) Towards the end of the battle, the 124th New York had made a daring bayonet charge, breaking the enemy line and capturing a number of Rebel prisoners, another event paralleled in the novel. There was even a real-life Jim Conklin, Henry's doomed best friend, in the 124th New York, although unlike his fictional counterpart, James Conklin survived the war and returned to Orange County. It is tempting, but ultimately unknowable, to think that he might have been one of the old soldiers to whom young Stephen Crane listened.[12]

If there was any doubt that Chancellorsville was the battle depicted in *The Red Badge of Courage*, it was answered by the most authoritative source—the novelist himself—in a later short story, "The Veteran." In the story, an aged Henry Fleming recounts his wartime experiences for a group of listeners sitting on soap boxes in a country store. "Mr. Fleming," says one of the listeners, "you never was frightened much in them battles was you?" "Well I guess I was," Henry answers. "Pretty well scared, sometimes. Why, in my first battle I thought the sky was falling down. I thought the world was coming to an end. You bet I was scared. . . . The trouble was, I thought they were all shooting at me. Yes, sir, I thought every man in the other army was aiming at me in particular, and only me. It seemed so darned unreasonable, you know. I wanted to explain to 'em what an almighty good fellow I was, because I thought then they might quit all trying to hit me. But I couldn't explain, and they kept on being unreasonable—blim! blam! bang! So I run. . . . That was at Chancellorsville."[13]

Another firsthand source for *The Red Badge of Courage* was Crane's history teacher at Claverack College in upstate New York. Despite its name, Claverack College was actually a quasi-military academy, and Crane spent two years there—"the happiest period of my life," he later said—preparing for the entrance exam to the United States Military Academy at West Point. (He never took the test; his older brother William convinced him that there was no future for him in the military, since there would not be another war in his lifetime. William, of course, was wrong.) At Claverack, Crane wore the Civil War-era uniform required by the school and drilled with old muskets and bayonets salvaged from the war. He rose to the rank of cadet captain, and once berated an unfortunate underclassman who dropped his gun for being an "idiot" and an "imbecile." He displayed, said the victim of the parade-ground abuse, "a perfectly hen-like attitude toward the rank and file."[14]

Under Crane's hard-driving leadership, his company won the school's coveted Washington's Birthday award for close-order drill. One of the judges was the school's history teacher and resident Civil War hero, Brevet Brigadier General John Bullock Van Petten. "General Reverend" Van Petten, like Crane's own father, was an ordained Methodist minister. Besides teaching history and elocution, Van Petten presided over one of the tables in the school dining hall, where, one of his former students recalled, "he often recounted some of his war experiences [and] became much excited as he lived over the old days." It is not known whether Crane was one of Van Petten's lunchroom charges, but as one scholar has conjectured: "It seems certain that . . . Van Petten, who had real war anecdotes to tell, was exactly the sort of man to whom Crane would have been responsive. Under these circumstances . . . Crane would surely have disregarded no opportunity to absorb further the lore of the battlefield from this veteran whose eyes had witnessed the scenes he so eloquently described."[15]

As chaplain of the 34th New York Infantry and lieutenant colonel of the 160th New York Infantry, Van Petten had seen action in a number of Civil War battles, including such hard-fought scrapes as Williamsburg, Fair Oaks, Malvern Hill, Second Manassas, Antietam, Port Hudson, and Winchester. Crane scholar Lyndon Upson Pratt has argued that Van Petten's experience at Antietam, the bloodiest single day of the Civil War, directly influenced *The Red Badge of Courage*. According to Pratt, Van Petten personally witnessed the rout of the 34th New York in the East Woods around Dunker Church at Antietam, including the death of the regimental color-sergeant and the rescue of the unit's flag by a young corporal (a similar episode near the end of *The Red Badge of Courage* marks Henry Fleming's transformation from coward to hero). Two years later, at the Battle of Winchester, Van Petten witnessed the rout of another Union regiment—this time not his own—and suffered a career-ending bullet wound to his leg. The general's biographer, Thomas F. O'Donnell, maintains that the latter battle made a deeper impression on Van Petten and, through him, on his students. There is, of course, no way of knowing what exactly Van Petten may have told Crane, but it is easy to connect the general's real-life regiment, the 34th New York, to Henry Fleming's fictional regiment, the 304th New York. All that's needed is an extra zero.[16]

Besides transmitting his own eyewitness experiences to Crane, Van Petten may also have put him on to an important literary source for *The Red Badge of Courage*. This was Union veteran John W. De Forest's 1867 novel, *Miss Ravenel's Conversion from Secession to Loyalty*, one of the very first fictional depictions of the war. Like Van Petten, De Forest was a Union infantry officer. He was also a friend and comrade of Van Petten's, having served with the reverend general in the Port Hudson campaign of 1862 and the Shenandoah Valley campaign of 1864. In his nonfiction account of his Civil War service, *A Volunteer's Adventures*, De Forest remembers Van Petten admiringly as "an officer of distinguished gallantry," yet sufficiently one of the boys to have run "foot races in his big boots with a private, to make the soldiers laugh at the unusual buffoonery." Again the evidence is circumstantial—Crane left behind few records of his outside reading—but as O'Donnell has suggested: "De Forest and Van Petten shared many adventures which the latter undoubtedly recalled later to student audiences that included Stephen Crane. Certainly a book from De Forest's pen . . . would have been strongly recommended by the history teacher who could vouch for the authenticity of the novel. . . . If Stephen Crane had never heard of De Forest, nor of *Miss Ravenel's Conversion*, before he came to Claverack in 1888, we may be certain that he heard of the man there, and that the novel was recommended to him by his history teacher, 'The Reverend General' John B. Van Petten."[17]

Perhaps inevitably given the period in which it was written, *Miss Ravenel's Conversion* is an odd mixture of traditional romance and hard-edged realism. The central focus of the book is an old-fashioned love triangle between a virtuous young woman, an honorable and adoring gentleman, and a dashing and colorful rogue. The lead characters are little more than stock figures: flighty heroine, solemn swain, caddish cavalier, avuncular father, interfering aunt. It is doubtful that the preternaturally modern Crane paid much attention to the book's main plot. What would have attracted his interest were the (comparatively few) scenes of Civil War combat that De Forest the veteran sprinkled through his narrative. Given his own novel's emphasis on cowardice and heroism, Crane would have been particularly interested in De Forest's depiction of skulking soldiers during the height of battle: "Grim faces turned in every direction with hasty stares of alarm, looking aloft and on every side, as well as to the front, for destruction. Pallid stragglers who had dropped out of the leading brigade drifted by . . . dodging from trunk to trunk in an instinctive search for cover. . . . One abject hound

. . . came by with a ghastly backward glare of horror, his face colorless, his eyes projecting, and his chin shaking. Colburne cursed him for a poltroon, struck him with the flat of his sabre, and dragged him into the ranks of his own regiment. . . . Further on, six men were standing in single file behind a large beech, holding each other by the shoulders." Compare this to a similar passage in *The Red Badge of Courage:* "The lieutenant of the youth's company had encountered a soldier who had fled screaming at the first volley. . . . The man was blubbering and staring with sheeplike eyes at the lieutenant, who had seized him by the collar and was pommeling him. He drove him back into the ranks with many blows. . . . Farther up the line a man, standing behind a tree, had had his knee joint splintered by a ball. Immediately he had dropped his rifle and gripped the tree with both arms. And there he remained, clinging desperately and crying for assistance that he might withdraw his hold upon the tree."[18]

There are other similarities between the two books. In one passage in *Miss Ravenel's Conversion*, the hero, Captain Colburne, relates a curious episode:

> I had just finished breakfast, and was lying on my back smoking. A bullet whistled so unusually low as to attract my attention and struck with a loud smash in a tree about twenty feet from me. Between me and the tree a soldier, with his great coat rolled under his head for a pillow, lay on his back reading a newspaper which he held in both hands. I remember smiling to myself to see this man start as the bullet passed. . . . The man who was reading remained perfectly still, his eyes fixed on the paper with a steadiness which I thought curious, considering the bustle around him. Presently I noticed that there were a few drops of blood on his neck, and that his face was paling. Calling to the card-players, who had resumed their game, I said, "See to that man with the paper." They went to him, spoke to him, touched him, and found him perfectly dead. The ball had struck him under the chin, traversed the neck, and cut the spinal column where it joins the brain, making a fearful hole through which the blood had already soaked his great-coat. It was the man's head, and not the tree, which had been struck with such a report. There he lay, still holding the New York Independent with his eyes fixed on a sermon by Henry Ward Beecher.[19]

In *The Red Badge of Courage*, Henry Fleming encounters a similar sight: "The captain of the youth's company had been killed in an early part of the action. His body lay stretched out in the position of a tired man resting, but upon his face there was an astonished and sorrowful look, as if he thought some friend had done him an ill turn." Such macabre sights were common on the battlefield, and Warren Lee Goss, in "Recollections of a Private," recounts yet another: "Advancing through the tangled mass of logs and stumps, I saw one of our men aiming over the branch of a fallen tree. . . . I called to him, but he did not turn or move. Advancing nearer, I put my hand on his shoulder, looked in his face, and started back. He was dead!—shot through the brain; and so suddenly had the end come that his rigid hand grasped his musket, and he still preserved the attitude of watchfulness—literally occupying his post after death."[20]

De Forest may even foreshadow Henry Fleming's famous wound, his ironic "red badge of courage," in another passage of his novel. Here, Captain Colburne witnesses another battlefield injury. "I had scarcely recovered myself when I saw a broad flow of blood stream down the face of a color-corporal who stood within arm's-length of me. I thought he was surely a dead man; but it was only one of the wonderful escapes of battle. The bullet had skirted his cap where the forepiece joins the cloth, forcing the edge of the leather through the skin, and making a clean cut to the bone from temple to temple. He went to the rear blinded and with a smart headache, but not seriously injured." Similarly, when Henry is wounded—actually, he is bashed on the head by another fear-crazed Union soldier—a friendly comrade checks his injury: "'Now Henry,' he said, 'let's have a look at yer ol' head.' The youth sat down obediently and the corporal, laying aside his rifle, began to fumble in the bushy hair of his comrade. . . . He drew back his lips and whistled through his teeth when his fingers came in contact with the splashed blood and the rare wound. 'Ah, here we are!' he said. . . . 'Jest as I thought. . . . Yeh've been grazed by a ball. It's raised a queer lump jest as if some feller had lammed yeh on th' head with a club. It stopped a-bleedin' long time ago. Th' most about it is that in th' mornin' yeh'll feel that a number ten hat wouldn't fit yeh. An' your head'll be all het up and feel as dry as burnt pork."[21]

Whether or not such similarities prove that Crane had read De Forest remains largely in the eye of the beholder. To be certain, De Forest read Crane. He observed to New York *Times* reporter Edwin Oviatt in 1898: "You have read Stephen Crane's *Red Badge of Courage?* It seems to me a really clever book, with a good deal of really first-class work in it. His battle scenes are excellent, though I never saw a battery that could charge at full speed across a meadow. His style is short, sharp, jerky; a style that never would have been tolerated in my day."[22]

One writer whose work Crane did read—we know because Crane tells us so—is Ambrose Bierce. Like De Forest, Bierce served in the Civil War—indeed, he probably saw more hard fighting than any other writer in American history, including his celebrated disciple Ernest Hemingway. He fought at Shiloh, Stones River, Chickamauga, Chattanooga, Resaca, Pickett's Mill, and Kennesaw Mountain, where he was almost killed by a Rebel bullet to the head. After the war, Bierce was one of the first writers to transmute his fighting experiences into fiction, producing a number of tense, terse, ironic short stories focusing typically on individual soldiers trapped in an unforgiving universe. Bierce, a noted cynic and misanthrope, did not think much of Crane—"the Crane freak," he called him, adding dismissively, "I had thought that there could be only two worse writers than Stephen Crane, namely, two Stephen Cranes." Crane, for his part, went out of his way to praise Bierce's writing, particularly his celebrated short story, "An Occurrence at Owl Creek Bridge." "That story has everything," Crane told a friend. "Nothing better exists."[23]

Bierce's influence is perhaps best seen in Crane's own short stories, particularly "A Mystery of Heroism," in which a Union private heroically fetches water for his comrades under fire, only to have two young officers carelessly drop the bucket he has so courageously brought them. In *The Red Badge of Courage*, the Biercian influence is seen primarily in the cool, somewhat sarcastic distance that Crane keeps from his main character, and in the overwhelming irony of Henry's being celebrated for a "red badge of courage" that he has received while running away. It should also be noted that many of Bierce's Civil War stories concern the problem of fear, either before or during battle. In one story, "One of the Missing," the protagonist actually dies of fright, while in two other stories, "A Tough Tussle" and "One Officer, One Man," the main characters die by their own hands rather than face the terrors of combat. A fourth story, "Killed at Resaca," concerns a young officer who dies performing an act of suicidal bravery after receiving a letter from his girlfriend accusing him backhandedly of cowardice. *The Red Badge of Courage*, of course, is concerned exclusively with Henry Fleming's internal and external struggles with his own fear.[24]

Other suggested sources for Crane's novel have ranged from the ridiculous to the sublime. It has been asserted, although never proven, that Crane was influenced by a popular 1887 novel, *Corporal Si Klegg and His "Pard,"* a fictionalized account of the Civil War service of Lt. Col. Wilbur F. Hinman of the 65th Ohio Infantry. Hinman's lengthy book—the length alone would seem to argue against anyone as restless as Stephen Crane wading through it—does include some similar episodes, including the familiar patriotic rush to enlist, the rigors and boredom of camp life, a bantering conversation with a Rebel picket, and the heroic rescue of a falling flag in the heat of battle. But Hinman's account is either broadly comic or sentimentally patriotic, two traits that are notably missing from *The Red Badge of Courage.* As Crane biographer John Berryman has observed, "Few of the correspondences rehearsed by H. T. Webster [author of an article on the subject in *American Literature*] look anything but inevitable." Moreover, Webster's contention that Crane modeled his use of vernacular after Hinman's rather less convincing depiction of countrified speech fails on two counts: first, there is no evidence that Crane ever saw Hinman's book, and second, he had already mimicked vernacular speech in *Maggie: A Girl of the Streets* and various newspaper articles, several years before he began writing *The Red Badge of Courage.*[25]

A far more artistic model for Crane's novel may have been Tolstoy's nonfiction book, *Sebastopol*, concerning the Russian siege during the Crimean War. Crane had read Tolstoy first while attending Syracuse University, and had remarked then that the Russian was "the world's foremost writer." After writing *The Red Badge of Courage*, he reiterated that view, telling William Dean Howells, "Tolstoy is the writer I admire most of all." Crane scholar James B. Colvert conjectures that Howells might have given the younger novelist a copy of *Sebastopol* when Crane called on him in the spring of 1893, a meeting at which Howells supposedly told a roomful of guests, "Here is a young writer who has sprung into life fully armed." There are a number of similarities between the two books, not altogether surprising, since they both concern young men at war. To Colvert, Tolstoy's primary influence on Crane was to demonstrate that "an appropriate dramatic method is to put the observing mind into the drama of experience—to describe the world not as it might be supposed to exist as objective reality but as it appears in the observer as a mental event. . . . [T]he crucial aim of the artist, as Tolstoy and Crane saw it, is to imagine and dramatize reality as emotional transmutations of experience."[26]

Ironically, eight years before *The Red Badge of Courage* appeared, John W. De Forest had praised Tolstoy to Howells for a different reason. "Nobody but he has written the whole truth about war and battle," said De Forest. "I tried and told all I dared, and perhaps all I could. But there was one thing I did not dare tell, lest the world should infer that I was naturally a coward, and so could not know the feelings of a brave man. I actually did not dare state the extreme horror of battle, and the anguish with which the bravest soldiers struggle through it." That task was left to Stephen Crane, and it was one at which he succeeded admirably, thanks in no small part to men such as Tolstoy, De Forest, Ambrose Bierce, Warren Lee Goss, and John Bullock Van Petten, men who, unlike Crane but very much like his fictional hero Henry Fleming, "had been to touch the great death, and found that, after all, it was but the great death."[27]

Notes

1. R. W. Stallman, *Stephen Crane: A Biography* (New York: George Braziller, 1968), p. 181. See also Sharon Carruthers, "'Old Soldiers Never Die': A Note on Col. John L. Burleigh," *Studies in the Novel* 10 (1978), pp. 158–160.
2. Quoted in Daniel Aaron, *The Unwritten War: American Writers and the Civil War* (New York: Oxford University Press, 1973), p. 211. Stephen Crane to Mrs. Olive Armstrong, April 2, 1893, in *The Portable Stephen Crane*, ed. Joseph Katz (New York: Penguin Books, 1969), p. 187. Bierce quoted in Linda H. Davis, *Badge of Courage: The Life of Stephen Crane* (Boston: Houghton Mifflin, 1998), p. 154. Joyce Milton, *The Yellow Kids: Foreign Correspondents in the Heyday of Yellow Journalism* (New York: Harper & Row, 1989), p. xii.

3. Corwin Linson, *My Stephen Crane* (Syracuse: Syracuse University Press, 1958), p. 13.
4. Linson, *My Stephen Crane*, pp. 36–37. Davis, *Badge of Courage*, p. 64.
5. Gerald F. Linderman, *Embattled Courage: The Experience of Combat in the Civil War* (New York: Free Press, 1987), p. 266. Aaron, *The Unwritten War*, p. 211.
6. Stanley Wertheim, "*The Red Badge of Courage* and Personal Narratives of the Civil War," *American Literary Realism* 6 (Winter 1973), p. 61.
7. Stephen Crane, *The Red Badge of Courage*, in *The Portable Stephen Crane*, pp. 189, 192, 197–98. Hereafter cited as *Red Badge*. Warren Lee Goss, "Recollections of a Private, II," *Century* 29 (December 2, 1884), p. 279. Goss, "Recollections of a Private, I," *Century* 29 (November 1, 1884), p. 108.
8. Goss, "Recollections of a Private, I," p. 108. *Red Badge*, p. 195.
9. Goss, "Recollections of a Private, III," *Century* 29 (March 5, 1885), p. 776. *Red Badge*, p. 212. Linson, *My Stephen Crane*, p. 37.
10. *Red Badge*, pp. 235–36.
11. Aaron, *The Unwritten War*, 211, 215. Stanley Wertheim and Paul Sorrentino, eds., *The Correspondence of Stephen Crane* (New York: Columbia University Press, 1968), p. 52.
12. Charles LaRocca, "Stephen Crane's Inspiration," *American Heritage* 42 (May–June, 1991), pp. 108–109. *Red Badge*, p. 257.
13. Stephen Crane, "The Veteran," in *The Portable Stephen Crane*, pp. 324–25. For a fuller discussion, see Harold R. Hungerford, "'That Was at Chancellorsville': The Factual Framework of *The Red Badge of Courage*," *American Literature* 34 (January 1963), pp. 520–531.
14. Wertheim and Sorrentino, *Correspondence of Stephen Crane*, p. 12. Harvey Wickham, "Stephen Crane at College," *American Mercury* 7 (March 1926), p. 294.
15. Lyndon Upson Pratt, "A Possible Source of *The Red Badge of Courage*," *American Literature* 11 (March 1939), pp. 1–10.
16. Pratt, "A Possible Source," pp. 4–5. Thomas F. O'Donnell, "John B. Van Petten: Stephen Crane's History Teacher," *American Literature* 27 (May 1955), pp. 196–202.
17. John W. De Forest, *A Volunteer's Adventures: A Union Captain's Record of the Civil War* (Baton Rouge: Louisiana State University Press, 1996), pp. 101, 182. Thomas F. O'Donnell, "De Forest, Van Petten, and Stephen Crane," *American Literature* 27 (January 1956), pp. 579–80.
18. John W. De Forest, *Miss Ravenel's Conversion from Secession to Loyalty* (New York: Penguin Books, 2000), pp. 250–51. *Red Badge*, p. 224.
19. De Forest, *Miss Ravenel's Conversion*, pp. 269–70.
20. *Red Badge*, p. 224. Goss, "Recollections of a Private, III," p. 776.
21. De Forest, *Miss Ravenel's Conversion*, pp. 251–52. *Red Badge*, pp. 264–65.
22. Edwin Oviatt, "J. W. De Forest in New Haven," New York *Times*, December 17, 1898. Reprinted in James W. Gargano, ed., *Critical Essays on John William De Forest* (Boston: G.K. Hall, 1984), p. 42.

23. For Bierce, see Roy Morris, Jr., *Ambrose Bierce: Alone in Bad Company* (New York: Crown, 1996). Ambrose Bierce, New York *Press*, July 25, 1896. Davis, *Badge of Courage*, p. 194.

24. Ambrose Bierce, *The Collected Short Stories of Ambrose Bierce* (Lincoln: University of Nebraska Press, 1970).

25. H. T. Webster, "Wilbur F. Hinman's *Corporal Si Klegg* and Stephen Crane's *The Red Badge of Courage*," *American Literature* 11 (November 1939), pp. 285–293. John Berryman, *Stephen Crane* (Cleveland: World Publishing Company, 1962), p. 79.

26. Wertheim and Sorrentino, *Correspondence of Stephen Crane*, 232. Berryman, *Stephen Crane*, pp. 54, 68. James B. Colvert, "Stephen Crane's Literary Origins and Tolstoy's *Sebastopol*," *Comparative Literature Studies* 15 (March 1978), pp. 74–75.

27. John W. De Forest, "Letter to Howells," *Harper's New Monthly Magazine* 74 (May 1887), p. 987. For Tolstoy's influence on Crane, see also J. C. Levenson, "Introduction: *The Red Badge of Courage*," in *The Works of Stephen Crane*, vol. 2, ed. Fredson Bowers (Charlottesville: University Press of Virginia, 1975), pp. xl–xlvi, liv–lxix.

PART III

"Let the Story Tellers Invent It All"

A Muckraker at Manassas

Upton Sinclair's Civil War Fiction

— Jessica A. Dorman —

A lifelong crusader for social justice, Upton Beall Sinclair died in 1968 at the age of ninety, the last and most prolific of the Progressive Era muckrakers. He published his first book in 1901 and his last—some eighty titles later—in 1962. Not until 1966 did poor health finally stanch the amazing flow of essays and letters that had long marked his presence on the American scene. Among Sinclair's works were more than fifty novels; a verse drama entitled *Hell;* a layman's guide to fasting; attacks on organized religion, alcohol, and the American university system; a treatise on psychic phenomena; four accounts of his 1934 foray into California state politics; two full-length memoirs; and biographies of O. Henry, Marie Antoinette, and Jesus.[1]

Despite the bulk and variety of his written output, Sinclair is remembered mainly for a single, youthful accomplishment: the publication, in 1906, of his controversial exposé novel, *The Jungle*. With its horrific descriptions of working conditions in the Chicago stockyards and the adulterated meat products emanating therefrom, *The Jungle* literally nauseated a nation. It also captured the attention of President Theodore Roosevelt, hastened the passage of landmark food and drug laws, and still remains the defining text of the muckraking movement, the only work of its genre still widely read today. Ironically, Roosevelt gave the movement its name and helped carry out many of its recommended reforms, without ever warming to Sinclair or his fellow muckrakers. "Some are Socialists, some are merely lurid sensationalists, but they are all building up a revolutionary feeling," the president said.

Because *The Jungle* is the best known of his novels, Sinclair is often identified merely as a chronicler of immigrant, working-class life. A quick perusal of his published fiction serves as an important corrective to that image. Far more typical than *The Jungle* are his novels purveying an "Americanized" brand of socialism, complete with American-born (and well-to-do) socialists. Prime examples are the novels that bookend *The Jungle*—*Manassas,* published in 1904, a story of the Civil War; and its sequel, *The Metropolis*, published in 1908. Stories of transplanted southerners, both novels draw heavily on Sinclair family lore, as the author made of his youth a working template, and discovered in socialism and soldiering a resolution for his youthful themes.

Descended on his father's side from the first governor of Louisiana and a long line of naval officers, Sinclair spoke proudly of belonging to a "pre-Revolutionary family."[2] By the time of his birth in 1878, the family had fallen on hard times. Upton Beall Sinclair, Sr., battled alcoholism all his life—this despite earnest prenuptial pledges of temperance to his intended, Priscilla Harden.[3] The Sinclairs shuttled between Baltimore and New York, moving from one shabby boarding house to another, their slum rounds interrupted occasionally by extended visits to wealthy Harden relatives. Their only child would later describe his boyhood as "a series of Cinderella transformations" marked by fluctuations in paternal solvency and sobriety. "No Cophetua or Aladdin in fairy-lore," he noted, "ever stepped back and forth between the hovel and the palace as frequently as I."[4]

Of the two environments, hovel and palace, it is the former that figures more prominently in Sinclair's memoirs. His two autobiographies, *American Outpost* and *The Autobiography of Upton Sinclair*, romanticize life among the lowly. Sinclair freely recalls skirmishes with bedbugs in Baltimore ("For thrills like this, wealthy grown-up children travel to the heart of Africa with costly safaris") and frolics on the sidewalks of New York ("I was one of Nature's miracles, such as she produces by the millions in tenement streets—romping, shouting, and triumphant, entirely unaware that their lot is a miserable one").[5] Misery, when it does intrude upon young Upton's consciousness, intrudes only on "palace" grounds. Even as a child, the author claims, he noticed the "atmosphere of pride and scorn, of values based upon material possessions" that enveloped his wealthy relatives. "I do not know how I came to hate it," he concludes, "but I know that I hated it with blazing fury from my earliest days."[6]

In 1892, Sinclair enrolled as a "sub-freshman" at the College of the City of New York.[7] Founded in 1847, City College charged no tuition and opened its doors to students barred by monetary or ethnic considerations from more elite institutions of higher learning. The "campus" where Sinclair attended classes consisted of a single building at 23rd Street and Lexington Avenue, which had housed the school since 1849. He was, in his own estimation, "a tiny chap in short pants and a shirtwaist, noisy and fond of jokes, with no smallest trace of that dignity which should have gone with the collegiate rank and station."[8] What he lacked in dignity, however, he made up for in fiscal responsibility. As "family fortunes happened to be at a low ebb," he set to work writing jokes for the comic press. For the next decade, he would support both his parents and himself with hackwork, producing under a variety of pen names a virtual storehouse full of puns and potboilers "equal in volume to the works of Walter Scott."[9] "My jokes became an obsession," Sinclair writes in his autobiography. "While other youths were thinking about 'dates,' I was pondering the jokableness of Scotchmen, Irishmen, Negroes, Jews. I would take my mother to church, and make up jokes on the phrases in the prayer-book and hymn-book. I kept my little note-book before me at meals, while walking, while dressing, and in college if the professor was a bore. I wrote out my jokes on slips of paper, with a number in the corner, and sent them in batches of ten to the different editors, and when they came back with one missing, I had earned a dollar."[10] In 1901, Sinclair published his first serious novel, *Springtime and Harvest*, under his own name. The book flopped. In 1902, he converted to socialism.

Sinclair's conversion came at a time when socialism was enjoying peak levels of popularity in America, but also engendering widespread distrust. Estimates of party loyalty vary: local and national counts of Socialist Party members, for example, fail to register those who could not afford to pay dues. The national party polled more than one million votes in the 1912 presidential election, while counting approximately 150,000 actual members.[11] Shaken by the Haymarket bombing in Chicago in 1886 and the assassination of President William McKinley by homegrown anarchist Leon Czolgosz in 1901, many Americans blamed immigrants for the influx of "radical" ideologies. (Needless to say, the size and strength of the "foreign" element was vastly overestimated.)[12] Liberal authors—Israel Zangwill, Jacob Riis, and Mary Austin, among others—responded—with literary works that attempted to normalize the foreign-born and welcome them into American society. Others, Sinclair among them, responded alternatively with radical portraits of the native-born. Rather than "Americanize" immigrants, they sought to "Americanize" socialism.

Sinclair would later boast that he had "absorbed American history—about a thousand volumes" as background for writing *Manassas*. "I think that is one of the things that marks me from most Socialists, that I know the history of this country," he told a friend.[13] The Civil War provided him with a perfect setting for his reform fiction, for, as he explained, "by contemplation of the heroism and glory of the past, America was to be redeemed from the sordidness and shame of the present."[14] On the surface, *Manassas* reads like a standard *Bildungsroman:* a young man grows up, goes to war, and grows up some more. The traditional coming-of-age plot cloaks a less traditional message: *Manassas* is a treatise on the omnipresence of narrative. Sinclair's characters apprehend their lives through story; they learn to love and to hate by the standards set out in popular myth. Simultaneously constructing and retracting myths himself, Sinclair challenges the wisdom of inculcating patriotism as moral imperative—and, along the way, questions the function of narrative itself.

Manassas opens on an antebellum tableau: the grounds of a Mississippi plantation in springtime. An old man sits, shaded by magnolia trees, spinning tales of bygone wars. His grandchildren cluster around him, eager to hear—though they know the stories "quite by heart"—of grand heroics on Revolutionary battlefields. As Grandfather Montague speaks, history converges with romance:

> So as with swift words he poured out his eager tale, to the little group around him it was like the waving of an enchanter's wand. They sat lost to all things about them, tense and trembling, clutching each other's arms when he made a gesture, crying aloud when he gripped his hands.

The old man concludes with an entreaty. "My children," he says, "you may live ever so nobly, you may die ever so bravely, but you will do nothing too good for your country." Sinclair provides the Montagues with a distinguished pedigree and a history of military service. The ranks of Montague heroes include the first Sir Leslie Montague, "who had defended his king so bravely at Marston Moor"; the second Sir Leslie, who "had come to Virginia to better his fortune and had been a famous Indian fighter and afterward a judge"; Grandfather Montague, with his Revolutionary War service; Henry Montague, a Harvard graduate; and a Montague uncle "who had given his life that Texas might be free."[15]

The epigraph to *Manassas* expresses hope "[t]hat the men of this land may know the heritage that is come down to them."[16] How, Sinclair asks, is heritage transmitted? How resisted? Grandfather Montague's death early in the novel heralds the ascendancy of a new generation, for whom love of region supplants love of country. Grandchildren, not grandfather, will conjure up the next battlefield. First encountered "tense and trembling" in the novel's opening scene, the young Montagues (Randolph, Ralph, Ethel, and their cousin Allan) grow to adulthood in a perpetual state of over-stimulation. Their loyalty is the prize sought by rival tale-tellers, north and south.

Sinclair structures the plot of *Manassas* along the educational trajectory of Allan Montague. Born in Mississippi and raised alongside his cousins, Allan is transplanted, at age twelve, to the home of maternal relations in Boston. As a boy in Mississippi, Allan meets Jefferson Davis and William Lowndes Yancey; later, in Boston, he hears Frederick Douglass speak, and is introduced to Abraham Lincoln and Charles Francis Adams; he happens by Harpers Ferry during John Brown's raid, and he arrives in Charleston as the first shot is fired on Fort Sumter.

From his Uncle Otis, and his Otis cousins, Allan hears tales—familiar in outline, yet strangely altered in import—that compel him to reject "the heritage that is come down" to him on the Montague side. *Manassas* thus unfolds as a conversion narrative: a chronicle of Allan's journey from south to north, and sin to salvation, with literature as precipitant.

For Allan, sentimental fiction, rather than scripture, provides a map to the conversion experience. Salvation follows hard upon reading—and "finding" himself in—*Uncle Tom's Cabin*. Growing up in the South, Allan had shared in the popular scorn for Stowe's "degrading negro sentimentalism." Once in Boston, however, his preconceptions falter. Surreptitiously, Allan buys the book and reads it in one "never-to-be-forgotten night." The story is familiar—but only to a point. Stowe paints a picture of the plantation life Allan knows and loves, but sets this picture in an unfamiliar and unflattering frame. As Allan reads, childhood certitudes recede, and "in the end he gave himself up to that story, and writhed and suffered, and turned away sobbing convulsively."[17]

Allan turns for guidance to his Uncle Otis, the abolitionist sage who functions, throughout, as an authorial spokesman. *Uncle Tom's Cabin* has left Allan hanging: what, he asks his uncle, happens next? The sequel to Stowe's novel, Otis explains, depends on the response of readers like Allan. Perhaps, Otis suggests, Allan will join the abolitionist brigade, "fighting slavery . . . for the wrong it does the white man."[18] Otis's remarks contain more than a tincture of racism, but they also—and, for present purposes, more importantly—contain the germ of Sinclair's philosophy on narrative, literary agency, and reform.[19] The goal of "story," Sinclair argues, is implication: binding readers or listeners into the plot, convincing them that outcome rests on audience participation. To resist a compelling narrative—as do those northern whites who deny accountability for slavery—is to evade duty. No crime, Sinclair suggests, trumps passivity.

As the novel continues, Allan reads pamphlets, attends lectures, forms opinions. Sinclair intrudes occasionally, to emphasize the perfidy of passivity and the power of popular literature. And then, after devoting more than three hundred pages to a celebration of stories and storytellers, from Grandfather Montague to Jefferson Davis to Frederick Douglass to Harriet Beecher Stowe, Sinclair pauses, in the book's final pages, and indicts the entire undertaking. Allan, now a young man of twenty-three, has enlisted in the Union army and finds himself surrounded by carnage at the first battle of Manassas. He watches his cousin Jack Otis die and witnesses the slaughter of Union troops. Gone is the "romance" and nostalgia of the book's opening, replaced by the sheer horror of war. Allan staggers away from the battlefield and, abruptly, the book ends.

War, Sinclair suggests, transcends the impedimenta of protagonist, plot, and conclusion. Stripped of possessions and personality, Allan stands alone, at Manassas, an individual without reference points. The novel's lack of closure challenges the reader to reassess the centrality of the individual in narrative. Although Sinclair would not strip the individual—through whom story may be transmitted, life perpetuated—of all power, he would question the assumption that national destiny may be determined by, or encapsulated in, the life story of any one person. Allan reaches maturity in *Manassas*, but the close of the novel finds him neither married nor dead, and utterly incapable of shaping or comprehending the events he witnesses. "What was a man?" Allan thinks, in the heat of battle.[20] Neither he, nor any storyteller, has the answer.

Sinclair originally intended *Manassas* to be the first of three Civil War novels, *Gettysburg* and *Appomattox* to complete the trilogy. Instead, *The Appeal to Reason* hired Sinclair to "do the same thing for wage slavery" that he had done for chattel slavery in *Manassas*. Selecting Chicago, the site of a recent stockyards strike, as his territory, Sinclair left his New Jersey farm for the Midwest in October 1904. Sinclair's first response to the Chicago strike, a manifesto, entitled "You Have Lost the Strike! And Now What Are You Going to Do about It?" appeared on the front page of *The Appeal to Reason* on September 17, 1904. "I went about, white-faced and thin, partly from undernourishment, partly from horror," he would recall in his autobiography. "It seemed to me I was confronting a veritable fortress of oppression. How to breach those walls, or to scale them, was a military problem." Infiltrating the meat-processing plants in the guise of a common workman, and scouring the district in the company of "lawyers, doctors, dentists, nurses, policemen, politicians, real estate agents—every sort of person," Sinclair breached the barricades and emerged with *The Jungle*.[21]

The Jungle appeared serially in *The Appeal to Reason* from February through November of 1905, was released the following February in book form, and brought its author fame, fortune, and utopia. With his newfound riches, Sinclair set out to establish a cooperative colony for "authors, artists, musicians, editors and teachers and professional men." Sinclair believed that in single-family homes, "[e]very person . . . lived his own little selfish life, wasteful, extravagant, and reactionary."[22] After several months of planning and location scouting, he purchased Helicon Hall, a former boys' school in Englewood, New Jersey, for $36,000. Set on nine-and-a-half acres overlooking the Hudson River, the main house featured a three-story glass-enclosed courtyard, an indoor pond, billiard and dining rooms, extensive living quarters, a dairy, and a poultry yard. Between November 1906, when the first colonists arrived, and March 1907, when a fire destroyed the building, more than seventy-five individuals made Helicon Hall their home. By the time Sinclair had settled insurance claims and sold off the property, much of his "first fortune" had dissipated. And so, eager to earn another, he set out to write a new best-seller.[23]

Some three years past, Sinclair had stranded young Allan Montague at Manassas, fully intending to return to him shortly. But rather than revisit historical terrain, Sinclair—his imagination, and reputation, now grounded in the present day—opted to set his Civil War sequel in twentieth-century New York.[24] As *The Metropolis* opens, Allan Montague, Jr., a young lawyer from Mississippi, moves to Manhattan and attends a meeting of the "Loyal Legion," Civil War veterans who had fought with his late father. As in *Manassas*, narrative and nostalgia (for war, glory, and honor) permeate the book's opening pages. Allan listens while an old soldier recites his "Recollections of Spotsylvania." He watches the reactions of the legionnaires: "While the Colonel read, still in his calm, matter-of-fact voice, you might see men leaning forward in their chairs, hands clenched, teeth set. They knew! They knew!"[25]

Upon leaving the meeting hall, Allan stumbles upon a socialist demonstration. He is in no mood to tolerate the disturbance. Flush with the Legion's "spirit of brotherhood and service" and associating such spirit with "democracy," Allan views socialism as an abomination. Yet he cannot help but notice that the street corner crowd is as stirred by oratorical attacks on "the system" as the Legion had been by "Recollections of Spotsylvania." And in time, as the novel unfolds, young Allan finds himself drawn into the radical fold.

Like *Manassas*, *The Metropolis* establishes itself as a narrative about the allure and divisiveness of narrative. Similar in their concerns, the two novels diverge in their conclusions. Whereas the former counsels against placing one's faith in any one tale or teller, the latter takes no such cautions. Young Allan finds the answer that his father, struck down at Spotsylvania, never had a chance to find—socialism.

Most critics have seen *The Metropolis* as a corrective to *The Jungle*, an effort to prove that Mississippi yields socialist converts as readily as Lithuania. Placed in its Civil War context, however, the novel's attempt to Americanize socialism appears less crude. Socialism, Sinclair suggests, is the true legacy of Spotsylvania, the only story that makes heroes of both street corner agitators and members of the Loyal Legion. Near the start of *The Metropolis*, one of Allan's companions observes that socialism may bring on "another civil war." Allan's initial dismay transmutes, by novel's end, into anticipation. He is ready and eager for battle. So, too, was Sinclair. Over the course of a long and multifaceted career, he would continue to remind American readers of the necessity of conflict. The location of the battlefield might shift—from the plantations of the Old South to the meat-packing plants of Chicago to the penthouses of Manhattan—but the battle, and the stories, would persist.

Notes

1. For a comprehensive list of Sinclair's writings, both published and unpublished, see the two excellent bibliographies compiled by Ronald Gottesman: *The Literary Manuscripts of Upton Sinclair* (Columbus: Ohio State UP, 1972) and *Upton Sinclair: An Annotated Checklist* (Kent: Kent State UP, 1973).
2. Sinclair's personal papers are divided into six collections at Indiana University's Lilly Library. In these papers, Sinclair traces his ancestry to Edward I, King of England. For this and other biographical material, see Box 1, Folder 1, Sinclair Papers I, Bloomington; see also Sinclair, Preface to "Theirs Be the Guilt," Box 4, Sinclair Papers IV, Bloomington.
3. Leon Harris, *Upton Sinclair: American Rebel* (New York: Thomas Y. Crowell, 1975), p. 98; William A. Bloodworth, Jr., *Upton Sinclair* (Boston: Twayne, 1977), p. 16; Bloodworth, "The Early Years of Upton Sinclair: A Study of the Development of a Progressive Christian Socialist," diss., U of Texas, 1972, pp. 13–28; Sinclair, *Love's Pilgrimage* (1911; Pasadena: By the Author, 1926), pp. 3–9.
4. Sinclair, *American Outpost* (New York: Farrar and Rinehart, 1932), p. 13.
5. Sinclair, *American Outpost*, pp. 4, 24.
6. Sinclair, *American Outpost*, pp. 13–17.
7. Box 1, folder 2, Sinclair Papers I, Bloomington.
8. Sinclair, *American Outpost*, pp. 31–32.
9. Sinclair, *The Autobiography of Upton Sinclair* (New York: Harcourt, Brace & World, 1962), p. 51.
10. Sinclair, *American Outpost*, p. 49.
11. Ira Kipnis, *The American Socialist Movement: 1897–1912* (New York: Monthly Review Press, 1952), pp. 5, 335–369.
12. Paul Avrich offers a corrective in *The Haymarket Tragedy* (Princeton: Princeton UP, 1984), in which he traces the American heritage of several Haymarket suspects.
13. Sinclair to Frank Harris, 10 September 1917, Sinclair Papers II, Bloomington.
14. Sinclair, *Autobiography*, p. 92.
15. Sinclair, *Manassas* (New York: Macmillan, 1904), pp. 3–14.
16. Sinclair, *Manassas* [epigraph].
17. Sinclair, *Manassas*, pp. 57–61.
18. Sinclair, *Manassas*, p. 71.
19. Sinclair's working-class sympathies did not translate easily across racial lines; *Manassas*, with its Southern setting, is more telling on this account than any of Sinclair's other early novels. Revealing, perhaps, more than he intended to in a 1917 letter, Sinclair mused that "If the civil war had not been fought out, if Horace Greeley and

the other pacifists had been able to call a truce, the chances are a hundred to one that I today should be a slave owner and a pro-slavery propagandist (Sinclair, "Letter of Resignation," 17 July 1917, printed in *Chicago Sunday Tribune*, 22 July 1917, 8: 8.)

20. Sinclair, *Manassas*, p. 404.
21. Sinclair, *American Outpost*, pp. 153–154.
22. Sinclair, *American Outpost*, pp. 177–188; see also Margaret Brown, "Not Your Usual Boardinghouse Types: Upton Sinclair's Helicon Home Colony, 1906–1907," diss., George Washington U, 1993, p. 43.
23. During his time at Helicon Hall, Sinclair wrote one new book, a work of "nonfiction" titled *The Industrial Republic*. In it, he predicted the winner of the 1912 presidential election (William Randolph Hearst over Roosevelt) and anticipated that a socialist revolution would follow shortly thereafter. Sinclair also published *A Captain of Industry* (December 1906) and *The Overman* (September 1907), both written years earlier, in the interval between *The Jungle* and *The Metropolis*. Sinclair, *American Outpost*, pp. 189–190; Harris, *Upton Sinclair*, p. 100; Gottesman, *Upton Sinclair: An Annotated Checklist*, pp. 34–38.
24. For a discussion of the Montague works, see Sinclair, "Preface" and "The Machine," in *Plays of Protest* (New York: Mitchell Kennerley, 1912).
25. The Montagues would appear in two additional works: a novel, *The Moneychangers* (1908), and a play, *The Machine* (1911). Sinclair, *The Metropolis* (1907; New York: Moffat, Yard, 1908), pp. 1–6.

Narrative Art and Modernist Sensibility in the Civil War Fiction of F. Scott Fitzgerald

— Marcia Noe and Fendall Fulton —

> We have learned that when Grant had decided to surrender his milkfed millions to Lee's starving remnants and the rendezvous was arranged at Appomattox Court House, Lee demanded that Grant put his submission into writing. Unfortunately, Grant's pencil broke, and removing his cigar from his mouth, he turned to General Lee and said with true military courtesy: "General, I have broken my pencil; will you lend me your sword to sharpen it with?" General Lee, always ready and willing to oblige, whipped forth his sword and tendered it to General Grant.
>
> It was unfortunately just at this moment that the flashlight photographers and radio announcers got to work and the picture was erroneously given to the world that General Lee was surrendering his sword to General Grant.
>
> The credulous public immediately accepted this story. The bells that were prepared to ring triumphantly in Loudoun county were stilled while the much inferior Yankee bells in Old North Church in Boston burst forth in a false paean of triumph. To this day the legend persists, but we of the Welbourne *Journal* are able to present to the world for the first time the real TRUTH about this eighty-year-old slander that Virginia lost its single-handed war against the allied Eskimos north of the Mason and Dixon line.[1]

This bogus newspaper report, which novelist F. Scott Fitzgerald persuaded the Baltimore *Sun* to dummy up as an article to send to his friends, is only one of many testaments to his lifelong fascination with the Civil War, an interest that has been well-documented by his biographers. Fitzgerald's southern sympathies were deep-rooted. His father was descended from an old Maryland family who could claim among its ancestors "The Star-Spangled Banner" lyricist Francis Scott Key, the author's namesake. Andrew Turnbull, whose own father was the Fitzgeralds' landlord in the 1930s, reports that Fitzgerald regaled him with the Civil War tales of his father, who reputedly rode with Colonel John Singleton Mosby's men and ferried Confederate spies across the river.[2] An entry in his *Ledger* for January 1902, suggests that Fitzgerald followed up his father's stories with some reading on his own: "He remembers Jack Butler, who had two or three fascinating books about the Civil War."[3]

During his teen years, Fitzgerald's enthusiasm for the Civil War and identification with the South did not diminish.[4] In 1911, he wrote and acted in a Civil War play, *Coward*, for St. Paul's Elizabethan Dramatic Club,[5] and in 1913 he enrolled in Princeton University, known as the southerner's northern university. Shortly after he did a stint in the army at Camp Sheridan, near Montgomery, Alabama, during World War I, Fitzgerald married Zelda Sayre, the town belle. A few years later, in a letter to Princeton classmate John Peale Bishop, Fitzgerald painstakingly pointed out errors of fact in Bishop's Civil War novel.[6]

Fitzgerald's interest in the Civil War did not wane as he matured. The specter of John Wilkes Booth haunted him all his life, perhaps because an ancestor by marriage on his father's side, Mary Surratt, provided the house in which the plot to assassinate Abraham Lincoln was hatched and later was hanged for her incautious hospitality.[7] As a teen Fitzgerald romanticized Lincoln's assassin, imagining in "The Room with the Green Blinds" (1911) that after he attacked Lincoln, the wounded Booth had been spirited away to a decaying mansion near Macon, Georgia. In 1935 Fitzgerald listed *Our American Cousin* as one of his ten favorite plays,[8] and in one of his last published stories, "The End of Hate," Fitzgerald imagines his protagonist unwittingly overhearing the Lincoln conspirators' final hurried meeting before the fatal event.

So perhaps it was only poetic justice that when he went to Hollywood to write for the movies, Fitzgerald was assigned to polish dialogue on the script of *Gone with the Wind*.[9] He also proposed a film script based in part on the Civil War exploits of one of his father's cousins.[10] Fitzgerald's mistress, Sheilah Graham, reported in her memoir of their time together, *Beloved Infidel*, that only after Fitzgerald was told that the pickets in the fence surrounding his Hollywood house resembled tombstones in a Confederate graveyard was he able to find it livable.[11]

For the past thirty years, literary scholars have traced the influence of Fitzgerald's obsession with the Civil War on his fiction, speculating about its significance as a matrix for theme and character. C. Hugh Holman asserts that the central image in Fitzgerald's southern stories is that of the southern belle. Sally Carrol Happer, Nancy Lamar, and their ilk "are the embodiments of a tradition that stretched back before the Confederacy and that enchanted and hypnotized men for a century, permanent embodiments of the dream of beauty and youth and the romantic aspiration of the aggressive male."[12] Such women, regardless of their geographical provenance, would preoccupy Fitzgerald throughout his career.

Scott Donaldson attributes Fitzgerald's "romance with the South" largely to his relationship with his southern-born wife and father. Donaldson finds that romance playing itself out in several stories that oppose the values and temperament of a young man from the North with those of a southern belle. He points out that the most significant story of this group, "The Ice Palace," focuses on just such a character, Sally Carrol Happer, who gains the audience's sympathy when her warm effusiveness is juxtaposed with her fiancé's cold intelligence and drive. Donaldson sees a developing complexity in Fitzgerald's portrayal of this Zelda-like character, pointing out that as Fitzgerald continued to write about the South in his Tarleton trilogy, he portrayed her as increasingly self-centered, irresponsible, fickle, and artificial, as exemplified by Nancy Lamar in "The Jelly Bean" and Ailie Calhoun in "The Last of the Belles." These characters, says Donaldson, reflect Fitzgerald's gradual disillusionment with the South and his beautiful southern wife.[13]

P. Keith Gammons links Fitzgerald's southern belle to the mythology of the Lost Cause, arguing that this character type becomes a medium through which the Old South can be constructed as the epitome of beauty, honor, and grace.[14] Like Donaldson, Gammons shows that Fitzgerald's disillusionment with the myth of the Lost Cause increased as his relationship with Zelda became more problematic. This disenchantment with the South became a synecdoche for the larger failure of the American Dream in *The Great Gatsby*, a novel in which a beautiful and charming southern belle, Daisy Buchanan, is shown to be morally deficient.[15]

These readings of Fitzgerald's southern stories are similar to that of John Kuehl, who sees Fitzgerald's affinity for the Civil War and things southern as seminal in his depiction of North/South polarities in "The Ice Palace" as a cultural contest between the warmth and inertia of the South and the coldness and energy of the North. This North/South conflict comprises additional binaries—masculine/feminine, mature/childish, and canine/feline—that add complexity and energy to the story.[16] Robert Roulston also engages the dualities of Fitzgerald's fiction, arguing that for him the South is either a lovely, romantic land filled with tradition and time-tested values or a place of inertia, failure, decline, and decadence, and that both attitudes are present in Fitzgerald's uncompleted final novel, *The Last Tycoon*.[17]

But by far the most thorough analysis of Fitzgerald's fictional treatment of the South and the Civil War is that of Frederick Wegener, who, in "The 'Two Civil Wars' of F. Scott Fitzgerald," quotes from the author's letters to show that Fitzgerald himself was well aware that the Civil War was dichotomized in his mind as both a romantic and chivalric quest and the source of great carnage and cruelty.[18] Wegener argues that for Fitzgerald, the Civil War was a more complex conception than those binaries suggest:

> Complicating any attempt at such an appraisal, however, is the fact that there turn out to have been "two Civil Wars" for Fitzgerald in more ways than one, or more than one pair of Civil Wars: not only the Civil War of romance and of realism, but also the Civil War in the North and in the South, the Civil War as tragic or farcical, the Civil War in fact and in memory, and the Civil War as actuality and as represented or reconstituted in writing.[19]

Thus, the subject of Fitzgerald and the Civil War is rather well-trodden territory. However, the four works of Fitzgerald's short fiction that employ Civil War settings, plots, and characters have escaped extensive analysis. This oversight is somewhat understandable; two of them, "A Debt of Honor" (1910) and "The Room with the Green Blinds" (1911) are very short, simplistic tales that the teenaged Fitzgerald published in the St. Paul Academy literary magazine *Now and Then*. Besides this juvenilia, however, there are two later Fitzgerald stories, "The Night at Chancellorsville" (1935) and "The End of Hate" (1940). While not among the author's finest, when read against one another they illuminate the ways in which Fitzgerald's narrative technique developed over the three decades of his writing career and also the ways in which his vision matured as the romantic ideals of boyhood gave way to a modernist concept of the human condition as characterized by ambiguity, disjunction, fragmentation, instability, and chaos.

"A Debt of Honor"centers on a green private, Jack Sanderson, who falls asleep on sentry duty but later redeems himself heroically in battle. The bulk of Jack's characterization relies on action, "one-time" events that Fitzgerald makes crucial indicators of Jack's character.[20] These events, although indicative of Jack's character at the time they occur, do not enable a well-rounded characterization, since the reader has no basis for comparison outside the immediate action. We are perhaps less convinced of their significance and probability, since we must take the meaning of these events at face value. The linear events of the story in themselves do provide some points of comparison. For example, Jack's failure to stay awake at his post can be compared to his prior eagerness to volunteer for the position, and the reader may assume that Jack is too new to the perils of war to know better. Likewise, Jack's headlong dash into the "bullet swept clearing" can be compared to his inability to hold his position while on sentry duty, and the reader might see some character growth or maturation.[21] The summation of Jack's character comes many weeks later with his charge against the enemy who "have possession of a small frame house" in a strategic location.[22] Here Jack proves his worth and pays the debt that gives the story its name.

Through his actions, Jack is used to exemplify familiar ideas of heroism and valor in the context of war. The events that advance the plot are meant by Fitzgerald to illustrate Jack's outstanding qualities, which are perhaps less outstanding because of a lack of substantial reference points, such as development of additional characters and use of dialogue. Dialogue serves only three times to give voice to Jack's character. Our introduction to Jack Sanderson is his eager offer to volunteer for sentry duty, responding "me, me" to his captain's request.[23] This is one of two times that Jack speaks throughout the story. When Jack is called to see General Lee after having been saved from execution, he responds in an overly formal manner, which is meant to convey his appreciation of "a new found life." "General, the Confederate States of America shall never have cause to regret that I was not shot."[24] Jack expresses emotion exuberantly while "drawing himself up to his full height," a description of "external appearance" that joins with dialogue in this instance to denote an aspect of characterization.[25] The reader is provided with information about Jack's youth and social class as General Lee reviews the situation of Jack's punishment and decides that execution is too harsh a punishment for "not much of an offense."[26]

"A Debt of Honor" does not develop a sense of environment, except as it pertains to Jack's situation. Fitzgerald relies on the reader's familiarity with the Civil War, and little description of the environment is given through which the reader can frame Jack's characterization. The pointed assertion that "it was getting dark—very dark" as Jack takes his sentry post aids in the reader's understanding of Jack's compromised situation. This look at Jack's immediate surroundings falls short of being a "trait-connoting metonymy" because it is a temporary situation and not sustained but rather an explanation for Jack's faltering.[27] Furthermore, Jack's thoughts, or internal environment, at this point in the story can be seen to be caused or at least bolstered by the external environment. The narrator tells us that Jack "never quite knew how it came about" as he realizes that "'number six' was such a long post."[28] This insight falls short of describing Jack's character, partly because the narration maintains the distance of the third-person point of view and because it is an isolated insight that does more to explain an action and evoke sympathy than to offer a parallel or metonymy.[29]

Twenty-five years later, Fitzgerald resumed writing Civil War fiction. "The End of Hate" and "The Night at Chancellorsville, " where connections are discordant and unstable, show a more mature and complex world view than is seen in the earlier Civil War stories, which emphasized honor, heroism, and courage. The ambiguity and indeterminacy typical of modernist texts dominate the later stories, conveyed through plot, with contested territory changing hands repeatedly as control vacillates between Union and Confederate forces, as well as through theme: identity is portrayed as unstable in contrast to the clear distinctions between Yankee and Rebel, comrade and enemy, that are made in the earlier tales.

"The End of Hate," finally published in *Collier's* in 1940, a few months before Fitzgerald's death and after many rejections from other magazines, once again features a Confederate protagonist, Tib Dulany, who is heroic and brave. But in this story Fitzgerald utilizes multiple environments not only to inform setting, but also to expand Tib's characterization through a sense of place. Setting is important in this story, since Dr. Pilgrim, his sister Josie, and Tib must cover a fair amount of ground to arrive at various key points in the plot. Not only does setting change; it is also used to frame characterization, as in the following description, which occurs when Josie and Dr. Pilgrim have been escorted to the southern Maryland farmhouse that shelters members of the Army of Northern Virginia who have suffered a disappointing battle against the Union's army:

> Suddenly Josie had a glimpse at the Confederacy on the vine-covered veranda. There was . . . a spidery man in a shabby riding coat adorned with faded stars. . . . Then a miscellany of officers, one on a crutch, one stripped to his undershirt with the gold star of a general pinned to a bandage on his shoulder. There was disappointment in their tired eyes. Seeing Josie, they made a single gesture: Their dozen right hands rose to their dozen hats and they bowed in her direction.[30]

The scene expands the focal point of the story for a moment and provides a larger context in which to place the protagonists. This is Fitzgerald's Confederacy—steeped in masculine tradition, quintessentially southern and genteel, yet also stripped down, shabby, and bandaged. It is a conceptualization in which romanticism and realism coexist to tragic effect, one that illustrates the dichotomy of the Civil War as perceived by Fitzgerald. This duality is crucial to understanding Tib, and the description helps inform both the reader's and Josie's positive perception of him.

Fitzgerald continues developing Tib's persona, layering elements that define him as poet, soldier, and displaced southerner. We learn that Tib had a life outside the Civil War, one that ended four years prior to the action of the story, and one that he attempts to continue after the war. Tib's history makes him a more complex and believable character than Jack in "A Debt of Honor." We learn, for example, that Tib wrote verse before becoming a soldier and thus his desire to "write a few lines sometime to express [his] admiration" of Josie is believable and leads the reader towards a better understanding of his temperament, which is one that is partly at odds with being a soldier.[31] This is made clearer when Tib expresses his dislike of shooting from ambush when he and Wash are confronted with a line of Union cavalry advancing on the farmhouse. The narrator's provision that "even after four years, Tib hated to shoot from ambush" puts the immediate situation in a larger context and allows us to see that this is not an isolated event but one that is consistent with Tib's character over an extended period of time.[32]

Since the story also jumps forward in time, we see how Tib must integrate his past with the present. This integration proves difficult since Tib's thumbs had to be amputated after he was hung by them when captured by Union troops; therefore, he cannot use the skills of his prewar life in his postwar life. Tib's plight reflects Fitzgerald's conceptualization of the instability that characterized the immediate period following the war, when northerners and southerners alike reshuffled their lives in order to move forward. Tib's postwar situation reflects a social problem: "his story was the story of men who have fought in wars. . . .[Tib and others like him] were a ruined lot."[33] Tib's mutilation marks him, and he cannot escape his new postwar identity. Tib's immediate response to the situation is revenge, until Josie offers a more conciliatory one: "To get a fresh start one had to even things up. Spew forth in a gesture the hate and resentment that made life into a choking muddle."[34]

The most difficult test of Tib's ability to forget the past comes when he sees Josie after he has ridden into Washington after the war. For Tib, Josie is symbolic of "those old nightmare hours. . . . And this had made her beauty a reminder of cruelty and pain."[35] Tib reflects on past experiences in such a way that the past and present are juxtaposed, heightening the reader's sense of his despair. Not only has Josie become symbolic of Tib's suffering, she is also indicative of a hopeful future promised to the victors of the war: "Her beauty had not gone unnoticed in Washington. She had danced at balls with young men on government pay, and now in this time of victory she should be rejoicing."[36] Fitzgerald uses Josie's appearance to reflect the good fortune of the victorious and to contrast the devastation with which Tib wrestles. She is "more beautiful than Tib had remembered. She was a ripe grape, she was ready to fall for the shaking of a vine."[37] On the other hand, Josie's inner landscape, specifically her heartache, evokes what, at least to Fitzgerald, seems to be at stake for a deeply divided nation: "[S]he had seen the Glory of the Lord hung up by the thumbs—and then left her heart in the street in front of this house eight months ago."[38] Josie, like Tib, has "lived between two worlds" that continue to be at odds until the past and present are reconciled at the end of the story.[39]

Where romanticism and suffering intersect in Josie and Tib, the sharply drawn parameters of North and South begin to break down. This intersection speaks to the dichotomization of the Civil War in Fitzgerald's mind as encompassing both romantic and violent elements. Josie's and Tib's need to find indisputable commonality supplants the polarization imposed by the conflict. This commonality, which Fitzgerald terms "human interest," is literally lifesaving.[40] It also indicates an artificiality inherent in identities imposed by the Civil War. This sentiment is reiterated when Tib turns to Josie after they have run away to ask, "What are you?" Josie replies, "Just another human being."[41]

The lines of distinction between Tib and Josie, North and South are further obliterated when Josie rescues Tib and they run away. After Josie has found a doctor to treat Tib and before Tib knows that his thumbs have been amputated, they stop to rest; the setting here signifies their blurred identities:

> Before they got into the buggy, Josie turned to him suddenly and for a moment they faded into the sweet darkness, so deep that they were darker than the darkness—darker than the black trees—then so dark that when she tried to look up at him she could only look at the black waves of the universe over his shoulder and say, "Yes, I'll go with you if you want—anywhere. I love you too."[42]

The universe, a symbol of infinite possibility, a blank slate in effect, trumps socially imposed differences that serve to isolate people from one another. In the dark, when nothing is distinct or sharply delineated, Josie and Tib are freed from the constraints of social identity. They only exist in this moment, to love each other, to blend together against the backdrop of the universe, the great equalizer. This image is at the heart of what is at stake in this story. In and of itself, it is quintessential romanticism. When viewed against the backdrop of the story's context, however, its impermanence indicates that balance must be achieved between this harmony and the discordant social world.

"The Night at Chancellorsville" reflects a similarly realist and modernist sensibility. Indeterminacy figures prominently in the story, in which the passengers on the train never really know which side is in control. Both Union and Confederate soldiers board the train, causing confusion and alarm, as the battle outside shifts again and again. In the context of this famously chaotic battle, Fitzgerald deals with socially relevant issues of class, gender, and cultural values. This story focuses not on a valiant soldier, but on a prostitute named Nora who is traveling by train from Philadelphia to Virginia with a number of her co-workers to minister to Union troops. As in "The End of Hate," the Civil War in "The Night at Chancellorsville" is notably different from that of Fitzgerald's early stories. This Civil War is gritty, noisome, and hard-edged, a far cry from the romantic backdrop of Jack Sanderson's heroic deeds in "A Debt of Honor."

Fitzgerald gives more importance to Nora's experiences on the train than to the events of the battle occurring outside the train, using the battle as backdrop for Nora's experiences and focalizing the Civil War through Nora's unique perspective. Nora relates her experiences to a man, presumably a client, to whom she says, "You only want to talk about the war, like all you men. But if this is your idea of what a war is—."[43] Clearly, Nora has different ideas about war than those promoted by the mainstream culture. Fitzgerald sets up this contrast by juxtaposing her characterization with social norms and assumptions pertaining to the Civil War. Immediately we are tipped off that this will not be a typical war story of valor and heroism.

As in "The End of Hate," the polarizing effect of socially prescribed identities is prevalent, and Fitzgerald contrasts Nora's character with the accepted social norms as they are represented by other characters in the story. On the surface, her view of the war is characterized by an ignorant detachment. She opens her account of events by saying that she "didn't have any notion what [she] was getting into."[44] This aspect of Nora's character reveals her status as "the other"—Nora does not display attitudes typical of members of higher social classes, as represented by the rich women or the soldiers on the train. Her emotional remoteness from the war is one aspect of this "otherness": "After *this* ride I don't care who wins."[45] Furthermore, Nora is only involved out of necessity: "[W]e've got to eat this summer."[46] Later in the story, a collective cry of outrage reveals the indignation of the sex workers at having been dragged into a perilous situation when a soldier threatens to throw them off the train to make room for the wounded: "Hey! We didn't come down to fight in any battle!" to which the soldier replies, "It doesn't matter what you came down for—you're in a hell of a battle."[47] One effect of this distance or lack of awareness on Nora's part is a deglorification of the Civil War.

The decay of the train is further evidence of this deglorification. Fitzgerald focuses on the interior of the train. He gives the setting such a strong sense of place that it plays an important part in constructing the sense of the story. Nora's displeasure at these surroundings is further evidence of her alienation from a war that seems removed or irrelevant to the daily vicissitudes of her life. Whereas Nora is "used to traveling nice," the train is "smoky and full of bugs."[48] The train's environment also reflects the larger context of the war, where provisions are limited. Nora has no water and no food except leftover bread and sausage. The smoky, rocking train car nauseates Nora and her colleagues. The passengers on the train are unable to see anything because of the mist outside. Other details, such as the bullet hole in the window, as well as the sounds of horses galloping and gunshots echoing, give a fragmented sense of what is happening outside the train.[49] (At one point, Nora is awakened by what she first perceives to be a storm but is actually cannon fire.)

The limited sensory perception of what is happening outside the train parallels the discord prevalent inside it. The action that occurs inside the train comprises personal, one-on-one interactions that emphasize the instability of identity. Officers don't look like dashing cavaliers; they are dirty, unkempt, mutilated, drunk, and obnoxious, like the one Nora meets on the train who tells her, "Maybe I'd be more pretty for you if I hadn't lost an eye at Gaines' Mill."[50] The prostitutes are repeatedly addressed as "ladies" but treated as whores by some of the soldiers, who inform the other passengers that "[y]ou're in terrible company, but we'll be there in a few hours."[51] This crisis of identity comes to a head when one officer tries to remove the prostitutes from the train car so that it can be used for the wounded, while another opposes him, stating, "These are northern women, after all," while his antagonist retorts, "These are—."[52] This interchange suggests that, at least from one perspective, Nora is expendable because her social status is marginal. Beginning with the story's title, which alludes to the battle in which Confederate General Thomas J. "Stonewall" Jackson was mistaken for a Union officer and fatally shot by his own men, the notion of identity is interrogated throughout the text. Indeed, as James H. Meredith notes, Fitzgerald applies "a heavy coat of modernist irony to the Civil War in order to strip away the patina of chivalric romance found in most literary representations of it."[53]

Nora's perceptions of the other characters inform the story's sense of problematic identities. Nora perceives and treats the soldiers differently than she does many of the other characters. She accords them a different set of standards. Nora sees another side of the soldiers than do the rich women who have gone to tend them. The soldiers' identities are more complicated than conventional notions are able to convey. The soldiers fulfill a duty to country but also sleep with prostitutes. To her they are "a bunch of yella-bellies."[54] Nora's attitude toward the soldiers reflects aspects of her profession. She knows soldiers in a different way than "normal" people do. Nora describes the soldiers who pop in and out of the train in terms that echo elements of her profession. She says of one soldier, "he looked pretty messy as if he'd just crawled out of bed: his coat was still unbuttoned and he kept hitching up his trousers as if he didn't have any suspenders on."[55] When two Rebel soldiers board the train, Nora says:

> One had on a old brown blouse sort of thing and one had on a blue thing—all spotted—I know I could never of let *that* man make love to me. It had spots—it was too short—anyway, it was out of style. Oh it was disgusting. I was surprised because I thought they always wore grey. They were disgusting looking and very dirty: one had a big pot of jam smeared all over his face and the other one had a big box of crackers.[56]

Her frank description jars with the common understanding of wartime hardships but echoes a familiar theme of indistinct identities. The soldiers are in various states of undress; their clothing indicates not the strict delineation of northern or southern identities but rather a state of chaos and ambiguity. At the heart of this chaos is the human condition, which Nora brings to light with her sympathetic statement, "They were just kids under those beards, and one of them tipped his hat or cap or whatever the old thing was."[57] Ultimately, what matters more than mere physical appearance is the flesh and blood hidden within a chaos of social identities.

Fitzgerald's Civil War stories put us in mind of the famous interchange between Nick Carraway and Jay Gatsby in *The Great Gatsby*. Nick says, "You can't repeat the past," and Gatsby immediately, almost desperately, replies, "Why, of course you can."[58] Like Gatsby, Fitzgerald approached the world with a "heightened sensitivity to the promises of life";[59] unlike Gatsby, he lived to experience the disillusionment, alienation, and dysfunction that characterize the modernist sensibility. While he wrote relatively few Civil War stories, his mature fiction reflects both attitudes; as his narrative skills matured, so did his world view. For Fitzgerald, as Faulkner's Gavin Stevens notes, "The past is never dead. It's not even past."[60] Fitzgerald viewed himself, his life, his family, his friends, and above all, his subject matter through the prism of American history, which inspired him with both a sense of romantic possibility and a keen awareness of its elusiveness, a tension that animates his best work.

Notes

"Narrative Art and Modernist Sensibility in the Civil War Fiction of F. Scott Fitzgerald," by Marcia Noe and Fendall Fulton, was previously published in volume 31 of *Midwestern Miscellany* (Fall 2003): pp. 53–71, which is published by the Society for the Study of Midwestern Literature.

1. Matthew J. Bruccoli, ed., *F. Scott Fitzgerald: A Descriptive Bibliography* (Pittsburgh: University of Pittsburgh Press, 1972), pp. 93–4.
2. Andrew Turnbull, *Scott Fitzgerald* (New York: Charles Scribner's Sons, 1962), pp. 5–6.
3. F. Scott Fitzgerald, *F. Scott Fitzgerald's Ledger: A Facsimile* (Washington: Bruccoli Clark, 1972), p. 156.
4. Turnbull, p. 41.
5. Turnbull, p. 42.
6. Andrew Turnbull, ed., *The Letters of F. Scott Fitzgerald* (New York: Charles Scribner's Sons, 1963), p. 163.
7. Turnbull, p. 6.
8. F. Scott Fitzgerald, "My Ten Favorite Plays," *New York Sun*, September 10, 1934, p. 19.
9. Jeffrey Meyer, *F. Scott Fitzgerald: A Biography* (New York: HarperCollins, 1994), p. 312.
10. Matthew J. Bruccoli, *F. Scott Fitzgerald: A Life in Letters* (New York: Charles Scribner's Sons, 1994), p. 430.

11. C. Hugh Holman, “Fitzgerald’s Changes on the Southern Belle: The Tarleton Trilogy,” in *The Short Stories of F. Scott Fitzgerald: New Approaches to Criticism*, ed. Jackson R. Bryer (Madison: University of Wisconsin Press, 1982), p. 56.
12. Holman, p. 61.
13. Scott Donaldson, “Scott Fitzgerald’s Romance with the South,” *Southern Literary Journal* 5, no. 2 (Spring 1973), pp. 3–17.
14. P. Keith Gammons, “The South of the Mind: The Changing Myth of the Lost Cause in the Life and Work of F. Scott Fitzgerald,” *Southern Quarterly* 36, no. 4 (Summer 1998), pp. 107–08.
15. Gammons, p. 109.
16. John Kuehl, “Psychic Geography in ‘The Ice Palace,’” in *The Short Stories of F. Scott Fitzgerald: New Approaches in Criticism*, ed. Jackson R. Bryer (Madison: University of Wisconsin Press, 1982), pp. 173–74.
17. Robert Roulston, “Whistling ‘Dixie’ in Encino: *The Last Tycoon* and F. Scott Fitzgerald’s Two Souths,” *South Atlantic Quarterly* 79, no. 4 (1980), pp. 355–56.
18. Frederick Wegener, “The ‘Two Civil Wars’ of F. Scott Fitzgerald,” in *F. Scott Fitzgerald in the Twenty-first Century*, ed. Jackson R. Bryer and others (Tuscaloosa: University of Alabama Press, 2003), p. 238.
19. Wegener, p. 239.
20. Shlomith Rimmon-Kenan, *Narrative Fiction: Contemporary Poetics* (New York: Methuen, 1983), p. 61.
21. F. Scott Fitzgerald, “A Debt of Honor,” in *The Apprentice Fiction of F. Scott Fitzgerald*, ed. John Kuehl (New Brunswick: Rutgers University Press, 1965), p. 38.
22. Fitzgerald, “Debt of Honor,” p. 37.
23. Fitzgerald, “Debt of Honor,” p. 36.
24. Fitzgerald, “Debt of Honor,” p. 37.
25. Fitzgerald, “Debt of Honor,” p. 37; Rimmon-Kenan, p. 66.
26. Fitzgerald, “Debt of Honor,” p. 37.
27. Rimmon-Kenan, p. 66.
28. Fitzgerald, “Debt of Honor,” p. 36.
29. Fitzgerald, “Debt of Honor,” p. 36; Rimmon-Kenan, p. 66.
30. F. Scott Fitzgerald, “The End of Hate,” in *The Price Was High: The Last Uncollected Short Stories of F. Scott Fitzgerald* (New York: Harcourt Brace Jovanovich, 1979), p. 742.
31. Fitzgerald, “End of Hate,” p. 744.
32. Fitzgerald, “End of Hate,” p. 744.
33. Fitzgerald, “End of Hate,” p. 748.
34. Fitzgerald, “End of Hate,” p. 748.
35. Fitzgerald, “End of Hate,” p. 748.
36. Fitzgerald, “End of Hate,” p. 749.
37. Fitzgerald, “End of Hate,” p. 749.

38. Fitzgerald, "End of Hate," p. 749.
39. Fitzgerald, "End of Hate," p. 749.
40. Fitzgerald, "End of Hate," p. 743.
41. Fitzgerald, "End of Hate," p. 746.
42. Fitzgerald, "End of Hate," p. 747.
43. F. Scott Fitzgerald, "The Night at Chancellorsville," in *Taps at Reveille* (New York: Charles Scribner's Sons, 1935), p. 211.
44. Fitzgerald, "Night at Chancellorsville," p. 211.
45. Fitzgerald, "Night at Chancellorsville," p. 213.
46. Fitzgerald, "Night at Chancellorsville," p. 211.
47. Fitzgerald, "Night at Chancellorsville," p. 213.
48. Fitzgerald, "Night at Chancellorsville," p. 211.
49. Fitzgerald, "Night at Chancellorsville," p. 214.
50. Fitzgerald, "Night at Chancellorsville," p. 212.
51. Fitzgerald, "Night at Chancellorsville," p. 212.
52. Fitzgerald, "Night at Chancellorsville," p. 213.
53. Fitzgerald, "Night at Chancellorsville," p. 193.
54. Fitzgerald, "Night at Chancellorsville," p. 211.
55. Fitzgerald, "Night at Chancellorsville," p. 213.
56. Fitzgerald, "Night at Chancellorsville," p. 214.
57. Fitzgerald, "Night at Chancellorsville," p. 214.
58. F. Scott Fitzgerald, *The Great Gatsby* (New York: Charles Scribner's Sons, 1925), p. 111.
59. Fitzgerald, *Great Gatsby*, p. 2.
60. William Faulkner, *Requiem for a Nun* (New York: Random House, 1950), p. 92.

“Let the Story Tellers Invent It All”

Col. John S. Mosby in Popular Literature

— Paul Ashdown and Edward Caudill —

Colonel John Singleton Mosby is remembered as “The Gray Ghost of the Confederacy,” a partisan ranger who bedeviled Union forces in northern Virginia during the Civil War. Historians still argue about Mosby’s impact on the war. Mosby biographer James Ramage explains Mosby’s use of fear as a “force multiplier.” It was not so much what Mosby did that mattered as much as it was what others thought he might do. He seemed to be everywhere, even when he was nowhere. “Time and time again,” writes Ramage, “Mosby danced on the nerves of opponents where they were most vulnerable.” Mosby, usually at the head of fewer than 400 men, led thousands of Union pursuers on a feckless quest to capture him or protect bridges, railroads, and military installations from his raids, drawing valuable troops away from other military activities.[1]

Beyond history, Mosby endures as a myth, largely of his own creation. Mosby lived longer than any other major Civil War figure, lectured extensively, and wrote *Mosby’s War Reminiscences and Stuart’s Cavalry Campaigns* (1887), *Stuart’s Cavalry in the Gettysburg Campaign* (1908), and *The Memoirs of Colonel John S. Mosby* (1917). He recognized that he had no patent on his own past. He sometimes dismissed the stories that had grown up about him as harmless fabrications, but he also spent most of his postwar life insisting on the accuracy of his version of events he thought important. He knew another story existed that was coeval with his own truth. He is a peculiar kind of figure for literary interpretation because, as he has told us, his own existence during the war was questioned. He was a mythical figure because it served his own interests to be thought of as ubiquitous, incorporeal, and evasive. And because he couldn't be captured by conventional strategies, it served the interests of his opponents and the recording press to either deny his presence or exaggerate his power. In this sense, the postwar popular literature about Mosby became fictions of a fiction.

Mosby's first appearance as a popular literary figure probably occurred during the spring of 1864 when a play, *The Guerilla, or Mosby in 500 Sutler Wagons*, was staged in Alexandria, Virginia. Mosby's friend Frank Stringfellow claimed he sneaked into the city to see a packed performance and returned to Fauquier County with published copies of the melodrama for Mosby. Stringfellow said he enjoyed the performance, but his qualifications as a theater critic are undocumented. Soon, a dime novel, *Jack Mosby the Guerilla*, depicted Mosby as a black-bearded sadist who tortures prisoners, induces his sweetheart to seduce Union soldiers and lure them into a trap, and tries to burn New York City by igniting a phosphorous-soaked bed at the Astor House.[2]

It was partly to refute such blather that Virginia novelist John Esten Cooke included Mosby in *Surry of Eagle's Nest*, a novel based on his own war experiences as one of General J. E. B. Stuart's staff officers, and *Wearing of the Gray*, a memoir, with sketches and portraits of Confederate heroes. Both volumes were highly popular after the war and well into the next century, and probably did much to sustain Mosby's wartime reputation in both the South and the North by including him among the primary figures of interest. As a fiction writer, Cooke wrote absurdly nostalgic, sentimental melodramas of little literary merit, although his nonfiction was more realistic. The Mosby of *Surry of Eagle's Nest* is a noble, jovial, and compassionate gentleman who attributes his "bloody wild-boar" image in the northern press to Union generals who make him out to be a bandit to excuse their ineptitude in fighting him as a legitimate soldier. In *Wearing of the Gray*, Cooke makes explicit reference to the Mosby of the dime novels, defends the legitimacy of his partisan command, and dismisses "any imputations upon the character of this officer, or upon the nature of the warfare which he carried on, as absurd." Mosby later told a reporter that Cooke's stories were all myths. "It isn't necessary that any history should be written; let the story tellers invent it all," he said.[3]

Clarke Venable's adventure novel *Mosby's Night Hawk* was published in 1931. The story involves a young Virginian who serves with Mosby and becomes a "night hawk," a scout known for his nocturnal rides. Although the novel contains some truly appalling literary racism, complete with happy, superstitious, loyal, groveling slaves who speak in comic dialect, *Mosby's Night Hawk* stays closer to the historical record than most of the other novels in which Mosby appears as a character. Mosby is described as "a myth with substance" and "a force without substance," suggesting the complexity of his elusive tactics. Edna Hoffman Evans's *Sunstar and Pepper,* a horse-and-boy historical novel, was published in 1947. While standing in front of his Magnolia Hill plantation in Virginia one day in 1862, sixteen-year-old Potter "Pepper" Pepperill spots Stuart, and joins the cavalry as a scout and courier. The action roughly spans the period between June 1862 and May 1863. Pepper and Mosby, who is portrayed as a kind of wise and gentle elder brother, scout behind enemy lines. As in most Civil War juvenilia, the emphasis is on reconciliation, and the growing awareness of both sides that peace is better than war, and sectional differences less important than building a stronger country. Mosby is the noble citizen-soldier, a virtuous hero young readers can embrace as a role model. The novel panders to all the stereotypical images of the plantation culture, including slaves who love the South and "ole Marster."[4]

Mosby also appears as a character in Garald Lagard's swashbuckling 1948 novel *Scarlet Cockerel*, a kind of *Captain Blood* meets *Gone with the Wind. Scarlet Cockerel* is part maritime adventure, part horse melodrama, but a skillful one. Lane Byrn is a young medical student returning to his Virginia plantation at his father's behest just as the war begins. He becomes embroiled in a gunrunning plot on the schooner *Whisper* and is befriended by its master, Captain Selmo. Also aboard the *Whisper* is the beautiful daughter of a Federal army officer. A romance ensues, Selmo and Byrn eventually join Mosby's partisans, and Byrn becomes the rooster-feathered Scarlet Cockerel. Mosby is a laconic, ruthless romantic, magnificently adorned in his scarlet-lined cavalry cape and ostrich-plumed slouch hat, but most notable for the "color and deep chill of his eyes. They were blue, hard as midwinter ice and as cold." Actual historical events such as the Berryhill Raid and Mosby's capture of Union general Edwin H. Stoughton are accurately recounted, but Lagard acknowledges that he takes liberties with chronology in order to structure the narrative. Selmo dies in a final bloodbath just before the partisans disband to end the war, and the Scarlet Cockerel is reunited with his lover as he tries to save the life of the Union officer who was his rival for her affections.[5]

No novelist has done more to gild the Mosby myth than Ray Hogan. Hogan was born in 1908 in Willow Springs, Missouri, where his father was the local marshal. In 1914 his father bought a hotel in Albuquerque, New Mexico, and Hogan picked up the plots for many of his later novels by listening to stories told by travelers. Hogan was in his fifth decade before he published his first novel. He wrote more than a hundred western novels and nonfiction books, hundreds of magazine articles, and film and television scripts.[6] Hogan had already written a dozen westerns when he began a series of books about Mosby in 1960. Mosby was an ideal subject for a western writer because the raider's irregular cavalry tactics, rustling, retributive hanging, horse stealing, trainwrecking, sharpshooting, robbery, and kidnapping could be props for stories set in Virginia as readily as in Texas. Indians could be converted to Yankees, and bushwhackers, spies, incompetent generals, deserters, and crooked sutlers could be substituted for black-hatted gunmen. Mosby had the advantage of acting like a western bandit while being portrayed as a courageous fighter for southern independence.

Hogan's first Mosby novel, *The Ghost Raider,* sets the parameters for the series. It begins with a meeting between General Robert E. Lee, J. E. B. Stuart and Mosby shortly before Gettysburg. Lee orders Mosby to undertake a secret mission to determine the size and disposition of Maj. Gen. Joseph Hooker's forces. Intelligence reports that Hooker is recruiting teamsters to deliver two hundred forage wagons to his army. Equally vital is Mosby's rescue of a captured Confederate officer, Major Curtis Sanford, who has mapped the area that Lt. Gen. Richard Ewell must penetrate during the first wave of the invasion. But Mosby blames Sanford for the deaths of his close friend Tom Ballenger and the men of his entire company. Lee reminds Mosby that a court of inquiry has exonerated Sanford. Mosby obeys reluctantly and declines Stuart's offer of troops for the mission, promising he can complete his assignment with just nineteen men. Hogan's plot develops with suitable melodramatic charm. Mosby plucks the sullen Sanford from the stockade, eludes capture, destroys wagons and blows up a troop train. After commandeering an ambulance, and escaping pursuing troops in a running gun battle, Mosby delivers Sanford to Lee and warns the commander about the size of Hooker's force. Sanford gives Lee false information, and presumably seals the fate of Lee's army.[7]

Given Mosby's reputation for battlefield heroics and his horse-opera adventures, it is surprising he hasn't appeared in more novels for young readers. An exception is an interesting novel by Joseph B. Icenhower, *The Scarlet Raider,* which appeared in 1961, just in time for the Civil War Centennial. Icenhower, a highly decorated retired Navy rear admiral and former World War II submarine commander, had written several sea stories and nonfiction books about submarine warfare before he took on the Civil War and Mosby. The story begins with fifteen-year-old Tim Morgan smuggling medical supplies through Yankee lines near Fairfax shortly before Gettysburg. Tim's father is a wounded veteran. He and Tim provide Mosby with needed supplies and vital information. Tim dreams that Mosby himself will come to collect the supplies, and Tim's father knows every Virginia youngster reveres the gallant raider. They hear the sound of horses outside their cabin, a knock on the door, and there stands the raider himself in his scarlet-lined cape and gray slouch hat with the famous ostrich plume and the two studded Colt pistols in holsters.

Tim tells Mosby he has been threatened by a Union corporal, Bull Ruffing, who wants Tim to smuggle contraband for profit. Mosby warns Tim to be careful, and gives him some stolen Yankee silver to swap for more supplies. He also gives Tim an undated appointment as a trooper in his command to protect the boy in the event he is captured as a spy. Tim then has a confrontation with Ruffing and is saved by a kindly Irish sergeant, predictably named Murphy, from New York, who discovers the contraband and warns Tim never to return to Fairfax. Tim then joins Mosby's Rangers, gets a magnificent horse named Midnight (his previous horse had, of course, been named Nellie), special training from Sergeant Hank Slaughter, and is ready for action. He and Slaughter sneak across the Potomac to scout Union defenses near Seneca Falls, where Stuart is expected to move into Maryland on his raid during the Gettysburg campaign. Although Slaughter is injured, Tim gets the information back to Mosby, who takes out the batteries defending the crossing after a sharp engagement. Tim becomes a hero, is mentioned in dispatches to Lee, and becomes perhaps the youngest corporal in the Confederate Army.

The main theme of this Centennial-year novel is honor among enemies. Mosby never gives way to hatred, and is a model of gallant compassion. In the end, it is the ability of both sides to work together that wins the day. Ruffing and his venal bushwhackers are portrayed in sharp contrast to the elegant partisans, who are wrongly branded as bushwhackers by their opponents. The genial and wise Irish sergeant, a stereotype in many Civil War novels, is rewarded for his earlier kindness to Tim, implying the possibility of grace, goodness and reconciliation even within the boundaries of war. Tim, of course, grows from boy to man within a matter of months, and the novel follows the familiar character-building formula.[8]

Mosby has been sighted in a number of literary haunts, raiding readers' sensibilities in various guises—a historical memory, a guerrilla professor-philosopher, an assassin, and even a cat. Mosby makes a cameo appearance in F. Scott Fitzgerald's famous novel *Tender Is the Night.* Fitzgerald's father, Edward Fitzgerald, spent his childhood near Rockville, Maryland. During the Civil War he had helped Confederate spies cross the Potomac and assisted one of Mosby's Rangers in escaping from Union-controlled territory. Fitzgerald, the great novelist and short story writer of the Jazz Age and the Lost Generation, grew up hearing the stories of his father's adventures. In the novel, Dick Diver sits in a Paris restaurant and reflects on the war: "Momentarily, he sat again on his father's knee, riding with Mosby while the old loyalties and devotions fought on around him." Mosby represents in the novel an idealized past, according to critic John

Limon, a "beautiful history" of a dignified war remote from the emptiness of the Lost Generation.[9]

The bestselling historical novelist John Jakes featured Mosby in a sprawling Civil War epic titled *On Secret Service*, published in 2000. The complex plot involves Pinkerton agents, spies, political and military figures, and culminates with the Lincoln assassination. Jakes used Tidwell's *Come Retribution* and other speculative sources as grist for his story. Mosby is aware of the failed mission, supposedly authorized by Davis, to kidnap Lincoln, and a new plan to blow up Lincoln and his entire cabinet at the White House. Cooperating with the Richmond authorities, Mosby assigns one of his men, who had previously found Mosby "unreliable; potentially violent, if not deranged," to help implement the plot by murdering an informer. When the soldier declines, and asks Mosby, "what have we come down to, sir?" Mosby replies: "I try not to ask myself that question, Lieutenant." The moral ambivalence of the war and its corrupting influence on both sides is a continuing theme of the novel, which reached a potentially much larger audience than any of the previous novels involving Mosby. Like Hogan, Jakes finds Mosby a useful character for a cloak and dagger tale.[10]

Mosby is a remarkably protean figure for fiction writers. He can be plotted as a cowboy hero, a spy, a villain, a metaphor, or a cat. He can be invoked on the boulevards of Paris or the mountains of Mexico. He can be an arsonist, a train robber, a kidnapper, a bomber, a torturer—even a rat killer. Or he can be a friend to children, a rescuer of distressed damsels, a patriot, a defense attorney, a savior, a lover, and even a prototypical Cold Warrior. He shows no signs of going away. He has continued to appear in popular fiction from the time of the Civil War to the beginning of the twenty-first century. No fiction writer, however, has come close to plumbing the depths of Mosby as a complex historical character. He is almost always one-dimensional, never fully human, cut to fit the needs of a specific narrative storyline. He has eluded fiction writers just as he eluded the Union Army. He is never a fully developed fictional character, but is usually made to seem ridiculous, capable of comic-book heroics and near-supernatural feats. Mosby in real life lived in a world conflated by classical mythology and the detritus of daily existence. As a popular literary myth, he has yet to achieve the legitimacy he sought throughout the war, and he remains a partisan. He always knew that if he wanted to be a character in his own creation myth, he was going to have to write the story himself.[11]

Notes

Parts of this essay were published in Paul Ashdown and Edward Caudill's *The Mosby Myth: A Confederate Hero in Life and Legend* (Wilmington, DE: Scholarly Resources Books, 2002), 145–176.

1. See, for example, Jeffry Wert, *Mosby's Rangers* (New York: Simon & Schuster, 1990), pp. 242–43; Dennis E. Frye, "'I Resolved to Play a Bold Game': John S. Mosby as a Factor in the 1864 Valley Campaign," in *Struggle for the Shenandoah: Essays on the 1864 Valley Campaign*, ed. Gary W. Gallagher (Kent, OH: Kent State University Press, 1991), pp. 107–26; Keith Poulter, "A Word in Edgeways," *North & South* 3, no. 1 (November 1999): pp. 18–19; Virgil Carrington Jones, *Ranger Mosby* (Chapel Hill: University of North Carolina Press, 1944; Virgil Carrington Jones, *Gray Ghosts and Rebel Rangers* (1956;reprint, New York: Galahad Books, 1995); James A. Ramage, *Gray Ghost: The Life of Col. John Singleton Mosby* (Lexington: University of Kentucky Press, 1999), p. 4.
2. James Dudley Peavey, ed., *Confederate Scout: Virginia's Frank Stringfellow* (n.p. , privately published, 1956), p. 50; John Esten Cooke, *Wearing of the Gray*, ed. Philip van Doren Stern (1867; reprint, Bloomington: Indiana University Press, 1959), p. 102; Russel Nye, *The Unembarrassed Muse* (New York: The Dial Press, 1970), pp. 43, 147.
3. John Esten Cooke, *Surry of Eagle's Nest* (1866; reprint, Ridgewood, NJ: The Gregg Press, 1968); Edmund Wilson, *Patriotic Gore* (New York: Oxford University Press, 1962), pp. 192–196, 315; Thomas E. Dasher, "John Esten Cooke," in *Antebellum Writers in New York and the South*, ed. Joel Myerson, *Dictionary of Literary Biography*, p. 3 (Detroit: Gale Research, 1979), pp. 64–70; Cooke, *Wearing of the Gray*, pp. 102–115; John O. Beaty, *John Esten Cooke, Virginian* (1922; reprint, Port Washington, NY: Kennikat Press, 1965), pp. 91–100; unidentified newspaper, n.d., John Singleton Mosby Scrapbooks, University of Virginia.
4. Clarke Venable, *Mosby's Night Hawk* (Chicago: Reilly & Lee, 1931); Edna Hoffman Evans, *Sunstar and Pepper* (Chapel Hill: University North Carolina Press, 1947).
5. Jere Hungerford Wheelwright, *Gentlemen, Hush!* (New York: Scribner, 1948); Garald Lagard, *Scarlet Cockerel* (New York: William Morrow, 1948); Wilson, p. 327.
6. "(Robert) Ray Hogan," *Encyclopedia of Frontier and Western Fiction*, ed. Jon Tuska and Vicki Piekarski (New York: McGraw-Hill, 1983), p. 179.
7. Ray Hogan, *The Ghost Raider* (New York: Pyramid Publications, 1960).
8 Joseph B. Icenhower, *The Scarlet Raider* (Philadelphia and New York: Chilton, 1961).
9. John Limon, *Writing after War* (New York: Oxford University Press, 1994), pp. 113–114; André Le Vot, *F. Scott Fitzgerald* (New York: Doubleday, 1983), p. 5.
10. John Jakes, *On Secret Service* (New York: Dutton, 2000).
11. Schlesinger is quoted in Michael Kammen, *A Season of Youth* (New York: Alfred A. Knopf, 1978), p. 152; quoted by Peterson, p. 34.

Hydra or Heracles?

Nathan Bedford Forrest in Civil War Fiction

— Paul Ashdown and Edward Caudill —

So many grotesque characters strut through stories about the South that it has become a cliché to say that southern fiction is obsessed with monsters. Richard Weaver has suggested that such monsters make literature relevant, because a belief in monsters is closely related to a similar belief in heroes. For every Centaur there is a Theseus, for every Hydra a Heracles. In Confederate general Nathan Bedford Forrest, southern fiction discovers both its Hydra and its Heracles, for he is at once monster and hero, dragon and dragonslayer.[1]

Forrest was one of the great fighting generals of the Civil War. A slave trader, planter, and Memphis politician of humble origins, he enlisted in the Confederate army as a private, raised his own cavalry unit, and rose to the rank of lieutenant general (the only soldier in either army to make such a monumental leap in rank). He fought at Shiloh, Chickamauga, Brice's Cross Roads, Franklin, and other western battles, sustaining several severe injuries and personally killing some thirty men. On April 12, 1864, his troops slaughtered hundreds of black soldiers and white Tennessee Unionists during his successful assault on Fort Pillow in western Tennessee. Forrest's culpability was never proved, although he was the subject of a congressional investigation and was widely condemned in the northern press.

After the war, Forrest entered the railroad business and briefly was a leading figure—some say the first Grand Dragon—of the Ku Klux Klan, which he later attempted to disband. Fort Pillow notwithstanding, Forrest was cited by many of the leading figures of the Confederacy as one of its greatest military figures. Statues of Forrest abound in the South. In Tennessee, many parks and schools are named for him, and his bronze statue stands on the lawn of the state capitol. Protesters have called for the removal of his image, if not his excision from history altogether. He remains, however, one of the most recognizable figures of the war, and has been the subject of numerous biographies, essays, and works of literature.[2]

Forrest first appeared as a fictional character in a story published in *Harper's Weekly* on May 7, 1864, just a few weeks after the assault on Fort Pillow. A black Union soldier, Daniel Tyler, survives the battle and recounts its horrors from the safety of a Union hospital. Tyler had been working in a field in Alabama when he saw Union cavalry approaching, and ran away to join them. Taken to Louisiana, he enlisted in a black regiment, and was among the fort's defenders when Forrest attacked. After the garrison repulses several charges, Forrest calls a truce and then breaches the fort's defenses when the Federals honorably lower their guns. The Rebels, described as savages, devils, and monsters, wantonly slaughter the black troops. Tyler is shot several times, clubbed, blinded, captured, and buried alive in a ditch. He claws his way out, swoons, awakens in the hospital, and tells how most of his companions were murdered by Forrest's riders. Like most *Harper's Weekly* stories, this tale did not carry the name of its author. Accordingly, readers probably did not distinguish between outright fictional accounts and purported eyewitness reports of the assault. In the story, Forrest is more wraith than flesh-and-blood character, a pattern often repeated in Forrest fiction.[3]

Joel Chandler Harris, the Georgia journalist best known for his Uncle Remus stories and local-color folk tales of the Old South, wrote contrasting profiles of Forrest in two novels he completed after he retired as an editor and columnist on Henry Grady's *Atlanta Constitution*. *Uncle Remus: His Songs and His Sayings* was published in 1880, and brought Harris international acclaim. The tales were popular fare as Americans embraced the romance of reunion and were eagerly receptive to a sentimentalized version of the Old South in which race had little to do with the Civil War. *A Little Union Scout* appeared after its serial publication in the *Saturday Evening Post* in February and March 1904. In it, Forrest shines as a chivalrous, avuncular, laughing figure given to homespun aphorisms. "It ain't what people think of you—it's what you are that counts," Forrest tells his scout, Carroll Shannon, the novel's narrator, who says Forrest's advice "rings true every time I repeat it to myself. It covers the whole ground of conscience and morals."

The Shadow Between His Shoulder-Blades appeared in 1909, following the success of *A Little Union Scout*. The story first ran serially in three November issues of the *Saturday Evening Post* in 1907. Billy Sanders, Harris's alter ego, tells tales as an old man about his wartime encounters with Forrest. Like a sort of military Uncle Remus, Forrest explains his technique of getting to the battle first with the most men, and pushing harder at the crucial moment when the troops "git the idee that they've done e'en about all they kin do an' might as well quit." Forrest appears as a tough customer throughout the story, a man who never liked or trusted blacks and never forgot a slight or a betrayal. When aroused, says Sanders, Forrest could be brutal. When Forrest hangs a turncoat and former business partner, Sanders says that "for days an' days—I could feel the shadder of that black, swingin' thing right betwixt my shoulder-blades, an' when I'm off in my feed I can feel it yit; sometimes it's cold, sometimes it's hot."[4]

Irvin Cobb, another journalist who used Forrest in his stories, was the son of a Confederate soldier. Born in Paducah, Kentucky, in 1876, Cobb became editor of the *Paducah Daily News* and wrote for the *Louisville Evening Post*, the *Saturday Evening Post* and *Cosmopolitan*. Cobb's "Judge Priest" stories were adapted for radio and film. He conceived of these stories as a rebuttal to northern stereotypes of southern life, which he claimed focused mainly on the gentry. They first appeared in the *Saturday Evening Post* in 1911, and continued to amuse readers in some 40 short stories and two novels. William "Fighting Billy" Priest is a former sergeant who rode with Forrest's cavalry and served into the 1920s as a circuit judge. Judge Priest presides over his domain as a benevolent despot with folksy wisdom and country humor, solving the problems of a cast of outrageous small-town characters. Most of the judge's cronies had served with him under Forrest. To these old soldiers, according to Wayne Chatterton, "Forrest is deified, and the war is a shrine which they must visit and revisit in their memories."[5]

Forrest figures at least tangentially in several works by Mississippi-born novelist William Faulkner, winner of the Nobel Prize for Literature in 1950. Although he is mentioned in nine novels and eight stories, Forrest is a principal subject in only one Faulkner story, "My Grandmother Millard and General Bedford Forrest and the Battle of Harrykin Creek," published in 1943. Grandmother Millard attempts to save the family silver from the Yankees by putting it in the privy, with an attractive young cousin posted to divert the plundering soldiers by claiming a young woman is inside. The Yankees ignore the warning, batter down the privy, only to find there really is a young woman, seated and screaming. But one of Forrest's officers, Lieutenant Philip St. Just Backus, shows up to save the girl, and immediately falls in love. Given the recent circumstances, the girl becomes hysterical at the mention of her rescuer's name. His subsequent reckless conduct provokes Forrest, who arrives at the summons of his old friend

Grandmother Millard. Together they contrive a fictitious report that the lieutenant, breveted major general, is "killed" at the putative "Battle of Harrykin Creek" during which he had rescued the girl. He's replaced by Lt. Philip St. Just Backus, and a wedding soon follows. Forrest is the only non-fictional character in the story, a spoof of the romanticism so dear to the South's self-image. Forrest is crude in appearance and language, but gallant and gentlemanly in demeanor and action. It is all mythical magnolias and lace set, tongue in cheek, against the harsh history of slavery, violence, and illiteracy.[6]

Caroline Gordon, the granddaughter of one of Forrest's soldiers, also made use of Forrest in the novel *None Shall Look Back*, published in 1937, one year after the publication of Margaret Mitchell's *Gone with the Wind*. Gordon's novel, although it skirts some of the same territory as Mitchell's tale, is a much richer epic.[7] Gordon was born in Kentucky in 1895. She married Allen Tate, one of the Nashville Agrarians. In 1934 she wrote to Maxwell Perkins at Scribner's and sketched the outline for her proposed novel. Gordon presented Forrest as an archetypal man of the southern states west of the mountains. Gordon's novel was to be based in part on her family's own story. "I rather want to have Forrest a character in the action, in somewhat the same way Napoleon is in *War and Peace*," she wrote, perhaps indicative of the epic she had in mind. In another letter she said she "wanted Forrest to be like a god." Scribner's had intended to publish the novel in 1936 but postponed it to avoid direct competition with *Gone with the Wind*. The book eventually appeared in February of 1937.

None Shall Look Back begins predictably enough with a Kentucky planter reposing in a summer house and sending a slave child scurrying off to fetch a julep. A large, interconnected family serves as a microcosm of the wider social order. Belles with fluttering eyelashes frolic in the rose garden and gambol beneath the leafy boughs of the hemlock trees with young fops—but soon the war pierces this Eden like a bayonet and the novel turns dark and bloody. They "had been playing a waltz and everybody was dancing and then suddenly they had heard the hoof beats down the road and a few minutes later the place was full of mounted men," the "black-browed Colonel," Nathan Bedford Forrest, in command. Soon the young men are off to war, and the women and the old men and the slaves, and the men with no fight in them, stay behind to protect their homes and provender as best they can.[8]

Gordon renders Forrest's famous battles in sanguinary detail. Forrest becomes the great mythical hero of the war, fighting the hated invader despite great odds. His ferocity becomes legendary among his men. "They said old Forrest himself carried a saber big enough for any two men and ground against all military regulations to a razor edge. A man in the Tenth had seen him whirl it in both hands and slice off a Yankee's head as if he'd been a gobbler on a block."

Southern soldiers are ennobled by their endurance and their allegiance to a great cause. At Murfreesboro, on December 7, 1864, Forrest seizes the colors from a fallen scout, Rives Allard, the scion of one of the principal families in the novel, and charges into the Union lines against the tide of retreating Confederates. "He raised amazed eyes to the milky sky. Death. It had been with him, beside him all the time and he had not known. . . . The rose-colored flag danced above him then dipped. It veiled his face for a moment from the men's sight but they heard his voice sounding back over the windy plain and saw him gallop toward the fort." Forrest carries the fight to the enemy but even he can't save the South.[9]

Faulkner called Shelby Foote's *Shiloh* "the damnedest book I have ever read and one of the best," and ranked it above *The Red Badge of Courage*. Published in 1952, *Shiloh* was Foote's fourth, and most successful, novel, and his best-known work before the historical trilogy, *The Civil War: A Narrative*, begun in 1958 and completed in 1974. *Shiloh* is told in the voices of eighteen soldiers who fought in the fields and woods above Pittsburg Landing, Tennessee, in April 1862. The novel alternates the perspectives of Union and Confederate combatants in seven sections. The speaker in the opening monologue, Lieutenant Palmer Metcalfe, an aristocratic aide-de-camp on General Albert Sidney Johnston's staff, reappears in the final chapter, and the penultimate chapter is composed of a dozen monologues by members of a single squad of Union soldiers. The collective voices serve as a doomed chorus moving through the landscape of battle, as the soldiers occasionally encounter one another as well as the generals, including Forrest, who seem to control their destinies.

Foote's prose is spare and laconic, befitting the prosaic and sometimes bemused reflections of unlettered young privates, sometimes Shakespearean, sometimes ironic, as if a cosmic tragedy were being invoked by a Greek poet and orchestrated by indifferent gods. Both Metcalfe and Sergeant Jefferson Polly, one of Forrest's scouts, observe the cavalryman's martial zeal with wonder. Polly recalls how he knew from the first time he saw Forrest that he was "looking at the most man in the world" and how he "followed him and watched him grow to be what he had become by the time of Shiloh: the first cavalryman of his time, one of the great ones of *all* time, though no one realized it that soon except men who had fought under him."[10]

The best novel about Forrest grew out of a student's honor's thesis at Kenyon College. As a boy growing up in Alabama, Perry Lentz saw what he later described as a "lurid contemporary engraving" of the Fort Pillow massacre reproduced in a biography of Forrest. What became *The Falling Hills* was written during the Civil War centennial and the gathering storm of the Civil Rights movement. "My principal intention," he later wrote, "was to recreate, with all the vividness and the historical accuracy that I could muster, what was once the most famous racial atrocity in a war that was caused by racist beliefs and by the peculiar institutions and cultures that had been built upon them in this nation."[11]

The Falling Hills is the story of Captain Leroy Acox, a reluctant officer in Forrest's cavalry, and Lieutenant Jonathan Seabury, a New England idealist who seeks to improve the lot of the black soldiers on garrison duty at Fort Pillow. Each becomes progressively disillusioned with the war, which reaches its climax at the ill-fated battle. Forrest again is more a force of nature than a human figure. To Union soldiers stationed in the Tennessee forts, Forrest is "wrathful and animal-like, his bare hands tearing through the doorway to get at the young men inside." In the quiet hours, "it was absolutely natural to assume that Forrest was coming at them, just as a man in the dark, when he knows there is something there, figures it is stalking him." Forrest sees Fort Pillow as a "cankering, infested boil on the men's minds and it stood for everything they hated and he was going to take them in swift and hard and they were going to lance it. It would be a relief and a purgation."[12]

The Confederate bloodlust stems from the treachery of the Unionist Tennesseans manning the hated fort, which "stood for the whole thing, Forrest knew." Behind the ramparts were "their own renegade flesh and blood" along with the despised blacks in Union uniforms. When the attack is ordered, Forrest's face is "a mask of anger and weary resignation and hatred, and the mood of the Tennessee woods . . . was upon him." The slaughter ensues, Seabury is killed trying to save a terrified black soldier, and Acox, while feeling a "great horror and a great guilt," succumbs to the violence because he believes it is "Forrest's orders that we kill them all." The slaughter was right, he reasons, because the fort stood for something and needed destroying. Forrest's culpability is never resolved, but is implicit. True to history, perhaps, but not to myth, because whatever happened at Fort Pillow is crucial to the way Forrest is perceived. If not guilty, he can be portrayed as something of a hero; if guilty, he is a monster. Lentz does not find many heroes in this story.

Two Pulitzer Prize-winning writers, in addition to Faulkner, have included Forrest in a short story. Both stories are about young men growing up with grandfathers who had served with Forrest. Robert Penn Warren, the most notable literary figure among the Agrarians, included "When the Light Gets Green," first published in 1936, in *The Circus in the Attic and Other Stories*. Peter Taylor's "In the Miro District" was published in the *New Yorker* in 1977. In Warren's story, a young southern man recalls his grandfather, Captain Barden, who had served with Forrest and now has "a long white beard and sat under the cedar tree." Barden, a reader of history, thought the South might have won the war if it had followed Forrest's advice and "cleaned the country ahead of the Yankees, like the Russians beat Napoleon." He also fought at Fort Pillow, and talked disparagingly about drunken black soldiers massacred under a bluff. In 1914, Barden has a stroke, and dies four years later, his own physical and emotional paralysis spanning another war. The paralysis is symbolic. Like the South, Barden is paralyzed, emotionally by tradition, physically by northern conquest. Barden is an emissary from Forrest's world who can be recalled only in the tangible accouterments of his existence, like the corncob pipe he smokes, while his essence, like Forrest and the war, is obscure, as in the reflection of the mirror.[13]

"In the Miro District" similarly explores a generational response to the men who fought the war. The setting is a Nashville upper-middle-class neighborhood in about 1925. The narrator recalls this year, when he was eighteen and his grandfather, Major Basil Manley, was an old man, from the perspective of late middle age. As a young man, he resented the grandfather with whom he was expected to bond by his social-climbing parents. Having a Civil War veteran around was considered socially desirable for persons of his parents' class, but the major didn't quite fit the expected role. He declined to speak much about his service with Forrest, except for an occasional anecdote. Instead, Major Manley was more likely to dwell on a more recent incident when he was kidnapped in 1912 by nightriders, escaped, and wandered through a swamp for ten days. This was the kind of authentic experience that mattered to the old man, who avoided Confederate reunions, "that gathering of men each year to repeat and enlarge upon reminiscences of something that he was beginning to doubt had ever had any reality."[14]

Their conflict widens after Major Manley intrudes upon his grandson's high jinks with young women "of the other sort" from those well-heeled young ladies who attended the prestigious Ward Belmont school. After finding the boy in the grandfather's room in a state of dishabille and hiding a naked girl from Ward Belmont, Major Manley storms out. After this incident, Taylor explained in an interview, Major Manley realized the grandson "no longer has any of the values he has. . . . [T]he world he had tried to be realistic about had lost its values." The grandfather assumes the expected role, grows a long white beard like Captain Barden in the Warren story, and begins attending Confederate reunions. He talks freely about the war, entertaining the friends of his daughter and son-in-law, and his grandson's classmates. Everyone adores him in his expected role, but the grandson senses something has been lost between them.[15]

These stories give insight into the meaning of Forrest and the Civil War for the generation that came of age in the early twentieth century. Warren and Taylor were both writing about the South in confrontation with modernity. Their grandfathers had been the vital link with the war, and they had been expected to perform a ritual they may not have wished to perform. The war for the grandfathers was something real, something unromantic, and something to be accepted and forgotten. Forrest had been a hard-fighting commander, morally complex, not a symbol but an unadulterated presence. The sons and grandsons wanted a heroic war that might have been won and might still be won if the South could hold to its agrarian values. The old soldiers retained a code and an independent spirit not necessarily compatible with the twentieth century. They form a bridge to a future when men like Forrest would become myths, not men.

Talented authors continue to bring Forrest to the attention of the general book-reading public. Elmore Leonard, one of the premier western and mystery genre writers, uses Forrest to good effect in *Tishomingo Blues*, his thirty-seventh novel. In *Tishomingo Blues*, Denis Lenahan, former professional high diving champion working the carnival circuit, sets up his act at a casino resort in Tunica, Mississippi, witnesses a murder, and gets mixed up with Detroit gangsters trying to take over the drug business from the "Dixie Mafia." Walter Kirkbride, a sleazy manufactured-home builder and Civil War reenactor blackmailed into laundering money for the Dixie Mafia, is obsessed with Forrest. Kirkbride, the other crooks, the diver and even a cop dress up in Union and Confederate uniforms and shoot it out with live ammunition during a reenactment of the Battle of Brice's Cross Roads. The novel mocks the reenacting craze and the gaming industry with all its attendant vices. Forrest, again, is portrayed as a high-minded avenger of mythical proportions. Kirkbride postures as a Forrest expert but passes on only legends and canards. He dresses up to look like Forrest, his hero, but behind the beard and the general's uniform he's just a counterfeit Confederate adrift, like the South, in a fetid cultural swamp far removed from the noble cause he thinks Forrest fought for.[16]

Howard Bahr's *The Black Flower* is an ethereal meditation about the Battle of Franklin. During the battle a frightened young woman visiting relatives in Franklin has an encounter with Forrest. When she looks in his eyes she sees "the shadow of a weariness that she knew he would never lose, and a dark wisdom she had no desire to own." He gives her the black ostrich plume from his hat as a remembrance. On the day after the battle she prays for a mortally wounded soldier, and tries to imagine God listening to her prayer. "She searched for an image of Him, found instead the face of General Nathan Bedford Forrest, looking just as he had on the stairs during the battle." Forrest, in a priestly role, offers her the assurance of grace and forgiveness. Years later the plume evokes the memory of Forrest and sanctifies the dead whose presence becomes real to her as she lingers over their graves. This image for her is in contrast to the hollow Lost Cause memorials that rise up all over the South. In time she accepts Forrest's "dark wisdom," which chooses courage and commitment over fear, the constructive power of repentance, and acceptance of God's will.[17]

In Padgett Powell's *Mrs. Hollingsworth's Men*, a fey, middle-aged southern woman out of sorts with an America that seems to have lost its mettle, sits down to write a grocery list at her kitchen table. The list gradually becomes a rant filled with surreal images that emerge from what she suspects is the fog of her demented mind. Although virtually ignorant of the Civil War, yet haunted by it, she finds that Forrest is "in her head like the hook of a pop-radio tune." The local high school bears his name, and the "idea had formed in her mind that he had been indomitable; he had been the War's Achilles. Achilles with pinworms and slaves besmirching his heroic profile." She invents a character who dreams of a man on a horse whom he knew to be representing the general. Forrest, ostensibly a projection of Mrs. Hollingsworth's discontent, is a Lost Cause icon in opposition to all that is wrong with postmodern America, or, at least, all that's wrong with Mrs. Hollingsworth. "No matter *what* you push, you get something." And that, perhaps, is the essence of Forrest—a doomed hero of a continuing, ill-fated war against the zeitgeist, a resistance fighter against the maladies of the spirit, an icon of all lost causes, however demented or noble. Forrest becomes a hologram of history, as familiar as a town square monument, and as spectral as an imagined reality.[18]

In *Last of the Dixie Heroes*, Roy Hill, the great-great grandson of Roy Singleton Hill, a Tennessee soldier who fought with Forrest, is a commodities trader for the Atlanta office of a giant corporation. He takes up with a group of Confederate reenactors who find living in a perpetual 1863 preferable to living in the spiritually dead, Yankee "occupied" South. Hill learns that Forrest called his ancestor the "Angel of Death," and gradually seems to assume the old soldier's identity. When he finds his great-great grandfather's uniform, carbine and diary, he discovers that he fought at Fort Pillow. The diary says:

> Twelve April 1864, Fort Pillow. Best day of this conflict so far. Forrest asks for unconditional surrender but they refuse. And thems tauntin' us from over the walls. So's we charge down from the east. . . . Now theys thinkin' twicet bout not surrenderin' but we has our orders from Forrest and they was to. . . ."

At that point the diary ends because the next page has been ripped out. Visiting his ancestor's homestead in Tennessee, Hill meets Ezekiel Hill, who claims to be a descendant of the Confederate soldier and one of his slaves. Roy Hill finds the last page of the diary in a coffin Ezekiel believes contains the ashes of their mutual ancestor. The diary continues: "kill the last God damn one of em. Was What Forrest says." The diary goes on to detail the Fort Pillow massacre of black soldiers with the added detail that "The Angel of Death" also killed his own slave Zeke. Roy burns the last page of the diary as he contemplates "where the line between the white Hills and the black Hills was drawn." The novel ends with Roy

Hill and his companions shooting it out with some Union reenactors who kidnap Hill's son. Roy Hill finds his manhood and his dignity by assuming the mantle of resistance to his untenable circumstances even as he accepts the ambiguity of war and his ancestor's role in it. Forrest is exposed, in fiction at least, as the culprit in the Fort Pillow massacre. As a killer and a man of his times, Forrest leaves the South with a legacy. The violence of the Civil War continues, and if there is meaning in the mayhem, it is that while the sins of the fathers are visited unto the next generations, fighting back is sometimes worth the struggle.[19]

Across the span of almost a century and a half, authors have appropriated Forrest for tales ranging from historical romance to alternative history and crime fiction. Although typically one-dimensional in fiction, Forrest appears in many guises. He has been portrayed as a cornpone philosopher, an agent of evil, a personification of impersonal nature, a holy fool, and a specter. Whether portrayed as a knight of a golden age before the South went soft and succumbed to Yankee lucre and morality, military genius, raptor-eyed homicidal maniac, Lost Cause icon, knight-errant, avenger, savior or rip-roaring racist, Forrest emerges with smoking breath and slashing sword as one of the most protean characters in all of literature. No mere mortal, often more epic hero or monster than man, Forrest is a fiction, a legend, and, ultimately, an American myth.

Notes

1. Richard M. Weaver, *The Southern Essays of Richard M. Weaver*, ed. George M. Curtis, III and James J. Thompson, Jr. (Indianapolis, IN: Liberty Press, 1987), pp. 68–69.
2. Jack Hurst, *Nathan Bedford Forrest* (New York: Alfred A. Knopf, 1994); Court Carney, "The Contested Image of Nathan Bedford Forrest, " *Journal of Southern History* 67, no. 1 (August 2001): 601–30; James W. Loewen, *Lies Across America: What Our Historic Sites Get Wrong* (New York: Simon and Schuster, 1999), pp. 258–61.
3. "Buried Alive," *Harper's Weekly*, May 7, 1864, in *To Live and Die: Collected Stories of the Civil War, 1861–1876*, ed. Kathleen Diffley (Durham, NC: Duke University Press, 2002), pp. 284–288; Kathleen Diffley, *Where My Heart Is Turning Ever: Civil War Stories and Constitutional Reform, 1861–1876* (Athens: University of Georgia Press, 1992), pp. xxvi–xxvii.
4. Paul M. Cousins, *Joel Chandler Harris* (Baton Rouge: Louisiana State University Press, 1968), p. 191; Joel Chandler Harris, *A Little Union Scout* (New York: McClure, Phillips & Co., 1904), pp. 120, 176–77; Joel Chandler Harris, *The Shadow Between His Shoulder-Blades* (Boston: Small, Maynard and Company, 1909), pp. 45, 62–66, 127, 132.
5. Anita Lawson, *Irvin S. Cobb* (Bowling Green, OH: Bowling Green State Univ. Popular Press, 1984); Irvin S. Cobb, "Preface," *Back Home* (New York: Grosset & Dunlap, 1912), p. x; Wayne Chatterton, *Irvin S. Cobb* (Boston: Twayne Publishers, 1986), p. 101; Irvin S. Cobb, "The Sun Shines Bright," in *Down Yonder with Judge Priest and*

Irvin S. Cobb (New York: R. Long & R.R. Smith, 1932); Irvin S. Cobb, "Forrest's Last Charge," in *Old Judge Priest* (New York: Review of Reviews Corp., 1916), pp. 280–323.

6. Dasher, *William Faulkner's Characters*; William Faulkner, "My Grandmother Millard and General Bedford Forrest and the Battle of Harrykin Creek," *Collected Stories of William Faulkner* (New York: Random House, 1950), pp. 667–99.
7. Jim Cullen, *The Civil War in Popular Culture: A Reusable Past* (Washington: Smithsonian Institution Press, 1995), pp. 65–107.
8. Caroline Gordon, *None Shall Look Back* (New York: Charles Scribner's Sons, 1937), pp. 27–28.
9. Gordon, *None Shall Look Back*, pp. 241, 340, 375.
10. Robert Brent Toplin, ed., *Ken Burns's The Civil War: Historians Respond* (New York: Oxford University Press, 1996), pp. xv, 33; Shelby Foote, *Shiloh* (New York: The Dial Press, 1952), pp. 145–146, 150.
11. Perry Lentz, *The Falling Hills* (New York: Charles Scribner's Sons, 1967; Columbia: University of South Carolina Press, 1994), preface to the 1994 edition, n.p.
12. Lentz, *The Falling Hills*, pp. 208, 216, 233.
13. Robert Penn Warren, "When the Light Gets Green," *Southern Review* 1 (Spring 1936): 799–806; Robert Penn Warren, "When the Light Gets Green," in *The Circus in the Attic and Other Stories* (New York: Harcourt, Brace and Co., 1947), pp. 88–95; Peter Taylor, "In the Miro District," *New Yorker* (May 14, 1977), pp. 34–48, collected in *In the Miro District and Other Stories* (New York: Alfred A. Knopf, 1977), pp. 157–204.
14. Taylor, *In the Miro District*, pp. 173, 180.
15. Taylor, *In the Miro District*, pp. 164, 185–186, 203; Taylor, interview with James Curry Robison, September 9, 1987, in James Curry Robison, *Peter Taylor: A Study of the Short Fiction* (Boston: Twayne Publishers, 1988), pp. 144–145; Catherine Clark Graham, *Southern Accents: The Fiction of Peter Taylor* (New York: Peter Lang, 1994).
16. Elmore Leonard, *Tishomingo Blues* (New York: HarperCollins, 2002).
17. Howard Bahr, *The Black Flower* (New York: Henry Holt and Co., 1998).
18. Padgett Powell, *Mrs. Hollingsworth's Men* (New York: Houghton Mifflin, 2000).
19. Peter Abrahams, *Last of the Dixie Heroes* (New York: Ballantine Books, 2001).

Tap Roots and the Free State of Jones

— Nancy Dupont —

Visitors to twenty-first-century Mississippi often learn of a legend that has endured since the state's darkest days in the nineteenth century. On the front of a brochure produced by the Jones County Chamber of Commerce, freely available at Mississippi welcome centers on interstate highways, are these inviting words: Discover the Free State of Jones. In the brochure, visitors read that, according to legend, Jones County seceded from the Confederacy at the beginning of the Civil War and became a sovereign nation, with its own laws, military units, and foreign ambassadors. As with most legends, the story of the Free State of Jones contains a bit of truth and much exaggeration. From Appomattox until today, historians have pored over countless Confederate and Union military records, personal letters, and private manuscripts to determine just how organized and sophisticated the Free State of Jones really was.

Often, however, the historical accounts ignore or give little attention to the two media that have spread the legend far and wide—newspapers and a popular book. Examining the stories that have been put into print for mass distribution provides the historian with clues as to the origins of the legend and the strength of its hold on the southern conscience. At the beginning of the secession crisis, Jones County, located in the Piney Woods section of southeastern Mississippi, was a sparsely populated county in a sparsely populated state. Only 3,323 people lived in Jones County in 1860, of whom only 407, or 12 percent, were slaves.[1] This made the county an anomaly; all Mississippi's 57 other counties had slave populations of at least 19 percent, and two counties, Isaquena and Washington, had slave populations of 92 percent.[2] Thus, residents of Jones County and the rest of the Piney Woods section lived far different lives than the wealthy planters of the Delta region. Piney Woodsmen produced livestock, and because their hogs, cattle, horses, and sheep were often free ranged, little work was required to care for them. The region's residents planted few crops, and their yields were poor.

Historian Grady McWhiney asserts that these untypical southerners were simply carrying on traditions long established in their Irish and Scottish ancestral homelands. These societal differences among antebellum Piney Woods residents left unfavorable impressions on many people who visited the region. Visitors complained of laziness or worse. "They are profane, and excessively addicted to gambling," observed one visitor. "This horrible vice prevails like an epidemic. Money gotten easily, and without labour, is easily lost."[3] That easily gotten money came from the vast supply of Piney Woods timberland, while the rest of Mississippi depended on cotton for cash. It is easy to understand why Piney Woods residents were not affected by the growing sectional crisis, the shifting power in American politics, and the debate over slavery. Many of them were not impressed with the reasons that led to the rise of the Confederacy, and they were even less pleased when the Confederacy asked and later demanded their service in the military.

The seed of the Free State of Jones legend was planted during the election of delegates of the Mississippi Secession Convention on December 20, 1860. Jones County sent J. H. Powell as its representative. Historians believe Powell was originally a cooperationalist, one in favor of waiting to secede until all the southern states could leave the Union together. This was a relatively conservative position, given that most delegates to the convention, from its first day on January 7, 1861, favored immediate, individual state secession.[4] By the time the final vote was taken, Powell had changed his position, casting his lot with the immediate secessionists. When word of his action reached Jones County, an angry, drunken mob gathered in the county seat of Ellisville. The crowd built bonfires and discussed how to punish Powell for his change of heart. The next day, a dummy was found hanging, accompanied by a sign: "Powell, the Anti-Secessionist Candidate."[5]

On July 12, 1864, the Natchez *Courier*, a newspaper that had editorialized against secession, printed a story that is now regarded as the legend's genesis. Under the headline "The Republic of Jones," the *Courier* wrote that Jones County had one year earlier seceded from the Confederacy and formed its own government, supposedly as a way to resist the Confederacy's conscription laws. Within a week, the article was reprinted in newspapers throughout the North and South. The New Orleans *Picayune* admitted in its July 17 edition that it had heard of the Republic of Jones but had assumed that the Confederacy had forced the county to cooperate with the war effort. But the *Picayune* now had information to the contrary, and it quoted the *Courier:*

> [Our correspondent] represented the people in the height of prosperity, and their army and navy complete, seeking to cultivate and enjoy the arts of peace. . . . The Confederacy has declared war against the republic, and sent an army under Col. Maury from Mobile to "crush the rebellion."[6]

The article went on to report the details of a "desperate battle"[7] against the Confederates which the Republic of Jones had won. It reprinted a dispatch declaring victory from Jones commander Major R. Robinson to the republic's secretary of war. Then, according to the article, the Republic of Jones appointed "ministers" to negotiate with the Confederacy. When that failed, the article stated, the Republic considered forming an alliance with the United States but it rejected the idea because the Union had demonstrated that it did not recognize the right of people to secede from their government.[8] The *Courier* admitted to its readers that the story seemed far-fetched, but it assured them "nevertheless it is true."[9]

At the time the article was published and reprinted, a band of Confederate deserters were hiding out in Jones County. The men, "owning no slaves, believing in the Union of Abraham Lincoln, hoped either to fight through the Confederate cordon and join the Federal forces, or hoped that the Yankee ranks would fight through to them."[10] The Confederates sent a band of men under the command of General Robert Lowry to catch the deserters. The man elected captain of this company of deserters was Newt Knight, who waited until the age of ninety-one to speak publicly about his Jones County company. His memories were published in the New Orleans *Item* on March 20, 1921. Knight described a rag-tag band of deserters who became furious with the Confederacy in 1862 after the passage of the Twenty Negro Law, which allowed any man owning twenty or more slaves to be exempt from conscription. Calling the conflict "A rich man's war and a poor man's fight," Knight deserted the Seventh Mississippi Battalion and returned to Jones County. "I felt like if they had a right to conscript me when I didn't want to fight the Union, I had a right to quit when I got ready," he said.[11]

The article in the New Orleans *Item* provided the second major newspaper account that gave life to the Free State of Jones legend. Knight's words wove a tapestry of rich detail about the small band of deserters and their efforts to attack Confederate conscription stations and stave off Confederate opposition. Knight admitted that there were never more than 125 in his company, and that in sixteen major battles with the Confederate forces, eleven men were killed. Lacking any formal military organization, the company often relied on its friends and its wits. Knight recalled:

> I recollect when Forrest's cavalry came a-raidin after us. They had 44 bloodhounds after us, those boys and General Robert Lowry's men. But 42 of them hounds just naturally died. They'd get hungry and some of the ladies, friends of ours, would feed 'em. And they'd die.[12]

At the core of Knight's objection to the Confederacy was the way it had come about. Rather than seceding from the Confederacy, Knight and his band of deserters believed they never seceded from the Union.

> When the Southern states was all taking vote on whether to secede, we took the vote in Jones County, too. . . . All but about seven of them voted to stay in the union. But the Jones County delegate went up to the state convention in Jackson and he voted to secede with the rest of the county delegates. He didn't come back to Jones county for awhile. It would a' been kinder onhealthy for him, I reckon.[13]

Although Lowry never completely suppressed Knight's company, the band of deserters had little success in reaching their goals. Knight claimed he sent a lieutenant to Memphis to volunteer his company for the Union army. The Federal band sent south to recruit Knight's company was attacked and forced to surrender to Confederate forces, according to Knight. He also claimed that the Union army sent rifles, which were confiscated by Confederate troops before they reached Jones County.[14] These assertions of contact with the Union army have support in various Confederate military dispatches, including one from Brigadier General W. L. Brandon to General Dabney Maury on August 14, 1864, claiming that a "Yankee lieutenant is now in Jones, entertained and protected by deserters.[15] Knight died less than a year after the *Item* article. His death was the end of a life that was unremarkable except for the legend that grew up around him.

Novelist James Street passed along that legend. Born in Lumberton, Mississippi, on October 15, 1903, Street was raised in Laurel in the heart of Jones County. He heard the legend of the Free State of Jones before he was six years old.[16] By the time he was fourteen, he was a newspaper reporter, holding down a part-time job at the Laurel *Daily Leader.*[17] At eighteen, he had a full-time job in Hattiesburg. He became a Baptist preacher, but returned to newspaper reporting after deciding he was not fit for the ministry. He worked at the Pensacola *Journal*, the Arkansas *Gazette*, the New York *World*, and the Associated Press before he began writing short stories and became a full-time freelance writer.[18]

Street's first telling of the Free State of Jones legend occurred in *Look Away! A Dixie Notebook*, published in 1936. The book was a compilation of stories he had learned as a child and during his years in newspapers. In "The Story of Ellisville," Street described a Newt Knight who could "squint across a creek and knock out a deer's eye with his muzzle-loader."[19] Street's Knight is quoted as declaring before the Civil War: "We ain't gonna fight dis wah. . . . Dis county now is de Free State of Jones."[20] Six years later, Street's fans would learn of another Jones County resistance leader, but this time he would be aristocratic, abolitionist, and the father of young woman beautiful enough to give Scarlett O'Hara a run for her money. Street's fifth novel, *Tap Roots*, was released in 1942. In it, he returned to the story of the Dabney family, a group of fiercely independent and affluent Mississippians living in a valley known as Lebanon. An earlier novel, *Oh, Promised Land*, had introduced Street's readers to the main characters; two other novels after *Tap Roots* would finish the chronicle.[21] *Tap Roots* was different, however, because it dealt with more than the economic, personal, and emotional problems of a southern family in the nineteenth century. *Tap Roots* was set during the sectional crisis and the Civil War, and each of the characters was forced to take a political stand.

In the foreword, Street makes it clear that the Lebanon Valley is in Jones County, Mississippi. However, he tells his readers that his characters are fictional and that he took many liberties with the legend. But Street makes it clear that his book is intended as an allegorical representation of the many pockets of resistance that existed in the Confederate States:

> It may surprise some of you to read that the South had many Unionists, Abolitionists and slavery haters. As a matter of fact, few Southerners owned slaves, and the South had its share of appeasers, copperheads, and draft-dodgers. The idea that the South rose to a man to defend Dixie is a stirring legend . . . and nothing more.[22]

His final words to his readers before beginning the story are a warning of what lies ahead: "If, in this story, you miss the oft-told tale of the Civil War of Gettysburg and Lee, then I am glad."[23]

The story opens with old Sam Dabney coming to grips with death under a tree (always referred to as "The Tree") on his property. He's thinking about ending life in the bosom of his extended family and with his dearest friend, Tishomingo, the only Choctaw Indian left in Lebanon. Sam's family consists of his son Hoab, who readers will learn is actually Sam's illegitimate nephew. Hoab and wife Shellie have five children. The eldest, Cormac; the beautiful young Morna; school-age twins, Aven and Bruce; and an adopted Cajun child named Kyd. The Dabneys are not slaveholders, but there are two free blacks who work for them. From the outset, the reader knows the Dabneys are a well-to-do family, owning timber land, a kiln, and the valley's only store. The other affluent family in Lebanon is the McIvors, who own slaves and plant their land in cotton. A McIvor son, Clay, is romantically linked with Morna, and the two families expect them to marry. The rest of the residents of Lebanon are poor Cajuns or Irish who work for the Dabneys or the McIvors.

The two Dabney patriarchs were split on the issue of slavery. "The only thing I've got against it is that it's unprofitable,"[24] Sam says before he dies. Son Hoab, however, is described as a "shouting abolitionist." After Sam's death, as the sectional crisis worsens, Hoab and a scheming Jackson, Mississippi, newspaper editor named Keith Alexander form an abolition society, but they realize it will be difficult to organize:

> The French of Louisiana, the Scots of North Carolina, the English of the hills, and the Irish of Mississippi had only one thing in common: poverty. The Natchez Crowd, as the South called the compromising and appearing Whigs of Natchez, were relatively unimportant. They owned thousand of slaves and were very rich, but their influence was negligible. The power was confined to the politicos, lawyers, preachers, and businessmen who owned a few slaves and who were willing to fight for the institution because the institution kept them in power.[25]

As the reader has been warned, the abolition society fails, but the seed is planted for a philosophical argument that will be made throughout the rest of the novel.

Like many novels set during the Civil War, the story in *Tap Roots* is anchored in a tale of love. Clay rejects Morna shortly after she is crippled by polio, and falls in love with her sister, Aven. The lovers go to Virginia and marry, leaving Morna with her unrequited love and jealousy. She gets attention from the scoundrel Alexander, the man with the bad reputation, but she cannot return his love because she is still in love with Clay. Only at the end of the novel will she agree to marry Alexander. In this plot structure, Street banks on the proven formula of *Gone with the Wind*, placing a hard-headed beauty in the direct path of an interesting, dangerous man. But unlike the opportunistic indifference of Rhett Butler to the southern cause, *Tap Roots*' Alexander is scornful of it and warns his newspaper readers of the price of supporting slavery:

> History will write that slavery caused this crisis. Slavery is a by-product of Southern society. It is a curse, a cancer. And unless the South cleanses itself of this sore, the world will say that it fought to keep men in bondage. You may holler high tariff and states' rights, the right of self-determination and the right of every man to revolt against an unjust government. Perhaps these are the real causes of the crisis, but the only visible cause is slavery.[26]

Hoab Dabney and Alexander turn their attention to preventing secession after Abraham Lincoln's election. Hoab decides that the senior McIvor, Doug, should run for election to the Secession Convention on an anti-secession platform. Doug is elected and Hoab warns him: "You got your orders from the people, and it is your duty to vote against secession until hell freezes over." McIvor votes with the secessionists, and when he is challenged by Alexander, McIvor shoots him in the back. Alexander is barely wounded, and McIvor, labeled a turncoat and coward, never returns to Lebanon.

Hoab decides that he and the residents of his valley will not pay taxes to Mississippi or to the Confederacy. Alexander declares: "He has in his own way proclaimed this valley to be free. Rebellion by any other name means the same. I doubt if he understands what he's done. Technically, he has set up a little monarchy. And somebody's going to get hurt."[27] The Confederacy soon comes to bring him to justice, and Hoab faces down a Confederate officer. "Go back to Jackson, sir," he tells the officer. "And tell your superiors that Hoab Dabney will pay no taxes to Mississippi. None of my money or the money of Lebanon will be used against the United States. I love the South as much as you do, but the South is wrong, and my sympathies and loyalties belong to the United States."[28]

The Confederate government in Richmond declares Lebanon in rebellion and blockades the entrances to the valley. Only by smuggling are Lebanon residents able to get weapons and newspapers. Hoab calls a Lebanon-wide meeting to inform the residents of the Confederate conscription law and the Twenty Negro Law, prompting one of the Irishmen to mutter, "It's a rich man's war and a poor man's fight and I'm not going to grease my trigger finger and risk my hide for any slaveholding bastard."[29] Hoab is encouraged by the resolve of Lebanon's poor, and he hopes that their numbers will be increased by Confederate draft-dodgers and deserters as well as Union soldiers who might hear about Lebanon and come to the aid of its cause. His wish is granted, but the immigrants are not the principle-loving patriots he is hoping for. As Lebanon's numbers increase, Alexander tells Hoab, "The scum of the world is coming in here."[30]

Soon the Confederacy sends a regiment to bring down Lebanon, and its leader is none other than Clay McIvor. Hoab believes the five hundred men in his rag-tag army will be ready soon, but he believes he needs six more hours. Morna, now restored to health, secretly gives her father the time by riding a horse to Clay McIvor's headquarters, where she seduces him and convinces him she still loves him. She even finds out what Clay will wear into battle the following day, information she gives to Alexander. The information is valuable; Alexander spots McIvor and kills him before the battle begins.

Street tells the story of the inevitable battle in fifty pages. The deserters, Unionists, and poor whites manage to come together in a common cause. "The idea of slipping through the woods, simply never entered their heads. They had a cause, and give any man a cause and he ceases to be a scheming little animal and grows to his fullness of spiritual manhood and becomes a crusader,"[31] Street writes. Lebanon loses the battle, but Hoab, Shellie, Morna, Bruce, Kyd and Alexander manage to survive by hiding out and moving through the swamps. At the end of the story, as Morna and Alexander pledge their love, the political statements are over and the futility of the fight is overshadowed only by the knowledge that the Dabney tree has deep tap roots in the soil of Lebanon.

The legend of the Free State of Jones reached its largest audience in 1948 with the release of the movie *Tap Roots,* starring Susan Hayward as Morna Dabney and Van Heflin as Keith Alexander. The Technicolor motion picture, directed by Walter Wanger, has been called "[the] attempt to prove that Susan Hayward could have played Scarlett O'Hara after all."[32] The film was shot on location in Asheville, North Carolina, a location too mountainous to have any resemblance to even the highest hills of Mississippi. There were elaborate antebellum period costumes similar to those worn in *Gone with the Wind.*[33] The movie has never been released for the home market. Street died of a heart attack in 1954, when he was fifty years old. Before his death, two more of his novels, *Good-Bye My Lady* and *The Biscuit Eater*, had been made into movies. The critics never liked his work, but the public did. He was praised for his "immense popular appeal . . . with a sure professional touch."[34]

Newspaper accounts and Street's novel have informed the world about the little county in Mississippi that said no to the Confederacy. Historians have argued for more than a century over whether Knight and his small band of deserters were truly seceding from the Confederacy, or whether they were merely hiding in the swamps of Jones Country trying to avoid military service. Historians ask if the men were truly committed to principle, or were merely uneducated cowards who had nothing else to do. But most of what the public knows of the Free State of Jones comes from the mass media, from the newspaper articles and the book that caused the legend to spread. The stories from the newspaper and the story from the book differ in major ways. First, it appears unlikely that Knight and company were abolitionists like Hoab Dabney, since anti-slavery material had been banned in Mississippi by the beginning of the Civil War. Second, while the Dabneys of *Tap Roots* had money, property, and servants, Knight had to scrape out a living by hunting his own game and growing his own vegetables.[35] Third, the sophistication of the organization and the size of the army are drastically different in the stories—the Dabneys had 500 men compared to Knight's 125.

But in other major ways, the stories are the same. In the newspaper versions of the legend, there is clearly stated opposition to Mississippi's secession from the Union and outrage that the county delegate had changed his position. In the novel, the opposition and outrage are the same. There is disgust at the Confederacy's Twenty Negro Law; Knight's description of the Civil War as a rich man's war and a poor man's fight is stated in both the newspaper and the novel. Perhaps most importantly, the lowly state of most of the men who fought for the

Free State of Jones against the Confederacy is the same in all the versions. They are poverty-stricken, hard-scrabble, independent sorts who know every inch of the woods and swamps in their county and are able to stay alive despite the forces of a major army arrayed against them.

No American seemed to have a set formula for meeting the sectional crisis of the mid-nineteenth century. In his classic essay, "The Blundering Generation," written only two years before *Tap Roots*, historian J. G. Randall asks how Abraham Lincoln's generation got itself into such a ghastly situation, which caused death and destruction at record levels. Among the elements or situations offered to explain the war, Randall lists a few: "the despairing plunge, the unmotivated drift, the intruding dilemma, the blasted hope, the self-fulfilling prediction, the push-over, the twisted argument, the frustrated leader, the advocate of rule or ruin, and the reform-your-neighbor prophet."[36] The residents of the Free State of Jones may have faced all or none of these, but their legend speaks of an even higher calling: defiance in the face of perceived error.

NOTES

1. Mississippi Power and Light Company (February 1983).
2. Ibid.
3. Timothy Flint, writing in *Recollections of the Last Ten Years*, ed. C. Hartley Grattan (1826; reprint, New York: Alfred A. Knopf, 1932), pp. 306–307, cited in Grady McWhiney, "Antebellum Piney Woods Culture," chap., *Mississippi's Piney Woods: A Human Perspective*, Noel Polk, ed. (Jackson, MS: University Press of Mississippi, 1986, p. 47.
4. Thomas H. Woods, "A Sketch of the Mississippi Secession Convention of 1860—Its Membership and Work," 6 (1902), p. 93.
5. This story, along with many others about the Free State of Jones, is told in Ethyl Knight, *Echo of the Black Horn* (Published by author, 1951).
6. "The Republic of Jones," New Orleans *Picayune*, July 17, 1864.
7. Ibid.
8. Ibid.
9. Ibid.
10. Meigs O. Frost, "South's Strangest Army Revealed by Chief," New Orleans *Item*, March 20, 1921.
11. Ibid.
12. Ibid.
13. Ibid.
14. Ibid.
15. (Washington, D.C: Government Printing Office, 1891), ser. I, 32, pt. 3, 632–633, quoted in Victoria E. Bynum, "Telling and Retelling the Legend of the 'Free State

of Jones,'" in Daniel E. Sutherland, ed. (Fayetteville, AK: The University of Arkansas Press, 1999), p. 25.

16. James Street, *Look Away! A Dixie Notebook* (New York: The Viking Press, 1936), p. v.
17. Stanley J. Kunitz, ed., *Twentieth Century Authors: First Supplement—A Biographical Dictionary of Modern Literature* (New York: The H.W. Wilson Company, 1955), p. 966.
18. Ibid.
19. Street, *Look Away*, p. 20.
20. Ibid., p. 23.
21. Max J. Herzberg, *The Reader's Encyclopedia of American Literature* (New York: The Thomas Crowell Company, 1962), p. 233.
22. James Street, *Tap Roots* (New York: The Dial Press, 1942).
23. Ibid., p. 11.
24. Ibid., p. 30.
25. Ibid., p. 123.
26. Ibid., p. 183.
27. Ibid., p. 268.
28. Ibid., p. 328.
29. Ibid., p. 387.
30. Ibid., p. 414.
31. Ibid., p. 486.
32. Robert Laguardia and Gene Arceri, *Red: The Tempestuous Life of Susan Hayward* (New York: Macmillan Publishing Company, 1985, p. 64.
33. Ibid.
34. Kunitz, *Twentieth Century Authors*, p. 966.
35. Frost, "South's Strangest."
36. J. G. Randall, "The Blundering Generation," *Mississippi Valley Historical Review* 27, no. 1 (June 1940), p. 11.

"Savage Satori"

Fact and Fiction in Charles Frazier's *Cold Mountain*

— Paul Ashdown —

Charles Frazier has said that he could write everything he knows for certain about his Civil War ancestor William P. Inman on the back of a postcard.[1] Frazier, however, was not much interested in history or biography when he wrote his novel *Cold Mountain*, which won the 1997 National Book Award. While offering "apologies for the great liberties I have taken with W. P. Inman's life," Frazier extrapolated just enough factual information from the shards of memory and scattered documents to invent a fictional Inman, "God's most marauded bantling," one of the great doughty characters in contemporary American literature.[2]

Rather than history, Frazier's real quest in *Cold Mountain* is the recovery of language and lost tradition. His work aspires to something richly mythopoetic. "Always in my mind, this was a book about language," he says.[3] That language is rooted in a tradition Frazier sees vanishing, if not already gone, but still worth remembering. "What I was interested in," he says, "was the old lost culture of the southern Appalachians."[4] Frazier's challenge as a writer is to place Inman, the fictional character, within the framework of actual events. Once he places Inman in a real past, he then becomes obliged to confront the historical context as far as possible. This raises questions about the accuracy of events as they are used in the narrative, especially as they relate to the real W. P. Inman.

Frazier, who grew up in the small western North Carolina towns of Andrews and Franklin, has long been interested in travel and the literature of the open road. One October day in the early 1990s, he hiked several miles along a creek called Caldwell Fork in a valley of the Smoky Mountains to look for two double graves on opposite sides of Mount Sterling. In the first grave are the bodies of two civilians killed near the end of the war by troops under the command of Colonel George Kirk, a Greene County Tennessean who had led two North Carolina mountain regiments mustered into the Union Army.[5] Kirk, considered a "bushwhacker" by the Confederates, had led numerous successful sweeps through the North Carolina mountains from his base in eastern Tennessee. Frazier does not say when the men were killed, but on April 25, 1865, Kirk left Asheville on a raid through the area, and Union cavalry fought an engagement with Confederate troops near Waynesville in early May in the last skirmish of the war in North Carolina.[6]

Frazier found another double grave on the other side of Mount Sterling. In it are the remains of a fiddler and a retarded boy killed by Confederate Home Guards under Captain Robert Teague, who figures prominently in the novel. "I was not then thinking about writing a Civil War novel," Frazier says. "What I am interested in are those two double graves and what they seem to represent."[7] According to Frazier, they were "most likely old Scots" whose ancestors were exiled after the defeat of the Jacobite army at the Battle of Culloden on April 16, 1746. During the Civil War they were caught in the crossfire of two economies and two cultures. "I knew a few such people as a child, but they were old, and I know no one remotely like them now," Frazier states.

To write about the lost culture Frazier needed a point of access. Not long after his visit to the graves, Frazier's father, Charles O. Frazier, told him the story of William P. Inman, Charles Frazier's great-great uncle.[8] Inman had deserted from the Confederate Army after he was wounded. He walked several hundred miles across North Carolina to return to his home and sweetheart near Cold Mountain.[9] The man who killed the fiddler was waiting for Inman when he reached the mountains, Frazier says. "The story seemed like an American odyssey and it also seemed to offer itself as a form of elegy for that lost world I had been thinking about. So I set out on Inman's trail and followed it for five years of writing."

To write the book, Frazier sought the solitude of the mountains that provided the locale for the story. His wife's parents made available an isolated cabin, where he wrote for up to a month at a time before returning home. When he was not writing, Frazier was doing some of the meticulous research that gives the book its authenticity. For example, in one episode the wandering Inman joins a group of gypsies for supper and is offered a bottle of Moët they claim they had taken in trade. This improbable offering is authenticated by the inventory at a general store in Murphy, North Carolina, where Frazier learned that more than forty cases of Moët were sold in one year in the 1850s.[10] To learn more about music so that he could develop the character of the mountain fiddler Stobrod, Frazier attended a fiddlers' convention in Virginia. To learn about William Bartram, the eighteenth-century naturalist whose *Travels* inspired both the author and his character, Inman, Frazier visited Bartram's home and gardens, now situated in a Philadelphia housing project.[11] To get the setting for the novel right, Frazier drew on his memory of childhood visits to Cold Mountain and hikes through a valley some thirty miles distant.[12]

Frazier attempted to create an authentic regional idiom for the book. This required a mastery of the archaism and technology of rural society. Few readers, unless they are acquainted with nineteenth-century equestrian lore, could untangle such a sentence as this: "A woman snubbed a big bay up to a birch trunk and then twitched it and poured lamp oil on the frog of its hoof and lit fire to it to curb a tendency to lameness." In this context "snubbed" means checking a line suddenly while allowing it to run out, especially by turning it around a fixed object such as a post. "Twitched" means a sharp pull of a loop of rope or strap tightened over a horse's lip as a restraint. "Frog" refers to the triangular elastic horny pad in the middle of the sole of a horse's foot.[13] His solution to the problem of dialect—which he avoided—was to convey the feeling of mountain speech obliquely. "I felt the music and the rhythm were the way to do it, rather than spell things funny."[14]

Although he says he is by ancestry triply qualified for membership in the Sons of Confederate Veterans, Frazier in writing his novel was "largely uninterested in the great movements of troops, the famous personality traits of the noble generals and tragic presidents."[15] He did not visit battlefields or participate in reenactments, and he professes a personal dislike for the long-cherished southern romanticism of defeat.[16] "When you grow up in the South," he says, "you get this concept of the war as this noble, tragic thing, and when I think about my own family's experience, it doesn't seem so noble in any direction. To go off and fight for a cause they had not much relation to: that's the part I see as tragic."

Frazier makes use of the historical record in *Cold Mountain* but feels no obligation to adhere to it slavishly in creating a work of fiction. In this sense he is true to the perspective of the descendents of the actual characters, including his own ancestors, caught up in Civil War. In his study of the Shelton Laurel massacre, which occurred in the western North Carolina mountains during the war, Phillip Shaw Paludan makes a useful distinction between what historians consider history and what the people who live in the mountains mean when they talk about the past.

> The residents are not particularly concerned about linking their past with the flow of greater events outside their valley. They are only slightly interested in the Civil War generally.
>
> The past they are involved in is personal; it focuses on fathers and mothers and grandparents and uncles and aunts and cousins and all their kin, as far back as anyone can remember. . . . When people in the valley talk about the Civil War, they care little about the conflict of cultures or the breakdown of politics or the wave of modernization. . . . [The people] are not interested in the war as history. . . . They do not care that you are a historian who might be able to put such events "in a larger context." They expect historians to get the facts wrong. . . . They may even resent history.[17]

The fictional Inman is never identified in the text as William Pinkney Inman or William P. Inman. Frazier does note his debt to the real W. P. Inman in his acknowledgments, but then, curiously, apologizes for taking liberties with his life story, even though he could hardly have done otherwise, owing to the fact that practically nothing is actually known about Inman's life. Moreover, the use of the last name throughout the book signifies a certain mythic universalism to the character, much like "the man with no name" who rides across the screen in Sergio Leone's famous spaghetti westerns. The point is not so much to detach Inman from the past as it is to detach him from the William P. Inman of historicity. We learn in the novel only the bare factual outline of Inman's life.

The roster of soldiers from Haywood County who joined Company F of the 25th North Carolina Regiment, which was organized in May 1861, includes the names of J. E. Inman, L. H. Inman and William P. Inman, who was wounded at Malvern Hill.[18] In *Cold Mountain*, Inman recalls four battles in particular as examples of "unwelcome visions," and Malvern Hill is first on his list. Inman is still pained by a hip wound incurred in that battle, but it is at Globe Tavern, near Petersburg, where he suffers the nearly fatal wound that brings him to a Raleigh hospital, ostensibly to die.[19] If Inman also was injured at Globe Tavern, that fact is omitted from the roster, perhaps because of his subsequent desertion.

Inman's desertion is given little explanation or context in the novel. During his recuperation in Raleigh he reads an announcement in the Raleigh *Standard* from the state government declaring that deserters and "outliers" would be hunted down by the Home Guard.[20] The names of all deserters would be put on a list, and the Guard would be on the alert in each county. The implication, for Inman, is that desertion is now widespread. He considers his options. Although he is still severely wounded in the neck, his legs feel strong. While "careful not to look too vigorous in front of a doctor," he knows he eventually will be considered sufficiently recovered to be sent back to the fighting in Virginia. He broods over his Cherokee friend Swimmer's admonition that "a man's spirit could be torn apart and cease and yet his body keep on living. They could take death blows independently. He was himself a case in point, and perhaps not a rare one, for his spirit, it seemed, had been burned out of him but he was yet walking. . . . His spirit, he feared, had been blasted away so that he had become lonesome and estranged from all around him."

He recalls Swimmer once having told him of a celestial forest accessible from the peaks of the highest mountains where dead spirits could be reborn. Inman tells Swimmer he has climbed to the top of Cold Mountain and not seen the healing forest. But although he has lost his belief in a literal heaven, Inman still holds to the probability of an invisible world, an alternative to "a universe composed only of what he could see, especially when it was so frequently foul." Cold Mountain looms in his mind "as a place where all his scattered forces might gather," and from that point on, the idea of returning home "one way or another" determines his future course. Having returned to his hospital bed, he awakens deep into the night and simply steps through a window that had been the focus of his attention during his first weeks in the hospital, when he was practically unable to move his head. He had imagined the window "would open onto some other place and let him walk through and be there." The window becomes the window of memory through which he conjures visions of Cold Mountain, of home and childhood, and of Ada Monroe, the young woman he barely knows but still loves. Ultimately, the window is his only means of escape from the intolerable memory of the war.[21]

Most readers will not understand the significance of the epigraph from Han-shan that precedes the first chapter of the novel. Han-shan was an eighth-century Zen Buddhist philosopher, poet and hermit best known through the translations of Beat poet Gary Snyder and Jack Kerouac's autobiographical novel, *The Dharma Bums.* According to Snyder's translation, han-shan means "cold mountain." In Han-shan's poetry "cold mountain" can mean either the poet himself or the remote mountain where the poet lived, or it can serve as a metaphor for the state of satori, a spiritual dimension raised above materialism and anxiety. Frazier quotes two lines from Han-shan, as translated by Snyder: "Men ask the way to Cold Mountain. Cold Mountain: there's no through trail." In the novel, Cold Mountain is both a real place that is difficult to reach as well as a place of enlightenment that is equally difficult to reach. Inman's decision to desert the army is also the beginning of a significant spiritual journey, a journey he soon realizes "will be the axle of my life."[22]

The novel fails to make explicit the extent to which desertion was a common occurrence. While North Carolina supplied between one-sixth and one-seventh of all the soldiers who fought for the Confederacy and suffered more than one-fourth of all battle deaths, the state had almost twice as many deserters as any other Confederate state.[23] General Robert E. Lee complained in a letter to

Confederate Secretary of War James A. Seddon on May 21, 1863, that desertion of North Carolina troops from the Army of Northern Virginia was becoming so "serious an evil that, unless it can be promptly arrested, I fear the troops from that state will be greatly reduced."[24] By the time Inman began his journey to Cold Mountain, about 40 percent of all Confederate troops had deserted.[25]

Objective causes for desertion in the Confederate Army included the inevitable litany of combat complaints, made worse by the eroding military situation: wounds, disease, hunger, extreme discomfort caused by lack of proper clothing and equipment, the inability to obtain furloughs, and lack of pay. Many wounded soldiers, like Inman, who recovered from their wounds simply chose not to return to their units. Subjective causes were also numerous. Morale deteriorated as casualties mounted and southern armies continued to retreat. Many soldiers were illiterate and were unable to understand or accept military discipline. These soldiers especially were susceptible to rumors and campfire gossip that weakened their resolve to continue to fight. Others were tormented by poignant letters from their families enumerating deprivations at home.

Lee and other military and political authorities blamed peace-minded newspapers, especially the Raleigh *Standard*, for encouraging desertions. What Lee called the "disgraceful 'peace' sentiment spoken of by the *Standard*" was initiated by the paper's editor, W. W. Holden, who had already been blamed for stirring up opposition to the war in the western counties.[26] Holden, a strident critic of Confederate President Jefferson Davis, initially urged the government to open peace negotiations with the Lincoln administration, then argued that North Carolina should initiate its own peace treaty.[27] It is significant that Inman is reading the *Standard* as he begins contemplating his own course of action. We can assume that he must be aware of the peace movement and of Holden's opposition to the war.

Inman's decision to desert, however, is not primarily political. For him, the war has become an unredeemed horror, both a personal tragedy and a long, unfolding disaster for the entire country. It is the slaughter of the Federal troops under Maj. Gen. Joseph Hooker at Fredericksburg, Virginia, that Inman retains as one of his many "unwelcome visions." This battle prompted a Confederate soldier near Inman to leap atop the stone wall Hooker's troops were assailing on Marye's Heights and shout, in mock derision: "You are all committing a mistake. You hear? A dire mistake." As the slaughter continued and the blue-clad bodies continued to pile up in front of the wall, Inman "just got to hating them for their clodpated determination to die."[28] The battle reminds Inman that the Union assault was more in keeping with what he saw as Lee's reckless tactics. Seeing Lee, Lt. Gen. James Longstreet and Maj. Gen. J. E. B. Stuart before the battle, Inman contrasts the three commanders:

> Longstreet looked like a stout hog drover. But from what Inman had seen of Lee's thinking, he'd any day rather have Longstreet backing him in a fight. Dull as Longstreet looked, he had a mind that constantly sought ground configured so a man could hunker down and do a world of killing from a position of relative safety. And that day at Fredericksburg was all in the form of fighting that Lee mistrusted and that Longstreet welcomed.[29]

What especially troubles Inman is Lee's famous remark at Fredericksburg: "It is well that war is so terrible or we should grow too fond of it." The remark, passed along the wall by the troops, is to Inman a "flight of wit . . . as if God almighty Himself had spoken." Inman believes that, to the contrary, "we like fighting plenty, and the more terrible it is the better. And he suspected that Lee liked it most of all and would, if given his preference, general them right through the gates of death itself." Inman questions Lee's belief that war clarifies God's will, and worries that such logic "would soon lead one to declare the victor of every brawl and dogfight as God's certified champion."[30]

After the battle, Inman walks among the dismembered corpses in front of the wall and hears a Confederate soldier say he wishes "everything north of the Potomac would resemble that right down to the last particular. Inman's only thought looking on the enemy is, Go home."[31] Going home, of course, is Inman's own desire. He wants to live a life "where little interest could be found in one gang of despots launching attacks upon another. Nor did he want to enumerate further the acts he himself had committed, for he wanted someday, in a time when people weren't dying so much, to judge himself by another measure."[32]

Inman's antipathy to the war raises the question of his initial motivation for enlisting in the Confederate Army. Asked why he fights, Inman says, "I reckon many of us fought to drive off invaders." The defense of slavery, he believes, is not at issue because "anyone thinking the Federals are willing to die to set loose slaves has got an overly merciful view of mankind." He has heard that soldiers are fighting against industrialism. A companion has "been north to the big cities, and he said it was every feature of such places that we were fighting to prevent." But Inman believes a better explanation for the initial zeal to enlist was simply the promise of change, an alternative to boredom, rather than any ideology. "The powerful draw of new faces, new places, new lives. And new laws whereunder you might kill all you wanted and not be jailed, but rather be decorated."[33]

Inman's explanation is plausible, given the situation that existed in the North Carolina mountains at the beginning of the war. Despite strong Union sentiment, 20,000 volunteers, including William P. Inman, out of a total white male population of 68,000 in the western counties, eventually joined the Confederate forces. Men enlisted at a rate initially higher than that of the Piedmont counties. William R. Trotter concludes that the "average yeoman farmer from the highland counties was utterly indifferent to the burning issues around which the secessionist movement coalesced during the 1850s. . . . But like most other North Carolinians, the mountaineers drew the line at the prospect of armed intervention by the Lincoln administration. When Lincoln called for troops, thousands of mountain men enlisted in the Confederate Army."[34] Whatever his reasons for marching away to defend the Confederacy, William P. Inman undoubtedly was caught up in the war fever that had swept through Haywood County.

The Confederate Home Guard that pursues and finally kills Inman had a reputation for savagery. Officially organized by the North Carolina General Assembly in July 1863 as the Guard for Home Defense, the Guards replaced militia units that had been mustered into regular service. The term "home guards" previously had been used loosely to designate the state militia. After 1863, it specifically applied to the hastily assembled cavalry and infantry units that were charged with protecting citizens from Union raiders and local marauders. Governor Zebulon Vance obtained specific authority from the General Assembly to use the state militia to detain Confederate deserters, and transferred that authority to the Guard after the militia was abolished. Guard units were usually untrained, poorly equipped, and unreliable. Those who served were usually unfit for regular service because of age or wounds and not uncommonly they were renegades avoiding conscription, which had drained the state of men capable of maintaining order in rural counties.[35] Some were actually Union sympathizers. In some counties the Guard was "zealous and bloodthirsty and actively feared, however inadequately armed; in other regions of the same county, it was cowed by or actively in league with the very people it was supposed to be arresting."[36]

Ada learns from a neighbor, Esco Swanger, that Kirk's Union raiders have looted farms near the state line. They are supposed to be liberators, Swanger says, but "our own bunch is as bad or worse. Teague and his Home Guard roaring around like a band of marauders. Setting their own laws as suits them, and nothing but trash looking for a way to stay out of the army."[37] The real Colonel Robert Teague, the Home Guard commander in Haywood County, had fought against Kirk over control of Big Creek, a center of Unionist sentiment in the northwestern corner of the country. Teague, according to Trotter's local sources, "had played cat-and-mouse with local deserters and had been fired on numerous times by snipers thought to have come to Big Creek." In the novel, Teague and his men are looking for information about a gang of outliers when they stumble upon the fiddler Stobrod and his companions, a retarded banjo player called Pangle, and a young deserter from Georgia.

According to local tradition, the real Teague did capture three outliers, George and Anderson Grooms and a boy named Caldwell, near the end of the war. Anderson Grooms, the model for Stobrod, believing he was being taken to jail, asked Teague if he could bring his violin. As Trotter tells the story,

> Teague said he could. Roped together, the three captives were forced to march over Sterling Gap to the Chattaloochie side of Sterling Mountain, a distance of about eight miles. Teague halted the party in deep forest. . . . "Play something for us, fiddler," commanded Captain Teague. Anderson Grooms took out his instrument and tucked it beneath his chin. In moments, the sad, minor-key melody of "Bonaparte's Retreat"—Grooms's favorite song—filled the gloom beneath the trees. Everyone in the party listened, spellbound; Grooms surpassed himself that day, infusing the tune with such indescribable longing that even his captors were moved. But not enough to bother marching their prisoners any farther. As soon as Grooms had finished his tune, all three men were lined up and shot. It is said that Grooms clutched his violin to his breast as he faced the muzzles of the firing squad. The men were left where they fell. Their kin from Big Creek came out at dusk and loaded the bodies into a sled drawn by an ox.
>
> Even today, "Bonaparte's Retreat" is known in that part of the mountains as "The Grooms Tune."[38]

Some of Inman's encounters with the Guard are also adapted from actual events. Inman and a preacher, Veasey, are captured by a Guard unit somewhere east of the mountains. Tied to fifteen other men, many of them either boys or "old greybeards" accused of being Unionists or deserters, Inman and Veasey are marched eastward for several days. Finally the Guard executes and hastily buries the captives. "When the firing was done, the Guard stood as if unclear as to what the next step might be. One of them seemed taken by some fit or spell, and he danced about and sang Cotton Eye Joe and capered until another man hit him at the base of his spine with a musket." Inman, however, is only wounded, and revives—somewhat implausibly—when he is uprooted by a wild boar.[39] This story is drawn from the Shelton Laurel massacre. In January 1863, fifteen suspected Unionists in Madison County ranging in age from thirteen to sixty were rounded up by troops under the command of Lt. Col. James A. Keith and marched toward Knoxville, where they were told they would face trial. Two escaped before the march. A few miles down the road the thirteen remaining prisoners were executed and buried in a shallow mass grave. A soldier danced above the bodies. Hogs rooted up a victim before families found the grave.[40]

As Inman draws ever closer to his reunion with Ada, the contrast between the two characters intensifies. We learn considerably more about Ada, a more fully realized character with a family lineage, Charleston roots, prejudices, preferences, and opinions on a range of subjects. Ada grows in ability, confidence and self awareness, learning that "just saying what your heart felt, straight and simple and unguarded, could be more useful than four thousand lines of John

Keats."[41] Inman, however, evaporates physically and emotionally as his journey progresses. He convinces himself that the redemption he seeks from the war, from history, from the world beyond the mountains, will be denied him, that it is "his lot to bear the penalty of the unredeemed, that tenderness be forevermore denied him and that his life be marked down as a dark mistake."[42] The best he can do is yield to the forces of nature, until finally he stops "at a place where the hemlocks stood black around him and made a world undifferentiated, with no compass degree preferable to another and with not a sound but snow falling on snow, and he reckoned if he lay down it would cover him and when it melted it would wash the tears from his eyes and, in time, the eyes from his head and the skin from his skull."[43]

When Inman finally meets up with Ada, she fails at first to recognize him. Inman accepts this disappointment stoically: "Entirely warranted, and in some way expected. He thought, Four years gone warring, but back now on home ground and I'm no better than a rank stranger here. A wandering pilgrim in my own place." And even when she does recognize and succor him, he warns her that he is "disordered" and "ruined beyond repair, is what I fear."[44] Ada believes there is a remedy of sorts, something that comes from within: "What she thought was that cures of all sorts exist in the natural world. Its every nook and cranny apparently lay filled with physic and restorative to bind up rents from the outside. And there was spirit rising from within to knit sturdy scar over the backsides of wounds."[45] She believes some people can be mended, and tells Inman, "I don't see why not you." Inman ponders the possibility, and decides that even if the rooted sorrow can never be removed, "we do well not to grieve on and on. . . . What you have lost will not be returned to you. It will always be lost. You're left with only your scars to mark the void. All you can do is go on or not." In Ada's love, at least, there is the beginning of redemption, the road to satori.

But history, which looms over the pages of the novel like the shadow of a malevolent black crow, has something else in store for Inman. The inevitable final confrontation with Teague and his Guard, ominously accompanied by a wolfhound and a bloodhound, occurs. Inman looks for a stone wall like the barrier that protected him at Fredericksburg, but there is to be no wall in this fight. Nor will words be of use—only cold-blooded, visceral violence is an option: "There was no sense talking with such men. Language would change nothing, no more than gabbling sound into the air." Inman, using the skills he has acquired in the war, kills them all, except for a strange boy called Birch, "a white-headed boy" who sports a nail on his left index finger "near as long as the finger itself, the way some people will grow them for cutting butter and dipping lard."[46]

The battle-scarred Inman studies this fey child-wraith, of whom he knows nothing except that he is one of Teague's riders.

> Inman could see that he had lost his hat. His head was white. He looked to have German or Dutch blood in him. Maybe Irish or some inbred product of Cornwall. No matter. He was now American all through, white skin, white hair, and a killer.

Inman tries to negotiate with Birch, who perhaps represents the war's corruption of innocence, and urges him to give up his pistol. "I'm looking for a way not to kill you," he says. "We can do this so that twenty years on, we might run into one another in town and take a drink together and remember this dark time and shake our heads over it." The boy refuses, and after he is knocked from his horse and lies sprawled in the snow, Inman stands close by and levels his LeMat pistol at him.

> The boy looked at him and his blue eyes were empty as a round of ice frozen on a bucket top. He looked white in the face and even whiter in crescents under his eyes. He was a little wormy blond thing, his hair cropped close as if he had recently been battling headlice. Face blank.

But Inman doesn't see the pistol in the boy's hand, and in a moment Inman is mortally wounded. Birch, an American killer, the pale rider of the Apocalypse, looks at his pistol and can only utter a backwoods blasphemy, "They God." When Ada reaches Inman, he dreams "a bright dream of a home. . . . Everything coming around at once. And there were white oaks, and a great number of crows, or at least the spirits of crows, dancing and singing in the upper limbs." Satori deferred, but perhaps not denied. Ada is carrying a child he will never see.[47]

Charles Frazier's ambitious novel succeeds at a number of levels. The author recovers a language and a culture often marginalized today, just as it was during the Civil War. His novel shows the plight of poor and ill-defended individuals, both cruel and merciful alike, swept up in terrible events that changed their lives and became the heritage of their descendents. The author, himself a child of that heritage, reminds us there is little romance in war. By making use of folklore, legend, and mythology as well as the limited documentary record, Frazier suggests that the past is a persistent story, a mutable memory, that really happened, although we can never know all that happened, or why. All we can know is that the past is never really over. If Inman represents something more than a historical actor, a surrogate Odysseus in a national creation myth, his story says less about the Civil War than it does about the search for the universal in the particular and the infinite in the strictures of time.

The two epigraphs point us in the right direction. Inman, like Han-shan, seeks the way to Cold Mountain, but there's no through trail. Standing on the threshold of modernism, emerging broken and bloodied from the trenches of Petersburg a mere half-century before the trenches of Flanders would swallow up another generation of young men, Inman clings to the subjective, romantic vision of nature he finds in the battered copy of Bartram's *Travels* he takes with him on his journey. Frazier reminds us that Darwin's dreadful but quiet war of organic beings makes the way to Cold Mountain a savage satori from which history offers no solace or exit. Only love can do that.

After the book was nearly completed in 1996, Frazier climbed the hill where his father told him the real Inman is buried. He found only rotted wooden markers and flat stones whose inscriptions had worn away. Still, says the author, "If he's there he has a fine view to the forks of the Pigeon River, where once stood a Cherokee town called Kanuga, not a trace of it left but potsherds in the river sand. His long view is up toward Cold Mountain. I am in his debt and I wish him peace."[48]

Notes

Parts of this discussion were first presented at the Symposium on the 19th Century Press, the Civil War, and Free Expression, in Chattanooga, Tennessee, on Nov. 6, 1998, and then as the Robert Foster Cherry Lecture at Baylor University on Jan. 27, 1999. A shorter version, "Tracking the Old Sow Bear: Fact and Fiction in Charles Frazier's *Cold Mountain*," appeared in the Fall 2000 issue of *Proteus* (pp. 29–31), and a book-length study, *A Cold Mountain Companion*, was published by Thomas Publications, Gettysburg, Pennsylvania, in 2004.

1. Tony Horwitz, "Celebrated in Fiction, Real Cold Mountain Is a Far Different Place," *The Wall Street Journal*, July 16, 1998, A1, A8.
2. Charles Frazier, *Cold Mountain* (New York: Atlantic Monthly Press, 1997), p. 53.
3. Maile Carpenter, "Hot Mountain," *News & Observer*, Raleigh, North Carolina, July 10, 1997.
4. Mel Gussow, "How a Family Tale Became a Word-of-Mouth Phenomenon," *The New York Times*, August 27, 1997.
5. Phillip Shaw Paludan, *Victims: A True Story of the Civil War* (Knoxville: University of Tennessee Press, 1981), p. 122.
6. John G. Barrett, *The Civil War in North Carolina* (Chapel Hill: University of North Carolina Press, 1963), pp. 391–392.
7. Charles Frazier, "Cold Mountain Diary," *Salon*, July 9, 1997.
8. Some press accounts confuse Frazier's great-great uncle with his great-great grandfather, also a Confederate soldier. See, for example, Malcolm Jones Jr., "A Yarn Finely Spun," *Newsweek*, June 23, 1997, p. 73.
9. Frazier, "Cold Mountain Diary."
10. Frazier, p. 98; Gussow.
11. Gussow.
12. Horwitz, A1, A8.
13. Frazier, p. 97. Definitions are from *Webster's New Collegiate Dictionary* (Springfield, Mass.: G&C. Merriam, 1975).

14. David Streitfeld, "Civil War Novel Strikes a Prize-Winning Chord," *International Herald Tribune,* November 20, 1997.
15. Charles Frazier, "Cold Mountain Diary."
16. Streitfeld.
17. Paludan, p. xii.
18. J. W. Moore, *Roster of North Carolina Troops in the War Between the States* (Raleigh, 1882).
19. Frazier, pp. 6, 18.
20. Richard Bardolph found that North Carolina newspapers were no longer running such advertisements in 1864 because of the extent of the desertion of North Carolina troops as well as the fact that earlier advertisements had been ineffective. Richard Bardolph, "Inconstant Rebels: Desertion of North Carolina Troops in the Civil War," *North Carolina Historical Review* 41:2 (April 1964), p. 170.
21. Frazier, pp. 1–19.
22. Frazier, p. 55.
23. Barrett, p. 28; *North Carolina Civil War Documentary,* ed. W. Buck Yearns and John G. Barrett (Chapel Hill: University of North Carolina Press, 1980), p. 125; Ella Lonn, *Desertion during the Civil War* (New York: Century Co., 1928), p. 231.
24. *War of the Rebellion: A Compilation of the Official Records of the Union and Confederate Armies* (Washington: Government Printing Office, 1880–1901), Ser. 1,25, Pt. 2: 814.
25. Bardolph, p. 165. See also Mark A. Weitz, *More Damning than Slaughter: Desertion in the Confederate Army* (Lincoln: University of Nebraska Press), 2005.
26. *Official Records,* Series I, XXVII, Part III, 1,052; *Official Records,* Series I, XLIX, Part 1, pp. 1034–1035. Barrett, p. 182.
27. Barrett, p. 171.
28. Frazier, p. 7.
29. Frazier, p. 6.
30. Frazier, p. 8.
31. Frazier, p. 9.
32. Frazier, p. 343.
33. Frazier, pp. 217–218.
34. William R. Trotter, *Bushwackers! The Civil War in North Carolina.* Vol. 2, *The Mountains* (Winston Salem: John F. Blair, 1998), 35–36.
35. W. Clark, "The Home Guard," *Histories of the Several Regiments and Battalions from North Carolina in the Great War 1861–'65. Written by Members of the Respective Commands,* ed. W. Clark (Goldsboro: Nash Brothers, 1901), pp. iv, 649; W. A. Joyce to Z. B. Vance, Sept. 10, 1863, Z. B. Vance Papers, North Carolina Department of Archives and History; Barrett, pp. 233–242.
36. Trotter, p. 107.
37. Frazier, p. 34.
38. Trotter, pp. 178–179.

39. Frazier, pp. 177–180.
40. Paludan, pp. 84–98.
41. Frazier, p. 272.
42. Frazier, p. 245. Clint Eastwood's western oeuvre suggests numerous similarities between Inman, "the man with no name," and many of Eastwood's most memorable characters, especially Will Munny, in the 1992 film *Unforgiven*.
43. Frazier, p. 316.
44. Frazier, p. 333.
45. Frazier, p. 333.
46. Frazier, pp. 290–291.
47. Frazier, pp. 345–353.
48. Frazier, "Cold Mountain Diary."

PART IV

"History with Lightning"

"History with Lightning"

The Legacy of D. W. Griffith's *The Birth of a Nation*

— Phebe Davidson —

Released in 1915, motion picture director D. W. Griffith's groundbreaking epic, *The Birth of a Nation,* represents a critical moment in both the history of the nation and the history of American film. The movie is generally credited with setting new narrative and technical standards for the film industry, including the pioneering use of tracking shots, panning, crosscutting, and close-ups. At the same time, the movie is criticized for reflecting and capitalizing on the worst aspects of the nation's uneasy racial climate. Even today, Griffith's film is a remarkably powerful and controversial document of American popular culture during the so-called Jim Crow era of legalized and *de facto* segregation.

The substance of the nearly three-hour-long extravaganza, drawn largely from Thomas Dixon's anti-black novel *The Clansman*, consists of a pair of love stories embodying the melodrama of post-Civil War Reconstruction and the crucial fable of the white race's return to power through the leadership of the Ku Klux Klan. The love stories provide for the romantic union of the white children of North and South, a favorite dramatic device for novels, movies, and plays in the post-war period. The melodrama of Reconstruction presents white southerners of the planter class being assaulted and humiliated by arrogant, foolish, and bullying blacks. The fable of the Ku Klux Klan posits that terrorist organization as the only saving and unifying force in a region beleaguered by rebellious and vengeful former slaves.

Like most of Griffith's work, *The Birth of a Nation* is plagued by his weaknesses as a director and storyteller. The characters are one-dimensional and artificial, the plots thin and obviously contrived. The story relies heavily on the use of didactic title cards and superimposed allegorical figures to direct the audience's thinking. Nonetheless, the movie retains a great deal of power because of the skill with which the director intertwines plots and particularly because of the innovative and masterful cinematic techniques he employs. With a running time of 165 minutes (subsequent to a nine-minute cut), *The Birth of a Nation* was the longest and most ambitious movie of its day.

The film makes more extensive and skillful use of crosscutting than previously had been seen in American movies. Griffith crosscuts not only between parallel stories, but also between stories and title cards,[1] and—most originally—between the broad action of the story line and close-ups of the individual characters involved. This serves to generate tension and suspense, as well as creating nuance and depth of expression. The imposition of allegorical figures, such as the one seen at the movie's close when the horseman of war dissolves into the prince of peace, may appear clumsy and overstated by today's standards, but in less sophisticated 1915 it was a stunning visual effect.

No brief summary can do full justice to Griffith's three hours of film, but some overview of the movie is necessary to assess its significance and effects. The movie is presented in two parts. The first deals with the Civil War and the events leading to Reconstruction; the second deals with Reconstruction itself. The people whose personal stories are used to illustrate the director's perspective occupy both historical periods in the film.

The parallel love stories involve two white American families, the Stonemans from the North and the Camerons from the South. These families represent the real (read *white*) America. The northern patriarch is Congressman Austin Stoneman, played by Ralph Lewis, modeled with great—one is tempted to say libelous—liberty[2] on the historical figure of Pennsylvania Congressman Thaddeus Stevens, a proponent of the harshest form of congressional Reconstruction. He is a liberal and thus a "bad" white man.[3] Devoted to the political and social advancement of African Americans, he cannot master his own lust for Lydia, played by Mary Alden, his opportunistic mulatto housekeeper. Of his two sons, the younger, Tod (Robert Harron), will die in the Civil War, ironically reunited with one of the Cameron sons. The elder son, Phil (Elmer Clifton), will survive and marry Margaret Cameron (Miriam Cooper), a true daughter of the South. Stoneman's one daughter is the beautiful Elsie, played by Lillian Gish.

The southern patriarch, Dr. Cameron (Aitkin Spottiswoode), is a wealthy planter who lives with his wife and children in a mansion located in Piedmont, South Carolina. If Cameron is the model southern patriarch, his wife (Josephine Crowell) is the model mistress of the planter class. Their five children include the eldest son, Ben (Henry B. Walthall) and his two younger brothers, Wade (George Beranger) and Duke (Maxfield Stanley). Like Tod Stoneman, these two younger sons will die in the Civil War. The Camerons also boast two daughters, of whom the elder, Margaret, ultimately to marry Phil Stoneman, is described as "a daughter of the old South trained in manners of the old school."[4] Her sister Flora (Mae Marsh), the youngest of the Cameron children, is described as "Flora, the little pet sister." She will leap to her death to escape the lascivious advances of a former slave.[5] Cameron's wealth, derived from the work of his many slaves, allows his family to live in mythic comfort and gentility.

As the stories of the northern and southern families develop and interconnect, the audience sees the older sons as school friends and the younger sons as chums. Later, of course, they will meet as adversaries on the battlefield, where the younger sons will die. The elder sons each fall in love with the beautiful daughter of the other family. These burgeoning love stories are nearly derailed by the Civil War, Emancipation, and Reconstruction. All obstacles are finally overcome, however, and both couples are united—a symbolic double marriage of North and South.

If the young people of the Stoneman and Cameron families appear as victims of the war, the same cannot be said of the major figures in the Reconstruction melodrama. In this plot, the audience is given two primary villains, the senior Stoneman and his mulatto henchman Silas Lynch (George Siegmann), who is appointed by Stoneman to be lieutenant governor of South Carolina. The plot is developed in a pastiche of scenes in which the old master, Cameron, is tormented by his former slaves, whose newfound freedom affords them the chance to abuse the same man who has, if the film is to be taken seriously, well cared for them in the past. Cameron is ultimately rescued by a "good" black, the family's mammy, who is identified in the film's cast list as "Mammy, *the faithful servant.*"[6]

An even more provocative subplot is developed in which Gus, "a renegade negro," makes advances to Flora Cameron. To escape him,[7] she leaps from a high cliff to her death. Meanwhile, Silas Lynch is pursuing Elsie Stoneman. Miscegenation, clearly, is perceived by the film's makers as a serious threat and an absolute evil.

The saga of the birth and rise of the Ku Klux Klan, introduced well into the movie's second part, is necessary to draw the preceding plots together and to establish the audience's perception of the heroic nature of the Klan itself, arising from the inherent necessity and rightness of white rule. By this time in the film, Ben Cameron has returned home from the war. He has recovered from his physical but not his emotional wounds, which include the loss of his family's wealth, the deaths of his brothers, and the loss of political power by white South Carolinians. He sits on a mountainside agonizing "over the degradation and ruin of his people."[8] A pair of white children come up the path, carrying with them a white sheet. They spy a group of four black children farther down the trail and hide under their sheet to wait. When the black children arrive, the white children begin making scary noises, swaying like a misshapen ghost. The black children run away, terrified, and Ben Cameron is struck with a sudden inspiration—the Ku Klux Klan is born.[9]

Subsequently, the Klan is shown throwing the fear of God into fractious blacks and avenges the implied violation of Flora Cameron by capturing and executing Gus.[10] When his dead body is delivered to Silas Lynch, bearing a note that says KKK, the accompanying title card bears the caption: "The answer to blacks and scalawags."[11] In this way the Ku Klux Klan makes the world, or at least this particular part of the South, safe once more for whites, whose rule is seen as the only way for the nation to achieve political stability underpinned by sound moral and ethical values.

Within the film industry, the influence of *The Birth of a Nation* has been tremendous—nearly incalculable. According to Everett Carter, the movie does indeed herald a birth, but not of a nation. Rather it is the birth "of an American industry and an American art; any attempt to define the cinema and its impact upon American life must take into account this classic movie."[12] The narrative pattern for the plantation tradition rests largely on the underpinnings of Griffith's film. In films up to and including *Gone with the Wind,* the Civil War remains the War of Northern Aggression, while the southern plantation is presented as an Edenic site where slaves and their owners live happily and harmoniously. White southern womanhood is genteel, lovely, and humane; white southern men tend to be dashing cavaliers. Anomalous figures (Jezebel, Scarlett O'Hara) serve merely to underscore the inherently correct and decorous social order represented by the white, aristocratic South.

Slaves in the genre are generally represented as being happy with their lot and endlessly loyal to their owners. To be sure, there are some flawed (rebellious) blacks, but they serve, like the anomalous white characters, to underscore the blissful nature of the southern plantation. As pointed out by film historian Ed Guerrero, *The Birth of Nation* exists for African Americans as the "starkly racist slander of 1915."[13] It was not until the late 1960s that Hollywood productions underwent a shift of perspective in the plantation genre, with such movies as *Drum* and *Mandingo,*[14] both of which presented the plantation as a nightmarish locus of perverse sex and physical abuse.

Drawing heavily on the already established literary tradition of plantation fiction, *The Birth of a Nation* offers numerous stereotypes that support the racist agenda of the genre. Within the southern point of view espoused by both Griffith and Thomas Dixon, who share writing credit for the movie, there are good whites (the Camerons) and bad whites (Congressman Stoneman). The good whites are southerners—Christian, chaste, and genteel. They have larger families and deeper loyalties than most northerners. They are good-looking, as the patriarchal Dr. Cameron demonstrates. "The kindly master of Cameron Hall,"[15] no longer young, remains tall and dignified, sporting a mane of silver hair and even features. The bad whites in the movie are northerners, victims of their own lust and easily manipulated by opportunistic blacks. They are not physically attractive. Congressman Stoneman, for instance, wears a bad wig and has a deformed foot that skews his gait—defects of the body that mirror defects of the soul. He is seduced by his mulatto housekeeper, a failing described in Griffith's title card as "The Great Leader's weakness that is to blight a nation."[16]

Within the same perspective, there are good blacks and bad blacks. The good blacks are loyal servants who rejoice in their lot and will do anything to help their owners. Typical representatives are the mammy, a substantial figure who brooks no nonsense from less contented blacks and who both mothers and otherwise supports her white family. Joining her in the gallery of black goodness are the loyal slave, exemplified by the field hands and house servants who do not betray their master after Emancipation, and the dancing buck, a variant on the happy darky of plantation fiction. Like the mammy who saves the aged and frail Dr. Cameron from a mob of vengeful former slaves, the happy darky is present on the Cameron plantation in the form of dancing bucks who dance away their two-hour dinner break for their own pleasure and to entertain the whites who happen by.

Mulattos form a subclass of blacks in the movie. Unlike other blacks, they are presented as being incapable of goodness. Stoneman's housekeeper, Lydia, is an example of the mulatto woman who trades on the combination of her light skin and black sexuality to ensnare—enslave?—Congressman Stoneman. According to one of Griffith's title cards, she is "roused from ambitious dreamings by Sumner's curt orders."[17] She later trades on her status as Stoneman's paramour to insult Sumner, who is more discerning than Stoneman himself. Similarly, Silas Lynch is in some way spoiled by his white blood, believing that even though he remains black in the eyes of society, he is now entitled to white privileges, including the sexual favors of a white woman (Elsie Stoneman) who has rejected him and whom he kidnaps in order to secure her submission. Gus, characterized by one of Griffith's title cards as "a renegade Negro,"[18] is a central character whose villainy serves to advance the dramatic action of the movie. In his desire to wed a white woman, he is the embodiment of an evil so terrifying to the movie's whites that they must destroy him, an act they perform with righteous enthusiasm under the aegis of the Ku Klux Klan.

Given the racially uneasy state of American life in 1915, it is not surprising that the film's impending release generated a firestorm of public response. The youthful National Association for the Advancement of Colored People (NAACP), founded in 1910 and already working actively to promote full social equality for American blacks, was to mount an important protest and boycott of Griffith's epic. At the same time, many whites in both the North and South subscribed to the belief that African Americans were inferior and had to be kept disenfranchised to the greatest extent possible. Among these whites was novelist Thomas Dixon, whose novel *The Clansman* was the starting point for *The Birth of* a *Nation.* Born in 1864, Dixon spent his early years in the vicinity of Shelby, North Carolina. At the age of eight, he would later claim, he witnessed a legislative session of the South Carolina state legislature comprised of "ninety-four Negroes, seven native scalawags, and twenty-three white men."[19]

A man of restless intelligence, Dixon was a graduate of Wake Forest College. He also spent some time at Johns Hopkins University, where he became a friend of future president Woodrow Wilson, who at that time was engaged in graduate work. At the age of twenty, Dixon served a term in the North Carolina state legislature. Subsequently, he tried his hand as an essayist, actor, lawyer, clergyman, and lecturer.[20] When he turned to literature, he enlisted the help of another school friend, Walter Hines Page of Doubleday, to secure publication of his novels. Dixon's purpose throughout his career was to inform the larger world of the "true" state of affairs in the South and to discredit what he believed was the skewed Yankee version of events during the Civil War and Reconstruction periods. His trio of novels about the Reconstruction—*The Leopard's Spots: A Romance of the White Man's Burden* (1903), *The Clansman: An Historical Romance of the Ku Klux Klan* (1905), and *The Traitor: A Story of the Rise and Fall of the Invisible Empire* (1907)—combined to give him credence as an expert on the period, someone whose direct experience underlay his work, even though he would have been far too young during Reconstruction to have remembered the events he recounted, many of which did not actually occur.

The most successful of his novels, *The Clansman,* he recast as a play, seeking a broader audience for the southern point of view regarding the Civil War, Reconstruction, and race.[21] Ultimately, he came to believe that motion pictures were the greatest movers of the masses and would be an excellent vehicle for his material. He was extremely lucky in finding D. W. Griffith. The director was himself a Kentuckian, the son of a Confederate cavalryman, and he already shared some sympathy with Dixon's perspective. Griffith had grasped the potential for increased scope in the cinema, and he was eager to make something larger and more ambitious than the typical one-reeler.[22] After six weeks of rehearsal, *The Birth of a Nation* began shooting on July 4, 1914 and took nine weeks to complete.[23]

Although the movie relies most heavily on *The Clansman* for its material, it also draws on Dixon's other novels to some extent. While some film analysts maintain the film contains a good deal of Griffith,[24] especially in its prewar sequences, historian John Hope Franklin asserts that the movie's content is "pure Dixon."[25] Whichever view is more accurate, the movie stands as a problematic cultural document. As racist fiction it is certainly objectionable to modern tastes, but *The Birth of a Nation* achieves its most troubling effects by presenting itself as a work of history, which is an outright lie. The movie's second title card holds the caption: "The bringing of the first African to American planted the first seed of disunion."[26] Following this card is the image of cringing blacks emerging from a ship to the sale block and passing before the raised arms and judgmental countenance of an ostentatiously praying New England Puritan. By implication, this places the blame for the South's peculiar institution on the North, an exculpatory over-simplification.

The second part of the movie is introduced by a title card that avers: "This is an historical presentation of the Civil War and Reconstruction Periods"[27] and is followed by selected quotations from Woodrow Wilson's *History of the American People,* arranged sequentially, on title cards in the movie:

> "Adventurers swarmed out of the North, as much the enemies of one race as the other, to cozen, beguile, and use the negroes. . . . In the villages the negroes were the office holders, men who knew none of the uses of authority except its insolences."
>
> "The policy of the congressional leaders wrought . . . a veritable overthrow of civilization in the South . . . in their determination to *put the white South under the heel of the black South.*"
>
> "The white men were roused by a mere instinct of self-preservation. . . . until at last there had sprung into existence a great Ku Klux Klan, a veritable empire of the South, to protect the Southern country."

These title cards are followed immediately by another, which lacks the "Woodrow Wilson" acknowledgment but carries the same historical authority:

> "The Uncrowned King. [Austin Stoneman]
>
> "The executive mansion of the nation had shifted from the White House to this strange house on Capitol Hill."

The implication of this sequencing is that all statements are factual, and all carry the same weight as the history written by the sitting American president. The suspect nature of Wilson's history in terms of adherence to fact would not have been within the purview of many moviegoers, large numbers of whom embraced the same attitudes about race as Wilson, and many of whom did not enjoy lives that encouraged them to read. Considering the weight given to his words, it is small wonder that Wilson said of the movie that it was "like writing history with lightning," concluding, "My only regret is that it is all so terribly true."[28]

Historical misrepresentations are deliberately manipulated in *The Birth of a Nation*, as in the use of historical facsimiles within the movie. Three such facsimiles are Ford's Theater, where the audience witnesses Lincoln's assassination; Appomattox Court House, where the audience witnesses Lee's surrender; and the House of Representatives of South Carolina. Each of these is introduced by a title card identifying the setting as a facsimile based on a historical documentation. In the first two facsimiles, the events presented match known facts. In the third, however,[29] the movie alleges that the House of Representatives was occupied by a helpless minority of twenty-three whites while the hundred plus black members took off their shoes, ate chicken, swilled liquor, and passed a law permitting the intermarriage of blacks and whites while the black lawmakers made eyes at the white women spectators in the gallery. There is no historical foundation for this scenario, and for Mast and Kawn these scenes are among the "most objectionable" in the entire movie.[30]

In fact, Dixon's purpose in bringing the filmed version of his novel to the public was not historical truth at all.[31] According to opponents of the film, one of Dixon's stated purposes "was to create a feeling of abhorrence in people, especially white women, against colored men."[32] He was also said to have "wished to have Negroes removed from the United States and that he hopes to help in the accomplishment of that purpose by *The Birth of a Nation*."[33]

There is no question that Dixon's aims were at least partially fulfilled. *The Birth of a Nation* attracted huge audiences, and ended up earning an unprecedented figure of $18,000,000 on its initial investment of $110,000.[34] On February 15, 1915, the movie was first screened at the Liberty Theatre near Times Square in New York, under the title of *The Clansman*. So powerful was the audience response to the emotionally packed epic that Dixon insisted the name be changed to *The Birth of a Nation*. Subsequent to its opening under the new title on March 3, the movie was shown 6,266 times in New York alone to a conservatively estimated 3,000,000 viewers,[35] and would be screened in thousands of other theaters across the nation.

Given its inflammatory nature, no one should be surprised that the movie attracted astonishingly vocal and active groups of partisans and opponents. Dixon, no stranger to opposition, enlisted the aid of his old friend Woodrow

Wilson, now president of the United States, arranging to screen *The Birth of a Nation* for him at the White House. He also sought to screen the movie for the Supreme Court, and was encouraged in this effort by the chief justice, himself a former member of the Ku Klux Klan. Dixon hoped that such an endorsement would enable the film to prosper despite the significant boycotts and protests mounted by the NAACP. He was not disappointed. Despite the best efforts of its opponents, the film was rarely suppressed, although Griffith did remove approximately nine minutes of film[36] consisting of 558 feet of film showing black soldiers attacking white women.[37] The Klan, more or less moribund prior to the movie's advent, was revived in Georgia. No fewer than 25,000 Klansmen in full regalia marched down Peachtree Street in Atlanta to celebrate the opening there of Griffith's movie,[38] and in one southern theater, the crowd was so enthusiastic that they actually shot up the screen[39] in a frenzy of participatory enthusiasm.

What is left when the dust has settled is a movie that still retains great power due to its technical proficiency and innovations, but which is at best the "record of a cultural illusion"[40] and not, despite its claims, of history itself. Even before the movie begins, the audience is faced with one of Griffith's didactic title cards.

> **A Plea for the Art of the Motion Picture**
>
> We do not fear censorship, for we have no wish to offend with improprieties or obscenities, but we do demand, as a right the liberty to show the dark side of wrong, that we may illuminate the bright side of virtue—the same liberty that is conceded to the art of the written word—that art to which we owe the Bible and the works of Shakespeare.[41]

Particularly chilling is to read *The Birth of a Nation*'s effect upon millions of viewers whose understanding of American history was thenceforward shaped not by any reality, but by the movie's deliberate misconstruction of events and their meanings. Even today, the battlefield scenes carry the same power as the famous Brady photographs, bringing the viewer into the experience of war in very immediate and powerful ways. Prior to *The Birth of a Nation*, no one had fully envisioned the power of feature length movies to sway the emotions. No one had fully understood their power to attract audiences.

If the movie's influence on the mainstream plantation genre film now seems predictable, other effects seem less so. The rise of independent black film companies could hardly have been a goal of Dixon or of Griffith, yet they were indeed formed and clearly arose in response to *The Birth of a Nation*. Thus, for instance, 1916 saw the creation of the Lincoln Motion Picture Company. Two years later came the release of *The Birth of a Race*, the first independent film production of Booker T. Washington's personal secretary, Emmett J. Scott, and the beginning of Oscar Micheaux's now legendary career as an independent black filmmaker. Less predictable, although it would probably appeal to Dixon, is the fact that the film remains in use today as "a recruitment piece for Klan membership."[42]

The trenchant lesson here is that the movies do not merely reflect their times and societies. They influence them in profound and unpredictable ways. *The Birth of a Nation* is, at best, a paradoxical exercise of freedom of expression, one we do well to examine for context as well as for content.

Notes

The title of this essay comes from Woodrow Wilson's description of *The Birth of a Nation* after its White House screening: "It is like writing history with lightning" (Gerald Mast and Bruce F. Kawn, *A Short History of the Movies* [Boston: Allyn and Bacon, 2000], 66; John Hope Franklin, "Birth of a Nation—Propaganda as History," in *Hollywood's America*," Steven Mintz and Randy Roberts, eds. [New York: Brandywine Press, 1993], 46).

1. Admittedly, title cards were a hallmark of silent movies. Under Griffith's direction, however, they served to heighten the drama of a sequence in the same way that drama is heightened by crosscutting to a clock's hands while a condemned prisoner waits for a last-minute pardon. For a particularly effective example of this, one has only to watch the assassination of Abraham Lincoln as presented in *The Birth of a Nation.*
2. Although Dixon publicly declared that he had revealed the real Thaddeus Stevens, the real Stevens was a childless bachelor, never went to South Carolina, and so far as is known, did not conduct an affair with his black housekeeper (Franklin, p. 49).
3. It is the vengeful Stoneman who says to Lincoln, after Appomattox, that the southerners' "leaders must be hanged and their states treated as conquered provinces" (*The Birth of a Nation*).
4. D. W. Griffith, *The Birth of a Nation*, hereafter cited as BOAN.
5. BOAN.
6. BOAN.
7. In the novel, Gus's crime is rape. In the movie, Flora's terror is sparked by Gus's unlikely statement that "You see, I'm a Captain now—and I want to marry" (*The Birth of a Nation*). The rape is implicit in the racist view of blacks that the film projects, and the audience is told by the following title card that "we should not grieve that she found sweeter the *opal gates of death*" (*The Birth of a Nation*).
8. BOAN.
9. Nothing in my reading supports this version of the Ku Klux Klan's origins. In fact, the Klan was born in Tennessee in 1866, not on a mountainside in South Carolina. That this sequence takes for granted a stereotypical perception of blacks as childish and credulous both derives from and supports the use of stereotypical figures in the plantation genre.
10. Before embarking on its mission to find Gus, the Klan witnesses a ritual dipping of the flag in the blood of the dead and dishonored Flora Cameron, surely a curious ritual for the knights of a good cause.
11. BOAN.

12. Everett Carter, "Cultural History Written with Lightning: The Significance of *The Birth of a Nation*" in *Hollywood as Historian*, Peter C. Rollins, ed. (Lexington: University of Kentucky Press, 1983), p. 9.
13. Ed Guerrero, *Framing Blackness* (Philadelphia: Temple University Press, 1993), p. 3.
14. There had been Hollywood challenges to at least some of the plantation stereotypes in such earlier movies as *Pinky* and *The Little Foxes*, but none of these were full-fledged plantation dramas.
15. BOAN.
16. BOAN.
17. BOAN.
18. BOAN.
19. Franklin, p. 43.
20. Franklin, p. 43.
21. Franklin, p. 44.
22. Franklin, p. 45.
23. Mast and Kawn, p. 63.
24. Louis Gianetti and Scott Eyman (in *Flashback: A Brief History of Film* [Englewood Cliffs, NJ: Prentice Hall, 1996]) maintain that "as a Southerner Griffith was actually something of a liberal—for his day. But he understood blacks only as a liberal nineteenth-century Southerner understood them: Negroes who were faithful . . . to their former masters were accorded respect and affection; blacks who were not loyalists were, by definition, slavering thugs with dangerous urges toward white women. Griffith's treatment of the race conflict and the Ku Klux Klan . . . to modern eyes, may appear insupportable. . . a measure of his restraint can be gauged by scanning his source material, an indescribably purple, extended rape fantasy whose author saw African-Americans as completely subhuman creatures who had to be either subjugated or exterminated" (32).
25. Franklin, p. 45.
26. BOAN.
27. BOAN.
28. Franklin, p. 47.
29. "An HISTORICAL FACSIMILE of the State House of Representatives as it was in 1870. After a photograph by the Columbia State" (*The Birth of a Nation*).
30. Mast and Kawn, p. 67.
31. The dedication of Dixon's novel *The Clansman* reads "To the memory of a Scotch-Irish leader of the South, my Uncle, Colonel Leroy McAfee, Grand Titan of the Invisible Empire of the Ku Klux Klan" (qtd. in Carter, p. 10).
32. Boston Branch of the National Association for the Advancement of Colored People, "Fighting a Vicious Film: Protest against 'The Birth of a Nation'" (1915), in *Hollywood's America*," Steven Mintz and Randy Roberts, eds. (New York: Brandywine Press, 1993), p. 79.

33. Mintz and Roberts, p. 80.
34. Gianetti and Eyman, p. 15.
35. Guerrero, p. 13; Carter, p. 9.
36. Mast and Kawn, p. 66.
37. Guerrero, p. 14.
38. Guerrero, p. 14.
39. Franklin, p. 15.
40. Carter, p. 15.
41. BOAN.
42. Tim Dilks, "The Birth of a Nation (1915)," p. 1, Aug. 5, 2000; http://www.filmsite.org/birt.html.

Hollywood Themes and Southern Myths

An Analysis of *Gone with the Wind*

— William E. Huntzicker —

By any measure, the 1939 movie *Gone with the Wind* has become one of the major classics of American cinema. Film critic Roger Ebert sums up the film's significance in three pages, noting that it presents a sentimental view of the Civil War, with the Old South replacing Camelot, and seems to suggest that "the war was fought not so much to defeat the Confederacy and free the slaves as to give Miss Scarlett O'Hara her comeuppance. We've known that for years; the tainted nostalgia comes with the territory. Yet after all these years, *GWTW* remains a towering landmark of film, because it tells a good story, and tells it wonderfully well."[1]

In its first 50 years, Margaret Mitchell's 1936 novel *Gone with the Wind* sold more than 25 million copies in 27 languages, and a special anniversary edition sent it back to the best-seller lists in 1986. In the first decade after its 1985 debut on video, *Gone with the Wind* earned more than $840 million in ticket sales, foreign rights, and sales. Susan Myrick, a journalist who had served as an adviser to the filmmakers on southern culture, claimed that 4,400 people worked on the film, which cost $4 million to make and grossed $37 million.[2]

The movie version *of Gone with the Wind* proclaims its pretensions with the opening words scrolling from bottom to top over an idyllic view of slaves driving horses and cattle silhouetted against a bright Technicolor red sky. The opening message reads:

> There was a land of Cavaliers and Cotton Fields called the Old South . . .
> Here in this pretty world
> Gallantry took its last bow . . .
> Here was the last ever to be seen
> of Knights and their Ladies Fair,
> of Master and of Slave . . .
> Look for it only in books, for it
> is no more than a dream remembered,
> a Civilization gone with the wind . . .

Mitchell, who thought she had written a realistic novel of the Old South, disliked the romanticism of the knights and cavaliers references, but film producer David O. Selznick saw the book—and movie—as a romantic story of a lost civilization.[3] The opening scene of the film says nostalgia with a shot of a long row of slaves hoeing a field; as they leave the field, they are silhouetted against a bright colorful sky that plays down the hardship of slavery. Author Alan T. Nolan has tied *Gone with the Wind* to Stephen Foster's idealized nostalgic moonlight-and-magnolias culture of the Old South on at least five subjects: slaves, Yankees, southern armies, vigilantes and Reconstruction. "That story idealized the men and women of the plantation class, suggested the superior valor of Southern manhood, and is strongly peopled with happy slaves and gentle and indulgent masters." Nolan is among many to note how the film plays down slavery as the cause of the Civil War. "The implication is that the war was not about slavery and the message is also that the slaves were well treated, happy, and did not care whether they were slaves or free people."[4] Along with other proponents of the Lost Cause myth, *GWTW* suggests that the Civil War was about more than slavery.

The Lost Cause myth emphasized southern virtue. Of course, the South never really lost the Civil War; it was merely overwhelmed by northern power and brutality. In the movie, Nolan writes, "a snaggle-toothed, evil looking Federal soldier has entered Tara to steal. Scarlett shoots him on the steps to protect herself from his rather obvious intent to assault her. The implication is that the Yankees were bushwhackers or guerilla warriors—bad people who were gratuitously and randomly upsetting the genteel and benign Southern culture."[5] Of course, Hollywood's penchant for creating a clear distinction between good and evil adds to this aspect of the Lost Cause myth. "The myth is that the defeat of the South was inevitable, that it was simply overwhelmed by massive Northern materiel and manpower and could not have won the war. The consensus among serious historians today discredits this myth."[6]

To give some credit to the filmmakers, they do express some ambivalence to elements of this myth—from the moment Rhett Butler, played by Clark Gable, makes his appearance. A bad boy from Charleston, Butler's social position is established when Scarlett asks about that "nasty, dark" man staring at them from the foot of the stairs, a mint julep glass in his hand. "That's Rhett Butler," Cathleen responds. "He's from Charleston—and he has the most terrible reputation!" To which Scarlett responds: "He looks as if—as if he knows what I look like without my shimmy!" A shocked Cathleen scolds Scarlett and tells her that Butler has to spent so much time in the North because "folks in Charleston won't even speak to him. He was expelled from West Point, he's so fast. And then there's that business about that girl he didn't marry."[7] That "business" is left vague, with a whispered revelation that the couple went for a buggy ride one afternoon without a chaperone.

Clearly, Butler is a man who does not fit into the polite society of the plantations Tara and Twelve Oaks, but his outsider status allows him to both reinforce and challenge the Lost Cause myth. His first speaking line comes after an invitation from Scarlett's father in the midst of excited anticipation about the impending war. "Mr. Butler's been up North, I hear," Gerald O'Hara says. "Don't you agree with us, Mr. Butler?" Stepping forward, Brett responds: "I think it's hard winning a war with words, gentlemen." During the conversation, he says, "there's not a cannon factory in the whole South," and even suggests that the North could win a war. "I'm saying very plainly that the Yankees are better equipped than we. They've got factories, shipyards, coal mines, and a fleet to bottle up our harbors and starve us to death. All we have is cotton . . . and slaves . . . and arrogance." (ellipses in original script) Such talk elicits gasps among this polite group anticipating a quick victory for southern virtue. The emphasis on arrogance both shocks the others and establishes Rhett as insightful outsider.

Melanie's brother, Charles Hamilton, eagerly challenges Butler for his "renegade talk," suggesting that the North could defeat the South and for calling southerners arrogant. Butler apologizes twice for his shortcomings and then, speaking to Ashley, excuses himself: "I appear to be spoiling everybody's brandy and cigars and dreams of victory." After Rhett leaves, Charles complains to Ashley that he refused to fight. "Not quite that, Charles," Ashley says. "He just refused to take advantage of you . . . he's one of the best shots in the country. As he's proved a number of times, against steadier hands and cooler heads than yours." Later, as Ashley leaves to join Rhett, Scarlett takes Ashley aside to declare her love for him, believing that once he knows that she loves him, he will not marry Melanie, whom Scarlett had described earlier as "a pale-faced, mealy-mouthed ninny—and I hate her!" Ashley admits that he loves Scarlett but calls her too passionate and too young to understand marriage. Besides, he and Melanie are much more alike. He leaves Scarlett angry and in tears, and she picks up a vase and throws it against a fireplace, breaking it. From a couch facing the fireplace, Rhett, who has overheard the entire exchange, rises and says his first words to

Scarlett: "Has the war started?"—appropriate words with which to begin their relationship.

Pouting about Ashley's marriage plans, Scarlett tells her father in their first scene together that she's not interested in Tara, even after he promises to give it to her. He cannot believe she is serious. "Land's the only thing in the world that matters!" Gerald O'Hara tells his daughter. "The only thing worth working for, fighting for, dying for! Because it's the only thing in the world that lasts!" In one of the film's famous silhouette shots with the camera backing away from the two forms against a bright sky, Gerald relates his love of land to their proud Irish heritage. "And to anyone with a drop of Irish blood in them, the land they live on is like their mother. But there, you're just a child. When you're older, you'll be seeing how it is. It will come to you, this love of the land. There's no getting away from it if you're Irish." Early on, her father establishes a major theme: her love of Tara.

This love of land is more than a sense of place, as is illustrated later in the film after the war. The importance of land also relates to the economic reality of the Great Depression, underway when the film was made. Of course, economic hardship visited Tara after the war. In affectionately telling Scarlett that Tara means more to her than even he does, Ashley picks up some of the red dirt and squeezes it into her hand. A few minutes later, the evil overseer-turned-carpetbagger Jonas Wilkerson shows up to offer to buy Tara before it is taken for back taxes. Scarlett's response is to throw the dirt in his face, saying that's all of Tara he'll ever get. Symbolically, the dirt stops the carpetbagger, but Scarlett becomes more practical by marrying her sister's beau, Frank Kennedy, so she will have the money to save Tara from the tax collector and carpetbaggers. Marrying Kennedy allows Scarlett both to keep Tara and to hold Ashley nearby. Kennedy, who arrived home a poor soldier after the war, has become a successful merchant in the postwar boom. Scarlett persuades Frank to allow her to run the fledgling lumber mill he had begun, and she hired Ashley, who had prospects in the North, to remain and manage it.

When Scarlett allows an Irish overseer a free hand to exploit convict labor, Ashley objects. "Scarlett, I don't like to interfere, but I do wish you'd let me hire free darkies instead of using convicts. I believe we could do better." Ashley protests that the foreman whips and starves the convicts: "I will not make money from the enforced labor and misery of others." To that, Scarlett snaps: "But you weren't so particular about owning slaves!" (This is, of course, one of the few places the word *slaves* appears in the film.) Ever the voice of the revisionist Old South, Ashley responds: "That was different. We didn't treat them that way. Besides, I'd have freed them all when Father died if the war hadn't already freed them." After Scarlett reminds him of the suffering of war and poverty, he responds that their friends are keeping *both* their honor and their kindness.

Scarlett's refusal to hire former slaves and her bootstraps mentality contribute to the creation of Shantytown, an encampment of homeless former slaves located between Atlanta and her lumber mill. Everyone, including Rhett, considers it a risky place for a woman to go alone. But one evening she ventures through Shantytown, and the contrasting ways in which the film and the novel handle the ensuing scene are instructive. In the novel, Scarlett encounters Big Sam, who, after a friendly exchange of greetings, escorts her through Shantytown. When leaving the mill, Sam fails to reappear, and Scarlett starts out alone in her buggy and soon is attacked by a white man and a black man. "What happened next was like a nightmare to Scarlett, and it all happened so quickly," Mitchell writes. "She brought up her pistol swiftly and some instinct told her not to fire at the white man for fear of shooting the horse. As the negro came running to the buggy, his black face twisted in a leering grin, she fired point-blank at him. Whether or not she hit him, she never knew, but the next minute the pistol was wrenched from her hand by a grasp that almost broke her wrist. The negro was beside her, so close that she could smell the rank odor of him as he tried to drag her over the buggy side. With her one free hand she fought madly, clawing at his face, and then she felt his big hand at her throat and, with a ripping noise, her basque was torn open from neck to waist. Then the black hand fumbled between her breasts, and terror and revulsion such as she had never known came over her and she screamed like an insane woman."[8] She struggles, bites the man's hand, and screams until Sam arrives and pulls the black man off her.

In the film, Scarlett is also stopped by two men, one white and one black, but the white man is the one who attacks her, while the other holds the horse. Big Sam hears her scream, runs to rescue her, grabs the white man, and knocks him to the ground. As that happens, the black man attacks Sam, who successfully knocks him off the bridge into the water below. During the fight, Scarlett rushes from the scene, and Sam runs after her. When she realizes who he is, she stops for him and they ride away in the buggy. At the end of the scene, he professes to be finished with those carpetbaggers. In Hollywood, one violent turn deserves another. Honorable southern men cannot let an attack on a white woman go unnoticed, especially when it comes from such unseemly people. Even Rhett Butler, a blockade runner and gambler who had proven himself a true southerner when he enlisted in the Confederate Army, again proves himself a southerner when he subscribes to the final element of the Lost Clause myth by helping the night riders to clean out the encampment of homeless former slaves and avenge the attempted rape of Scarlett.

Mitchell's novel is not at all subtle about the issue of vigilantism, but Selznick's film is more careful. Selznick accepted the vigilante theory of justice, but he was reluctant to name outright the Ku Klux Klan. In a long memo to screenwriter Sidney Howard, Selznick said he was uninterested in conveying Mitchell's image of the KKK: "It would be difficult, if not impossible, to clarify for audiences the difference between the old Klan and the Klan of our times. (A year or so ago I refused to consider remaking *The Birth of a Nation*, largely for this reason. Of course we might have shown a couple of Catholic Klansmen, but it would be rather comic to have a Jewish Kleagle; I, for one, have no desire to produce any anti-Negro film either. In our picture I think we have to be awfully careful that the Negroes come out decidedly on the right side of the ledger, which I do not think should be difficult.) Furthermore, there is nothing in the story that necessarily needs the Klan. The revenge for the attempted attack can very easily be identical with what it is without their being members of the Klan. A group of men can go out to 'get' the perpetrators of an attempted rape without having long white sheets over them and without having their membership in a society as a motive."[9]

As in the novel, the attack in Shantytown is the most repulsive thing Scarlett ever experienced, but her subsequent rape—or near-rape—by Rhett Butler is not so unpleasant. "Their on-again, off-again romance differs slightly from Miss Mitchell's account," Ronald Haver writes, "in that in the film Rhett tells Scarlett several times that he loves her—something he doesn't do in the book until the end. He does try to convince her that 'we belong together, being the same sort,' and after they finally marry she taunts him with the fact that 'I shall always love another man,' whereupon he does the only thing a frustrated husband could do—carries her up the stairs for a night of forced passion. Their scenes have an erotic tension and frankness daring for the time, especially in a costume picture, where everyone usually behaved with decorum and good manners."[10]

Only after this passionate night does Scarlett awake happy—perhaps beginning to realize and perhaps too late—that she really loves Rhett, who arrives to announce that he is leaving and to apologize for forcing himself upon her. Again they get into one of their periodic spats, and he storms off. When he returns, she is pregnant as a result of their night of passion. She seems truly worried. "But, Rhett, if you go, what shall I do? Where shall I go?" To respond to her questions, Selznick received special exception from Hollywood's Production Code rule against swearing to allow Clark Gable, as Rhett Butler, to deliver the most famous line in Hollywood history: "Frankly, my dear, I don't give a damn."

The electricity Gable and Leigh provided on screen related to their personal relationships, as Ebert notes. "Clark Gable and Vivien Leigh were well matched in the two most coveted movie roles of the era. Both were served by a studio system that pumped out idealized profiles and biographies, but we now know what outlaws they were: Gable, the hard-drinking playboy whose studio covered up his scandals; Leigh, the neurotic, drug-abusing beauty who was the despair of every man who loved her. They brought experience, well-formed tastes, and strong egos to their roles, and the camera, which often shows more than the story intends, caught the flash of an eye and the readiness of body language that suggested sexual challenge."[11]

Scarlett, as the center of all young men's attention, repeatedly pokes her finger in the eyes of Georgia's pretentious and hypocritical high society, whose world she clearly exploits. With Rhett's help, the self-centered Scarlett risks her life to get Melanie and her baby out of Atlanta as the city burns in the background, even while telling herself that it was only because she promised Ashley to care for them. Arriving to Tara and finding that it survived attacks, she rebuilds it through hard work and marrying for money. The courageous socialite and ruthless businesswoman who makes cutthroat deals while exploiting convict labor finally decides that what she really needs is a man—Rhett Butler. To conclude the film, Scarlett leaves Atlanta and her ostentatious home she built with Rhett to return to Tara for renewal and to contemplate how to win back the man she's decided she loves after all. She concludes with the words she always uses to put off important quandaries: "After all, tomorrow is another day!"

An interesting story with engaging and not completely virtuous characters, *Gone with the Wind* blends Hollywood themes and southern myths to give it remarkable staying power. Of course, the film romanticizes about the Old South and suffers from the nostalgia of the Lost Cause, with its view of an innocent South attacked by a brutal, overpowering North. For its day, however, the movie created complex characters—both white and black—and successfully used the grand sweep of a dramatic bygone era as a perfect backdrop for a glitzy, crowd-pleasing romance. For many viewers, it remains the most vivid and enduring image of the antebellum South.

Notes

1. Roger Ebert, *The Great Movies* (New York: Broadway Books, 2002), p. 199.
2. No author, *Margaret Mitchell: The Book, the Film, the Woman* (Atlanta: Atlanta-Fulton County Public Library Foundation, 1996), unnumbered pages.
3. Ronald Haver, *David O. Selznick's Hollywood* (New York: Bonanza Books, 1980), p. 297.
4. Alan T. Nolan, "The Anatomy of the Myth," in Gary W. Gallagher and Alan T. Nolan, *The Myth of the Lost Cause in Civil War History* (Bloomington: Indiana University Press, 2000), pp. 17, 30.
5. Nolan, pp. 30–31.
6. Nolan, pp. 30–31.
7. Some quotes from the movie are taken from Sidney Howard, *Gone with the Wind*:

The Screenplay (New York: Delta Books, 1989), but some in the film do not appear in the Howard script.

8. Margaret Mitchell, *Gone with the Wind* (New York: Warner Books, 1964), pp. 780–81.
9. Rudy Behimer, ed., *Memo from David O. Selznick* (Hollywood: Samuel French, 1989), p. 147.
10. Haver, p. 291.
11. Ebert, p. 200.

Knights in Blue and Butternut

Television's Civil War

— Paul Ashdown —

It is hardly surprising that the Civil War, the most traumatic event in American history, would become a major theme for books, magazines, songs, movies, and television. Early television writers, in particular, were influenced by the way Civil War stories had evolved in movies. The first silent films emphasized conflict and assigned blame. Films made after World War I avoided causes and issues and viewed the Civil War as bad for both sides. There were few battles. Individual heroes and the healing of sectional divisions took priority. When something about the war was attempted on early television, the result was similarly bland. *You Are There: Grant and Lee at Appomattox* (1955) created the impression that the Civil War was

> a war free of ideology, and that with the conflict ending, the nation would soon be unified again. . . . The bitterness that was felt on both sides was downplayed to the degree that the viewer is left with the impression that there were no enduring philosophical or political differences between the North and the South.[1]

Some 139 westerns appeared on television from 1946 to 1978.[2] Only two attempted to connect the Civil War to the time and place it was fought. *The Gray Ghost*, which appeared during the 1957–1958 season, was the first television series to focus on the military aspects of the conflict. *The Americans* (NBC,

1961) recounted the adventures of two brothers from Harpers Ferry, Virginia, fighting on opposite sides. The series was soon canceled. Most westerns skipped the war and avoided the controversy by focusing on Civil War veterans. Writers working this genre mined the mother lode of epic narrative, drawing on tales of wandering veterans from Ulysses to Ingmar Bergman's chess-playing knight of *The Seventh Seal*. Television westerns usually were set during the years between 1865 and 1890 rather than earlier periods of frontier history. Stories occurring before the war had to confront slavery. Stories placed during the Civil War required battle scenes and had to confront messy ideological issues. Stories set after the war emphasized reconciliation and renewal.

As script writers worked to develop plausible plots and characters to fit the quarter-century time frame, the Civil War was a narrative bank from which they could make frequent withdrawals. The war had produced thousands of rootless veterans accustomed to violence. They had drifted west to territory ravaged by brutal fighting, much of it instigated by lawless bands of marauders who had little allegiance to either side. The war in the west never really ended, and created the Wild West.

Westerns were full of characters perpetuating the vengeance and vandalism they had wrought during the conflict, as well as others who continued fighting against them. Some doughty and deranged characters emerged, including:

> **Vint Bonner**, *The Restless Gun* (NBC, 1957–1959), a western drifter who had served in the Civil War. Because of the war he hated violence, but as the fastest gun in the West, he engaged in retributive and morally ambiguous combat, a cinematic plot device employed from *Shane* (1953) to *Unforgiven* (1992).
>
> **Paladin**, a black-clad knight-errant whose calling card bore the name of the series, *Have Gun, Will Travel*, which ran on CBS from 1957 to 1963. Paladin was a Montaigne-quoting former Union cavalry officer who read newspapers in the Hotel Carlton in San Francisco to find potential clients in need of a mercenary.
>
> **Maverick** (ABC, 1957–1961), Bret and Bart, larcenous card-playing brothers who avoided conflict by comic cunning and guile. Heroism was not in the family bloodline. When Bret and Bart left for the Civil War their Pappy had told them: "If either of you comes back with a medal I'll beat you to death." He also told them, "work is all right for killin' time, but it's a shaky way to make a livin'." A movie remake of the series appeared in 1994.
>
> **Lucas McCain**, *The Rifleman* (ABC, 1958–1963), a Union Army veteran whose specialty was a modified Winchester rifle with a large ring that cocked the hammer when he drew.
>
> **Yancy Derringer** (CBS, 1958–1959), an ex-Confederate soldier, card sharp

and Mississippi riverboat captain (a sort of Cajun Rhett Butler), who prowled the Vieux Carré in New Orleans as special agent to the city's civil administrator.

Bronco (ABC, 1958, 1962), Bronco Lane, an ex-Confederate Army captain, who sometimes stopped "tearin' across the Texas Plains" long enough to battle Texas outlaws.

Colonel Ranald S. Mackenzie, commander of *Mackenzie's Raiders* (Syndicated, 1958, 1959), who led secret missions into Mexico under orders from President Grant and General Sheridan to suppress marauders, many of whom were veterans or deserters from both the Union and Confederate armies.

The Rough Riders (ABC, 1958, 1959), two former Union soldiers and an ex-Confederate soldier reconciled and chastened by battle, who roamed the Dakota Badlands as a gunslinging trinity.

The Rebel (ABC, 1959, 1961), Johnny Yuma, an angst-ridden Confederate veteran who wandered the West in bitter exile from his vanquished homeland. *The Rebel* was in some ways both a "rebel" of the 1950s and a ghost of the defeated Confederate army.

In these and other westerns, the war motivated the characters, many of whom obviously suffered from what veterans of later conflicts would call shell shock, post-traumatic stress syndrome, or simply insanity. Directors occasionally used stock footage of Civil War battles borrowed from the Hollywood movie vaults when a character needed to recall the war. With the exception of *The Gray Ghost*, the Civil War as mid-century television text was predominantly a western genre dealing with the aftermath of sectional rivalry and the struggle of the combatants to override the landscape of traumatic memory. But as writers sought ways to integrate the post-bellum anguish of the characters into the standard frontier-romantic tradition, themes dwelling on repentance, reconciliation, and healing gradually gave way to more conventional morality plays staged in frontier cattle towns like Dodge City.[3] The western landscape became mythic and moral rather than place- or time-bound. That the historical concerns of mid-century America could be projected on a sagebrush landscape indicates a "synchronization between qualities inherent within the genre and values relevant to American life at the time."[4]

The Gray Ghost was the exception to the displaced Civil War veteran narrative in the western genre. *The Gray Ghost* was based on the Civil War adventures of an actual Confederate partisan, Colonel John Singleton Mosby (1833–1916), whose audacity in the Virginia theater of war was said to have extended the life of the Confederacy by about six months. Virgil Carrington "Pat" Jones, a Virginia journalist and historian, contended that Confederate guerrillas in Virginia had been far more effective than previously thought. Encouraged by historians Douglas Southall Freeman and Bruce Catton, Jones wrote *Ranger Mosby* and *Gray Ghosts and Rebel Raiders.* Lindsley Parsons, a producer of western films, read these books and told CBS executive Tom Moore that Mosby had commercial potential. "He and I were talking about various kinds of folk heroes and this seemed like a good idea," Moore recalled.[5]

CBS did not buy book rights, but did hire Jones as a historical consultant. Parsons advised Jones that the first thirty-nine scripts would make use of some fiction, but that later scripts could adhere more to history. He told Jones he could review each script for accuracy before it went into production. Jones said the pilot film used to sell the series "wasn't too bad, except one scene that showed Mosby seated in a tent, with his name on a placard attached to the outside. I told them that, to my knowledge, Mosby never used a tent as a guerrilla leader and, had he done so, I was sure he never would have put his name on it."[6]

At the outset, CBS could not find national sponsors. Moore said: "There was some apprehension that a favorable Confederate was not in keeping with the times. A few years before, CBS had taken *Amos 'n' Andy* off the air. We tried to sell it to all the networks but they all had the same apprehension." CBS Television Sales, Inc., an autonomous unit of CBS, put the series out for syndication or sale to individual television stations. At this point, the producers found they had a hot property. During its first season, the series was lavishly praised in southern newspapers. The president of the United Daughters of the Confederacy made a five-minute TV film commending *The Gray Ghost.* Tod Andrews, a New Yorker who played Mosby "in handsome wooden fashion," made a promotional tour of the South in the spring of 1958. "They greeted me as if I were Robert E. Lee reincarnated," he told *Newsweek.*[7] The program appealed to audiences in many regions, especially the South.[8] In June 1958 it was the third most popular syndicated program, based on a weighted survey of the top twenty-two national markets.[9]

Several factors contributed to the program's appeal. It preceded the Civil War centennial by only three years, and this was a factor in the original decision to produce it. Awareness of the war was growing, and would continue to grow for the next several years. But television's Mosby faced some unexpected difficulties. In May 1954, the Supreme Court ruled that racial segregation of public schools was unconstitutional. The next decade was turbulent in the South.

In September 1957 the desegregation controversy reached a climax when national guardsmen called out by Arkansas Governor Orval A. Faubus barred nine black students from entering all-white Central High School in Little Rock. Faubus complied with a court order to remove the guardsmen, but the threat of mob violence caused President Dwight D. Eisenhower to send 1,000 federal paratroopers to protect the black students just as *The Gray Ghost* was beginning to appear on television screens across the South. CBS grumbled that the show would have been booked solid if Little Rock hadn't scared away some northern sponsors. Jones expected the series to continue, and screenwriter Jack DeWitt had already completed outlines for another year's scripts. Jones recalled: "Before the year was out, CBS informed me that I should remain ready to go back to Hollywood at any time. Two or three times I received phone calls alerting me. Then, to my surprise and disappointment, I was informed that the series would not be continued."[10]

Parsons felt that "the pros and cons of the Civil War belonged to history, and that entertainment with a historical background would be welcomed. It was. But that was before the Little Rock court decision."[11] Parsons also attributed the cancellation to NAACP pressure on sponsors. "Some of the blacks said *The Gray Ghost* glorified the whites and white supremacy," he recalled. DeWitt said he also encountered pressure from blacks. "A delegation came to me and said they didn't want blacks depicted as servants. I told them that if we used them we would use them as they were during the war. When they didn't accept that I told them we wouldn't use them at all. That was unfortunate because in the next season's shows we had two or three episodes in which blacks were heroes. I told them there would be no attempt to put them down."[12]

Critic Richard F. Shepard said that sponsoring a Civil War theme "when Federal troops were in Little Rock seemed as perspicacious an idea as one to serialize the life of Joseph Stalin as a situation comedy."[13] J. Fred MacDonald assessed the importance of the program in his history of African-Americans in television:

> There is no doubt that *The Gray Ghost* was a casualty of the segregation issue. Although it never dealt with the slavery problem in the Civil War, the premier of the series in September 1957 coincided with the inflammatory confrontation at Central High School in Little Rock. Even local sponsors were fearful that mounting civil rights tensions might precipitate a misunderstanding of the sponsorship of a series in which the white southern heroes seldom lost. Just as advertisers shunned association with black causes, they also avoided open affiliation with white southern intransigence.[14]

In September 1958 *The Gray Ghost* was being carried on 190 stations, but the lack of new episodes began eroding its popularity. The decision not to produce more episodes had in effect killed the series. "Again," *Newsweek* said, "the South had won the battles but lost the war." Southerners protested. AIN'T THIS LIKE THOSE DAMN YANKEES? asked The Raleigh *Times*. "TV should smarten up," said the Birmingham *News*. "With the coming of the 100th anniversary of those stirring times, interest is mounting to a new high." The Little Rock *Gazette* thought the cancellation amounted to a kind of censorship, noting: "The notion that because Mosby's Rangers will not be on tv this season, they can be presumed never to have lived or not to live today in the history books. . . . It seems unlikely that we have come to pass where sectional shooting could be touched off by a tv show, no matter how stimulating to the old glands and juices." CBS received 2,500 letters protesting the cancellation. DeWitt claimed the governors of five southern states went to CBS and tried to keep the show on the air. He said they contended *The Gray Ghost* was the only program on the air the South could be proud of. DeWitt bemoaned the network's lack of sensitivity to historical programming: "CBS hasn't any more courage than a dead chicken. They canceled the show. The U.S. has a history, an exciting history, but nobody has ever done anything with it."

The termination of *The Gray Ghost* shows how much television history must be compatible with commerce and contemporary social values. Although the cavalier myth appealed to youthful audiences, and *The Gray Ghost* was ostensibly just another romance featuring the exploits of dashing heroes on horseback, some sponsors thought the cavalier conjured up images of southern plantation aristocracy and its supporting system of slavery. The presentation of the Civil War from the southern point of view seemed out of place to many after thousands of African Americans had died defending the United States in World War II and the Korean conflict. While attempts had been made to separate slavery and racism from the Civil War, it ultimately proved impossible to disassociate entertainment from ideology. As Thomas J. Pressly concluded in his 1954 study of the way Americans remember the war, "disagreement over the meaning of the Civil War experience was matched, in the middle of the twentieth century, by sharp controversy in the arena of politics over issues related to those of Civil War days."[15]

Undoubtedly many of those who enjoyed the series saw the gallant rangers as resistance fighters in a continuing struggle to preserve not only noble southern traditions but also white supremacy, the military establishment and the supremacy of state over nation, regardless of the intention of the program's producers. Nor was it reasonable to blame African-American organizations or sponsors for objecting to *The Gray Ghost* even if there was little or no explicit racism in the series. The program was implicitly racist in its glorification of those who defended slavery even if their primary motivation was the defense of their state's right to separate from the Union. In the context of the times, any program resurrecting the Confederacy carried within it the manifest content of sectionalism and the historical baggage of the period. This does not suggest, however, that history can never be successfully presented as commercial entertainment, nor does this imply a retroactive judgment on the past. Mosby, once asked if he admitted fighting on the wrong side, answered obliquely: "I do not—I may have fought on the side that was wrong, but I fought on the right side."[16] For his part, Parsons doubted another Civil War series could succeed. "The emerging minorities would make the thing very difficult. You'd have to straddle a lot of issues."[17]

And yet the Civil War has reemerged from time to time on the television screen. David L. Wolper's *Appointment with Destiny* documentary series (1972), miniseries and movies such as *The Blue and the Gray* (1982), *North and South* (1985–86), *Gettysburg* (1993), and *Andersonville* (1995) were well-received by television audiences, if not always by historians. *Roots* (1977) and *Roots: The Next Generations* (1979) were the most widely watched miniseries in history, with estimated audiences as high as 140 million. *Roots* not only addressed the Civil War but attempted to tell the full story of slavery and its legacy. The nine episodes of Ken Burns's documentary *The Civil War* (1991) became the most widely watched series in the history of PBS and probably did more to stimulate interest in Civil War history than any production since *Gone with the Wind.* Many critics and historians, however, were less than enchanted.

Television's Civil War, then, is not one war but many wars. Television interprets the Civil War both mythically and historically, sometimes seriously, sometimes frivolously, and, after *The Gray Ghost*, cautiously. As historian, television sometimes simplifies, distorts, and trivializes the war, transports it to safer times and places, and brings it into a historical present where it contends against politics, commerce, and culture. The television history of the war has tended to emphasize themes of reconciliation and consensus. Television has ennobled and sanctified the war and challenged cultural boundaries. Television history sometimes just reminds Americans that they have a history, that they fought a Civil War that was "the crossroads of our being, and it was a hell of a crossroads," and that history, like television, is a treasury of many stories.[18]

Notes

Portions of this paper appeared, in somewhat different form, in "Confederates on Television: The Cavalier Myth and the Death of the Gray Ghost," *Studies in Popular Culture* 2 (Spring 1979), pp. 11–22, and in Paul Ashdown and Edward Caudill, *The Mosby Myth: A Confederate Hero in Life and Legend* (Wilmington, DE: Scholarly Resources Books, 2002). Parts of this discussion were presented by Ashdown and Caudill at the Symposium on the 19th Century Press, the Civil War, and Free Expression, in Chattanooga, Tennessee, on Nov. 14, 1997.

1. Robert F. Horowitz, "History Comes to Life and You Are There," in *American History American Television: Interpreting the Video Past*, ed. John E. O'Connor (New York: Frederick Ungar, 1983), 89.
2. Rita Parks, *The Western Hero in Film and Television* (Ann Arbor, Michigan: UMI Research Press, 1982), 159–161.

3. Civil War tensions even reached television's Dodge City. A *Gunsmoke* episode originally aired on July 21, 1956, involved Confederate veterans squaring off with a former Union soldier in U.S. Marshal Matt Dillon's town.
4. J. Fred MacDonald, *Who Shot the Sheriff* (Chicago: Nelson-Hall, 1983), p. 1.
5. Tom Moore, telephone interview, July 5, 1978.
6. Virgil Carrington Jones, personal letter to author, May 19, 1976.
7. *Newsweek*, August 4, 1958, 65.
8. For example, *Variety*'s Telepulse rating system for June 2–9, 1958 as reported in the Aug. 6, 1958 issue showed an audience rating of 21.2 and a share of 44 in Houston based on 351,000 television homes. This means 21.2 percent of the 351,000 homes—some 74,500 homes—representing 44 percent of all sets in use at the time, were tuned to *The Gray Ghost*. In Charlotte, the figures were a 21.3 rating and a 39 share based on 62,000 homes; in Oklahoma City, a 15.7 rating and a 40 share based on 121,000 homes; and in Corpus Christi, a 28.3 rating and a 49 share based on 51,000 homes.
9. *Variety*, July 30, 1958.
10. Jones, personal letter.
11. Lindsley Parsons, telephone interview, July 24, 1978.
12. Jack DeWitt, personal letter to the author, July 24 , 1978.
13. Richard F. Shepard, "The Gray Ghost Rides Again," *The New York Times*, September 28, 1958.
14. MacDonald, p. 69.
15. Thomas J. Pressly, *Americans Interpret Their Civil War* (Princeton: Princeton University Press, 1954), 360.
16. John Singleton Mosby to Alexander Spottswood Campbell, February 25, 1909, Special Collections, University of California, Santa Barbara.
17. Lindsley Parsons, telephone interview, July 5, 1978.
18. Shelby Foote, in *The Civil War*, Geoffrey C. Ward, with Ric Burns and Ken Burns (New York: Alfred A. Knopf, 1990), p. 260.

History Thrice Removed

Joshua Chamberlain and *Gettysburg*

— Crompton Burton —

The small wooden box with the glass window in the lid arrived at the Maine State Museum one day in 1969. Part of a transfer of materials and artifacts from the adjutant general's office, it was accompanied by a note stating simply, "Flag, 20th Maine Regiment, (very fragile in box)." During the ensuing three decades, museum staff routinely opened the box and examined the Stars and Stripes peeking back from within, but dared not remove the banner for fear of damaging the relic. Running short of conservation funds, the museum was finally able to interest the Army Historical Foundation in underwriting its restoration, and in 1998 curator of Historical Collections Douglas Hawes hand-delivered the box to a textile conservation laboratory in Sharpsburg, Maryland.[1]

What followed was an impressive combination of forensic investigation and painstaking preservation that yielded compelling evidence that the flag was almost certainly the one defended to the last by Union troops on Gettysburg's Little Round Top on the afternoon of July 2, 1863. Particles and chemicals from the silk of the standard were collected and sent for microscopic examination in Illinois. The results revealed soot, ash flakes, and seeds peculiar to the state of Maryland, and suggested that the bleeding of the red dye into the white stripes possibly came from the post-battle downpour. All facts pointed to the flag as being the one around which the 20th Maine rallied under the command of Colonel Joshua Lawrence Chamberlain. Said conservator Fonda Thomsen, "There is a 99.9 percent chance this is the same flag."[2]

For millions of Americans, mention of Chamberlain and his regiment's heroic stand on the rocky outcropping on the Army of the Potomac's exposed left flank conjures images of desperate combat, inspired leadership, and triumph in the face of overwhelming odds. All those elements were present on Little Round Top late on the afternoon of July 2, 1863, but popular and enduring perceptions of the engagement's pivotal moment come not from the official records of the Civil War, a Mathew Brady photograph, or even guided tours of the hallowed ground. They come, instead, from actor Jeff Daniels's portrayal of Chamberlain in the contemporary movie *Gettysburg.* One could argue that the big-screen presentation of the defense of Little Round Top is actually history thrice removed. From the actual engagement to reports, narratives, memoirs, historical fiction, and the motion picture's screenplay, the thread of the story makes its way from the pages of official records to the flashing lights of the movie marquee.

The screenplay calls for Chamberlain (Daniels), out of ammunition and unable to repel another assault, to summon his company commanders and hurriedly weigh the regiment's limited options. Says Chamberlain: "Well, we can't run away and if we stay here, we can't shoot. So, let's fix bayonets. We'll have the advantage of moving down the hill. They gotta be tired, the Rebs, they gotta be close to the end if we are, so fix bayonets." Chamberlain turns to his trusted field officer, Captain Ellis Spear, and explains, "Ellis, you take the left wing. I'll take the right. I want a right wheel forward of the whole regiment." Spear questions, "What, you mean charge?"[3]

Exchanging cold steel for hot lead was exactly what Chamberlain had in mind. In the film, the 20th Maine prepares to execute the movement and hurl itself down the hill on Chamberlain's command: "Left wing, right wheel. Charge!" While the regiment dramatically seizes the initiative and secures the position, taking dozens of prisoners, proper credit for launching the charge of the regiment remains a question for historians rather than moviegoers to this day. For the paying public, Chamberlain barked, "Charge!" Researchers and even some of those present on Little Round Top that day under the command of the college professor-turned-colonel aren't so certain.[4]

Screenwriter Ronald Maxwell, for his part, is sure of one thing—his obligation to balance history and the record of the engagement along with a pressing need to recreate the moment in such a way that Hollywood can tell its own version of the story. Says Maxwell: "The last thing the world needs is a mindless, glossy entertainment on the Civil War. None of us wants that, so it is important to accept the seriousness of this challenge: to keep our eyes wide open, to be relentlessly honest, to refrain from perpetuating myth and folklore, to get to the truth of the matter. Nothing will be more dramatic and nothing will be more worthwhile."[5]

More than one historian disputes the screenwriter's pledge to maintain the historical record. William B. Styple advances the theory that it was actually one of Chamberlain's lieutenants who initiated the offensive movement of the 20th Maine. In documenting the role of Lieutenant Holman Melcher, Styple questions the conventions that have placed the regiment's colonel at the forefront and counters, "It has been long believed, (regardless of the truth) that the legendary hero Colonel Joshua Lawrence Chamberlain led the charge of the Twentieth Maine down the rocky slope of Little Round Top." Styple, a stickler for authenticity himself as a Civil War reenactor, laments those abuses of the record that come as a result of exhaustive treatment in a variety of genres and media. "The Battle of Gettysburg, through its estimated 150,000 surviving participants and countless historians, has spawned an incalculable number of books, articles, poems, paintings, songs, speeches, film epics, and prize-winning novels," he says. "Of all these, the last is perhaps the most damaging to the truth."[6]

Historian Edward G. Longacre also disputes Maxwell's portrayal of Chamberlain as catalyst of the desperate charge. "No participant ever testified to that effect, except for some postwar reunion speakers who gave the colonel credit for everything the 20th Maine accomplished that day," Longacre maintains. "Although he did take part in the movement, it is doubtful that Chamberlain, who had been twice slightly wounded including in the right instep, could have gotten in front of everyone else to lead the way."[7]

Examination of the historical record attached to Little Round Top reveals no shortage of material upon which to attempt a reconstruction of the actual events that have prompted so much debate and discussion in the decades following the engagement. Indeed, determining where to begin can be a challenge by itself. For such noted historians as Bruce Catton and Shelby Foote, the key moment in the battle remains elusive. Catton's *This Hallowed Ground* prefers to address the general ebb and flow of Gettysburg's second day: "East of Devil's Den there was Little Round Top, swept by Southern rifle fire, defended by last-minute Federal reinforcements who ran panting along the uneven hillside to drive back the Confederates who had swept through Devil's Den."[8] For his part, Foote approaches the pivotal moment atop the rocky outcropping from a distinctly southern perspective. His widely acclaimed *The Civil War: A Narrative* quotes the commander of the 15th Alabama, Colonel William Calvin Oates. Recognizing that his continued assaults on the Union position would remain unsupported by reinforcements, Oates orders a withdrawal just as the 20th Maine came storming down the hill. Says Oates, "When the signal was given we ran like a herd of wild cattle."[9]

Capturing the true course of events requires the researcher to reach well beyond the record as put forward in general Civil War histories. Thorough examination of official records, regimental histories, personal recollections and post-war correspondence holds the key to knowing what can be known of Little Round Top. There is significant evidence to suggest that Chamberlain did indeed shout "Charge!" just as Maxwell portrays it in his docudrama. Perhaps some of the most compelling support for belief that the film is true to the moment in question comes from Chamberlain's own battle report, originally authored less than a week after the engagement. In the narrative, once believed lost and not the document upon which the eventual official record was based, the colonel of the 20th Maine recalled, "As a last, desperate resort, I ordered a *charge*." He went on to repeat the claim in a number of post-war venues, including a speech and in his contribution to a collection of memoirs for recipients of the Medal of Honor.[10]

Two members of the regiment who fought alongside Chamberlain had similar recollections of the action. William Livermore was a member of the regiment's color guard, and in his diary he described a distinct order: "We stood until our center had lost half our men, and we knew we could not stand longer. We were ordered to charge them when there were two to our one." Another member of the detail assigned to protect the regiment's battle flag, Corporal Elisha Coan, recalled: "Then Col. C. gave the order 'Forward'. This was heard by but a few but it spread along our lines and the regt. with a yell equal to a thousand men sprang forward in a wild mad charge."[11]

Further confirmation comes from the 20th Maine's flanks. The battle report of Colonel James Rice, commander of the 44th New York in support of Chamberlain, offers corroboration. "At length the enemy pressed so strongly upon the left flank of Colonel Chamberlain's regiment that he wisely determined to change the order of battle, and commanded his left wing to fall back at right angles to his right," Rice reported. "He then ordered a charge and repulsed the enemy at every point."[12] Further evidence that Chamberlain's defining military moment grew from the legendary order appears in the widely referenced *Army Life: A Private's Reminiscences of the Civil War* by Theodore Gerrish. In the work, often quoted or utilized as a source for other research, Gerrish describes the desperate measures taken by his commanding officer: "The order is given 'Fix bayonets!' and the steel shanks of the bayonets rattle upon the rifle barrels. 'Charge bayonets, charge!'"[13]

Taken in combination, there is significant argument that the moment Maxwell describes, or something akin to it, did indeed take place on Little Round Top on the afternoon of July 2, 1863. It is tempting to stop there, congratulate Hollywood on resisting the urge to extend the dramatic moment too far in support of the screenplay, and move on to other issues, such as the true nature of the military maneuver that Chamberlain claims his regiment executed to turn the tide in favor of the Union. Unfortunately, the historical record does not allow for closing the case so easily, and evaluation of equally compelling evidence that suggests that Chamberlain never did utter the order cannot be ignored. Chamberlain's official report, the one upon which the official records are based, refutes the colonel's earlier assertion that he did indeed shout the order. In fact, Chamberlain's account suggests that he himself did not have to exclaim anything more than to prepare to move: "At the crisis, I ordered the bayonet. The word was enough. It ran like fire along the line from man to man, and rose into a shout, with which they sprang forward upon the enemy not thirty yards away."[14]

A 1913 article in *Hearst's Magazine* authored by Chamberlain adds weight to the contention that he never got beyond the order to fix bayonets. Said Chamberlain: "It was vain to order 'Forward.' No mortal could have heard it in the mighty hosanna that was winging the sky, nor would he wait to hear." The 20th Maine's commander went on to recount, "The grating clash of steel in fixing bayonets told its own story; the color rose in front; the whole line quivered for the start; the edge of the left wing rippled, swung, tossed among the rocks, straightened, changed curve from scimitar to sickle-shape; and the bristling archers swooped down upon the serried host—down into the face of half a thousand! Two hundred men!"[15] Consistent with these accounts, Chamberlain resisted the nostalgic temptations of the 1889 reunion at Gettysburg, during which the regiment's monument was dedicated. Addressing the controversy in his usual straightforward fashion, the ex-governor of Maine stated, "In fact, to tell the truth, the order was never given, or but imperfectly."[16] At that same ceremony, the regiment's quartermaster, Howard L. Prince, acted as unit historian offering up a narrative that included yet another disclaimer: "The lines were in motion before the word of command was completed, and Colonel Chamberlain does not know whether he ever finished that order."[17]

The account of Ellis Spear does nothing to end speculation that the movement was born of a single Chamberlain order of resorting to the bayonet. Removed from the center of the line on the regiment's left, Spear remembers, "Suddenly, in the midst of the noise of musketry, I heard a shout on the center, of 'Forward,' and saw the line and colors begin to move. I had received no orders, other than to hold the left and guard the flank and did not understand the meaning of the movement."[18] Several other accounts seem to confirm the theory that the movement was more spontaneous than anything else. Definitive biographies, such as Alice Trulock's *In the Hands of Providence* and Willard Wallace's *Soul of the Lion*, support the argument that the advance was not born from a single and dramatic command, as Hollywood would have us believe.[19]

In fact, the weight of evidence begins to shift the spotlight away from Chamberlain to one of his subordinates. John J. Pullen's regimental history,

The Twentieth Maine: A Volunteer Regiment in the Civil War, is widely credited with popularizing Chamberlain and his role decades before the story found its way to the big screen. In his detailed account, Pullen not only corroborates the assertions of those documenting the impulse of the regiment to advance, but transfers potential laurels to another. "Chamberlain stepped to the colors and his voice rang out, 'Bayonet!' There was a moment of hesitation along the line, an intaking of breath like that of a man about to plunge into a cold, dark river. But along with it there was the rattling of bayonet shanks on steel. Intent on his wounded, Lieutenant Melcher sprang out in front of the line with his sword flashing, and this seems to have been the spark. The colors rose in front. A few men got up. Then a few more."[20]

The role of Melcher is reflected in a variety of narratives, memoirs and histories. Harry Pfanz's definitive *Gettysburg: The Second Day* describes Melcher's approach to Chamberlain asking permission to recover his wounded and being asked to return to Company F and await the order to move forward. It is a thread that finds its way into numerous explorations of the struggle for Little Round Top but does not feature the stuff of docudrama.[21] Note for instance the fact that Chamberlain authored *multiple* battle reports with conflicting detail. While the most commonly referenced report is dated July 6, 1863, it actually was submitted in 1884 after editors compiling the official records requested a rewrite of the colonel from Maine. His recreation from memory has more than a single discrepancy from the original.[22]

Another oft-quoted source, Gerrish's *Army Life*, suffers from the fact that its author was actually in hospital at the time of the defense of Little Round Top rather than in a position to describe both Chamberlain's order and Melcher's exhortation. Beyond this compromising of Gerrish's first-person account, there is the more cumulative effect of the work's being widely quoted and passed along from source to source as definitive. In his introduction to a reprint of *Army Life*, Pullen acknowledges that "I can recall half a dozen recent books about the 20th Maine Regiment, Joshua Chamberlain and the Battle of Gettysburg which all use Gerrish as a source."[23] Perhaps a final word on Gerrish should be included from the writings of the 15th Alabama's commander, Colonel Oates. Said Oates of Gerrish, "He was, I believe, the chaplain, and not present to see it. Doubtless he was at prayer a safe distance in the rear."[24]

Tracking the accuracy of the historical record, researchers encounter even more challenges. For instance, even as *Maine at Gettysburg* suffers from inconsistencies in the roll of the 20th Maine at Little Round Top, so too the author of its account of the engagement, Captain Howard L. Prince, must himself be located as being behind the lines at the critical moment. His "The Regiment Engaged," while widely accepted as definitive in its own right, was compiled from the observations of others, as Prince was actually escorting a consignment of shoes to the troops in his role of quartermaster sergeant in the regiment. In his address during the dedication of the regiment's monument at Gettysburg in October 1889, Prince was candid in admitting he was within the sound of the guns, but not actually in a position to see for himself the events unfold in front of the 20th Maine.[25]

No less an authority than Harry W. Pfanz, former chief historian of the National Park Service, suffers from a challenge to his narrative in *Gettysburg: The Second Day.* While the *New York Times* hailed the work as "meticulous research," Pfanz mistakenly represents Lt. Melcher's first name as Homer when in fact it is Holman.[26] Oliver Norton, long thought to have represented accurate detail in *The Attack and Defense of Little Round Top*, appeared to have been in a superior position to offer clarity from among the contradictions when he published in 1913. As bugler to Colonel Strong Vincent, the brigade commander who ordered the Maine regiment onto the field on the second day, Norton chose to compile battle reports of prime participants. Still, even he was moved to disclaim that while there is general agreement that the contested ground was pivotal to the Union position: "But here the agreement ends. No two writers agree in their statements of what actually took place."[27]

The historiography of Little Round Top gains consensus only from those who freely admit that it is impossible to be one hundred percent certain of what took place on the Union left with the Alabama regiments pressing home the attack on the 20th Maine. In the introduction to his memoirs, Oates wrote, "No two men can participate in a great battle and see it just alike."[28] Spear cautioned his family and descendants not to believe everything they read in examining the record of the war, warning, "The general movements, the strategy and tactics of the Army of the Potomac in which I served are matters of history, which is not always accurate in details since it is made up of reports colored sometimes, more or less, by personal interest."[29]

So where does the published record, replete with contradiction, controversy, and conflict, leave Maxwell's screenplay? Lost reports, absentee authors, and Hollywood renderings of historical events create at least the suggestion that there is no true history or account that one can rely upon to represent what actually happened. Indeed, David Lowenthal offers: "As the past no longer exists, no account can ever be checked against it, but only against other accounts of the past; we judge its veracity by its correspondence with other reports, not with events themselves. Historical narrative is not a portrait of what happened but a story of what happened."[30] Lowenthal further qualifies that which we can know of such events as the defense of Little Round Top when he states, "It is impossible to recover or recount more than a tiny fraction of what has taken place, and no historical account ever corresponds precisely with any actual past."[31]

Such must be the case in exploring what really happened on Little Round Top. Later in life, Chamberlain claimed to have yelled, "Charge!" even though his official report, flawed as it may have been, ultimately never made such a reference. Pullen offers an interesting perspective in his biography of Chamberlain, authored in 1999, in which he addresses the screenplay against the backdrop of pure history. "This novelized and filmed version has been set upon by some historians, who seem to forget that they are quarreling with a fiction and who also forget that no matter what the truth is or what they write in its elucidation, this is the way the event will be remembered by 98 percent of the general public who are aware of it," he writes. "This is the way mythology proceeds—carrying forward essential truths unencumbered by factual details."[32]

As defined by Michael Real, the docudrama is the retelling of history through dramatic reenactment. Quoting Robert Rosenstone, Real marks some boundaries of critique of the film genre as a form of historical delivery: "The historical film must be seen not in terms of how it compares to written history, but as a way of recounting the past with its own rules of interpretation."[33] Taken in this context, Maxwell's screenplay qualifies as a significant form of historical interpretation. Few sources, as the events on Little Round Top demonstrate, are beyond question, and just as historians triangulate between accounts of the event, memory of participants and other narrative, so too does the filmmaker enjoy the same freedom to construct a script and choreograph scenes of such momentous events in history as the repulse of the 15th Alabama.

As Mark Twain once wrote, "When I was younger, I could remember anything, whether it happened or not, but I am getting old, and soon I shall remember only the latter."[34] In later years, Chamberlain and many veterans of the 20th Maine battled the advance of time upon their recollection of Little Round Top, just as they once contested the advance of the 15th Alabama. Perhaps Melcher himself comes closest to capturing the reality of the moment when he recalled that Chamberlain "gives the order to 'fix bayonets,' and almost before he can say 'Charge!' the regiment, with a shout of desperation leaps down the hill and close in on the foe, which we find behind every rock and tree."[35] While Hollywood producers needed more to work with in order to position Chamberlain as the hero of Little Round Top, their version of the dramatic moment has almost as many supporters as those who would dispute its accuracy.

Popular perceptions of Chamberlain's heroism and the 20th Maine's place in history based upon a film portrayal suffer no greater disservice than those created by revisionist rewrites of the record or reminiscences clouded by the passage of time. Thomas A. Desjardin, in framing the context for his own work, *Stand Firm Ye Boys from Maine,* points to the fluid nature of historical study: "In this sense, perhaps the greatest contribution this volume could make would be to stimulate further study and discussion of these highly significant events."[36] Rosenstone observes, "Film neither replaces written history nor supplements it. Film stands adjacent to written history, as it does to other forms dealing with the past such as memory and the oral tradition."[37] In this light and based upon the balance of evidence discovered to date, the screenplay can and should occupy a similarly legitimate place in the body of historical interpretation.

NOTES

1. Maine State Museum, "The 20th Maine's Battle Flag," [World Wide Web site of 20th Maine Flag Exhibit, Maine State Museum]. [cited 12 December 1998]. Available from www.state.me.us/sos/arc/general/admin/20flag.htm. Also, Laurie LaBar, Curator of Historical Collections, Maine State Museum, email exchange with author, 2 October 2002.
2. Ibid.
3. Ronald F. Maxwell, *Gettysburg: The Screenplay* (Sherman Oaks, CA: Person to Person Films, Inc., 1992), p. 108.
4. Ibid., p. 109.
5. Ronald F. Maxwell, "Poetic License in Historical Films," [World Wide Web site of Ron Maxwell]. [cited 19 March, 2002]. Available from www.ronmaxwell.com/ggenerals_plicense.html.
6. William B. Styple, ed., *With a Flash of His Sword: The Writings of Major Holman S. Melcher, 20th Maine Infantry* (Kearny, NJ: Belle Grove Publishing Co., 1994), p. vii.
7. Edward G. Longacre, *Joshua Chamberlain: The Soldier and the Man* (Conshohocken, PA: Combined Publishing, 1999), p. 140.
8. Bruce Catton, *This Hallowed Ground* (New York: Doubleday & Co., 1971), p. 311.
9. Shelby Foote, *The Civil War: A Narrative, Fredericksburg to Meridian* (New York: Random House, 1963), p. 505.
10. Longacre, *Joshua Chamberlain*, p. 141.
11. Styple, *With a Flash of His Sword*, pp. 77–78, 84.
12. Oliver Willcox Norton, *The Attack and Defense of Little Round Top, Gettysburg, July 2, 1863* (Gettysburg, PA: Stan Clark Military Books, 1992), pp. 206–207.
13. Theodore Gerrish, *Army Life: A Private's Reminiscences of the Civil War, A History of the 20th Maine Infantry Regiment* (Baltimore and Gettysburg, PA: Butternut and Blue and Stan Clark Military Books, 1995), pp. 109–110.
14. U.S. Department of War, *The War of the Rebellion: A Compilation of the Official Records of the Union and Confederate Armies* (Washington: U.S. War Department, 1880), Series I, Volume XXVII/1, p. 624.
15. Joshua Lawrence Chamberlain, *Through Blood & Fire at Gettysburg, General Joshua Chamberlain and the 20th Maine* (Gettysburg, PA: Stan Clark Military Books, 1994), p. 23.
16. Thomas A. Desjardin, *Stand Firm Ye Boys from Maine: The 20th Maine and the Gettysburg Campaign* (Gettysburg, PA: Thomas Publications, 1995), p. 162.

17. Ibid.
18. Abbott Spear, Andrea C. Hawkes, Marie H. McCosh, Craig L. Symonds, and Michael H. Alpert, eds., *The Civil War Recollections of General Ellis Spear* (Orono, ME: The University of Maine Press, 1997), pp. 34–35.
19. Alice Rains Trulock, *In the Hands of Providence, Joshua Lawrence Chamberlain and the American Civil War* (Chapel Hill, NC: The University of North Carolina Press, 1992), p. 148. See also Willard M. Wallace, *Soul of the Lion, A Biography of Joshua Lawrence Chamberlain* (New York: Thomas Nelson & Sons, 1960), p. 102.
20. John J. Pullen, *The Twentieth Maine: A Volunteer Regiment in the Civil War* (Dayton, OH: Press of Morningside Bookshop, 1984), p. 124.
21. Harry W. Pfanz, *Gettysburg: The Second Day* (Chapel Hill, NC: The University of North Carolina Press, 1987), p. 234.
22. Longacre, *Joshua Chamberlain*, pp. 140–141.
23. John J. Pullen, introduction to *Army Life: A Private's Reminiscences of the Civil War, A History of the 20th Maine Infantry Regiment* by Theodore Gerrish, p. ii.
24. Glenn LaFantasie, *Gettysburg: Lt. Frank A. Haskell, U.S.A., and Col. William C. Oates, C.S.A.* (New York: Bantam Books, 1992), pp. 98–99.
25. John J. Pullen, *Joshua Chamberlain: A Hero's Life and Legacy* (Mechanicsburg, PA: Stackpole Books, 1999), p. 140.
26. Pfanz, *Gettysburg: The Second Day*, p. 234.
27. Oliver Wilcox Norton, *The Attack and Defense of Little Round Top, Gettysburg, July 2, 1863* (Gettysburg, PA: Stan Clark Military Books, 1992), p. 13.
28. LaFantasie, *Gettysburg*, p. 2.
29. *The Civil War Recollections of General Ellis Spear*, p. 3.
30. David Lowenthal, *The Past Is a Foreign Country* (New York: Cambridge University Press, 1985), p. 215.
31. Ibid., p. 214.
32. Pullen, *Joshua Chamberlain*, p. 142.
33. Michael R. Real, "Historical/Ethical Interpretation: Reconstructing the Quiz Show Scandal," in *Exploring Media Culture: A Guide* (Thousand Oaks, CA: Sage, 1996), p. 224.
34. Pullen, *Joshua Chamberlain*, p. 135. Originally found in Styple, *With a Flash of His Sword*, 133.
35. Styple, *With a Flash of His Sword*, p. 133.
36. Desjardin, *Stand Firm Ye Boys from Maine*, p. xiii.
37. Robert A. Rosenstone, *Visions of the Past: The Challenge of Film to Our Idea of History* (Cambridge, MA: Harvard University Press, 1995), p. 77.

"Ain't Nobody Clean"

Glory! and the Politics of Black Agency

— W. Scott Poole —

"History is, I am convinced, not something to be left to historians." So wrote Warren Susman in *Culture as History*, a seminal work in the cultural studies movement. Susman should be a happy man, since we now live in a world where history never simply belongs to historians. This fact emerges clearly when we examine the creation of historical mythologies, the rendering of the messy details of the historical process into epics of gods and heroes. Such myth-making allows humans both freedom and absolution from the sins of history.[1]

The American Civil War has been a veritable womb of national and folk myths. Robert Penn Warren wrote that the war "reaches in a thousand ways into our bloodstream and our personal present."[2] The white South had its myth of the Lost Cause, the tale of a traditional society's epic struggle against the industrial might of the North, a struggle lost in the fighting but forever covered with glory. The North had its own myths, embodied and preserved by the influential veteran's organization, the Grand Army of the Republic, and by northern evangelical churches as well.[3] Religion and popular culture embodied the northern myth of reconciliation, a myth in which the Union army squelched the South's barbaric tendencies and then offered a helping hand of reconciliation, inviting former Confederates to share a successful century of American empire-building. Nina Silber has argued that these myths often coalesced into a rather muddled epic narrative of brave and noble white southerners who were yet rebels, and devoted northern Union men who welcomed these rebels quickly back into the fold with "malice towards none."[4]

These myths have endured in the filmography of the Civil War. The patient critic could write reams detailing bad Civil War movies—bad from cinematic, historical, and even moral perspectives. American popular culture in the twentieth century was in love with a dreary succession of fragile belles on fertile plantations (or was it fertile belles on fragile plantations?) and noble southern gentleman drawling endlessly about the ever-oncoming Yankees while a literally supporting cast of African Americans makes the supper, binds the corsets, and marches off happily to work in unseen cotton fields.[5]

Remarkable in this consistent outpouring of popular myth is the sheer weight of whiteness, the degree to which white actors—both literally and figuratively—preoccupy writers and producers. The movie *Gone with the Wind* and such television demi-epics as *North and South* represent ludicrous examples of this tendency. A more telling case is the highly controversial 1975 film *Mandingo*, which in its conscious attempt to deconstruct the plantation myth, never quite escapes a fascination with white agency. White men and women are still the engines of private and collective history in *Mandingo*, although they are shown now to exhibit a sexually predatory nature. African Americans remain victims, if rebellious ones.[6]

The 1989 film *Glory!* seemingly represents a cinematic repentance for earlier failures to do justice to the black experience of slavery and the Civil War. Ultimately it is a failure, albeit a magnificent one—a fine film that teaches the important truth that 178,000 African-American men served the Union cause and 37,000 of them died in that cause. Moreover, even the failures of *Glory!* expose the fault lines of both race and class in contemporary America, at moments becoming a kind of parable for the strange configurations of these variables since the Civil War.

Glory! tells the story of the 54th Massachusetts, a regiment of African Americans organized near Boston in 1862. Robert Gould Shaw, scion of a prominent Boston abolitionist family, led the regiment. Although not the earliest of the African-American units, the outfit's heroic if suicidal 1863 assault on Battery Wagner near Charleston, South Carolina, served as proof of the fighting mettle of black soldiers, a point on which not all white northerners had yet been convinced. The story of the regiment captured the imagination of New England, in particular, when Shaw died leading his men in the attack. A monument raised on Boston Common in the 1890s forever glorified Shaw and the 54th in what has been called America's "most elite" memorial. Built with money raised by Boston Brahmins, designed and produced by the well-regarded French sculptor Augustin

Saint-Gaudens and dedicated in a ceremony with orators such as William James, the memorial managed, as Kirk Savage has noted, to both glorify Shaw and make the men of the 54th something other than "a foil for whiteness."[7]

Glory! not only attempts to tell the story of the 54th Massachusetts, it also reflects a number of current concerns among some in the African-American community, showing the roots of these concerns in the antebellum and Civil War era. The character of Thomas, for example, embodies a bookish, northern free black male who attaches himself to the regiment because of abolitionist ideals and a heightened racial consciousness honed in the parlors and lecture halls of Boston instead of the cotton rows and slave quarters of Mississippi or South Carolina. He is made the friend of Robert Gould Shaw, who is used to illustrate Thomas's class position. After Thomas receives a wound in the regiment's first engagement, for example, the colonel reassures him by saying that he will soon be "back in Boston reading Hawthorne by the fire."[8]

Thomas raises the issue of class within the African-American community. He clearly sees himself as superior to his comrades, joking with one of the white officers about their unwieldy conversational skills and finding it difficult to enter into the emotional fervor of evangelical religion common to former slaves. *Glory!* does a great service in raising this complex issue, an issue that historians have not always covered in their emphasis on the unity created by racial consciousness. In a twist that would have startled freedmen in the late nineteenth century, however, Thomas is shown gradually joining the former slave community in its songs and sentiments. This, of course, represents a complete reversal of the hopes of black leaders such as W. E. B. DuBois, whose "the talented tenth" would bring "racial uplift" to the former slaves and working-class blacks.[9] Again, reflecting somewhat anachronistic concerns about identity, Thomas slowly rediscovers his "blackness" toward the film's conclusion, even taking part in a sort of "hush arbor" religious meeting.

Thomas's opposite number is Trip, portrayed by the inimitable Denzel Washington, whose performance garnered him an Academy Award. Trip embodies the angry young black male, a runaway slave from Tennessee whose scarred back bears witness to his status as a "bad Negro," in John Blasingame's plantation typology. Mocking Thomas's class position by repeatedly calling him "snowflake" and challenging the order of the Union Army by standing up to the regiment's brutal Irish drill sergeant, Trip strikes out again and again at a world that has literally struck him—the world of whiteness, whether the Confederates he joined up to fight or the officer corps of the Union Army itself.

A significant thread of the film's narrative concerns Trip's "redemption" from a destructive streak of rebellion into a studied defiance of all the varied machinery of white supremacy. To their credit, the filmmakers show us a character who learns to channel his anger, directing it not against his fellow soldiers in the 54th, but rather against the Federal government, which asks black soldiers to fight and die like white men but refuses to pay them like white men, and against the Confederates, who fight for the slaveholding republic. However, *Glory!* also shows us Trip suffering for his defiance, even being wounded in the house of his friends. In one disturbingly violent scene—disturbing both because of the subject matter and the sheer power of Washington's performance—Trip receives a lashing on his already scarred back. Shaw orders the punishment himself, to preserve order and discipline in the regiment, and looks on with a mixture of pain and dismay while it is carried out.

Undoubtedly, the decision to include such a scene in the film derived from the need to show the horrors and indignities suffered by African Americans. But why choose this humiliating means of punishment? Why portray committed abolitionist Robert Gould Shaw looking on while one of his men is beaten to a bloody pulp, an incident he never would have stood for, much less ordered? African-American soldiers did suffer discrimination within the ranks of the Union Army and, like many white soldiers, often suffered some degree of physical abuse. But never did they suffer what their brethren endured at the hands of slaveholders. This scene suggests almost a moral equivalency between the slaveholding South and the Union, a notion pleasing perhaps only to neo-Confederates and the Black Panthers.[10]

The episode challenges one of the central messages that director Edward Zwick hoped to convey. Its inclusion works mischief within the narrative itself, suppressing and literally flogging the notion of black agency. The beating of Trip prepares the way for the breaking of Trip. His sufferings become part of a kind of redemption narrative. White characters also change during the course of *Glory!* Shaw moves from a syrupy paternalism toward his men to the respect born of shared dangers by the time of the assault on Battery Wagner. However, it is not too much to say that Tripp's transformation from "bad Negro" into "faithful Negro" occupies the narrative center of the film. Viewers may watch sadly as the proud if abrasive Trip is broken first by the lash, then by the intervention of Morgan Freeman's character, Sergeant Rawlins, who strikes him across the face and, in a speech that would have pleased Booker T. Washington, castigates him for being little more than a "swamp-running nigger." The final climatic scenes have Trip accepting the role as flag-bearer in the heat of combat, a flag he had refused to carry earlier because he had joined the fight for black freedom, not for a white man's nation.

The breaking of Trip did not result from an unconscious racism on the part of the filmmakers, but from the need to resolve a narrative dilemma they themselves created within the film. Making use of a black rage defined more by the 1965 Watts riot than by the Civil War-era black massacres at Fort Pillow or Milliken's Bend, the filmmakers needed to show the reality of black soldiers participating fully and bravely in the fight for their freedom. Trip, therefore, had to be broken, to reach the point where he would charge, flag staff in hand, alongside Robert Gould Shaw, the man who had ordered him beaten like a slave. The making of this narrative point required the filmmakers not only to show a series of ritual humiliations of Trip at the hands of white officers, but also to significantly reconstruct black attitudes towards the idea of American nationalism and its symbols. In Denzel Washington's character, they incarnate the black liberation movements of the 1960s rather than the men who fought for "Freedom and Union" in the 1860s. Trip's anger at the entire white establishment, and not merely white slaveholders, represents an anachronism matched by Trip's unlikely use of inner-city lingo.

A wholly different, and perhaps superior, approach to telling this story would have been to accurately portray the demographics of the historical 54th Massachusetts Regiment. *Glory!* portrays these soldiers primarily as runaway slaves, when in fact the historical regiment was composed almost entirely of northern blacks who had been free from birth and whose parents, and in some cases grandparents, had also been free. The anger of a character such as Trip would have been out of place among these men, whose lives and thought had been shaped by the experience of freedom, the thriving life of black northern institutions, and republican rhetoric that had led to emancipation in the state constitutions of the North after the Revolutionary War. Black rage would have been present, to be sure, but it would have been a rage directed against the slave power of the South—not American institutions and ideals.

Trip's refusal to carry the American flag in combat offers one example of the unfortunate direction the filmmakers are led by historical inaccuracy. In truth, African-American soldiers proudly carried the flag, understanding that waving of the banner and wearing the blue uniform of the Union were in themselves subversive acts that would forever change the nature of the United States. "Oh Give Us a Flag" became one of the most popular camp songs for black troops because they understood that their actions meant the United States would never again be a slaveholding republic built on a bundle of compromises containing fugitive-slave clauses. Frederick Douglass, whose two sons were real sergeants in the real 54th Massachusetts, understood this when he wrote that "the American flag is the flag of freedom for those who really stand under it and defend it with their blood." There was no angrier black man in nineteenth-century America than Frederick Douglass, and yet he understood the power of bearing the flag and what it would mean for 37,000 African-Americans to wash the flag in their own blood. Speaking to a doubtful white audience in New York City in

1863, Douglass insisted: "They are ready to rally under the stars and stripes at the first tap of the drum. Give them a chance, stop calling them 'niggers' and call them soldiers."[11]

How could a better film have been made of the African-American Civil War experience? One answer is that the film could have focused even more on the experience of battle, rather than simply the politics of the campfire and Shaw's bureaucratic struggles with his recalcitrant superiors. This might seem a strange answer for historians, who frequently complain about the focus on battlefield action in historical epics, a focus often detrimental to the examination of deeper cultural, social, and moral issues. But battle itself served as the central issue for African-American soldiers, who wanted to be able to say, as Trip does after the regiment's first engagement, "We men now, ain't we . . . we men!" As *Glory!* suggests, even many northerners had doubted this fact from the beginning. One Boston newspaper in 1862 had suggested that the government enlist black soldiers simply "to occupy the yellow fever posts" along the Mississippi River, implying that it was better for black men to be sacrificed to disease than white ones.[12]

A film that spent less time breaking a proud black man and more time showing these same proud black men carrying Enfield rifles against the forces of the Confederacy would have been more historically accurate, while also achieving the filmmakers' purpose of exploring the true significance of black soldiers in the Civil War. *Glory!* leaves the viewer with the impression that the 54th died with its colonel at Battery Wagner, when actually it went on to bravely acquit itself at numerous engagements in the final two years of the war. More attention to those details would have prevented moviegoers from seeing the experience of the 54th as a kind of fluke, an experiment that ended with the death of a brave white colonel. In short, the story could have been told as what it was: an assertion of agency and humanity by black soldiers afraid neither of the white Confederates nor deterred by the clumsy paternalism of northern whites.

Director John Sayles once observed that he had often had the experience of seeing a so-called "historical film," only to discover that the real events were far more interesting that those portrayed on film.[13] *Glory!* certainly serves as a case in point, an intriguing and even educational film that nevertheless does not quite escape the restriction of black agency so common to the genre of Civil War films. White paternalism, in the form of the young abolitionist prancing on his steed, remains the dominant ethos of the film. Seemingly filled with attempts to deconstruct the white myths of dominance, the breaking of Trip actually symbolizes the continued unwillingness to make a Civil War film that not only is full of black men but is in a real sense *about* black men. Robert Wiegman has written that representations of African Americans in film, at least since the civil rights era, have often manifested the egalitarian dream of the era while at the same time creating "narrative scenarios that reaffirm white masculine power."

Glory! follows this unfortunate tendency. Edward Zwick, in commenting on criticism of his film and the message he hoped to convey, has responded that if the film's "iconography" contains "a certain degree of liberal fantasy, well, so be it." Zwick's motivations were certainly well intended, but the men of the 54th Massachusetts deserve to be more than the icons of white liberal fantasy.[14] "It stinks," Trip tells Robert Gould Shaw in one of the most powerful scenes in *Glory!* "and we all mixed up in it—ain't nobody clean." This simple statement, so aptly describing the burden of race in America, prompts Shaw to ask Trip what the solution to the dilemma could possibly be. "Kick in," Trip tells him, "we all got to kick in." *Glory!* suggests that there are some subjects on which historians must be more than scholars, and filmmakers more than entertainers.

Notes

1. Warren Susman, *Culture as History: The Transformation of American Society in the Twentieth Century* (New York: Pantheon: 1984), 5.
2. Robert Penn Warren, *The Legacy of the Civil War* (Cambridge, MA: Harvard University Press, 1961), 101. Warren's slim volume is the place to begin reflecting on the meaning of the Civil War and its myths; the two bests works on the meaning of the southern Lost Cause are Charles Reagan Wilson's *Baptized in Blood: The Religion of the Lost Cause, 1865–1920* (Athens: University of Georgia Press, 1980) and Gaines M. Foster, *Ghosts of the Confederacy: Defeat, the Lost Cause and the Emergence of the New South* (Oxford: Oxford University Press, 1986);
3. See Edward J. Blum's "Gilded Crosses: Postbellum Revivalism and the Re-Forging of American Nationalism," *Journal of Presbyterian History* 79 (Winter 2001): 277–292.
4. Nina Silber, *The Romance of Reunion: Northerners and the South, 1865–1900* (Chapel Hill: University of North Carolina Press, 1993), 48–65.
5. Edward D. Campbell, *Celluloid South: Hollywood and the Southern Myth* (Knoxville: University of Tennessee Press, 1981) offers a good introduction to the portrayal of southern stereotypes in film. The new directions in such scholarship are best seen in Grace Elizabeth Hale's *Making Whiteness: The Culture of Segregation in the South, 1890–1940* (New York: Pantheon Books, 1998); see especially 154ff and 277–79.
6. See Daniel Lieb, *From Sambo to Super-Spade* (Boston: Houghton Mifflin, 1975) for a discussion of the relevant filmography.
7. Surprisingly, scholars have not dwelt very much on the important story of this regiment. One place to begin is Russell Duncan's Introduction to *Blue-Eyed Child of Fortune: The Civil War Letters of Colonel Robert Gould Shaw*, ed. Russell Duncan (Athens, GA: University of Georgia Press, 1992); Kirk Savage, *Standing Soldiers, Kneeling Slaves: Race, War and Monuments in Nineteenth-Century America* (Princeton: Princeton University Press, 1997), 193–203.

8. All quotes from the film are draw from *Glory!* prod. Freddie Fields and dir. Edward Zwick, 122 min., videocassette (Tri-Star Pictures, 1989).
9. W. E. B. DuBois, *The Souls of Black Folk* (New York: Dover Publications, 1994), 55ff.
10. Joseph T. Glatthaar, *Forged in Battle: The Civil War Alliance of Black Soldiers and White Officers* (London: The Free Press, 1990) notes some instances of physical, and many instances of verbal, abuse of black soldiers by the white officer corps. Significantly, "whipping" was not one of the abuses, likely because of its association with slavery. Moreover, white officers were frequently court-martialed in the Union army for the ill-treatment of black troops, often based on evidence given by those troops. See especially 90ff.
11. Quoted in Duncan, Introduction to *Blue-Eyed . . .*, 21.
12. Quoted in Dudly Taylor Cornish, *The Sable Arm: Negro Troops in the Union Army, 1861–1865* (New York: W.W. Norton and Company, 1966), 9.
13. "A Conversation Between John Sayles and Eric Foner," in *Past Imperfect: History According to the Movies,* Mark C. Carnes, ed. (New York: Henry Holt Co., 1995), 11.
14. Robert Wiegman, "Black Bodies/American Commodities: Gender, Race and the Bourgeois Ideal in Contemporary Film," *Unspeakable Images: Ethnicity and American Cinema,* ed. Lester Friedman (Urbana and Chicago: University of Illinois Press, 1991), 312; Edward Zwick quoted in Jim Cullen, "A Few Good Men," *The Civil War in Popular Culture: A Reusable Past* (Washington and London: Smithsonian Press, 1995), 141.

Alex Haley's *Roots*

The Fiction of Fact

— William E. Huntzicker —

Forty years after *Gone with the Wind* provided the Old South's strongest antidote to *Uncle Tom's Cabin*, the plantation novel seemed to get its long-overdue racial makeover with the phenomenal success of Alex Haley's *Roots: The Saga of an American Family*. The book appeared as the finishing touches were completed on a spin-off television miniseries—eight of the most successful programs in television history. On his dedication page, Haley claimed he had no idea his personal history would take him twelve years to research and write. "Just by chance it is being published on the Bicentennial year of the United States," he wrote. "So I dedicate *Roots* as a birthday offering to my country within which most of *Roots* happened."[1] Haley's patriotic gift of 1976 put slaves at the center of the plantation narrative in the most dramatic way since *Uncle Tom's Cabin* and elevated genealogical research to a national pastime.

Celebrating their national bicentennial, Americans seemed in a self-congratulatory mood in 1976. A hungry actor, Sylvester Stallone, had launched his own road to stardom by writing a script about the rise of fictional boxer Rocky Balboa. The resultant movie, *Rocky*, in which Stallone sealed his fate as both superstar and typecast not-too-bright, monosyllabic tough guy, was filmed for around $1 million and yielded more than $250 million at the box office, spawned at least four sequels, and won the year's Oscar for best picture. The following year, the motion picture industry moved the classic American western story from the past into the future to "a galaxy far, far away," where a quantum leap in special effects gave Luke Skywalker special powers to rescue Princess Leia from the evil Darth Vader in the first *Star Wars* film.

Haley tried to inject his family story into the enormous success and lasting popularity of the likes of Rocky, Luke Skywalker and Darth Vader. Like these popular movie icons, Kunta Kinte, the proud Mandinka warrior Haley claimed as his first African ancestor brought to America as a slave, also entered our personal lives and conversations. Rather than achieving success in one lifetime, Kinte became the centerpiece of Alex Haley's rags-to-riches story that spanned two centuries through seven generations from freedom to slavery to freedom to successful author and celebrity. Kunta Kinte's story appeared in book form in September 1976 and on television in January 1977. Haley gained immediate recognition, especially after appearing at the end of the series in one of the most watched television programs ever.

Haley credited his story—and his success—to the conversations he heard as a child listening to his Grandma Cynthia Murray Palmer, Cousin Georgia Anderson, and other old ladies on Grandma's front porch in Henning, Tennessee (population 500, about fifty miles north of Memphis).[2] The stories mentioned the proud African—Kunta Kinte—and contained remnants of African words. His book culminates in Haley's "peak experience" of visiting Juffure, a Gambian village of about seventy people, where a *griot*—the village storyteller—recited the lineage and history of the village for him. After about two hours of recitation, the old man came to the story of Kunta, the eldest of four sons who was kidnapped by slavers one day when he left the village to chop wood.

"I sat as if I were carved of stone," Haley wrote in his book. "My blood seemed to have congealed. This man whose lifetime had been in this back-country African village had no way in the world to know that he had just echoed what I had heard all through my boyhood years on my grandma's front porch in Henning, Tennessee . . . of an African who always had insisted that his name was 'Kin-tay'; who had called a guitar a 'ko,' and a river within the state of Virginia, 'Kamby Bolongo'; and who had been kidnapped into slavery while not far from his village, chopping wood to make himself a drum."[3]

After Haley showed the worn notebook pages with his grandmother's story to an interpreter, everyone in the village became excited. Haley and the men of the village prayed in a mosque: "Praise be to Allah for one long lost from us whom Allah has returned." People of the village cheered, cried and celebrated with him. "Let me tell you something: I am a man," Haley wrote. "A sob hit me somewhere around my ankles; it came surging upward, and flinging my hands over my face, I was just bawling, as I hadn't since I was a baby. *'Meester Kinte!'*

I just felt like I was weeping for all of history's incredible atrocities against fellowmen, which seems to be mankind's greatest flaw." On the way home, Haley wrote, "I decided to write a book. My own ancestors' [*sic*] would automatically also be a symbolic saga of all African-descent people—who are without exception the seeds of someone like Kunta who was born and grew up in some black African village, someone who was captured and chained down in one of those slave ships that sailed them across the same ocean, into some succession of plantations, and since then a struggle for freedom."[4]

Thus, Haley claimed to tell not only his personal family story but also the history of African Americans in the United States. He worked with television producer David L. Wolper, who hoped for cross-media synergy, to boost both the book and the related television series. Filming for the television series began in April 1976 and was nearly completed in August—about a month before the book was distributed. Wolper had heard about Haley's research in 1972 and pursued purchasing film rights. Haley, who was telling his story in lectures and magazine articles, had not yet finished the book. After acquiring the rights, Wolper hired producer Stan Margulies and writer William Blinn to began formulating episodic television scripts from portions of the book as Haley completed them. Writers Ernie Kinoy, James Lee and Max Cohen joined the project to work feverishly through the summer of 1975 to complete the script—more than a year before the book was finished. Fred Silverman, who had just joined ABC as vice president for prime-time programming, heard about the project and offered $6 million for a twelve-hour miniseries. Silverman had already shown that dramatic African-American programs could succeed with the acclaimed made-for-television movie *The Autobiography of Miss Jane Pittman* in 1973.[5]

Putting Haley's project on film was particularly challenging, Wolper recalled. "All in all, when Alex's book first came to us in rough draft, it was over two thousand pages. In cutting the book down to six hundred pages, a lot of characters were lost, some of whom we had already incorporated into our film scripts." In addition, characters like the wrestler and the fiddler were created to provide television dialogue giving inner feelings that an author can provide through a book's narrator. Film and television normally provide emotional experiences, while a book provides an intellectual experience. At their first meeting, Wolper found Haley to be "the most dynamic, fabulous, unbelievable person I have met in my life," and Haley told him he wanted to reach the greatest number of people. Television would be their medium and Wolper bragged that he produced a "middle brow" program appealing to large numbers of people.[6]

But the actual numbers shocked everyone involved. An estimated 130 million people—more than half the nation—watched at least some of the television series. The book had immediately hit the bestseller list when it was published, and sales grew after the television program aired in January, making it the best-selling nonfiction book of 1977. By the time the program aired, the book had sold 750,000 copies, and on Tuesday of the week of the broadcasts, it hit a one-day sales record of 67,000 copies. By March, one million copies were in print. One day in Los Angeles, some 3,000 people lined up to have Haley autograph copies of the book. Haley, who had been the ghost writer for the bestselling *The Autobiography of Malcolm X* in 1964, was in no way prepared for the celebrity he achieved. As the series ended with the family's escape to Tennessee, Haley appeared on camera briefly to trace Kunte's lineage from then to the present. That program, episode 8, aired on January 30, 1977, became the most watched program in television history at the time, with an estimated 98 million people tuned in.[7] By the time Haley died in 1992, *Roots* had sold 1.5 million copies in hardcover and 4 million in paperback.[8]

Like Haley's book, the miniseries focused primarily on the Old South through the end of the Civil War. After his capture at the age of seventeen, Kunta Kinte takes a life-threatening voyage on a slave ship to Annapolis, Maryland, where he is purchased by a Virginia plantation owner. In Virginia, he is given the name Toby and the master's last name of Waller. Eventually, he marries Bell, another slave, and they have a daughter, Kizzy, who is taught the African traditions by her father and is taught to read and write by a white child who had Kizzy as a playmate. For that crime and for forging a pass in a futile attempt to help a beau escape, Kizzy is sold to a crass plantation owner, Tom Lea, who rapes her on her first night at his place. The birth of Chicken George results from that union; George's handle comes from his role as trainer of Lea's gamecocks. In 1827 Chicken George married Matilda, and their son, Tom, was born in 1833. When Tom Lea's fortunes decline, he sells off the slaves, except for an aged Kizzy and Chicken George, on loan to a British aristocratic cock fighter. Because Tom was sold to the Murray plantation, he takes that last name and marries a half-Indian slave, Irene. (On television, the family name was changed from Murray to Harvey.) At the end of the Civil War, this family moves to Henning, Tennessee, where they buy land with Chicken George's winnings from fighting chickens in England. The family reunion and move to Tennessee become the happy ending of the miniseries.

In filming *Roots*, the African-American actors felt profound emotions as they relived what they saw as their own history. LeVar Burton, an untested film student from UCLA, received the role of the young Kunta Kinte. Lou Gossett portrayed Fiddler, an older slave who taught him English and ways to survive on the plantation. As overseer, white actor Vic Morrow whipped Kinte for escaping and for refusing to give up his African name and accept his slave name of Toby. During the scene, actor Burton was about eighteen and he had makeup to look like blood on his face for the whipping. Asked whether he should be caught when cut from the tree after the beating, Burton said he'd just fall. "When he hit the ground like that," Gossett recalled, "he hit it hard, I mean *hard!* When he finally said he was Kunta Kinte—they were trying to make him say his name now was Toby—I just stood there in awe. When they cut him down, I looked at him and said to myself, 'Damn, is he dead?' . . . All of a sudden it started to come up—the tears, the crying, I could feel it coming—and I thought, 'I'll never be able to say my lines.' So I started saying my lines and tears started to come, then I lost control, but that's what actors dream about. Actors dream about doing something so pure that it is involuntary."[9]

The *Roots* television series ended its eight nights in January 1977 with records—eight of the thirteen most viewed television shows in history up to that time. Significantly, the movie *Gone with the Wind*, broken into two parts for airing on prime-time television the previous November, held the previous record for television audience. Clearly, the story of the Old South still had currency, rivaling only the Super Bowl in getting the nation's attention. In addition, a Southern governor, Jimmy Carter of Georgia, had been elected president in 1976. News about *Roots* reflected the enthusiasm of its audience. Wolper, however, had feared that race riots could result from the strong material. *Time* magazine reported that some black leaders saw the series as the most important event since the Selma civil rights march.

In the mass media, success spawns more of the same. ABC ran a sequel in February 1979 called *Roots: The Next Generations.* As they did for the first series, the producers and writers of the sequel worked from Haley's notes. Writer Ernest Kinoy worked with one thousand pages of Haley's rough manuscript to trace Haley's family from emancipation to the present. The credits for the sequel, which ran for seven nights, said it was based on Haley's *Roots* and *Search*, a book that was never written. Audiences arrived in huge numbers, but not like the original. *Roots II* peaked at a 32.7 percent rating and 50 percent share for the third episode.[10] *Roots: The Next Generations* follows Haley's family from Reconstruction through the present.

Ironically, education and family values supported by both the book and television series are not reflected in Haley's personal life. In fact, the series glosses over some of his personal life. In her doctoral dissertation, built upon interviews with Haley, Mary Siebert McCauley acknowledged that *Roots II* covers Haley's marriage and an affair. "Since Haley had actually been married twice, he was asked why he told about only one marriage in *Roots II.* He explained, 'Well, simply because it would have been duplicative or repetitive to use two marriages. That's all. From a film point of view, it wasn't a documentary as such. We had to compress. Remember we were telling a hundred years in fourteen hours."[11]

After the television and publishing success, however, Haley's life took on more aspects of a holy war than of nirvana. As awards poured upon the book and television series—including a special Pulitzer Prize for the book—lawsuits also proliferated. "Like so many who've made it big—financially as well as professionally—I've become a sitting duck for lawsuits. . . . No matter how unfounded, each and every lawsuit has to be fought—at an enormous cost, in money, in time and in psychic wear and tear."[12] Strangely, Haley himself initiated one of the first lawsuits. In April 1977, Haley sued his publisher for $5 million, claiming that Doubleday had failed to promote the book sufficiently and that, further, it had made a sweetheart deal with the paperback publisher, Dell, later a division of Doubleday, to publish the paperback version too soon. The suit was settled.[13]

Two authors sued Haley for plagiarism. Novelist Margaret Walker, who had written a celebrated Civil War novel in 1966 about the life of the daughter of a slave mother and a white plantation owner, claimed in federal court that parts of *Roots* came from her novel *Jubilee*.[14] Her suit was dismissed on a summary judgment. Philip Nobile, who reviewed Haley's plagiarism cases, said that Walker proved her copyright infringement but that she was the "victim of a biased federal judge who thought Haley was above suspicion."[15]

Novelist Harold Courlander charged that Haley lifted eighty-one situations from his 1967 slave novel, *The African*. Haley settled this case for $650,000, and, in court, admitted other "trespasses"—mostly from historical books in the public domain. "Alex Haley acknowledges and regrets that various materials from *The African* found their way into his book, *Roots*," Haley admitted as part of the settlement. In interviews, Haley said many people offered him notes and some of them could have included the questionable passages. "There were passages from the book that appeared verbatim in my notes," Haley said. "And it was futile to try to defend myself. I honestly can't recall what was in my mind when I wrote something at 3 a.m. five years ago."[16]

Haley's *Roots* begins with historical specificity that gives it credibility: "Early in the spring of 1750, in the village of Juffure, four days upriver from the coast of The Gambia, West Africa, a manchild was born to Omoro and Binta Kinte. Forcing forth from Binta's strong young body, he was as black as she was, flecked and slippery with Binta's blood, and he was bawling." Growing up in an idyllic Africa, Kunta Kinte loved his freedom, living innocent of the evils of the larger world—until slavers captured him at the age of seventeen. He was unfamiliar with Europeans and ships. (On television, he even had a run with then-popular O. J. Simpson in a playful scene in a lush green countryside near Savannah, Georgia, standing in for Africa.)

Within months of the miniseries, Haley found himself on the defensive for his anthropology, history, genealogy and even his own personal story. Mark

Ottaway, a travel writer and reporter, attacked the very idea that Haley had actually traced his roots to a specific village. The Gambian village of Juffure in 1767 differed dramatically from Haley's description. "Far from being a remote Eden untouched by white civilization, the real Juffure was a white trading post surrounded by white colonization." Such residents were more likely to be collaborators than victims of slavers. The capture of a Juffure resident by slavers was unlikely in 1767, a date Haley selected on the basis of his research in the United States, not Africa. And the African information, Ottaway contended, came not from a *griot*, but an unofficial historian who knew in advance what Haley wanted to hear and provided the desired information.[17]

Ottaway quoted Haley's response: "This book is also symbolic. I know Juffure was a British trading post and my portrait of the village bears no resemblance to the way it was. But the portrait I gave was true of nearly all the other villages in Gambia. I, we, need a place called Eden. My people need a Pilgrim's Rock. I wanted to portray our original culture in its pristine state, and I know it is a fair portrayal." Thus, Haley was not missing his calling to be a preacher. Haley again defended his research a few days later from Gambia. "It was like somebody walked up to you and said your dead father had not actually been your father. . . . It all began to roll in on me—glimpses, memories, scores of memories, the researching, the digging of researching that I went through to check and cross-check. Then I got angry. I flew across the ocean. . . . Here we have all these blacks, these millions of American blacks. Can't we blacks have one case where we are able to go back to our past without someone taking a cheap shot to torpedo it?"[18]

Nonetheless, Ottaway had concluded his story saying that Haley maintains "with some justification that the 'symbolic truth' of 'Roots' remains untarnished." Thousands of men like Kunta Kinte were sold into slavery. "If his grandmother's story was correct, Haley has demonstrated his forefather was such a man. But he has not demonstrated that his name was Kunta Kinte, that he lived in Juffure, or that he was captured by slavers in 1767."[19]

As the *Roots* book was released, Haley admitted to gaps in his history and personal story, even before the criticism and before he became a celebrity. "Although it's advertised as nonfiction, perhaps we should call it 'faction.' Every statement in 'Roots' is accurate in terms of authenticity—the descriptions of the culture and terrain are based on valid material. The beginning is a re-creation, using novelistic techniques, but as it moves forward more is known and it is more factually based." As he stated in the book and in repeated interviews, Haley was inspired to write his book after seeing the Rosetta Stone in the British Museum and thinking about how a few words and characters could unlock history and culture. And seeing other people in the National Archives working hard on their own family histories further inspired him to seek his own roots. "It occurred to me that they were really trying to find out who they were."[20]

Historian Willie Lee Rose related Haley's search to "the particular pain of not knowing shared by most Afro-Americans whose history was so curiously mislaid" and who did not have "Haley's good fortune in having a Grandmother Cynthia, or for that matter an original Afro-American parent who troubled to stitch American places and things into the memories of his progeny with African names." Despite the many clues passed on, Haley's history left much to be desired, from the idyllic Gambia to colonial Virginia in a tobacco-growing region depicted in the book as cotton country. Haley gives the slaves words not appropriate to the time and place. Such petty anachronisms are so numerous, Rose found, that they "chip away at the verisimilitude of central matters in which it is important to have full faith."[21]

Rose saw "factional" as a way to suggest "that the primary incidents and historical moments are true, but that in reconstructing the emotions of his personalities in the grip of their fates, in supposing their motives, indeed, in filling their mouths with conversation, he has done the best he could, as other writers of historical fiction try to do." But this is neither history nor fiction. Rose contended that it is appropriately called a saga. "Sagas are usually told in episodes, and for that reason *Roots* is particularly well adapted to television." Already portions of Georgia were being prepared to stand in for Africa. Prophetically, Rose wrote, "Success for Haley, and for Georgia, on the scale of *Gone with the Wind*'s, seems secure."[22]

Where some journalists and historians found spiritual legitimacy in Haley's story, some genealogists were less forgiving. Genealogist Elizabeth Shown Mills and history professor Gary B. Mills attacked Haley's genealogical research by revisiting many of the sources for *Roots* and contended that he failed at the typical family challenge of reconciling oral tradition with documentary evidence. "Historical evidence indicates that Mr. Haley has been heir to the same frustrations faced by untold numbers of other amateur genealogists who seek to document family traditions and legends, and he has fallen victim to the same psychological hangup that has entrapped many others: a reluctance to accept any truths that deviate from the cherished family legend." The researchers found many of the names Haley used. For instance, one Waller slave named Topy, one of several who could have been Kunta Kinte, had died before the arrival of the *Lord Ligonier*, the ship which Haley said brought him to the United States. "In truth, those same plantation records, wills, and censuses cited by Mr. Haley not only *fail to document* his story, but they *contradict* each and every pre-Civil War statement of Afro-American lineage in *Roots!*" The Millses found records from the plantations mentioned in *Roots* but the records did not fit Haley's facts. "The degree of discrepancy which exists between the Haley family chronicle and documentable facts inevitably calls into question both the legitimacy of *Roots* as 'history' and its very essence as an expression of one family's heritage." Further, the trend toward oral history, they wrote, "has obscured for many the basic fact that *there is no such thing as The Gospel According to Aunt Lizzie*." They argued for the application of the same rigorous standards as historians; otherwise, researchers become frustrated and disillusioned when their own personal legends are not neatly borne out by the facts they find.[23]

A year after Haley's death and on the eve of CBS's three-part miniseries *Queen*, which was based on an unfinished novel about Haley's father's side of the family, Philip Nobile looked at Haley's plagiarism, sloppy chronology, factual errors, and concluded that *Roots* was a hoax. "Historians are reluctant—cowardly—about calling attention to factual errors when the general theme is in the right direction." Haley built "the church of *Roots*" upon his visit with Kebba Fanji Fofana, the supposed *griot* of Juffure on May 17, 1967. "Kunta Kinte, the only African American ancestor to survive the genealogical erasure of the Atlantic slave trade, was Haley's meal ticket in hundreds of subsequent lectures and kept Doubleday keenly involved with the project despite a decade of editorial upheavals and deadline disappointments." Nobile contends that George Sims, Haley's researcher for thirty-two years, and Murray Fisher, his editor, deserve credit for Haley's publications, but both denied it. Sims said he collected stories from Henning for a book that never appeared; Sims said they were his stories, but Haley told them better. Haley kept having money problems and missing deadlines and the alleged plagiarism resulted from the rush to finish the book before the television show was aired.[24]

Appearing in the mid-1970s, *Roots* enjoyed the benefits of an academic culture that had experienced a dynamic revisionism on slave historiography. In the first major historical work on the slave South, Ulrich B. Phillips in 1918 had seen slaves as docile and happy with their situation. As recently as 1959, Stanley Elkins accepted and perpetuated this stereotype by emphasizing the trauma of the slave ship and plantation life to explain the Sambo stereotype of the docile slave.[25] Even Harriet Beecher Stowe knew that slaves, to be left alone, would put forward a face that the masters wanted to see. Haley gave faces and names to those levels of personal rebellion and deceit. As historians began to look at history from the bottom up in the 1960s and 1970s, they found slave sources that exposed a rich alternative culture with many levels of acceptance and rebellion.[26] Haley's family was not typical; it was privileged—from their status in Juffure to their ability to form and maintain a family from slavery to freedom. In a book that appeared the same year as *Roots*, historian Herbert Gutman estimated that as many as one in six or seven slave families were ended by force or sale.[27]

While Nobile has campaigned to have the Pulitzer committee remove Haley's special prize, others have sought greater recognition for Haley, whose star seems to have faded in the academic community. While acknowledging that *Roots* has been compromised as history, David Chioni Moore says that it may have to wait until histories of the 1970s are written to achieve its proper place as a "foundational text" of the culture. Slavery and racism forced millions of people to give up their languages, their identities, and even their own names. Outlawing their stories robbed slaves of their history. "Alex Haley and his bridge called *Roots,* whatever its shortcomings and whatever its construction, promised to redeem that crime of history." *Roots* should be regarded as a sacred text, he argued, and then its "facticity must be placed in the background" and the silence can end. Helen Taylor characterized Haley as a Tennessee *griot* who told a vital apocryphal story that invites both resistance and identification. Moore and Taylor argued that the story spoke for millions of people a symbolic truth that was more important than the literal truth of its facts.[28]

Clearly, Alex Haley had been around the world—and around the block. He both trivialized genealogy and took it too seriously. Once he broke the ground for African Americans to trace their roots, he said, what remains is "just a matter of filling in the blanks—which person, living in which village, going on what ship, across the same ocean, slavery, emancipation, the struggle for freedom." Thus, the trivialization, as the Gary and Elizabeth Shown Mills pointed out, created the expectation that these blanks can be easily filled in and that they will conform to family legend. On the other hand, he contributed to a massive assumption that genealogy was the same as a person's identity. He assumed, as noted above, that finding one's roots was the same as finding oneself—a gross oversimplification that does not seem to be addressed in any of the literature on *Roots.*

African Americans had been denied access to their roots in an effort to deny their identities; thus Haley's perceived accomplishment is an act of both triumph and rebellion. It acknowledges the generations of suffering under slavery. It affirms the importance of a strong black Muslim tradition and grants permission for subsequent products of popular culture to have strong, even rebellious black heroes with whom the entire audience can identify. The hero instills pride in the struggle against overwhelming odds and ultimately winning a victory, if not for himself, but for subsequent generations. In him, the ultimate trickster makes his culture survive through passing along clues that allow Haley to make the ultimate genealogical link.

Haley's phenomenal success indicates that his message resonated with contemporary culture. Despite allegations of fakery and the melodrama, Alex Haley reached into the American soul across racial lines—not an easy task, even in the 1970s. He affirmed the survival of family values against overwhelming odds at a time the nation was anxious about the security of its family values. He affirmed that, even the most rootless among us can find our roots and our identities. At the same time, *Roots* helped Americans to confront the difficult issues around slavery. It allowed us to see and name the issues and identify with the suffering[29] As Fiddler nurses Kunta Kinte after he's cut down, actor Burton described the characters as "irreparably and forever bonded in this moment." Like Scarlett in *Gone with the Wind*, Fiddler tells Toby (Kunta) that "There's going to be another day."[30]

Notes

1. Alex Haley, *Roots: The Saga of an American Family* (Garden City, N.Y.: Doubleday & Company, Inc., 1976), dedication page.
2. Alex Haley, "My Furthest-Back Black Person—'The African'," *New York Times Sunday Magazine,* 16 July 1972, 12.
3. Haley, chapter 120, 679. In this and subsequence notes, chapter numbers will be used with page numbers for ease of locating quotes in other editions.
4. Haley, chapter 120, 681.
5. David L. Wolper with Quincy Troupe, *The Inside Story of T.V.'s "Roots"* (New York: Warner Books, 1978), 34–35, 44–45, 50–51.
6. Wolper and Troupe, 46, 58–59.
7. Wolper and Troupe, 152–154, 156.
8. Eric Pace, "Alex Haley, 70, author of 'Roots,' Dies," *New York Times,* 11 February 1992.
9. Quoted in Wolper and Troupe, 128.
10. The rating is the percent of television households tuned to the program; the share is the percent of sets in use tuned to the program. When three commercial networks competed for most of the audience, a share of more than 33 meant you were drawing more than your competitors. The first night of the sequel received a 27.8 rating and 41 percent share; the second night reached a 29.3 rating and 41 share. With the third episode, the numbers picked up to a 32.7 percent rating and 50 percent share. The fourth night garnered a 31.8 rating and 48 percent share; the fifth night, 31.7 and 48; sixth night, 28.9 and 47; and the seventh, 28.6 and 40. Rating and share numbers are from http://www.davidlwolper.com.
11. Mary Siebert McCauley, "Alex Haley, a Southern Griot: A Literary Biography" (Ph.D. diss., Vanderbilt University, 1983), 204.
12. Alex Haley, "There Are Days When I Wish It Hadn't Happened," *Playboy,* March 1979; Fisher, 451.
13. Wolper and Troupe, 164–165.
14. Walker died in 1998. See "Margaret Walker Alexander, 83, Professor and Author of 'Jubilee'," *New York Times,* 4 December 1998.
15. Philip Nobile, "For History's Sake: Three Pulitzers That Should Be Revoked," speech to the Columbia University graduate students, 5 April 2002, at www.mobylives.com.

16. Philip Nobile, "Uncovering Roots," *Village Voice* 23 February 1993, 32–33; *The Tennessean*, 15 December 1978, quoted in McCauley, 198–199; Arnold H. Lubasch, "'Roots' Plagiarism Suit Is Settled," *New York Times*, 15 December 1978, A1, B8.
17. Mark Ottaway, "Tangled Roots," *Sunday Times of London*, 10 April 1977, 17, 21; Robert D. McFadden, "Some Points of 'Roots' Questioned; Haley Stands by Book as a Symbol," *New York Times*, 10 April 1977, 1, 29.
18. Ibid.; John Darnton, "Haley, Assailing Critic, Says 'Roots' Is Sound," *New York Times*, 19 April 1977, 3.
19. Ottaway, 21.
20. Mel Watkins, "A Talk with Alex Haley," *New York Times*, 16 September 1976, BR1, BR10.
21. Willie Lee Rose, "An American Family, *New York Review of Books* 23:18 (11 November 1976).
22 Ibid.
23. Gary B. Mills and Elizabeth Shown Mills, "*Roots* and the New 'Faction': A Legitimate Tool for Clio?" *The Virginia Magazine of History and Biography* 89:1 (January 1981): 6, 23, 26.
24. Philip Nobile, "Uncovering *Roots*," *Village Voice* (23 February 1993): 32, 37–38.
25. Ulrich B. Phillips, *American Negro Slavery* (Baton Rouge: Louisiana State University Press, 1966); Stanley M. Elkins, *Slavery: A Problem in American Institutional and Intellectual Life* (Chicago: University of Chicago Press, 1959).
26. See, for example, Eugene D. Genovese, *Roll, Jordan, Roll: The World the Slaves Made* (New York: Pantheon Books, 1974); John W. Blassingame, *The Slave Community: Plantation Life in the Antebellum South*, 2nd ed. (New York: Oxford University Press, 1979); Lawrence W. Levine, *Black Culture and Black Consciousness* (New York: Oxford University Press, 1977).
27. Herbert G. Gutman, *The Black Family in Slavery and Freedom, 1750–1925* (New York: Pantheon Books, 1977), 318.
28. David Chioni Moore, "Routes: Alex Haley's *Roots* and the Rhetoric of Genealogy," *Transition: An International Review* 64 (1994): 10; Helen Taylor, "'The Griot from Tennessee': The Saga of Alex Haley's *Roots*," *Critical Quarterly* 37:2 (Summer 1995): 59, 60.
29. Georg Stanford Brown in commentary on *Roots* DVD, episode 5.
30. LeVar Burton in commentary on *Roots* DVD, episode 2.

A Voice of the South

The Transformation of Shelby Foote

— David W. Bulla —

One day you are a struggling artist, trying to win fame and fortune. The next day you are a major celebrity. How did you get to such a place in your career? In the case of southern author Shelby Foote, the answer is remarkably simple—television. Once upon a time, Foote was a novelist with a book contract but no mass audience. Then came Ken Burns's 1990 television documentary, *The Civil War*. Suddenly, Foote was the star he had always imagined being—not as a novelist, but as a venerable mouthpiece for the Civil War in general and southern culture in particular. This was ironic, since the Memphis-based Foote always thought his writings, especially his novels, would propel him to major celebrity. Instead, his fame came after he appeared as a guest expert on Burns's nine-part documentary, an appearance that propelled the author of the three-volume, million-and-a-half-word *The Civil War: A Narrative* into the unsought and somewhat uncomfortable role of principal spokesman for America's bloodiest war.

Born November 17, 1916, Foote rose to minor literary prominence in the late 1940s and early 1950s as a novelist writing about the Civil War and racial and class relations in his native Mississippi. Foote attended the University of North Carolina at Chapel Hill from 1935 until 1937, where he wrote features, book reviews, and short stories for *Carolina Magazine*, served in the military during World War II, and then wrote briefly for the Associated Press before turning full-time to novel-writing in the late 1940s. In 1952, his novel *Shiloh* received glowing reviews. The Civil War-era novel focuses on the character of southern general Nathan Bedford Forrest. *The Saturday Review* called *Shiloh* "a superb story of war," and the *New York Times* hailed Foote as "a promising novelist who has arrived."[1] The reviewer in *The Atlantic* said *Shiloh* was better than Foote's first three novels (*Tournament*, *Follow Me Down*, and *Love in a Dry Season*) and called it "a true accomplishment," adding, "The author's achievement is that he has fused the landscape, the weather, the generalship, the fighting, the atrocious suffering of the wounded, the thoughts and feelings of the living, the shattered bodies of the dead into a single dramatic entity, which takes possession of the reader."[2]

Given such reviews, Foote thought his book might make him a literary giant. "The coming success of SHILOH is going to be a great help," he told his lifelong friend, fellow-novelist Walker Percy.[3] Later, however, Foote was forced to admit that the book had received "nothing like the prominent attention I thought it would."[4] He brooded, "I have nothing but contempt for myself in the shape I am in," and told Percy that he feared he would be nothing more than a minor writer.[5] In 1953, however, Foote's credentials as a Civil War expert caused him to receive a gem of a literary invitation. Random House publisher Bennett Cerf commissioned the Mississippian to write a piece on the Civil War in observance of the conflict's upcoming centennial. Cerf gave Foote plenty of time—almost a decade—to write the piece, and he only expected approximately 200,000 words from the author. Foote, too, thought the project would take a few years, perhaps five at the most. However, once he started to research the war and its many engrossing historical characters, he quickly realized that the project would take much longer. *The Civil War* would become, in time, Foote's magnum opus, the work that defined his entire career.

While working on the first volume of what would become a three-volume set, Foote received perhaps the greatest endorsement any Mississippi writer could receive when an aging William Faulkner touted him publicly as an up-and-coming novelist of talent. Foote's association with Faulkner went back to his college days. When he was nineteen, Foote rode with Percy through Faulkner's hometown of Oxford, Mississippi, on a trip from Chapel Hill to Greenville. In Oxford, Percy stopped his car in front of Rowan Oak, Faulkner's antebellum-style home. Percy refused to go inside, saying he did not want to bother America's most famous writer. Foote, however, had no such qualms. He knocked boldly on the front door and was greeted by Faulkner's two fox terriers, a Dalmatian, and a small, shirtless, barefoot man. Foote asked the great novelist where he could get a copy of *Marble Faun*, Faulkner's first book.[6] The writer said his agent might be able to help. It was a short visit, like hundreds of other intrusions the literary giant received at his home each year, but the two men gradually built a friendship, and Faulkner accompanied Foote to the hundredth anniversary of the Battle of Shiloh in southern Tennessee in April 1962. It was one of the last trips Faulkner would make—two months later, he died suddenly of a heart attack.

Despite Faulkner's encomiums, Foote struggled mightily to meet the deadline for his Civil War book. The problem was that Foote, a careful outliner of plots, typically wrote only 500 words per day. He did not come close to finishing the book on time. In fact, it took him more than twenty years to complete the work. Because of the book's unrivalled depth, Foote became sort of a literary hero when *The Civil War: A Narrative* was finally completed and published in 1974 as a three-volume set. The first two volumes had been published in 1958 and 1963, respectively, to solid reviews, but the best reviews came after volume three came out in 1974. The reviewer in *National Review* praised Foote for giving "a balanced emphasis on the war in the West."[7] The *New York Times* commended *The Civil War: A Narrative* for being "a monumental, even-handed account of the country's tragic, fratricidal conflict."[8] Historian Richard N. Current agreed and added that the book's greatest strength was its ability to put the reader on the battlefield. "The reader puts down the book with the feeling that he actually has met and known the actors," Current wrote. "He feels, too, that he has experienced the events they took part in. . . . This sounds like history written by a novelist, and in fact it is."[9]

Some critics took Foote to task for a supposed lack of academic rigor. John Cournos, writing in *Commonweal*, castigated Foote for not using footnotes, "the very thing a careful reader may want. He may want to know on what authority the author has made this or that statement and has drawn certain conclusions therefrom."[10] Foote countered that "footnotes would have totally shattered what I was doing. I didn't want people glancing down at the bottom of the page every other sentence."[11] Phoebe Adams, the *Atlantic Monthly* reviewer, was not sure *The Civil War: A Narrative* was even a narrative, or that the author was "a proper historian," but she praised Foote for being "a splendid historian" and cited the book's rich detail.[12] She felt, however, that it would only get a small audience response.

James I. Robertson, a history professor at Virginia Tech, countered Adams's claim by predicting that Foote's work would appeal to a broad base of readers. Robertson also commended Foote's pen: "His prose is powerful, tending more toward the overwhelming than toward the incisive . . . [his prose] alternately brims with natural movement, constructed excitement, allegory, color and force."[13] The history professor, who would go on to write the definitive biography of Confederate general Thomas J. "Stonewall" Jackson, agreed with the criticism of Foote's lack of documentation, saying Foote's narrative was a bit shallower than the work of Bruce Catton, who also wrote a comparable, critically acclaimed three-part history of the war. Fellow historian C. Vann Woodward offered the most precise description of Foote's massive work, calling it "narrative military history."[14]

After he completed the mammoth military work, Foote returned to novel writing with *September, September* (1978), but his reputation languished for more than a decade even while *The Civil War* was selling approximately 4,500 copies a year in the 1980s.[15] "Although reviews have praised his novels," James E. Kibler wrote in 1978, "Foote is still largely neglected by critics. He is not as yet popular with writers for the scholarly journals or with teachers in the classroom."[16] Foote had to wonder if he would ever make a major hit with the critics. He complained to Percy that his most original novel, *Follow Me Down*, had been misunderstood. "No reviewer has pointed out that the book is (what I clearly think it is) 'the best constructed American novel since *Gatsby*,'" Foote wrote. "That's what I am waiting to hear them says. Looks like I'll have to wait a long time."[17]

When filmmaker Ken Burns began planning a massive documentary on the Civil War for the Public Broadcasting Service, he asked twenty-four historians, including Foote, to confer with him in Washington, D.C. There, they carefully went over Burns's manuscript for the documentary. "We went over it page by page," Foote noted. "If anyone questioned anything, or said, 'that's not accurate,' Ken threw it out, no matter how dramatic or important Ken thought it was."[18] Then Burns, who had been tipped about Foote's encyclopedic knowledge of the war by Robert Penn Warren, talked to the historians individually. The director interviewed Foote for eight hours, four of which were taped, in preparation for the 1990 airing of the documentary. After the lengthy interviews, it became clear that Foote would be, as Burns later put it, "the presiding spirit of the series."[19] The director added, "We'd keep jumping out of the van and turning on the camera, because he kept opening his mouth and blowing us away with what a great man he was."[20]

The single most important factor in Foote's rise to celebrity was his personal presence. Increasingly, Burns focused his film's narration on the gentlemanly historian-writer from the Mississippi Delta. Each night of the film's original airing in the fall of 1990, Foote was charming, humorous, and incisive. He was at his best when he was relating humorous anecdotes or when he put the war into a larger perspective—623,000 dead, 5 percent of the male population of the country at the time (a comparable dead figure in World War II would have been 2.5 million). Foote stressed that the Civil War was the country's most significant event because it defined what America would be. "This country was into its adolescence at the time of the Civil War," he noted. "Like all traumatic experiences that you might have had in your adolescence, it stays with you the rest of your life, certainly in your subconscious, most likely in your conscious, too. The Revolution provided us with a constitution. It broke us loose from England. It made us free. But the Civil War really defined us. It said what we were going to be and it said what we were not going to be."[21]

Foote, for his part, was surprised by his newfound celebrity.[22] He told C-SPAN's Brian Lamb: "It vaulted me into the public attention, which had been minuscule before that and I had all kind of reactions to that happening. But it sold books and that is the glorious thing about it. The *War* stayed in hardcover, but it also came out in Vintage (paperback) and it took off like a skyrocket after this television program."[23] The Washington *Post* reported that Vintage printed 10,000 copies of each volume of *The Civil War* the week after Foote appeared in the film, selling half that total in the first week.[24] The reclusive author, who had rarely even signed autographs in the past, was now recognized in public. "I get this star quality reaction from people, which I find rather unpleasant, really," he said. "Crossing an airport or going somewhere to dinner or something, there are people who come over and say how much they enjoyed the war."[25] Foote was in demand on the talk-show circuit, in glossy magazines, and on National Public Radio, PBS, and C-SPAN. *People* magazine did a profile on him in October 1990.[26]

The awards that had once eluded Foote now began to flow into his Memphis home. In 1992 he won the Charles Frankel, St. Louis Literary, and Nevins-Freeman awards. Then, between 1991 and 1999, he received honorary doctoral degrees from the College of William & Mary, the University of South Carolina, the University of North Carolina at Chapel Hill, Millsaps College, Notre Dame, and Loyola of New Orleans. Before the 1990s, Foote had received just two honorary doctoral degrees, from the University of the South and from Southwestern University. He continued to appear frequently on television and radio. He appeared on C-SPAN's *Booknotes* with Brian Lamb, NPR's *Weekend Edition* with Scott Simon and Liane Hansen, and on PBS's *The News Hour with Jim Lehrer.* Lamb interviewed him three times, once after the publication of the Modern Library's *Stars in Their Courses*, after Doubletake Books (a subsidiary of W.W. Norton) published *The Correspondence of Shelby Foote & Walker Percy*, and in 2001 at his home in Memphis. Lamb also had Foote on live during a C-SPAN Fourth of July celebration when they discussed the Gettysburg and Vicksburg campaigns.

On Memorial Day 2000, Foote appeared on PBS's *News Hour with Jim Lehrer* discussing the Confederate battle flag that flew over the state house in Columbia, South Carolina. Jim Hodges, South Carolina's governor, had just signed a bill to remove the flag from the legislative building. Foote characteristically lamented Hodges's decision. The author said: "The flag is a symbol my great grandfather fought under and in defense of. I am for flying it anywhere anybody wants to fly it."[27] In 1994, Hansen had Foote on her Sunday morning NPR show to discuss a proposed Walt Disney Civil War theme park to be built in northern Virginia near the Manassas battlefield. Foote opposed the park primarily on artistic grounds. "Anything Disney ever does is loaded with sentimentality," he said. "That's all right in fantasies like *Snow White* or *The Lion King*, but if he [Disney CEO Michael Eisner] starts messing with American history and presents these people the way he does those people in the Disney films and at the theme parks, you're going to have a misidentification of history."[28] The author also commissioned the missile cruiser USS *Shiloh* and unveiled a bronze statue of William Faulkner in Oxford.

Meanwhile, Percy biographer Jay Tolson said that *The Civil War: A Narrative* received a major boost from the film: "Shelby showed me a little account book with yearly earnings from his books. The difference between the pre-Burns years and the post-Burns years was huge." Tolson suspects *Shiloh* also received a shot in the arm after the film. Random House sold approximately 400,000 copies of *The Civil War: A Narrative* through the summer of 1991, and Foote made nearly a million dollars in royalties.[29]

Despite—or because of—the continuing attention, Foote was most comfortable at his home in Memphis. In his last few years he left the impression that his public persona irked as much as pleased him. "When you're on television, you belong to whoever turns the set on to evoke your presence," he said. "I don't want to sound insane, but they act like they can do it again at any moment. They write or call and say, 'Would you come to dinner next Thursday night. We enjoyed your program so much we'd like you to visit our home.' And they live in Wyoming."[30] He stopped answering his fan mail and agreed to only one in twenty invitations to appear in public, wryly telling one reporter that he might best be remembered for editing "the best high school paper in the country."[31] In a more sober moment, Foote said, "I've faced the fact that I probably am more apt to be known for writing this three-volume history than anything else."[32]

In an increasingly unliterate world, Foote may have been the last great southern historian-writer. In such a world, more than a decade removed from the first airing of Burns's popular masterpiece, it is not clear whether Foote's three-volume war epic will long outlive his celebrity. Many historians still see it as a reliable work of history, even though it does not have footnotes. Foote challenged his readers to gauge the accuracy of his account of the war. "The professional historians have criticized it, but what they haven't done is point out any errors," he noted. "I'm not saying there are no errors, but there are damn few, fewer than most history books that are just loaded with footnotes."[33]

In the end, Foote's voice, presence, expertise, and attractiveness—especially since he was in his seventies and a large portion of *The Civil War*'s audience was elderly—made him famous. Yet Foote's celebrity also stood for something else that is powerful in American pop culture: the cult of the individual. As social critic P. David Marshall puts it, the cult "celebrates the potential of the individual and the mass's support of the individual in mass society."[34] Foote was one such individual, a relatively obscure writer who through the power of television came to be associated with the Civil War in general and his native region in particular. In many ways, as fellow historian James McPherson phrased it, "Shelby Foote was the South."

Notes

1. James E. Kibler, "Shelby Foote." *Dictionary of Literary Biography,* vol. 2: *American Novelists since World War II,* ed. Jeffrey Helterman and Richard Layman (Detroit, MI: Gale Research Co., 1978), p. 150.
2. Charles J. Rolo, "Men Fighting," *Atlantic Monthly* 189(5) (May 1952): 82.
3. Jay Tolson, ed., *The Correspondence of Shelby Foote and Walker Percy* (New York: Doubletake, 1997), p. 85.
4. Tolson, p. 89.
5. Tolson, p. 94.
6. Paul Grondahl, "Fleshing out the Stories of History," *Albany, N.Y., Magazine.* Online: http://www.albany.edu/writers-inst/albymag.html#foote. Accessed 31 May 2000.
7. M. E. Bradford, "Else We Should Love It Too Well," *National Review* 27 (14 February 1975): 173.
8. Nash K. Burger, "The Blue and Gray Ran Crimson," New York *Times Book Review,* 15 December 1974, p. 2.
9. Richard Current, "A Novelist as Historian Shows Blue and Gray in a Mighty Panorama," New York *Herald Tribune Book Review,* 23 November 1958, p. 5.
10. John Cournos, "Bright Book of the Civil War," *Commonweal* 69(15) (9 January 1959): 393–94.
11. William C. Carter, ed., *Conversations with Shelby Foote* (Jackson, MS.: University Press of Mississippi, 1989), p. 233.
12. Phoebe Adams, Review of *The Civil War: A Narrative (Vol. II), The Atlantic Monthly* 212(6) (December 1963): 156.
13. James I. Robertson, Review of *The Civil War: A Narrative, Civil War History* 22(2) (June 1975): 173.
14. C. Vann Woodward, "The Great American Butchery," *The New York Review of Books* 22(3)(6 March 1975): 12.
15. Carter, *Conversations with Shelby Foote,* p. 233.
16. Kibler, p. 153.
17. Robert L. Phillips, *Shelby Foote: Novelist and Historian* (Jackson, MS.: University Press of Mississippi, 1992), p. 16.

18. Kathleen Nelson, "Overnight Success 'Ironic' for Shelby Foote," St. Louis *Post-Dispatch*, 5 November 1992, 1E.
19. Susan Howard, "The Civil War Expert Finds Similarities with Today's Conflicts," New York *Newsday*, 24 January 1991, p. 75.
20. Mark Muro, "Shelby Foote Makes His Presence Felt in PBS Epic," Boston *Globe*, 26 September 1990, p. 47.
21. Brian Lamb, Shelby Foote interview on C-SPAN's *Booknotes,* 11 September 1994. Online transcript (22 pages): http://booknotes.org/transcripts/10141.htm, p. 4. Accessed 3 June 2000.
22. Elizabet Kastor, "The Civil War Drama: For Filmmaker Ken Burns, the Culmination of a Five-Year Crusade," *Washington Post*, 23 September 1990, G1.
23. Lamb, p. 4.
24. Charles Truehart, "The Historian Storyteller: Civil War Expert Shelby Foote, Gaining Acclaim for His Role in the PBS Series," Washington *Post*, 2 October 1990, E1.
25. Lamb, p. 3.
26. Michelle Green and David Hutchins, "The Civil War Finds a Homer in Writer Shelby Foote," *People Weekly*, 15 October 1990, pp. 61–62.
27. Elizabeth Farnsworth, "Debating the Flag," *The News Hour with Jim Lehrer,* transcript from Public Broadcasting Service, 29 May 2000. Farnsworth led the roundtable discussion. Online: http://www.pbs.org/newshour/bb/politics/jan-june00/flag_5–29.html. Accessed 4 June 2005.
28. Liane Hansen, "Civil War Historian Foote Objects to Disney's America," *Weekend Edition* Sunday with Liane Hansen. Online. Lexis-Nexis Universe. Transcripts: National Public Radio. 18 September 1994.
29. Jay Tolson, interview, 1 September 2005. Foote was not hurt by the fact that Burns turned his Civil War documentary into a cash cow. Burns, his brother Ric Burns, and Geoffrey Ward wrote a $50 book published by Alfred Knopf, owned by Random House, that served as a companion to the film.
30. Jeff Bradley, "Shelby Foote's 'Civil War' work may have helped Clinton," Denver *Post*, 8 November 1992, 1E.
31. Nelson, p. 1E.
32. Lamb, p. 11.
33. Carter, 233. As a historian of Civil War press suppression, I can testify that Foote's study is reliable. While I dispute his claim that approximately three hundred cases of suppression occurred in the North—I maintain the number is higher—Foote characterized the degree with a greater degree of precision than most academic historians.
34. David P. Marshall, *Celebrity and Power: Fame in Contemporary Culture* (Minneapolis, MN: University of Minnesota Press, 1997), p. 43.

Index

About the Editors

David B. Sachsman holds the George R. West, Jr. Chair of Excellence in Communication and Public Affairs. He came to the University of Tennessee at Chattanooga in 1991 from California State University, Fullerton, where he had served as dean of the School of Communications. Previously, he was chair of the Department of Journalism and Mass Media at Rutgers University. Dr. Sachsman is the director of the annual Symposium on the 19th Century Press, the Civil War, and Free Expression, which he and Kit Rushing founded in 1993. Dr. Sachsman is an editor of *The Civil War and the Press,* a book of readings drawn from the first five conferences, published by Transaction Publishers in 2000. Dr. Sachsman also is known for his research in environmental risk communication and for the three editions of *Media: An Introductory Analysis of American Mass Communications*, for which he wrote the history chapter.

S. Kittrell Rushing is the Frank McDonald Professor and head of the Communication Department at the University of Tennessee at Chattanooga. Before joining the UTC faculty more than twenty years ago, Rushing taught for several years at the University of Mississippi. Dr. Rushing's most recent publication is the re-release by the University of Tennessee Press of Eliza Frances Andrews's (1840–1931) first novel, *A Family Secret* (2005). The work is a fictionalized account of Andrews's experiences during the last year of the Civil War. In 1876, the novel was the top-selling work of fiction in the United States. Rushing's interest in the works of Fanny Andrews began with his discovery in the University of Tennessee at Chattanooga library archives of Andrews's 1870–1872 diary. The diary with notes and an introduction was published in 2002 by the University of Tennessee Press.

Roy Morris Jr. is the editor of *Military Heritage* magazine and the author of four well-received books on the Civil War and post-Civil War eras: *Fraud of the Cen-*

tury: Rutherford B. Hayes, Samuel Tilden, and the Stolen Election of 1876 (Simon and Schuster, 2003); *The Better Angel: Walt Whitman in the Civil War* (Oxford University Press, 2000); *Ambrose Bierce: Alone in Bad Company* (Crown, 1996); and *Sheridan: The Life and Wars of General Phil Sheridan* (Crown, 1992). He also edited and wrote the introduction for a popular new edition of Ambrose Bierce's *The Devil's Dictionary* (Oxford University Press, 1999). A former newspaper reporter and political correspondent for the *Chattanooga News-Free Press* and the *Chattanooga Times*, he was founding editor of *America's Civil War* magazine, which he edited for 14 years.

About the Contributors

Paul Ashdown

Paul Ashdown is a professor of journalism and electronic media at the University of Tennessee. He is a former newspaper and wire service journalist and continues to write columns. His research interests include international communications, 19th and 20th century American history and literature, literary journalism and popular culture. He has written extensively about the works of James Agee and teaches an interdisciplinary honors seminar on the legacy of the Civil War.

Menahem Blondheim

Menahem Blondheim is a member of the departments of American Studies and Communications at the Hebrew University of Jerusalem. He earned his B.A. from the Hebrew University and his M.A. and Ph.D. degrees from Harvard University. His research into the history of communications is currently focused on intersectional communications in the Civil War.

Edward J. Blum

Edward J. Blum is an assistant professor in the Department of History at San Diego State University. He is the author of *Reforging the White Republic: Race, Religion, and American Nationalism, 1865–1898* (Baton Rouge: Louisiana State University Press, 2005), which was a nominee for the Bancroft Prize, and coeditor (with W. Scott Poole) of *Vale of Tears: Essays on Religion and Reconstruction* (Macon, GA: Mercer University Press, 2005). Blum's most recent publication is a religious biography of W. E. B. Du Bois entitled *W.E.B. Du Bois, American Prophet* (University of Pennsylvania Press, 2007).

Sarah Hardin Blum

Sarah Hardin Blum holds her Ph.D. in history from the University of Kentucky. She teaches history, rhetoric, and writing at San Diego State University.

David W. Bulla

David Bulla focuses his research on the history of U.S. journalism, examining limitations on press performance. His dissertation explored press suppression in Indiana during the Civil War. Bulla earned a Ph.D. in mass communications from the University of Florida in 2004, an M.A. in journalism from Indiana University in 2001, and a B.A. in English from UNC-Greensboro in 1983.

CROMPTON BURTON

Holding a BA in Radio-TV production from the University of Arizona and MSJ from Ohio University, Crompton Burton has enjoyed a career first in commercial broadcasting as a sports anchor and reporter and, most recently, in college communications and marketing. He now serves as associate vice president of Alumni and College Relations at Marietta College in Ohio. His master's thesis focused upon the role of a Maine newspaper in hometown coverage of the American Civil War, and his contributions to journalism history scholarship include paper presentations on such varied topics as Copperhead editor Marcellus Emery, the war bulletins of Edwin M. Stanton, the Kingfield Rebellion and the press relations of General George B. McClellan.

EDWARD CAUDILL

Edward Caudill is a professor of journalism and electronic media at the University of Tennessee, Knoxville. His scholarship has focused on the history of ideas in media. His books include *Darwinian Myth: The Legends and Misuse of a Theory, Darwinism in the Press, The Myth of Nathan Bedford Forrest* (co-authored with Paul Ashdown), *The Mosby Myth: A Confederate Hero in Life and Legend* (co-authored with Paul). His most recent work has looked at the role of the press in creating cultural myths and legends surrounding popular or unpopular ideas and individuals.

LLOYD CHIASSON, JR.

Lloyd Chiasson, Jr., a former reporter with daily newspapers in Vermont and Louisiana, is a professor in mass communications at Nicholls State University in Thibodaux, Louisiana. Dr. Chiasson co-authored *Reporter's Notebook*, and served as editor and co-author of *The Press in Times of Crisis, The Press on Trial,* and *Three Centuries of American Media.* In 1999, Dr. Chiasson visited Latvia as a Fulbright scholar, where he taught at the University of Latvia and Riga Stradina University.

PHEBE DAVIDSON

Perhaps best known as a poet, Phebe Davidson is also a literary critic with a strong historical bent and is the author of *American Movies and Their Cultural Antecedents in Literary Text* (Edwin Mellin Press, 2001). Since moving to South Carolina fifteen years ago, she has become an engaging scholarly analyst of Southern culture and literature. Her work involves artifacts as seemingly disparate as colonial captivity narratives and popular movies, current syntax and social order. She is a distinguished professor emerita at USC, Aiken.

JESSICA A. DORMAN

An aspiring journalist from the age of seven—when she caught the bug from Woodward and Bernstein—Jessica Dorman served as president of *The Harvard Crimson*. She later diversified her journalistic credentials as a sports writer for the *New Haven Register* and assistant to a nationally syndicated gossip columnist. Opting to sling gossip in the past tense rather than the present, Dorman earned her doctorate in the History of American Civilization from Harvard. She has taught American studies at Trinity College and Penn State, and has acted as director of Publications at the Historic New Orleans Collection since 2004.

EVE DUNBAR

Eve Dunbar is an assistant professor of English at Vassar College. Her scholarship and teaching focus on late-nineteenth and twentieth-century African American literature and culture. She at work on project entitled *Passing As Citizens: African American Citizenship and the 20th Century Rise of the Passing Narrative*, which tracks the development of the racial passing narrative and themes of citizenship in African American literature and culture. Her essay in *Memory and Myth* grows out of her graduate work at the University of Texas-Austin, and was first published in *The Southern Historian* (vol. 24).

NANCY DUPONT

Nancy McKenzie Dupont is an assistant professor in the Department of Journalism at the University of Mississippi. Her research interests are the secession era and Civil War reports. She has written several book chapters and has published in *Louisiana History*, the *Journal of Radio Studies*, and the *Professional Studies Journal*. She has presented papers at the Association for Education in Journalism and Mass Communication and the American Journalism Historians Association, and is a regular contributor to the Symposium on the 19th Century Press, the Civil War, and Free Expression.

FENDALL FULTON

Fendall Fulton is a senior English major at The University of Tennessee at Chattanooga, where she is pursuing a concentration in creative writing. She also teaches creative dance to kindergarteners and first graders. In 2005, she won third prize in UTC's Women's History Month poetry contest.

ROBERT BLAKESLEE GILPIN

After writing his BA/MA on hobos and the American West at Yale University, Robert Blakeslee Gilpin was the 2001 Mellon Fellow at Clare College, Cambridge, where he earned an M.Phil in British history. He is currently a Ph.D. candidate at Yale. His dissertation, tentatively titled "Monster and Martyr: Tracing John Brown Through American Memory," looks at the infamous radical abolitionist from the period immediately preceding his death until the middle of the twentieth century.

William E. Huntzicker

William E. Huntzicker is an assistant professor of journalism and mass communications at St. Cloud State University in central Minnesota. Upon graduation in history from Montana State University, he went to work for the Associated Press in Minneapolis. Subsequently, he received a master's and doctorate in American Studies from the University of Minnesota-Twin Cities. He has taught journalism and mass communication courses at the University of Minnesota, University of Wisconsin-River Falls, Bemidji State University and St. Cloud State University. He is the author of *The Popular Press, 1833–1865* and several book chapters and articles on stereotypes in nineteenth-century newspapers and on journalism in the American West.

Roy Morris Jr.

Roy Morris Jr., the editor of *Military Heritage* magazine, has written extensively about the Civil War and nineteenth-century history. He is the author of *Ambrose Bierce: Alone in Bad Company* (Crown, 1995). For the past several years he has been at work on a new biography of Stephen Crane for Oxford University Press.

Marcia Noe

Marcia Noe is a professor of English and coordinator of Womens Studies at The University of Tennessee at Chattanooga, where she teaches undergraduate and graduate courses in American literature, drama, and women's studies. She is the author of *Susan Glaspell: Voice from the Heartland* and seventeen other articles, reviews, and reference book entries on the Pulitzer Prize-winning playwright Susan Glaspell. In 1993 she was Fulbright senior lecturer-researcher at the Federal University of Minas Gerais in Belo Horizonte, Brazil. She is the co-author, with Junia C. M. Alves, of *O palco e a rua: a trajetória do teatro do Grupo Galpão* (Pontifica Universidade Catolica, 2006).

W. Scott Poole

W. Scott Poole is a South Carolina native. He received his M.T.S. from Harvard University in 1997 and his Ph.D. from Ole Miss in 2000. He is the author of *Never Surrender: Confederate Memory and Conservatism in the South Carolina Upcountry*

(University of Georgia Press, 2004) and *South Carolina's Civil War: A Narrative* (Mercer University Press, 2005). He is also co-editor (with Edward Blum) of *Vale of Tears: Essays on Religion and Reconstruction* (Mercer University Press, 2005).

DEBRA REDDIN VAN TUYLL

Debra Reddin van Tuyll is associate professor of communications at Augusta State University. She is author of *The Southern Press in the Civil War* (Greenwood Publishers, 2005) and co-editor of *The Civil War and the Press* (Transaction 2000). She is currently working on projects that look at dissent among newspapers in the Civil War South and that examine newspaper and magazine readers in antebellum North Carolina and what they were reading.

BERNELL E. TRIPP

Bernell E. Tripp is an associate professor of journalism in the College of Journalism and Communications at the University of Florida. Her research interests include the abolitionist press, antebellum African-American women journalists, and the nineteenth-century African American press in the United States and Canada. Her chapter in *Memory and Myth* resulted from her research into the white abolitionists interaction and personal relationships with several members of the African-American press. She has written several book chapters, books and papers on these topics, and her current project is an overview of African American press development in the nineteenth and twentieth centuries.